A SHEARWATER BOOK

Gifford Pinchot

and the Making of Modern Environmentalism

GIFFORD PINCHOT

and the

Making of Modern Environmentalism

Char Miller

ISLAND PRESS / Shearwater Books

Washington / Covelo / London

A Shearwater Book
Published by Island Press

Copyright © 2001 by Char Miller

Shearwater Books is a trademark of The Center for Resource Economics.

Library of Congress Cataloging-in-Publication Data
Miller, Char, 1951–
Gifford Pinchot and the making of modern
environmentalism / Char Miller.
p.   cm.
Includes bibliographical references (p.   ).
ISBN 1-55963-822-2 (hardcover)—ISBN 1-55963-823-0 (pbk.)
1. Pinchot, Gifford, 1865–1946. 2. Conservationists—United
States—Biography. 3. Politicians—United States—Biography.
4. Conservation of natural resources—United States—History. I. Title.
s926.p56 m55 2001
333.7'2'092—dc21   2001005665

Printed on recycled, acid-free paper

Manufactured in the United States of America

10 9 8 7 6 5 4 3 2

Frontispiece: Gifford Pinchot sometime in the 1930s, keeping abreast
of Pennsylvania politics while relaxing on the East Terrace of his home,
Grey Towers, in Milford. (Grey Towers NHL)

For Judith Lipsett

Contents

Prologue

GIFFORD PINCHOT had long wanted to visit the Yosemite Valley. An avid outdoorsman from his youth, and a future architect of the conservation movement of the early twentieth century, Pinchot had heard of the park's beauty, of its granite-studded landscape, from friends and relatives; their verbal impressions had reinforced the visual renderings of the park collected in the popular books of photographs that were the coffee-table volumes of his class and time. He knew what a tourist would and should observe in this treasure of the Sierra Nevada, the glacially carved canyons set within those mountains that John Muir twenty years earlier had anointed as the "Range of Light." So it was with great anticipation that on Thursday, May 7, 1891, the twenty-five-year-old traveler climbed into a stagecoach in Raymond, California, at the edge of the Sierra foothills, to ride north and east to Wawona, gateway to Yosemite.

That the coach was not built with Pinchot's body in mind—he stood a storklike six-foot-two—came as no surprise. On the long journey west from his home in New York City he had crammed himself into the narrow seats of railroad passenger cars, had been sandwiched between other passengers in a series of packed stagecoaches, and had even bounced along trails into the Grand Canyon astride a low-slung mule, his feet trailing on the rough ground. Nor was it surprising that Pinchot immediately took to those aboard the Raymond stage. He was a gregarious, amiable, and confident young man, as charmed by a recent Princeton graduate, Albert Edward Kennedy, as he was by an older woman "who thought the Carboniferous Age just grand." What with the pleasant company and good conversation, enveloped in a landscape of "magnificent forest growth," his journey into the Sierra proved a "very instructive drive."[1]

When Pinchot finally entered the valley, however, his first impression was that Yosemite did not live up to its much-vaunted reputation. Oh, the valley *was* beautiful, but not overwhelmingly so. His enthusiasm for the Mariposa Grove of redwoods, for example, in which he spent all of Friday riding and hiking, was tempered by his earlier encounters with other, more substantial groves in southern California. The Mariposa, he recorded in his diary, was "less fine" than the Tulare Grove; its trees did not inspire him as had their more southerly counterparts. "Who shall describe the Sequoias? Their wonderful beauty to me is far more wonderful than their size," he had declared in his diary after hiking through the Kaweah Giant Forest. "The perfect shape, the massive columns, but above all the marvelous coloring of the bark make them surely the most beautiful trees in the world." None of the Yosemite redwoods, not even the much-revered "Grizzly Giant," in the shade of which he ate his lunch, soared as high as the mammoth "Karl Marx."[2]

The trees were not the only things that suffered in comparison. Early the next morning Pinchot hurried up to Inspiration Point, there to encounter for the first time the valley's astonishing vista framed by El Capitan to the north, Bridalveil Falls to the south, and the massive Half Dome anchoring the eastern horizon. It was a rare tourist who did not fall sway to this landscape's prescribed "poetic appeal," who would not concur with Ralph Waldo Emerson that this was the only site (and sight) in the world "that comes up to the brag and exceeds it."

Pinchot was that rarity. He conceded that the point "is well raved indeed," its view "marvelous," and even acknowledged, as did most visitors, that he did not have the capacity to capture his feelings in words. "Can't describe it at all," he noted laconically.[3]

But at least he was able to pinpoint why he failed to see Yosemite on its own terms: "Wish I had seen it before seeing the Grand Cañon," he wrote.

"Everything is tame after that. Not that the Valley is not wonderful and wonderfully beautiful, but it can't touch the Cañon."[4]

Yosemite's grandeur, as Pinchot would soon discover, could gradually overwhelm its visitors, even those who had been first to the Grand Canyon. For the next two days he crisscrossed the valley floor, scaled rock walls, and tramped along mountainous trails, his long gait covering more than twenty-five miles a day. Pinchot may have been a young man in a hurry— he usually was—but little escaped his attention. Before long, he began to recognize that it was in this more tactile, intimate way that Yosemite beguiled. Even its much-touted "views" could still surprise and astound, it dawned on him, if approached in the proper manner. The "clear reflection" of Mirror Lake was at its best just before daybreak, he found; at that hour, by slowly circling the body of water, he could catch myriad sunrises. Nevada Falls was less kaleidoscopic but no less forceful in its impact on his imagination; he was transfixed as he clambered up beside it and into its rainbow-hued spray. "Nothing so fine, so graceful, so great and yet so delicate ever came in my way before," he wrote later that evening in his room at the Stoneham Hotel. By turns he was exhausted and exhilarated by his interactions with Yosemite, ultimately declaring, "I wish I could spend a month in the valley."[5]

He packed that month into just one more day. Sunday morning began with a brisk hike to Mirror Lake and Glacier Point, sites to which he would return later in the day as he moved up and down the valley, trying to absorb all he could before his departure. That he toured on the Sabbath initially gave him pause, but his mode of transport eased his guilt: "Sorry to travel about Sunday, but as I walked it was not so bad." His actions became somewhat more irreverent when he set off that afternoon for Yosemite Upper Falls, with Mr. Kennedy, the Princetonian, in tow.

Melting snow and spring rains had replenished the Yosemite Creek's high country watershed, so that the falls were thunderously full as they plunged more than 1,700 feet to the point where Pinchot and Kennedy stood, before then tumbling down a second and shorter cascade into the valley below. Warned that it would be impossible to cross under the crashing waters, the two young men were undeterred; together they leaped into the "maelstrom of wind and water." Blinded by the torrent and stunned by its force—"[we] could only see at intervals and moved by sighting a rock and running to it"—they managed to cross to the other side and then to return. With sore muscles and drenched clothing, with the water's roar resounding in his ears, Pinchot knew that this was what made Yosemite "worth crossing the continent to see."[6]

That it took this natural baptism to wash away his initial disappointment with Yosemite, that his encounter with its many water courses—from Bridalveil to Nevada and Vernal Falls, from Yosemite Creek to the Merced River—were what led Pinchot to appreciate the valley for what it contained, is consistent with other pivotal moments in his life. Like John Muir's favorite bird, the dipper, the aptly named water ouzel that works the streams of the Sierras, "flitting about in the spray, diving in foaming eddies, whirling like a leaf among beaten foam-bells," Pinchot was most at home when he was awash.[7]

This image of a playful Pinchot communing with nature in the wilds of the Yosemite Valley runs smack up against the usual story, told over and over, about his relationship with this sacred Sierran landscape. Water is also the central focus of this narrative, but in this case the emphasis is not on water's exhilarating wildness, within which a person could be engulfed, but on harnessing its turbulent flow for human consumption.

The tale goes something like this. In the first years of the twentieth century, after founding the Forest Service in 1905 and while serving as its first chief, Pinchot acted as the main publicist for what historians call "utilitarian conservationism," the belief that natural resources such as lumber, coal, and water should be sustainably used and that the federal government should regulate use. This philosophy had two groups of detractors. One encompassed entrenched economic interests, which believed in a laissez-faire exploitation of nature's bounty and regularly challenged the imposition of federal regulations on resource-rich public lands. Equally skeptical were those later dubbed aesthetic conservationists or preservationists, men and women who advocated the maintenance of wilderness *as* wilderness.

These conflicted views of natural resource use came to a head over the proposed construction of the O'Shaughnessy Dam in the Hetch Hetchy Valley. The valley, located in a remote northern section of Yosemite National Park, was a cherished place, especially for the eminent naturalist

John Muir, Pinchot's friend and mentor and a leading proponent of preservationism. Muir sharply opposed inundating Hetch Hetchy's stunning landscape. Pinchot countered that its beauty was of less importance than its utility as a much-needed reservoir for San Francisco; the city would gain a publicly controlled water supply and free itself from the monopolistic private water purveyors who dominated the market. So involved was the protracted dispute over Hetch Hetchy—after a series of bruising congressional debates, the dam was finally built in 1913—that subsequent commentators have argued that it marked the first sustained national discussion of the limits of economic development. So heated was the debate over the fate of this alpine valley that it destroyed the friendship of Muir and Pinchot.[8]

Although their confrontation over Hetch Hetchy is legendary, the very legend has turned these two actors into caricatures, foils who serve as polar opposites in a dramatic narrative. A more subtle evaluation of Pinchot's perspective emerges in an examination of the two moments in which he and Yosemite connect. Taken together, they reveal Pinchot's ability to maintain what might seem to be contradictory impulses—the desire to live simultaneously within and on nature, to exult in its splendors while exploiting its resources. These positions seem incompatible only if one accepts, as Pinchot did not, that to preserve nature humanity must live apart from it. He knew that such segregation was impossible, and believed too that the survival of any organism—human included—depended on its ability to utilize the surrounding environment to its advantage. "We live on the Earth," he told an audience in 1924, "and from the Earth." Nothing he encountered as a forester, or as an inveterate hunter and angler, or as an elected official, suggested otherwise. Human behavior mirrored the natural life struggle.[9]

So Pinchot would reflect one evening in the teens while camped beside another, more tropical body of water, on "a narrow neck of land with the great stretches of the Bay of Florida on either side of it." He could not sleep because there was a leak in the inflatable "rubber bed" on which he had stretched out, and "every thirty minutes it let me down on as fine a collection of cobble stones as you would care to see." The comic rise and fall of his bedding was a mercy, he noted, for it "kept [him] wakeful and attentive to the great show the fish put on."

What he heard in the "darkness of that interminable night" he could not forget, for the water "all about us was crowded with great schools of mullet" and their predators. In the pitch black, Pinchot could not determine what was attacking the mullet (though he guessed that a combination of sharks, tarpon, and porpoises were in on the hunt), but the sound of the assault was deafening: "Every instant, on one side or another, or on both, some big fish would smash into these schools, hundreds of thousands of mullet would spring into the air in a wild effort to escape, and the roar as they tore out of the water and broke in again was like . . . the thunder of one hundred drums." Until daylight, the air reverberated with the "long drumroll of the mullet as they left the water, the crash of the big fish that drove them into the air, and the louder roll again as the multitudes fell back." The excited Pinchot could not guess how "many millions of living creatures there were within reach of our ears that night." He knew only that he been a lucky witness to "the diapason of life and death," into which at dawn he immersed himself, swimming "in the blood-warm water made roily by the multitude of fish."[10]

Pinchot's was a thrilled recognition of nature's often brutal harmonies, and of his place within them. What he remembered of this and similar episodes was "the marvelous intimate glimpse of wild life, as the tarpon and the mullet lived it and died—wild life in action, furiously busy with its own concerns, with survival and extinction, with capture and escape, and wholly unaware of the human onlooker." His engaged role as participant in and observer of this wildness complicates the moral calculus by which some have come to judge him. That calculation depends on a deification of wilderness, a concept whose roots stretch back to nineteenth-century Romanticism, and one that reinforces an artificial and politically charged distinction between the human and the natural. "Idealizing a distant wilderness," argues historian William Cronon, has given rise to a troubling "set of bipolar moral scales in which the human and the nonhuman, the unnatural and natural, the fallen and unfallen, serve as our conceptual map for understanding and valuing the world." It is on this scale that critics of Gifford Pinchot have found him wanting.[11]

Articulations of Pinchot's failure have been particularly evident since World War II, as the utilitarian conservationism with which he is too closely associated, and which appeared triumphant with the erection of the

O'Shaughnessy Dam in 1913, have steadily fallen from favor. This decline has accelerated since the 1960s, as environmental activists and scholars have critically analyzed the forester's public activities, challenged the fundamental guidelines of the profession he did so much to advance, and, by extension, questioned his integrity.

Much of this has been accomplished by setting Pinchot up in opposition to Muir, who serves as a more obvious precursor to the contemporary, preservation-oriented environmental movement. This "Son of the Wilderness" had a spiritual appreciation for the Earth that speaks directly to the movement's current ideals; his "religious ideology," as one sympathetic historian called it, dovetails with their scholarly perceptions and political needs.[12] With Pinchot there has been no such match. How could there be when his politics were born of materialism? Pinchot "didn't care to see Hetch Hetchy; his decision was not based on the value of the valley *for itself*," Michael Cohen scolded in *The Pathless Way: John Muir and American Wilderness*. "He was more interested in the welfare of San Francisco,"[13]

Other critics have suggested that this pragmatic orientation reflected a psychological flaw in Pinchot's character. There "was a spareness to him more than physical," historian Frederick Turner has asserted. "The woods were not home to him, and he seems never to have been touched by their mystery." Not a lyrical man, Pinchot was thus out of synch with contempo rary sensibilities, at least as they have been defined by Muir's intellectual heirs. When the National Wildlife Federation established its Conservation Hall of Fame in the mid-sixties, the forester's status had crumbled so much that he was but its eighth nominee, chosen well after John Muir. "Among conservationists and the general public," Stephen Fox wrote, "Muir had finally won his quarrel with Pinchot."[14]

Only after he was no longer thought a threat to Muir's preeminence could Pinchot begin to receive considered analysis of his place in the intellectual history of American environmentalism. That at least is one possible conclusion to be drawn from the work of Roderick Nash and Stephen Fox, whose writings in environmental history have done so much to establish Muir's status. On Pinchot's contributions to environmental thought, the two tend to agree. His insights have been limited because he had "little sympathy for or understanding of ecology and the land ethic" that grew out of John Muir's writings, that ecologist Aldo Leopold built upon, and that reached fruition in the environmental activism of recent decades. In this view, Pinchot is significant only as a transitional figure; what "Pinchot and his utilitarian conservationism did," Nash asserts, "was to provide the necessary bridge from a pioneer to an ecological perspective."[15]

This critical assessment modifies Pinchot's own overblown estimation of his stature in the conservation movement and, by tempering some of the animosity the forester has generated during the past three decades, allows a more precise rendering and balanced understanding of his work's impact. Yet Nash's metaphor also freezes Pinchot intellectually, and it restricts his contributions chronologically. Fox, too, contends that one need take Pinchot seriously only during "his prime time, from 1895 to 1910," just before and during his career as a public servant in the Department of Agriculture. The forester might have helped construct a bridge to an ecological vision, but he is not allowed to cross it.[16]

That assessment of Pinchot's legacy is inaccurate and unjustified. His biography demonstrates the evolution of a complicated set of perspectives. This grandson of a lumberman did much to develop the profession of forestry and to craft the conservation agenda of the Progressive Era. The regulations he enacted while chief of the Forest Service restrained the devastating clear-cutting strategy that people like his grandfather, Cyrille Pinchot, had pursued in eastern Pennsylvania during the Antebellum Era. In time, Pinchot would reform even forestry's utilitarian emphases, creating a more inclusive vision of conservationism. In the 1920s and 1930s, he embraced ecological principles to better understand the growing pressures on the nation's forested estate.

His political vision also evolved. Born into a family of great wealth and privilege, Pinchot early on recognized that the conservationist ethos must oppose social discrimination and economic inequality. Reinforcing these commitments was his experience as a two-term governor of Pennsylvania, during which he not only fought hard to restore cut-over lands, but helped to define and defend the rights of workers, women, and children. Concluding that the land and its people must be treated equitably, Pinchot came to believe that poverty was a form of pollution.[17]

True, Pinchot never learned to think, in Aldo Leopold's arresting phrase, like a mountain. But then, few have, making Pinchot a more representative figure than his many critics acknowledge. Perhaps he simply lacked the imagination. His *Breaking New Ground* does not "read like a typical memoir by a conservationist or nature lover," Fox asserts. "That is, one finds no fond descriptions of early baptism in the natural world" nor any "lyrical descriptions of nature contact and excursions undertaken in adulthood." Most damaging of all, apparently, is that the book contains "no speculations about the proper human place and significance in the grand scheme of things, designed to curb human hubris and induce greater humility in us all."[18]

Fox is right about *Breaking New Ground,* an intensely political tract. But he is wrong about Pinchot's being insufficiently in awe of nature, wrong too in claiming an absence of wonder in his writings. Some of the most vivid examples of Pinchot's sensibilities emerge in *To the South Seas,* a chronicle of the Pinchot family's cruise to the Pacific aboard the schooner *Mary Pinchot* in 1929. Early one morning, for instance, while preparing to depart Hiva Oa, one of the Marquesas Islands in French Polynesia, Pinchot watched as the first light struck "the great square peak of Temiti, its precipices and towers glorious in the sunrise." Soon his view of the mountain was obscured by gathering clouds, "and here and there showers fell across the steeps." Meanwhile, "over the neighboring island of Tahu Ata, less high but more rugged than Hiva Oa, a rainbow of extraordinary brilliancy and vividness suddenly appeared. Its bands of misty color grew swiftly in height and reach, until, almost before we knew it, it had bridged the two mile gap between the islands and rested with a foot on either one." Pinchot was stunned: "We watched it spellbound. It was the sight of a lifetime. Two such islands joined by a bridge made a vision of glory for which I have no words. Then it died away, and somehow left us breathless."[19]

When the usually voluble Gifford Pinchot admits he is at a loss for words, one must take notice. But one must also take care, for the wild and exotic setting, and the peace it evoked within him, were at once deeply felt and a literary contrivance. That, of course, is the point. Gifford Pinchot was no more immune to the aesthetic imagery and natural symbolism that are staples of Western culture than were John Muir and his legatees—all have imbibed the same tradition. Fox, in short, read the wrong book.[20]

Porpoises swimming off the coast of the Florida Keys would have confirmed that Pinchot could be humbled. He had gone to the islands to hunt the mammals, loving the fight that they gave him as he balanced precariously in a canoe, and braced for the furious energy they unleashed when he struck them with a harpoon. If he struck them, that is. For what he found was that porpoises were no easy mark, and that even if he did manage to sink his iron, the porpoise almost always won the ensuing battle of strength and will. But that is not why these tests quickly lost their allure. Rather, as Pinchot put it in a collection of essays, *Just Fishing Talk* (1936), his close observations of dolphin behavior forced him to rethink his own.

Plying the aqua waters of south Florida, Pinchot was frequently startled when one of his prey would surface just out of harpoon range, and would "examine us with one eye, then turn and examine us with the other, obviously disapprove of us, and then make off. If they had spoken out," Pinchot mused, "they could not have been more definite in their opinion." Shamed, he forswore the chase. "Since I got to know about them . . . I've gone no more a'hunting," he affirmed. Any porpoise could parade "across the bow of my canoe in perfect safety. He's free of the seas for all of me." Pinchot also had gotten himself off the hook through this affirmation, yet another sign that this dam advocate had constructed a deeply complex relationship with the natural world.[21]

His appreciation of nature's complexity owes much to his remarkable adaptation to a protean environment. Born in August 1865, shortly after the close of the nation's bloodiest war, he died in October 1946, a little more than a year after the blinding flash that marked the end of World War II and the birth of the Atomic Age. Over this span, he worked for, offered counsel to, and battled with every president from Grover Cleveland to Harry S. Truman. As modern America emerged, Pinchot was among its creators.

In the late nineteenth century, the American agricultural empire reached the Pacific coast, setting the stage for the exploitation of the region's natural resources to feed the explosive industrial revolution. The speed with which grass, timber, and minerals were consumed helped foster the growth of a conservation movement that set the context for Pinchot's subsequent efforts to regulate grazing, logging, and mining. Some of the central principles of this movement were imported from Europe, a transatlantic migration of ideas that he participated in when he studied the science of forestry in France, Germany, and Switzerland, bringing home with him the European emphasis on the importance of state regulation of resources.

Alongside, and of a piece with this regulatory effort, was the rise of a national administrative structure within the United States, in which the executive branch dominated the other two branches of the federal government; this new political arrangement gained strength during the presidency of Theodore Roosevelt. The prime marker of the executive branch's consolidation of authority was the establishment of a federal Forest Service in 1905, to which Pinchot devoted considerable energy.

He was no less engaged in the growth of the welfare state. Although it was largely attributable to the reactions of the Franklin D. Roosevelt administration to the deprivations of the Great Depression, Pinchot also contributed to its emergence. As governor of Pennsylvania in the mid-1920s, and again during a second term in early 1930s, he restructured the Keystone State's bureaucratic apparatus and its ideological bearing so that it would better respond to the increasing needs of its population, especially its marginalized citizens. Dedicated to the American experiment, Gifford Pinchot was very much a man of his times.

He may even have been at one with ours. About this, Pinchot might have caviled, for he accepted that there were ephemeral limits to his influence; there would come a time, he believed, when he would not matter. "No one better understood that the battlefields of the future in certain respects must take different forms from those of the past," Cornelia Pinchot confirmed when she spoke at the dedication of the Gifford Pinchot National Forest in Washington State, a ceremony held on October 15, 1949, shortly after the third anniversary of her husband's death. "He insisted that conservation must be reinvigorated, revived, remanned, revitalized by each successive generation, its implications, its urgencies, its logistics translated in terms of the present of each of them."[22]

Although such an expression of humility is not normally associated with the oft-zealous Gifford Pinchot, it adds an essential layer to our understanding of a life story as intricate as any of the riparian habitats, alpine meadows, or hardwood forests through which he tramped. That acknowledged, given the chronological range of his life and the breadth of his career it would be odd indeed if his experience did not at least speak to the conditions that confront those living at the beginning of the twenty-first century. His conviction that the power of politics and government (at all levels of human society) must be employed to expand the benefits of democracy to those often excluded from civic life remains an article of faith among contemporary progressives. Relevant too is Pinchot's certainty that social justice was partly secured through economic expansion, and that this was keyed to the nation's ability to protect and to use in a sustainable fashion Earth's bounty. In this quest for sustainability, Pinchot's vision was not narrowly nationalistic. Recognizing early the global dimensions of resource development, he was at the forefront of those seeking international agreements to check environmental devastation. In many ways, Pinchot's activism helped bring to life the world we live within.[23]

Part One

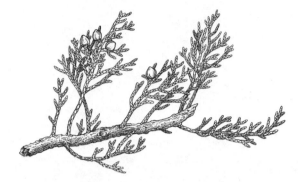

FAMILY
TREE

The World of His Father

THE SILLIEST tale Gifford Pinchot ever told about why he became a forester and an avid conservationist hinged on the gift of a red sled. That sled was all a young Gifford could think about, an obsession that grew each winter, when "with eyes of untold envy . . . I watched the bigger boys go careering about on their steel-shod steeds of gravity." Each winter he lobbied his father for a sled of his own, and each year his father refused. Many years later, when he was forty-seven years old, Gifford would concur with his father's decision: "Red sleds," he would say, "are dangerous things for small boys to operate and there is the possible emergency of crashing into a curb or tree when going down a long hill at the rate of thirty miles an hour." James Pinchot had only had his son's best interests in mind, Gifford came to believe.[1]

But his father had a heart, too, finally giving a sled to the grateful Gifford in the winter following the boy's tenth birthday. "Fortune smiled that first Christmas of the sled," Gifford later noted, for "the snows were deep and persistent." The red sled was "the Christmas present that I have loved best of any that have come to me throughout life."

The moral of this story, as Pinchot recounted it in 1912 to a newspaper reporter, was not simply that delayed gratification is good, though that was also true. "It was probably because of this long period of anticipation that the sled was so highly appreciated when it came." The story had another significance in its teller's eyes. His devotion to the art of sledding, "and the joy of the outside it had a tendency to develop, may have had something to do with the career that the man chose when he came to maturity."

This "creation story" is a bit of a stretch, but one element rings true, at least in a biographical context. The central role that James Pinchot played in the gift of the sled supports Gifford's long-standing claim that it was actually his father who was *the* "father of conservation," having encouraged his son to become one of the nation's first foresters. Bestowing paternity on James Pinchot confirmed Gifford's sense of his own preeminent place in the history of forestry and conservation, conferring genealogical sanction upon and precedence for his activities within these movements. But it is somewhat overstated, for there were a number of prominent American scientists, naturalists, and publicists in the late nineteenth century who developed the idea of conservation and encouraged the growth of a receptive public. Among these were forester Bernhard Eduard Fernow, George Bird Grinnell, who was editor of *Forest and Stream,* naturalist John Muir, and Harvard botanist Charles Sprague Sargent—a distinguished roster on which James Pinchot does not belong.[2]

James nonetheless figured prominently in all of Gifford's theories about why he chose his profession. The most sustained "creation story" that the son would write was entitled "50 Years Ago" and was a narrative of the Pinchot family's 1879 excursion into Keene Valley, in New York's Adirondack Mountains. It reveals why Gifford felt so compelled to equate conservation with his father.

It was on this trip, when he was thirteen years old, that Gifford had his first brush with wilderness, a brush that he would later remember as being critical to his life course. This was a civilized wilderness, to be sure—or, rather, one that was in the process of being domesticated. His parents, like other urbanites of means, repaired to the mountains to escape New York City's heat and humidity, its dirt, clamor, and disease. This seasonal migration had particular resonance for members of the post–Civil War generation, who at once benefited from but felt uneasy about living within the industrializing metropolitan economy.

Their ambivalence was understandable. In the postwar years, American cities had mushroomed in physical size, population density, and economic might. The industrial revolution produced a staggering array of goods and services for these new consumers, but the grimy, fetid, and massive urban areas that spread out and around the new factories swallowed up what was once open space and robbed the citizenry—native and immigrant alike—of any breathing room. No wonder that in the 1870s many newly rich Americans, who yearned to escape the turmoil of modern urban life, sought release in a grand tour of the North Woods.[3]

The Pinchots thus followed a well-beaten path into this wild land, traveling along the new rail lines and roadways that penetrated the woods, staying in boardinghouses and hostelries constructed to lodge summer guests, and plying the region's many clear lakes and rushing streams in canoes and guide boats. The ample presence of these tourist services suggested just how popular the Adirondacks had become within a decade of their "discovery." The Pinchots' two-week excursion was social—their letters reveal that they bumped into friends and acquaintances, or people much like those they knew—and, in that sense, familiar. Not for them a sylvan solitude.[4]

The Adirondacks furthermore offered little respite from familiar bodily complaints. Neither the constitution of Gifford's mother, Mary Pinchot, nor that of his younger sister, ten-year-old Antoinette, improved much during their summer travels; rather, they did daily battle with a parsimonious landlady whose meals were as small as they were unappetizing (complaints echoed by other travelers). Grumbling stomachs undercut the meditative calm and rustic charm of this forested landscape.[5]

There was a moment on this 1879 trip, however, when Gifford and his father were able to slip away from the domestic troubles they had helped carry into the woods and, hiking up and out of the Keene Valley, made camp along the Upper Ausable Pond. Before setting off on their journey, which bore all the marks of a male initiation ceremony, James gave his son a present—a fly rod, Gifford's first. The young man had come of age, at least in his father's eyes, a psychological transition that Gifford would acknowledge a half-century later when he offered a detailed description of his father's gift. "The rod my father gave me had a hickory butt, a second joint of ash, and a lancewood tip. What became of the other joints, I'll never tell you," he wrote whimsically; but "the butt reposes, ferrule gone, in my rod rack, and, like the old horse turned out to grass, in its senectitude has naught to do but enjoy its well-earned rest."[6]

In 1878, however, the rod and boy were young and untested. That his emerging manhood was twined with this expedition is as clear as the reflections of sublime "gigantic mountain sentinels" that played across the surface of the Upper Ausable Pond; these images, one contemporary guidebook put it, evoked a scenery "of remarkable wildness," and Pinchot himself was struck by "the steep dark mountain slope" that rose from the opposite shore "in full view of our camp by day." A better backdrop for self-discovery could not have been imagined.[7]

Like all such passages, Gifford's began with a journey away from the family or, more precisely, away from his mother, sister Antoinette, and five-year-old brother, Amos. An arduous trek it was, too, beginning with its first stage. "The road from Keene Valley to the Lower Ausable Pond has loomed in rocky grandeur all my life as the roughest road I ever traveled," Pinchot later recalled. "My father and I walked over it rather than sit in the bucking buckboard, and so did Judge William Hammersley of Hartford, the third member of our party." After a tough ascent covering about eight miles, the group, which included two brawny local guides, loaded their boats and rowed nearly two miles to the mouth of an unnavigable stream flowing down from the upper pond, which they then reached after a mile portage. Once on the Upper Ausable Pond, the company selected its campsite, constructed a lean-to near the shore, and built "deep and delicious balsam beds" into which a tired thirteen-year-old boy gratefully tumbled.[8]

The days and nights that followed were less strenuous physically but not emotionally, for each moment was packed with the hitherto unknown trappings of adult male experience, with new sights, tastes, and sounds. There was the time, for instance, when the group had to ford a rock-filled stream that the less than nimble Judge Hammersley, "no lightweight in mind or body," could not negotiate. Gifford was astonished when one of the guides, "who had spent much of his life with a travelling circus, picked up the Judge's 250 pounds or so and carried him across . . . with the greatest of ease."

The youthful onlooker was equally excited by the camp fare, especially the daily flapjacks, which he had never eaten before, sweetened by another novelty, maple syrup, made each morning by heating up chunks broken off from a cake of maple sugar. The landscape itself contained surprises both gentle and wild. As he washed up in the morning or waded in the pond's cool water at midday, chubs would gather just beneath the surface, waiting for scraps. The fish "would even run in and out between my fingers in search of food," Gifford found. "I could feel them and even catch one now and then if I tried." This sense of wonder, this recognition of nature's palpable presence, was offset by its ability to inflict pain, as innumerable "black flies, midges, and mosquitoes worked their wicked will upon us. They were like a cloud by day and needles of fire by night." But what really impressed Gifford were the "calls of the wild" that echoed off the mountain on the far shore's mountainside. One night he heard what the guides identified as the roar of a bear. "Whether they were right or not, I do not know," Pinchot wrote. "At any rate I have never heard its like again." Most riveting of all was the sleep-shattering scream of a panther, the memory of which "will remain till my very substance is worn away."9

For Gifford, this had been an unforgettable journey on which he gained a "new and lasting conception of the wilderness" and his place within it. Every night the men would gather around the campfire, passing time by telling "stories of hunting and fishing . . . till the booming of the bullfrogs sent me to bed," Pinchot remembered. These stories gave him insight into the nature of the hunt, the refining of outdoor skills, and the character of the sportsman's code.10

The more the young Gifford embodied these adult behaviors and attitudes, the more he was allowed to fish on his own. It was while he was soloing early one morning, in silent pursuit of "a one-pound trout" he thought he had spied lurking in a pool shaded by the branches of an alder, that his father let slip a compliment about the boy's abilities that the son forever treasured. The cast had been tricky and he never landed the elusive trout, but his efforts had not gone unnoticed. James Pinchot and Judge Hammersley, "in another boat a long bow shot away," had observed Gifford's technique and tenacity, and at one point the young man overheard his father comment, "The boy doesn't fish as if he were only thirteen." That compliment, Gifford later wrote, "gave me something to stiffen my backbone then and now and all the years between." He concluded that the significance of this memory "is not hard to read: Whenever you go, and whenever you can, take the youngster along."[11]

What had made James Pinchot's words so delicious, however, was not simply that they affirmed Gifford's maturity but that Gifford believed he had listened in on a private, adult conversation—"My father never knew I heard him, but still waters carried the sound, as still waters do." But still waters also run deep, especially in the often controlling and manipulative James Pinchot. It is quite likely that he had staged this particular moment with the same care with which he had managed the whole trip; he intended his son to hear his encouraging words. That calculated compliment, like the earlier gifts of the shiny red sled and the fly rod, were of a piece, elements of the elder Pinchot's deliberate effort to mold his firstborn son into the man he would have him become.[12]

AN AMERICAN TALE

Becoming Gifford Pinchot had much to do with James Pinchot—about this, Gifford was correct. But the context of his maturation also had much to do with his paternal family's long history, a heralded past whose roots drew upon a complex network of French and American cultural legacies.

In 1816, members of the Pinchot family were forced to cross the Atlantic to America because Napoleon Bonaparte had taken to the seas, breaking out of his exile on Elba in late February 1815 and sailing north on the Mediterranean toward the southern coast of France. Within twenty days of Napoleon's landing in France, in what is now known as the "flight of the eagle," the self-proclaimed "Man of Destiny" swept into Paris to loud acclaim. Fearing the outbreak of civil war and concerned for his own safety, Louis XVIII had already fled to Belgium, opening the way for Napoleon to proclaim a new constitution and begin his second reign.[13]

Among those who were overjoyed that the eagle had landed was Gifford's grandfather, Cyrille Constantine Désiré Pinchot. Then only sixteen, he lived with his parents in Breteuil, a small, prosperous community hugging the banks of the Noye River, approximately sixty miles north of Paris. If this youth "warmly espoused" the Bonapartist cause, the European powers of the Congress of Vienna did not. Labeling Napoleon "an enemy and disturber of the peace of the world," they gathered their armed forces to confront him. Napoleon, unable to convince his enemies of his pacific intentions, launched an offensive into Belgium in June to challenge those arrayed against him. Young Pinchot hoped to come to his emperor's aid. One family legend held that his hopes went unfulfilled because he was under enlistment age. Another linked his dashed hopes to bad timing. His father, Constantine, a dry-goods merchant and political figure in Breteuil, raised a detachment of troops, placed Cyrille at its head, and then sent them off to battle, but they failed to reach the French army before its disastrous defeat at Waterloo. Either way, the Pinchots' political allegiance proved costly, for with the return of Louis XVIII to the French throne in 1815 and Napoleon's subsequent exile to St. Helena, the family fell victim to the White Terror, a short-lived period of persecution that marked the Bourbon Restoration. When a cousin, said to have been an "uncompromising Bourbon adherent," denounced Cyrille to the royal authorities, he, his father Constantine, and his mother Maria fled first to England and then to the United States, hoping that the New World would be a safe haven.[14]

Unlike many Europeans who took shelter in America, these new French immigrants came well-heeled and were able to cushion the shocks of the transatlantic migration. Constantine apparently had sold his mercantile concern in Breteuil, but he also brought a considerable stock of goods with him, material that enabled him to reestablish himself in New York City. Three years later he sold his business, and with the profits purchased four hundred acres of prime farmland outside Milford, Pennsylvania, and a town lot on which he erected a store and a house. Located in the northeastern corner of the state, at the head of the Delaware River Water Gap, the Milford region was home to an increasing number of French émigré families, no doubt one reason that the Pinchots moved there in 1819. But they had no intention of simply replicating French provincial life. They were eager to exploit this rich land and in the process refashion themselves as sturdy republicans.[15]

Exploit the land they did. Anything but simple yeoman farmers, the Pinchots took advantage of the economic interaction between the community's dusty commercial byways and the bountiful harvests of corn and other grains that their tenants reaped from the farmlands on which the Pinchots would never live. Profits, not purity, guided their actions and defined their ambition.[16]

They made the earth pay, too. Constantine and Cyrille, for example, embarked on a series of entrepreneurial projects that over time brought them considerable wealth and social prestige. The family's store was the cornerstone, and it could not have been sited more advantageously, standing as it did at the crossroads of Milford, a political and economic hub. This county seat was also a linchpin in the overland and riparian transportation of goods and services between the agricultural frontiers of western New Jersey, northeastern Pennsylvania, and central New York State and the seaports of New York City and Philadelphia. The store's counters, then, served as points of interchange; across them flowed local and regional agricultural produce, finished goods—cloth, linens, and tobacco—from the cities, and raw material from distant settlements. One local eminence would later cast a baleful eye on the character of this bustling economic activity: "When my father moved [to Milford] in 1821 or 1822," William Bross wrote, "there were certainly not as many righteous men in the town as there were in Sodom. The stores were all open on the Sabbath, and the streets were full of teams loaded with lumber from the back districts, or those from New Jersey exchanging their produce from lumber. In fact, Sunday was the great market and gala day of the week." The material benefits of this lucrative, if less than pious, trade enabled the Pinchots to purchase more arable land and hire more tenant farmers to work it, so that by the time of Constantine's death in 1826, a decade after his family's flight from France, the Pinchots were among the largest landholders in Pike County. Waterloo had been a blessing in disguise.[17]

Cyrille seemed particularly blessed, at least materially. With his mother, he successfully built upon his father's mercantile endeavors. Maria Pinchot ran the family store, freeing her son to plunge into the grand sport of the nineteenth century—land speculation. Although his business records are spotty, those that remain reveal his skill at expanding his land holdings throughout northeastern Pennsylvania and New York State, and later in Michigan and Wisconsin. At times he served as a middleman, especially between French speculators and American landed interests, but usually he invested his own monies. Pinchot was particularly interested in forested lands. To maximize profits he, like other lumber investors of his day, clear-cut the woods, set up temporary sawmills to process the lumber, secured the resulting logs and boards together into rafts, and then, during the spring, shipped them down rain-swollen rivers to market in various port towns along the Delaware River, Philadelphia being the most important.

The trip downriver was complex and tricky, and the markets were unstable from one year to the next, as Pinchot's partner, John Wallace, advised him in 1834. That spring Wallace himself rode the rafts down the Delaware, stopping to sell them in New Hope, Trenton, and other towns. Unlike previous years, when buyers had flocked to the riverbanks to inspect the wood, this year—a year of tight credit—they stayed away, and Wallace found that he was "running after them." By the time he landed in Philadelphia, the credit crunch had discouraged most buyers. Three years later, however, during the Panic of 1837, Pinchot hit it big, receiving an order for 100,000 board feet of hemlock joists. Regardless of the size of the monetary returns, however, each year he reinvested his capital in another set of timber stands, and the cycle would repeat itself.[18]

The environmental consequences of this cycle, so emblematic of the preindustrial pattern of lumber development, were considerable. Unregulated by anything beyond market demand, lumber entrepreneurs cut a swath through the American wilderness, leaving behind denuded hills, eroded terrain, and silted rivers. The scars in the landscape deepened between the 1830s and 1860s when, to feed the insatiable appetite for wood sparked by the so-called transportation revolution, which included an expanding network of turnpikes, canals, and railroads, Pinchot and others employed more technologically advanced and efficient means to cut, mill, and transport the trees of America.

New, more powerful saws that made more efficient use of water power accelerated the harvesting in northeastern Pennsylvania and elsewhere. During the peak of pre–Civil War production in Pike County, noted early twentieth-century historian James Elliot Defenbaugh, "sawmills dotted every mountain stream; lumber, manufactured and in the log, covered the banks wherever an eddy could be found suitable for rafting, and in the spring and fall a majority of the male population were floating their hard

earned products down the Delaware in search of a market." By the end of
the 1860s the county, once lushly "covered with a dense forest of white and
yellow pine, oak, ash, and hickory" and containing some of "the best hemlock land in the State," was cut clean. The machine in the garden was a
powerfully destructive force, one that later generations of Pinchots would
work assiduously to control.[19]

In Cyrille Pinchot's view, however, the machine was a constructive
engine. It enabled him to harness nature's energies to enhance his material
world and to contribute to the growth of the republic. By the 1850s, he had
become the largest taxpayer in the community as well as the township's tax
collector; he inhabited a stately Greek Revival house across the street from
which stood the family store, said to be the community's most prosperous.
His political connections were paying off when he was selected to represent
the United States in settling Indian claims to western lands. In him were
private good and public service conjoined.[20]

Cyrille's awareness of this interplay between the environment, economic
activity, and political advantage had emerged fully some years earlier in the
curious incident of the Milford railroad bridge. At stake in its construction
was the community's continued prosperity, at least as defined by its role as
a regional transshipment point for goods heading to urban markets along
roads that stretched out to the east, or in Delaware River port towns to the
south.

Until the late 1840s, the Delaware River and its watershed had sustained
the region's transportation needs and economic growth, a pattern that Pinchot and others had reinforced through their investments in land transportation, specifically in stage lines and in the construction of the Milford
and Owego Turnpike. Their productive marketing of Milford was threatened in the late 1840s when a new, more efficient, and ultimately cheaper
form of transportation pulled over the horizon: the Erie and Delaware
Railroad. By 1848, its tracks snaked northeast from New Jersey and connected with the eastern bank of the Delaware River at Port Jervis, New
York—eight miles to the northeast of Milford. The railroad's charter then
called for its lines to cross the river at Matamoras, Pennsylvania, and follow
the river valleys to Binghamton, New York, and ultimately to Buffalo and
Lake Erie. In its geographical wanderings lay a critical message. The rail-

road would redirect the region's economy along a new axis that would bypass Milford.[21]

But not without a fight. Cyrille Pinchot and other prominent local entrepreneurs sought to obtain a spur line running between Milford and Matamoras so that their market might have direct access to the Erie's trunk line. There was only one problem. Engineers for the Erie discovered that it would be prohibitively expensive to enter Pennsylvania at Matamoras, for to continue the railroad's northerly path would require blasting a three-mile rail bed through the massive outcropping known as the Glass Factory Rocks (estimated cost: $100,000 per mile).

They suggested that the railroad span the river at Sawmill Rift instead, four miles north of Port Jervis, thereby avoiding the stony obstacle. To do so, however, would require a formal change of the railroad's charter with the Pennsylvania legislature. But the Erie's request for this contractual alteration was stalled by Milford's opposition to the plan. Because the railroad could not afford a delay, it agreed, despite the expense, to build "a double bridge across the Delaware at Matamoras, arranged for both the passage of wagons and for a railroad track, to maintain the bridge forever, and to lay a track from the station at Port Jervis to and across the bridge."[22]

Milford was saved—or so its boosters thought. Yet the Erie's directors had no interest in building the bridge and tried to avoid doing so; not until 1854, after years of legal wrangling, did the Erie finally erect the bridge. Its construction stood as a symbol of the active role that local capital (and capitalists) could play in transcending geography and nature, and in shaping the contours of a nationalizing industrial economy. Tiny Milford, with a population of fewer than two thousand, had worked the levers of democratic politics and parlayed its political influence to bend railroad tracks to meet its needs. Cyrille Pinchot's contribution to this adaptive response to changing circumstances, with its beguiling sense of power and of possibility, suggested how thoroughly he had adopted the American character.

The bridge took on a different meaning, however, if one stood on the Matamoras side and pivoted 180 degrees from the shiny track pointing toward Port Jervis and faced the village of Matamoras on the Delaware's western bank. This new vista was a letdown, for leading away from the bridge was a simple, rough wagon trail that meandered toward Milford, some six miles to the south and west. There was no railroad line, and none would ever be built between the two communities. This critical project never got off the ground because in its bruising battle with the Erie, Milford had lost many of the very human and financial resources it had fought so hard to retain.

The dimensions of the town's Pyrrhic victory are glimpsed in a letter that Frederick Bailey, secretary of the Milford and Owego Turnpike Company, sent to Pinchot in 1851 in the midst of the protracted political struggle over the bridge. Pinchot had urged the company to help underwrite the cost of building a Milford-to-Matamoras rail line, a proposal Bailey fully appreciated. "It would seem but natural and reasonable that the Road Company should assist in this matter," he responded, and indeed "the Will is good, but the flesh or means is very Weak." It was weak, he noted, precisely because of the boom in railroad construction on which Pinchot had hoped to capitalize. To the north, the expanding operations of the Erie, which by this time had pressed beyond Binghamton, New York, had diverted commerce to such an extent that the turnpike's "tolls have shrunk more than half"; to the west, another railroad was moving out of the Pennsylvania coal country to connect with the Erie at Great Bend, New York, "and the attention of our citizens is now drawn to the making of Plank Roads and other improvements . . . so as to intersect and avail themselves of this thoroughfare." In this context, a bridge or railroad to the east in Milford—indeed, Milford itself—would be of little value to those living farther west.[23]

The Milford and Owego Turnpike was devalued, too. In light of the railroad's tremendous competitive advantage, the turnpike company was forced "to throw open [the] gates to the public," and a decade later the road's charter was officially repealed. That legal denouement masked just how swiftly the Erie Railroad had rearranged the region's economic structure and transportation systems; within three years of its arrival in Port Jervis, the railroad had come to dominate entrepreneurial activity within the Delaware River watershed. No better demonstration of this was its willingness to build the Milford bridge and leave it standing: empty of purpose, so full of meaning.[24]

This reversal of Milford's fortunes was demographic as well. Down the

Erie's rails went any number of the community's ambitious sons and daughters, seeking greater prospects in the larger world. William Bross was one of those who headed west, settling in Illinois, where he would become both lieutenant governor and one of Chicago's leading journalists. The Pinchots also contributed to the brain drain. Three of Cyrille and Eliza Pinchot's five children—Edgar, James, and Mary—left home. Mary married an attorney and moved to Bridgeport, Connecticut. James, like Edgar, migrated to New York City, seeking to make his mark in its burgeoning antebellum economy. He did so, too, achieving a level of financial success that allowed him to retire shortly after Gifford's birth in 1865 and to spend freely to refurbish Milford, thereby contributing to its economic transition from a fading entrepôt to a booming tourist mecca.[25]

The Rise of James Pinchot

James Pinchot's goal was to reinvent Milford's past by reconfiguring its built environment. Beginning in 1863, when he razed a building next to the Pinchot family's store to make way for a new post office, he constantly schemed to gentrify the scruffy village in which he was raised. To enact those schemes required extensive land ownership, and he urged his father, who had invested in rural holdings, to now buy village real estate outright or to control it through the purchase of mortgages.

James evidently planned to build a chapel and a library on some of this land, uplifting symbols of morality and social beneficence. His good friend, artist John Weir, was certain that the chapel would "be an attraction," but only if "it fulfills the aesthetic demand that associates religion with beauty," an association he knew Pinchot grasped: "Your own life and surroundings say that [you do], so you can't get away from it!"[26]

James's aesthetic sensibility had been encouraged on a tour of the summer-green English countryside in 1871, where he had continually marveled at the contrast between its clean lines and neat fences and Milford's dust and blight, writing his mother that he wished "every one in Milford could see [these hamlets] to know how much could be done in beautifying our village."

Dusting off the villagers was also part of the plan. James was repeatedly

struck by the clash between the ugliness of human life and the Edenic countryside. This was as apparent to him in Ireland, whose "peasantry is about
what we see at home," as it was in Italy, where the distinctions were even
greater. Amid the Italian gardens, in which he inhaled the tangy scent of
orange and lemon groves, Pinchot also sniffed the more pungent, sweaty
aroma that marked the country's "squalid, dirty, ill-looking . . . lower
classes." He had firm hopes that a redesigned Milford would scrub away
similar affronts to gentility; a refined land meant a refined people, precisely
the kind of environment in which to raise his children.[27]

Pinchot was not alone in his distaste for the great unwashed or in his
hunger for refinement. As with other members of the American cultural
elite, he built these concerns into the very architecture of his country estate
in Milford, construction for which began in the mid-1880s, when his oldest
son, Gifford, was twenty. He hired celebrated architect and close friend
Richard Morris Hunt, whose designs catered to the tastes of the upper
crust. Hunt housed the elite in sumptuous abodes in New York City's high-
end residential neighborhoods, built their summer "cottages" in Newport,
Rhode Island, and, most remarkably, was the architect for George W. Vanderbilt's palatial manse Biltmore, in Asheville, North Carolina. On its vast
forests in the early 1890s, Gifford Pinchot would launch his forestry career.

For the Pinchot family's country estate in Milford, dubbed Grey Towers,
Hunt constructed a Norman-Breton bluestone manor that dominated the
physical and social landscape. Its imposing, fortresslike exterior, complete
with three sixty-foot turrets, was matched by an impressive interior that
held a medievalized great hall, twenty-three fireplaces, and forty-four
rooms, each crammed with furnishings that hearkened to those "of the old
baronial days." The manse's siting on a "commanding eminence" overlooking the village of Milford and the Delaware River intensified its visual
impact. The sheer size and scale of this "summer castle," and its self-conscious evocation of the Pinchots' French ancestry (a bust of Lafayette,
tucked in a niche in its eastern wall, gazes across the rolling hills of western
New Jersey to the Atlantic and beyond), drew all eyes—tourist and local
alike—upward.[28]

James was not to this manor born. Grey Towers was the crowning
achievement of the twenty-five years he had spent working in New York

City, work that had brought him considerable wealth. As a result of an advantageous marriage to Mary Eno, his fortunes grew; with this affluence came a heightened awareness of the social function of the cultural elite.

Whether these were James's aspirations at age nineteen when he sallied forth to New York is anyone's guess. But it is clear that even before he departed Milford, James Pinchot displayed a marked ability to use friendships and contacts to the family's and his own advantage; it was a skill he would hone throughout his life and would later seek to inculcate in his children.

During his adolescence, for instance, James boarded for a time at Goshen Academy in Goshen, New York, some seventy-five miles east of Milford. One of his teachers and mentors there, Henry Fitch, left Goshen in the late 1840s to join the Erie Railroad Company as its first general passenger and ticket agent. He is credited with structuring the rail line's complex timetable, regularizing the conduct of its passenger services, and formulating a ticketing system that stabilized the company's finances. In 1849, shortly after Fitch had begun this work, James Pinchot, now eighteen, contacted his former teacher about selling lumber to the Erie for use in the construction of its bridges and track. This contact dovetailed with Cyrille Pinchot's political maneuverings to compel the Erie to build a bridge from Port Jervis to Matamoras.

Fitch, who presumably knew nothing of the elder Pinchot's activities, happily supplied James with a detailed list of the Erie's purchasing agents, and in so doing gave the Pinchots access to a new, regular, and more rational market for their lumber than the fickle and seasonal ones that they had been chasing along the banks of the Delaware River. James Pinchot was learning that the personal touch was critical to the successful pursuit of mammon.[29]

He touched Fitch once more when, in 1852, two years after moving to New York, James hit upon a method by which to regularize the sale of Pinchot farmlands throughout northeastern Pennsylvania. "You will remember that Mr. Fitch, my old teacher, is in the employ of the N.Y & E.R.R.," he advised his father, and "knowing he must be necessarily acquainted with the agents through whom the emigrants are influenced to go west by the Erie R.R., I called on him to see if he could not assist me in some way." He could. Fitch apparently agreed to use his influence with "the agent of the German Society" to channel emigrants to Milford to buy land from the Pinchots for $17 or $18 or more per acre. The Pinchots' share of the sale would be $15 per acre, James had proposed, and the Erie would skim off the rest, a deal with which Mr. Fitch was reportedly "much pleased." These were handsome prices, and these sales had the added benefit of encouraging in-migration to Pike County and therefore bringing new consumers to the Pinchots' Milford store. James recognized that it never hurt to have good friends in high places, a point he would drive home with his sons Gifford and Amos when, partly in honor of his well-placed mentor, he sent them to Fitch's alma mater—Yale College.[30]

In other ways, James Pinchot proved a quick study during his first decade in New York City, successfully pursuing a number of lines of commerce while developing an extensive social network. He initially clerked in a mercantile establishment, then struck off on his own into the business of interior furnishings: first as Partridge, Pinchot & Warren, then just as Pinchot & Warren. The companies sold a broad array of wallpaper, window shades, and curtains from their Courtland Street store, located in the hub of New York's commercial center; these goods either were manufactured in plants in New York State and Pennsylvania or were imported from England and Europe.

The customer base for James's business expanded sharply throughout the 1850s, reflecting the city's own surge in population—from 515,000 in 1850 to nearly 814,000 ten years later—that rapidly moved outward from lower Manhattan into the island's northern sections and on to the Bronx, spilled across the East River into Brooklyn, and west across the Hudson, into New Jersey. Much of this migration was in search of better housing, and these residential consumers, rich and middling alike, used ever-larger amounts of disposable income to redecorate their homes.

Established businesses and the emerging corporations, which were beginning to construct the first grand, multilevel office buildings, were also entering the market for furnishings, though the biggest single purchasers of Pinchot & Warren's wares appear to have been the massive "pleasure palaces"—hotels—that came to dominate the antebellum skyline of New York. The material benefits derived from this boisterous market in interior decoration were, Pinchot would later confess, "so out of proportion with the amount of capital invested" that he hesitated to speak of them.[31]

At the same time, Pinchot used his newly acquired wealth to indulge the philanthropic impulses that marked him as a rising gentleman of means and standing. One example of these impulses was his support of contemporary American landscape art, and his budding friendships with artists Sanford Gifford (after whom James would name his first son), Jervis McEntee, Eastman Johnson, and Worthington Whittredge. As Pinchot's financial successes mounted, he purchased examples of his friends' work and loaned them for exhibitions in the United States and Europe; he later donated some of his collection to museums, bringing these artists greater public attention. His patronage was linked to the development of cultural institutions, too, for he believed, as did other members of the mercantile elite, that commercial New York needed the cosmopolitan gloss of London and Paris. He was active in the affairs of the National Academy of Design—like his brother, Edgar, he became a Fellow for Life—and was among those who early on subscribed to the establishment of the American Museum of Natural History. While still in his thirties, James Pinchot thus had emerged as one of the city's important agents of culture.

So consumed had he been during the 1850s with the building of his fortune that his health—spiritual and physical—periodically broke. In late 1854, for instance, he acknowledged in a letter to his parents that he had set aside his religious faith but had then been challenged by the famed Reverend Ward Beecher, whose Plymouth Church in Brooklyn Pinchot occasionally attended. "I went to Church with Ed [Pinchot] this morning at Beecher's, and heard a very superior sermon. It was on the duty of Christians and made a strong impression on me." Beecher evidently had scolded his congregants for "keeping all our religion for Sundays and particular occasions, and said these things should not be so." It was a classic Beecher rebuke, for the minister had gained a considerable reputation for confronting the wealthy, and those who wished to be, with the potential immorality of trade. "The Devil teaches Christians to use the world's selfish maxims," he once asserted; "it is here that he persuades them to smother their conscience." Recognizing that this blanket indictment covered him, Pinchot cried out to his parents that unless "in some way reminded of our continued worldliness ... we are continually carrying our worldliness too far. In fact I have lately almost entirely neglected everything else."[32]

Among those things James Pinchot neglected was his physical health, which had collapsed briefly several months earlier. His recovery had not been complete, and he associated his spiritual malaise with bodily maladies—another Beecher-like idea. For the next couple of years, the topic was a consistent thread in his correspondence home. In response to yet another distress call in 1855, his father finally urged extended rest. "What if you should do nothing for one year. Where would be the damage[?] Perhaps it will prove the best spent year in your life," Cyrille Pinchot concluded. "You can come home and raise chickens." But James Pinchot drove on, only acceding to his father's advice when, four years later, he suffered from what physicians diagnosed as "hemorrhages of the lungs." He spent the better part of 1859 traveling on horseback throughout the South; now no longer saddled with worldly cares, and enjoying sustained and rigorous exercise, Pinchot revived.[33]

As part of his resurrection, he began to dance—or at least to participate in the social whirl of New York's grand society: its fetes, cotillions, and balls. The invitations were numerous for a bachelor like Pinchot, who moved easily among the civic elite, was comfortably situated in the masculine world of the city's leading literary and social clubs (the Century and Union), helped flog its cultural ambitions, and cut a prosperous figure. Portraits reveal him to have been a man of powerful if slightly rotund frame, with a soft face and a light set of muttonchops. He was a presence—even in his absence. As artist Launt Thompson reported to a vacationing Pinchot during the summer of 1863, there had been "many inquiries after you," and so insistent were they that Thompson said he was "rather forced by experience to believe that the mammas regard you with considerable favor, if not more." The press of the mamas' affection was not altogether maternal. "We don't want our future wife to be a mamma before we get to her," Thompson winked salaciously. "Daughters sometimes are rebellious, sometimes mammas." Still, Pinchot's friend concluded, "I think the daughters like you too."[34]

A most eligible bachelor, James nonetheless caught many of his artist friends off guard in May 1864 when he married Mary Eno, the eldest

*James W. Pinchot
(1831–1908), Gifford's
father, was a successful
merchant, art collector,
and avid promoter of
his son's career.*
Grey Towers NHL

daughter of Amos R. Eno, a wealthy merchant and land speculator in New York. How the couple first met is unknown; evidently they moved in similar social circles, and may have come to know one another through propinquity. His residence at 128 West 22nd Street was within blocks of her parents' home at 26 East 23rd, and was around the corner from one of her father's most important enterprises—the upscale Fifth Avenue Hotel, site of innumerable soirees. Wherever they may have met, in Mary James met his match—she was a striking beauty, shrewd, ambitious, supportive, and of most good fortune.

Apparently it was not Mary's character and quality that so surprised James's compatriots, but the timing of the couple's nuptials. Most of them managed to miss the grand event held at the Madison Square Presbyterian Church—Eastman Johnson overslept; Jervis McEntee was out of town; and Launt Thompson confused the late May date with another. McEntee at least understood the significance of being newly wedded: "I can appreciate all your bright anticipations," he wrote James. "Believe me when I wish you all the real happiness you have as good a right to expect, that the wedding day shall not be the coming joy, but that time shall but confirm and fulfill all the promises of today." One of those promises was quickly fulfilled: on August 11, 1865, Mary gave birth to their first child, the future chief forester of the United States. James could barely contain his exultation. "The people of Milford . . . plied me with about a hundred questions about the baby — our baby," he wrote his wife while visiting his parents a month later, "all of which I answered in a modest, becoming manner."[35]

There was nothing demure about his wife's aspirations for this new family, however. Over the years, Mary Pinchot would urge her husband to raise his sights still further. "I believe you capable of a higher development than you will get if tied down to paper hangings," she advised in the late 1880s. "I think it a mistake that a man of such noble aspirations and large capacity should not fill a larger sphere." That she offered this particular advice to her husband at the exact moment the Pinchot and Eno families were involved in an extensive discussion about Gifford's future is significant. Amos Eno had been pressing his talented twenty-two-year-old grandson to join his commercial ventures and thus increase the family's wealth. But Mary, James, and Gifford were resisting, hoping that the young Yale graduate might pioneer the then-unknown field of forestry. How much more convincing would their rebuttal be, Mary reasoned, were James to retire and establish himself as a model of engaged public service for his son, thereby deflecting her father's pressure.

That shortly thereafter James stepped away from the daily grind is a sign of his wife's influence; that Gifford, and later his younger brother, Amos, took up public careers speaks just as loudly of the degree to which her expansive plans shaped her "children's position in the future." That it was Mary Eno Pinchot who most frequently voiced concerns on this topic qualifies Gifford's later public affirmation that it was his father who determined his life course. About this issue, his mother would have as much to say as her husband, using words that would be of greater consequence than the gift of a swift red sled.[36]

Relative Power

I N T H E S U M M E R of 1913, a year before Mary Eno Pinchot would die, her nearly forty-eight-year-old son Gifford suffered a personal blow that probably only this mother could (and would) correct. Theodore Roosevelt had gone back on his word, withholding much-promised praise from his autobiography for the outstanding work Pinchot had done as chief forester during his administration. The mother and son had discovered the offending lacuna during a most companionable moment—sitting together in the library of Grey Towers on a warm June evening, Gifford reading aloud the work's page proofs for his mother's amusement. But she was not amused. To his diary, the slighted Pinchot confided that his mother "was indignant at the scant mention of me," and he confessed to sharing some of his mother's anger, "especially in view of [Roosevelt's] declarations that he would give me much credit, several times repeated."[1]

Certainly Pinchot deserved the credit he sought: no one had been more intimately involved with the president's thinking on conservation matters nor had worked as hard to turn those thoughts into political reality. Pinchot had been among a coterie of federal scientists and bureaucrats who had devised and implemented the aggressive conservationist agenda that has done so much to define Roosevelt's continuing legacy in environmental politics. The number of national parks doubled from five to ten; the first eighteen national monuments were set aside, including the spectacular Grand Canyon; and more than fifty bird sanctuaries were established. Roosevelt also signed off on the creation of the Forest Service and its jurisdiction over a rapidly expanding national forest system. Securing these forests, and developing the agency to manage them, had occupied much of Pinchot's time and energy. He was also instrumental in organizing the May 1908 National Governors' Conference on the Conservation of Natural Resources and countless other national and regional conferences. From these podia Roosevelt proclaimed his administration's allegiance to the conservation movement, proclamations Pinchot often ghostwrote. The close relationship between the two men had been one reason why Roosevelt had asked Pinchot to draft an earlier version of the autobiography's chapter on conservation; once drafted, TR was to have inserted the words that honored his valued colleague.[2]

When Roosevelt failed to keep his side of the bargain, and counseled his disappointed friend that "he had intended to treat me as he did himself [in his autobiography] by merely reciting facts," Pinchot felt boxed in, unable to respond. Those in the know, that bully of a man had implied, would recognize the significance of Pinchot's many contributions.[3]

Mary Pinchot would have none of this manly reticence. As soon as her son had finished reading the chapter, the seventy-five-year-old mother moved slowly to her writing desk, picked up a pen, and, with her "right hand stiff with rheumatism," a painful fact she just happened to convey to her correspondent, wrote a scathing rebuke. "We have been reading tonight this chapter on Conservation for the 'Autobiography'—I am wondering if you know how little importance is given there to Gifford," she began. Warming to her task, she said she could not imagine how it was possible that "he who was the soul and fount of Forestry is scarcely mentioned by name," leaving the impression, which she was confident Roosevelt knew to be false, that her son "was only incidentally connected" with the great policies of his administration. Gifford would not ask that the president correct the record, she wrote—"[h]is own modesty and generous way of regarding what others do, always prevents his taking credit for what is justly his due"—but she was under no such restraint. This "is history you are writing," she counseled, "and so far as I know, there is little record of him except the shameful treatment of the last [Taft] administration and the vituperation of those who, being envious of righteousness and truth, hate him." Her son's intense devotion to Roosevelt's conservation ideals, which in 1910 had led William Howard Taft to sack him from his position as chief of the Forest Service for insubordination, should have impelled the former president to reestablish Gifford's reputation. Since it had not, she was reminding him of his duty. "It is for future generations that I wish [Gifford's] name to be vindicated and his services honored."[4]

Mary Pinchot's angry words found their mark. She knew they would, for she had reminded Roosevelt that her claims for her son were cut from the same cloth as the ambitions that had driven him "to seek the publication to the world of the truth" of his presidential accomplishments. Boosting Gifford would also elevate TR.[5]

The former president rose to the challenge and revised the text so that it contained the flattering words the Pinchots longed to read. "Gifford Pinchot is the man to whom the nation owes most for what has been accomplished as regards to the preservation of the natural resources of our country," Roosevelt now averred. The "moving and directing spirit in most of the conservation work" in which Pinchot "was practically breaking new ground," and Pinchot's "tireless energy and activity" earned the former president's great respect. "I believe it is but just to say that among the many, many public officials who under my administration rendered literally invaluable service to the people of the United States, he, on the whole, stood first." [6]

For restoring her son's standing, Mary Eno Pinchot was grateful. "You told me I would be satisfied with your chapter on Conservation, and so I am," she responded after reading the published version. "I thank you for your admirable tribute to Gifford."

Where did Mary Pinchot learn how to cow this Rough Rider, and to do so with language that simultaneously appealed to private, affective ties and public, abstract principles? How did she know to demand of "My dear Colonel" that he right a personal wrong to avoid a larger historical slight? And when had she acquired such a commanding presence that even her middle-aged son would sit quietly by and allow her to protest on his behalf?

Mary Eno Pinchot's skills had been honed through a lifetime of involvement in the national political arena, a masculine realm in which she never had a vote but came to wield a share of influence. These skills were also an inheritance of sorts—her close study of her family's illustrious heritage would regularly embolden her to define, extend, and defend familial honor. She could also so act because of her financial independence, an independence born of her father's fortune. Money and power, along with her forceful personality, would enable her to exert a remarkable influence on those whose lives intersected with hers, none more so than her son Gifford.

MOTHERLODE

She just could not restrain herself. A young Mary Eno, walking in New York's Battery Park, accompanied by the family nurse who was cradling Mary's baby sister in her arms, spied a cute dog—"a little black and tan, lying on the grass asleep"—and rushed over to it. She put her "hands on his head," she later remembered, cooing, "Come little doggie, won't you come home with me?"—a plea that made sense for someone for whom so many dreams had already come true. But not this one. The "little dog, angry at being disturbed" from its own reverie, "caught my hand in his mouth and bit it severely." The injured child was swooped up by a gentleman who, with the nurse leading the way, and a "crowd of people" surging behind, carried her home, where a physician cauterized "the several wounds." Mary was, the good doctor averred, "a brave little girl." [7]

She was also a bit self-centered, which was amply confirmed in her later retelling of this incident. For days, she said, a worried crowd had gathered before her home, a crowd so large that "every doctor in town" had to push through the gawkers to inquire after Mary's health. By this fuss she was not surprised. "The City of New York was at this time very small, clustering mostly around the vicinity of the Battery," she noted, "and of course such an event produced profound excitement." Why "of course" it should do so she never explained, but then she never felt the need. Around her always "a great commotion naturally ensued." [8]

So it had throughout her family's history. Both her maternal and paternal ancestors had made things happen, had forced people to take notice of them, as Mary Eno Pinchot was delighted to discover when, in her later years, she began to dig through the families' correspondence and develop their impressive genealogy. This archival research did nothing but confirm her sense of collective achievement, if not inherited greatness. Both the Phelps and Eno families, out of whose union she was born, were marked by an expanding set of financial resources and matched by widening social aspirations—traits that were leavened by a longstanding commitment to the commonweal. They led lives of privilege and purpose.

The Phelpses were the more politically active of the two branches, an activism dating from their arrival in the mid-1600s in the frontier "plantation" of Simsbury, Connecticut, a farming community that straddled the Farmington River and lay twelve miles to the north and west of Hartford. The Phelps family helped to clear the plantation's forests and plow its fields, and then had fought and died in the town's defense during King Philip's War and the later French and Indian Wars. Their commitment to this place perhaps reached its most intense expression when Noah Phelps, Mary Eno Pinchot's great-grandfather, signed Simsbury's Declaration of Independence in 1774 shortly after British troops had sealed off Boston Harbor. Although the document swore loyalty to King George, it denounced the British Parliament's actions against Boston, demanded the establishment of a Continental Congress to govern colonial affairs, and called for aid to the beleaguered citizens of Boston, a declaration that quickly turned into a call to arms. Having secured enough land and accumulated sufficient wealth, the Phelpses were able to raise their own company from the Simsbury region to fight in the War of Independence, with Noah Phelps in command. By war's end he had risen from lieutenant to major general, signals of both his tactical skill and political acumen. In peacetime, these same qualities would enable him to expand the family's landholding and extend its local influence.[9]

His children—most notably his son Elisha, Mary Pinchot's grandfather—fully mined the prospects offered by an emerging republic. Born in 1779, Elisha was raised to pursue a career in public service, itself an indication of the Phelpses' increasingly comfortable financial status. His path led to his admittance to Yale College's class of 1800, one of the first to matriculate under the ever-watchful eye of President Timothy Dwight. Brought to Yale in 1794 to subdue what the college's trustees felt was an unruly, irreligious student body, the Congregational minister wasted no time before confronting undergraduate impiety; he hacked away at its intellectual roots, which drew heavily upon European enlightened skepticism—Thomas Paine's *The Age of Reason* (1794) was said to have been the rage on campus—and American Deism. At Dwight's Yale, God and Federalism were one.[10]

Elisha Phelps divined no such unity, and inhabited a more complex cosmos; this Congregationalist was a devout Republican. He clearly enjoyed the struggle associated with maintaining this equilibrium, for following his graduation from Yale he entered yet another Federalist redoubt, Tapping Reeve's celebrated school of law in Litchfield, Connecticut. Reeve and his co-educator, James Gould, were vocal opponents of Jeffersonian Republicanism; Phelps could not have selected a more hostile environment in which to study law.[11]

Yet Litchfield had its allure. Its founders were in the vanguard of those jurists seeking means by which to integrate the practices of common law with the principles of popular sovereignty. Their resolution was radical, and, given the Federalist disenchantment with the populace, they concluded that a state had the "supreme power" to command "what is right, and [prohibit] what is wrong." That conclusion enhanced the power of the judiciary, too: in theory "courts make no law," the Litchfield lawyers acknowledged, "but in point of fact they are legislators." Their students did not miss the political implications of this fact: in the new republic, lawyers ruled.[12]

And Litchfield lawyers especially ruled, to judge from the lofty positions the school's graduates secured; two became vice presidents of the United States, three were appointed associate justices of the U.S. Supreme Court, and innumerable others became Cabinet officers, senators, congressmen, and state legislators. Not all were Federalists. Since most of these posts were elected, Republicans such as Elisha Phelps could gain office and thus shape law and social policy. The Simsbury native followed a well-beaten path, then, when, shortly after being admitted to the Connecticut Bar in 1803, he leaped into local and state politics.[13]

For the next thirty years or so, Elisha alternated between practicing his profession and campaigning for office, serving in the Connecticut House of

Representatives for ten terms and as its Speaker for two, as well as holding a state senatorial seat for several more. This Republican's aspirations for national office were stymied, however, by the Federalist Party's dominance. Phelps and his Republican peers were finally able to break their rivals' hold through sweeping reforms legislated by the state's Constitutional Convention in 1818; as one of its twenty-four elected delegates, Phelps had helped draft laws that expanded the electoral franchise and disestablished the Congregational Church. These legal maneuvers opened the way for two-party politics, and Phelps quickly capitalized on the opportunity in that year's fall elections, becoming the first non-Federalist to serve Connecticut in the U.S. House of Representatives. He would follow up this triumph with another; in 1835 he was appointed a commissioner to revise and codify the whole of the State of Connecticut's statutes. In so doing, he turned the tables on his Litchfield law professors, using their Federalist precepts about judicial preeminence to ensure a Republican outcome.[14]

All the while, Phelps grew richer. The bulk of his income came from his law practice, allowing him to invest in a series of local improvement schemes; these included a failed canal system that was to have linked Simsbury to transportation routes running between New Haven, Hartford, and western Massachusetts, and a more successful wool-card manufacturing concern sited not far from his sprawling mansion, which overlooked the placid waters of the defunct canal. It was to that estate, built on land that members of the family had purchased in the 1640s, that Phelps's granddaughter, Mary Eno, would come each summer; it was there that her first child, Gifford, would be born in 1865. She loved the manse and loved dallying in "its old fashion garden, with its straight wide paths, bordered with beds of all sorts of flowers. . . ." She did more than just take in the heady scent: it was on these extended visits that she first came to appreciate what seemed to her to be an enduring bond between the Phelpses' social status and the family's political heritage.[15]

For Mary, journeying to Simsbury was like taking a trip back in time in many ways. Its furniture was as antique as those who inhabited the old estate, and it testified to the family's cultural standing; Mary played on the piano that Noah Phelps had hauled into the colonial outpost, and walked on wool rugs imported from Brussels. Further evidence of the Phelpses' eminence could be seen in Elisha Phelps's daily activity in his retirement. Each morning Mary witnessed the flow of petitioners and friends who rode up the hill to the house seeking her grandfather's advice, drawing upon his experience, and exchanging the latest political gossip. These visible reminders of his magnetism, when set within the stories she heard about his arduous labors as a congressman, impressed her no end.[16]

Impressive, too, was her uncle, the Honorable John Smith Phelps (D-Missouri), who would provide her with an even more thorough introduction to American politics. After studying at Hartford's Trinity College in the mid-1830s and apprenticing in his father's law office, he had been bitten with what the family called "western fever" and, in 1837, lit out for the territories. He got as far as Missouri, settling in Springfield, seat of Greene County, Queen City of the Ozarks. He had been lured there not by the expanding frontier's agricultural opportunities but by its open politics. Within three years he had gained a seat in the Missouri state legislature, and in 1844 he won the first of nine straight elections to the U.S. House of Representatives. That November, after an absence of seven years, John Phelps returned to Simsbury for a Thanksgiving family reunion.

Mary Eno could not wait to meet her uncle, a man for whom she held a "great curiosity" because he was her mother's favorite sibling and because he lived in close proximity to the Indians. On the day of his arrival, Mary remembered, suddenly "the door of the dining room opened and my uncle came out to meet us," but his opening remarks stunned them all: "he welcomed us to China instead of to our own home." Realizing that he was delirious, the family put him to bed, but "before morning he was dangerously ill, so that the Thanksgiving Day, to which the family had looked forward with such joy, was now a very sad one." [17]

Happily, he recovered, and thereafter the Phelps and Eno families frequently exchanged visits; John Phelps's trips to New York, Mary related, "were always times of great rejoicing." No wonder. Phelps was charming and energetic, a polished speaker and a vivid conversationalist, a man whose career within the Democratic Party and on Capitol Hill showed considerable promise. A staunch supporter of western expansion, he helped underwrite the development of the trans-Mississippi West as a member, and later chairman, of the House Ways and Means Committee. Many colleagues expected him to become Speaker of the House, but he never secured that post—because, some contemporaries believed, by the late 1850s his zealous defense of the Union sounded too Republican (and northern) for the Democratic (and southern) leadership of his party. As had happened to his father, John Phelps's maverick positions impeded his career.[18]

His niece was nonetheless enthralled by Phelps's time within the national spotlight, and the reflected glory that fell upon those within his circle. When John Quincy Adams's funeral procession wove through New York City in early March 1848, Mary and her family gathered at her father's office on Broadway to watch the casket pass by. Out of one of the accompanying black carriages leaped Congressman Phelps, who was serving as an honorary pallbearer. He waded through the onlookers to speak to the Enos, "a proceeding," Mary later commented, "that seemed to me very exciting at the time."[19]

More electrifying still was her extended visit to Washington in late February and early March of 1853 for the inauguration of President Franklin Pierce. She recalled standing in the East Portico of the Capitol, situated perfectly to take in the lengthy celebration, but its oratorical charms were not what caught her attention. "I suppose I heard the inaugural speeches, but to tell the truth they interested me much less than the assemblage of people present." Among those powerful figures in whose shadow she stood, and to whom her uncle introduced her, was yet another impressive relative, Senator Samuel Phelps of Vermont, and the ever-fascinating Sam Houston, whose drawl, "long hair and gilt buttons" remained vivid even with the passage of time. By her uncle's side, Mary had learned an essential lesson— politics was a matter of knowing who to know.[20]

MONEY TALKS

Those of wealth and standing gained access to those in the know. That was the lesson she would absorb from her father, Amos Richard Eno, who piled up a vast fortune as a merchant and land speculator during New York City's tumultuous growth before, during, and after the Civil War. His lucrative ventures—he reportedly controlled more than $25 million worth of prime Manhattan real estate at his death in 1898—gave him the power to join with others in defining what constituted the fashionable sections of the nation's largest city. This manipulation of land use patterns was no less obvious in his philanthropic munificence, which reinforced the refinement of not only the urban landscape but also that of his ancestral homeland, Simsbury, Connecticut. Town and country would bear his impress.[21]

Amos Eno's French Huguenot forebears would themselves have been impressed. Having fled to England in the sixteenth century, members of the Eno family—whose name was apparently shortened from the original "Henno" once in the New World—then migrated to Connecticut, arriving in Windsor, of which Simsbury was a part, in the late 1640s. There they earned their capital the hard way—by working the land. Fortunately, theirs contained good, arable soil, well watered by the Farmington River and its tributaries, and the family prospered. Their economic successes allowed them to add to their holdings, as did their repeated service in defense of the community, for which they received additional grants of land. By the late 1600s, the Enos were among the area's largest landholders, regularly held important community posts, and were exemplary members of the local Congregational church, a level of status that they enhanced over the next century. By then, Salmon Eno, Amos Eno's father, was a prosperous farmer, but unlike the Phelpses, his neighbors and relatives—the two families had intermarried several times by the late eighteenth century—he did not parlay his local eminence into a statewide or national political career. He represented Simsbury but once in the Connecticut state legislature.[22]

Neither would politics attract his second son, Amos Richard, born in 1810. Commerce did, but Simsbury's limited horizons—it was a hamlet of less than 2,000 souls, with modest industrial activity—were not enough to sustain his mercantile ambitions. He rebelled at the town's social provinciality, moreover, confiding to his fiancée, Lucy Phelps, that "most of its inhabitants" embodied a "staid puritanical character" he could not abide. In 1830 he moved, with his cousin John J. Phelps, to the more vibrant, regional economic hub of Hartford, the state's capital.[23]

They stayed several years, toiling as clerks in a successful downtown dry goods concern. Their work gave the young men insight into the complexities not only of the business world but of working in a city that, despite its growth in population and economic activity following the War of 1812, would remain a middling entrepôt, trapped between the two major urban centers of the eastern seaboard, New York and Boston; to the south lay another, ambitious rival, New Haven, whose splendid port enabled it to dominate trade throughout the Connecticut River valley. The advent of the railroad only pressed home Hartford's relatively precarious position. By the mid-1830s, rail links between New York, New Haven, and Boston were on the drawing boards and heavily financed; Hartford, by contrast, was slow to respond to the challenge. Symptomatic of this was the timing and manner in which Amos Eno and John Phelps left the community: in 1833 they caught a stagecoach to New Haven and then traveled by steamboat to the nation's first city, there to establish a partnership in the dry goods trade. Eno and Phelps's immediate success would prove that New York was everything that Hartford and Simsbury were not.[24]

The triumph of the Phelps-Eno partnership, to hear Walter Barrett tell it, was part of an enduring American legend, the rise of the sons of small-town America to national prominence. The cousins had "small means, small credit, but big hopes," Barrett observed in *The Old Merchants of New York City* (1863), a chatty and discursive multivolume assessment of the lives of Gotham's rich and famous. Hope was their only currency, for when they opened their tiny establishment and prepared to stock its shelves through auction sales, they ran up against a system of exchange stacked against new, unknown merchants. "In those days almost every purchaser was required to give an endorsed note for the amount of his purchase," but "Eno & Phelps could not do it. Nobody would endorse for them." Forced to purchase goods on credit, a far more risky venture, they nonetheless prevailed, so that in less than one year they had become the largest auction purchasers. So coveted were they that when they were "present at sale, auctioneers became anxious for them to buy, and would call on them to bid," a powerful position that they exploited to the hilt. When they retired from commercial activities they were, Barrett reported, "supposed to be worth over a half a million dollars each," quite a tidy sum.[25]

The story of their success, when tied to the other, similar tales that Barrett recounted, contributed greatly to the classic nineteenth-century fable about the social origins of New York City's merchant princes. Each had come from limited means; each prospered as a result of his prudence, diligence, and probity. The mere existence of their massive wealth enhanced democracy, moreover, for their individual success gave credence to the notion that this was a land of endless opportunities. Barrett, consciously or otherwise, used Amos Eno and others to underscore Alexis de Tocqueville's broad claim that, in America, the rich men were formerly poor sons.[26]

Yet neither Eno nor Phelps had a ragged past. Not only did both come from families of some consequence in Simsbury, but as Barrett's own evidence indicates, they developed business connections and social networks with other sons of northern Connecticut, many of whom hailed from Hartford County. Thus they lessened their risks and facilitated one another's expansion, promoting a rise that was collective, not individual. Moreover, what Barrett did not appreciate was that one of the opportunities that amassing great wealth provided was the chance to widen the divide between rich and poor, a gap maintained through differences in income and savings, and shored up through distinctions in housing, education, and culture. Amos Eno's economic success both expanded and narrowed the contours of the world in which his children and grandchildren would later come of age.[27]

Those economic distinctions were written into the land itself. Beginning in the 1840s, Eno began to invest in high-end real estate and, capitalizing upon its manifold possibilities, soon retired from the wholesale dry goods business to devote his full attention to this brisk speculation. He was particularly adept at forecasting and encouraging the northern thrust of commercial and residential development on Manhattan Island, especially as it moved into the undeveloped regions lying above Washington Square.

At times his ventures seemed excessive, even mad. In 1855, for instance, he plunked down a reported $170,000—at the time, an astronomical sum—for fourteen lots covering the intersection of Fifth Avenue and Twenty-third Street; one of these, an odd, narrow, triangular lot formed by the confluence of Broadway, Fifth Avenue, and Twenty-third Street, alone cost $25,000. These prices led the *New York Tribune* to wonder at the judiciousness of such investments, concluding that "the secret" of these "high prices we presume lies in the . . . idea . . . that no lots on this island are fit to place magnificent structures upon except those situated upon the narrow strip lying between Fourth and Sixth avs and Tenth and Fortieth-sts." Eno was banking on that presumption. It paid off handsomely. Take that triangular lot, on which he erected what would become known as the original Flatiron Building: he "was content to hold on to this valuable site," the *New York Times* later reported, "for the reason that [its] rentals yielded him annually as much as he paid for the property"; the yield dramatically escalated when, upon his death, its sale reaped nearly $700,000, an approximate thirtyfold increase in value. Fifth Avenue had become New York City's gold coast, and Eno one of its most successful prospectors.[28]

Yet the prospects were not so certain in the early 1850s. When Eno purchased nearly a full block between Twenty-third and Twenty-fourth Streets, fronting on Madison Square, and proposed to build an elegant hotel in the then-undeveloped neighborhood, the press quickly dubbed the project "Eno's Folly." When local bankers refused to underwrite the construction, Eno drew on his substantial assets and secured funding in Boston; once completed in 1855, the hotel quickly became a spectacular economic success. Its profits were rumored to have been a quarter of a million dollars a year; more importantly, its sheer presence generated further waves of land speculation, as well as office and housing construction that increased the value of Eno's other properties in the neighborhood.[29]

That success bred success is a neat economic rebuttal of Tocqueville's egalitarian forecast for Jacksonian America. Eno could not be counted among the common men. Commoners in turn would not be found traipsing along the corridors, or supping in the richly appointed dining room, of the Fifth Avenue Hotel, which, upon its opening in 1859, became the social, cultural, and political hub of elite New York. Why it became so, *Harper's Weekly* could not say, for it found the hotel's decorative touches a bit much. Its white marble exterior, dark red and white marble flooring, drawing rooms decked out with "heavy masses of gilt wood, rich crimson or green curtains, extremely handsome rose-wood and brocatelle suits [and] rich carpets . . . the whole presenting about as handsome and as comfortless an appearance as any one need wish for."

But the magazine's upper-crust readers understood the hotel's drawing power, flocking to purchase goods in its boutique-like shops or eating in its vast dining room with adjoining tearooms and smoking parlors. They made it a point to sweep down the series of wide promenades with other

members of the city's elite and influential visitors from home and abroad.
That the lobby—or, more precisely, one section of it, the "Amen corner"—
was also the headquarters of the state's Republican Party added to the
hotel's cachet, as did the fact that in nearby residential neighborhoods lived
such luminaries as the elder Theodore and Martha Roosevelt, parents of
the future president. More, having "a room at the Fifth Avenue Hotel, with
the related right to pass regularly through its parlors," historian Richard
Bushman has observed, "made a public claim to personal refinement." By
this standard, none were so refined as the Enos, and later the Pinchots, who
lived on the hotel's premises for many years.[30]

A highly visible point on New York's map of respectability and refinement, the hotel was only one of many ways Eno contributed to and located
himself within the geography of the genteel. He joined some of the city's
most important social and civic clubs and was involved in the establishment
of a number of others, including Groliers, Players, the Union League, and
the Reform, to which he would later sell his massive Twenty-third Street
home. As did his future son-in-law, James Pinchot, Eno contributed money
and artifacts to the city's emerging cultural institutions, such as the Metropolitan Museum.

Eno's philanthropy was generous and a definitive statement of his gentility, qualities that also characterized his munificence toward his native
town of Simsbury. There, he purchased his father-in-law's substantial
home along the Northampton canal, turning it into a country estate complete with white picket fences, tall elms, and a green sweep of lawn. He
rebuilt the town too, donating considerable funds to construct what a Simsbury historian labeled a "dignified and appropriate colonial style Library"
and to fill its shelves with edifying literature. He provided as well the
wherewithal to refurbish the Congregational church and then purchased
an old farm, retrofitting it to serve as an asylum for the town's indigent.
Such benevolence cleansed the social landscape and reordered the spatial
terrain, making Simsbury a more refined village from which to have come,
and to which to return.[31]

UPTOWN GIRL

With the power to improve came an uplifted sense of station, a sensibility that Amos Eno's daughter, Mary, took to heart as she moved through the Simsbury and New York her father had transformed. The movement, as her memoirs reveal, was always upward, an ascension that she marked by noting the family's changes of address and circumstance. Her earliest recollections were of living in a house near the Battery in the early 1840s, but within a few years her father's fortunes increased to the point that they could afford to leave the compactly settled neighborhood and join others in their flight up-island. They landed in a home on Fourth Street, near Washington Square, in the then-fashionable Fifteenth Ward, "where we children, of whom there were now four, had a great deal of pleasure." Their joy consisted, she remembered, of playing in "a beautiful garden, taking up a whole block, which was just opposite us," and in developing playground friendships with other children of New York's rising commercial and professional families; she kept note, too, of each of her associations with these families, tracking her childhood status.

When Amos Eno decided that, fashionable or not, Washington Square was too distant from his place of business, and migrated back to an older, lower Manhattan address, Mary took comfort in his purchase of the fabled Leeman Reed house; Wendell Barrett had gushed that it was once "the wonder of its day," and the same could have been said for its address, 16 Greenwich Street, which in the late 1820s and early 1830s was the heart of New York's wealthy residences. Mary would later admit that she had never lived in as fine a house, and was forever entranced by its solid, dark mahogany doors, its door frames, baseboards, and fireplaces of white Italian marble, and its "beautiful, although not very large garden," complete with large marble cisterns that collected rain for the family's water supply. The impressive edifice also contained an art gallery, on whose walls Reed had hung the work of Thomas Cole and other early American landscape artists for whom he had served as a patron. One set of canvases that Mary recalled viewing was Cole's riveting series "The Course of Empire," an allegorical exploration of the struggle between humanity's relentless civilizing quest and the indomitable power of nature.[32]

The world outside this sanctuary, however, suggested that civilization was losing ground, though not to nature. Pleased that her family's residence enabled her to forge friendships with members of old New York families, Mary was aware that the neighborhood had seen better days. Her new friends began to move away, at once intensifying and profiting from the decline by selling their large homes to developers. So, in time, did the Enos, who remained "until we were surrounded by immigrant boarding houses," only to add to their number through the sale of the Reed homestead. The peripatetic family then returned to the Washington Square region, and in succeeding years moved ever northward, finally building an impressive mansion on East Twenty-third Street, fronting Madison Square. Through all these moves, one thing remained constant: the names of those families with whom Mary Eno associated. She kept good company.[33]

Amid this entourage, she gained a sense of entitlement, an unstudied expectation that to her should come the fine things of life. She never knew otherwise, for her education was as cloistered as her homes. In keeping with the pattern of her class, she was raised by nannies and educated by governesses. As she entered adolescence, her schooling remained private, sometimes in concert with friends or alone with a tutor; one of these was her mother's close friend, the writer Caroline Kirkland, with whom Mary studied literature and with whose daughter she studied music. Beyond these academic endeavors lay the more engaging give-and-take of "society," the whirl of which formed the core of her memoirs. In them she detailed her meeting of the Italian contralto Albioni and, later, that "very fine looking man, with a soft hat of rather a peculiar shape," the Hungarian patriot Louis Kossuth. With painstaking exactness she remembered the impromptu parties at the homes of friends and neighbors, and the far more formal coming-out dances she attended, the clothes she wore to them, and the emotions they provoked.[34]

That she also knew how to obtain what she wanted was never more manifest than during her years of courting. "In those days, society was very much less formal than it afterwards became," she remarked about the mid-1850s, so "we young people could do very much as we liked," a situation that many women, of society and not, found advantageous.

Mary Eno's attributes were considerable. Given her beauty and energy,

*The daughter of a wealthy
New York City land spec-
ulator, Mary Jane Eno
Pinchot (1838–1914)
was a commanding force
in her children's lives,
especially Gifford's.*
Grey Towers NHL

and her family's wealth and connections, her home, especially its balconies, became "the great resort for the young men of the neighborhood." This traffic overran her father's insistence "upon our not going out or receiving company at home without someone in attendance," and so did her frequent excursions on horseback to Central Park. "The park was at that time in an incomplete state, and not as well guarded . . . so that we had many wild rides in the unfrequented parts of the park without any notice from the policeman." She also knew how to put ill-advised suitors in their place, much as she did one ardent young man from St. Louis. He was "about a foot shorter than I—so that I was not willing to dance with him," but, once he was elevated on a horse, and perhaps believing "he was at better advantage than under ordinary circumstances," he pressed his suit anew. It failed. Shouting "No! No! I could never think of it," Mary Eno whipped her steed "and galloped away as fast as [she] could, leaving that gentleman far behind. . . ."[35]

She would not be reined in during her long and happy marriage to (a presumably taller) James Pinchot, either. It was after she was a married woman, in fact, that she was best able to display her ability to take the lead in public matters, leadership that intertwined the political activism of the Phelps family with the Enos' financial muscle. This remarkable combination of powers enabled her, in one particularly dramatic instance, to enter the civic arena in defense of her family's name and reputation.

The drama unfolded in the spring of 1884 when her younger and much-loved brother, John Chester Eno, did something really stupid—to his father. Four years earlier he had been tapped to be president of the Second National Bank of New York, a bank in which the Eno, Phelps, and Pinchot families were heavily invested. The bank was conveniently located in a corner of the Fifth Avenue Hotel, where one would think that all could keep a close eye on it—but not so, apparently.

Although the bank's assets were said to total $4 million in 1884, that was an inflated figure, because over the previous two years John Eno had been stealing the bank's ready cash and then investing heavily in the stock market, especially in risky railroad ventures. When these investments went bust, Eno stole ever-larger quantities of the bank's assets, including an alleged $1.5 million of his father's securities—thefts that, when they came to light in May 1884, totaled more than $4 million. He then compounded his problems by fleeing to Canada.

This massive defalcation, which nearly broke the Second National Bank, and the subsequent extradition proceedings were the focus of a more than decade-long set of court battles, some of the technicalities of which were ultimately resolved by the U.S. Supreme Court. John Eno had become a household name for all the wrong reasons.[36]

His family set financial matters aright. Amos Eno and the other directors made good on the bank's losses, with the elder Eno ultimately paying back each director, a payoff that totaled more than a quarter of his considerable wealth. While staggering, the financial problems were nevertheless more easily resolved than the legal complications that young Eno faced. He would face them nearly alone, too, for no one in his immediate family, infuriated as they were by his duplicity and theft, was willing to come to his defense—except Mary Eno Pinchot.[37]

It is quite likely that Mary helped her brother evade the police surveillance of his Manhattan home so that he could escape to Canada. Her grand design was for him to slip across the Atlantic and set up a life in Europe, beyond the judicial reach of the federal and state governments. To that end, Mary Pinchot initiated an extended correspondence with William Tecumseh Sherman, a close family friend, seeking advice about how to deflect the Justice Department's inquiries and parry its legal maneuvers. With letters of introduction from the Civil War hero and influential member of the Republican Party, she gained access to important congressmen, held meetings with relevant Cabinet officials, and, over the years, pleaded her brother's cause at the White House, meeting first with President Chester Arthur and later with Grover Cleveland and Benjamin Harrison. She was not above suggesting that the executive branch commit a fraud of its own. She hoped President Arthur, for instance, would persuade his secretary of state, Frederick T. Frelinghuysen, to "shut his eyes for half an hour" so that John Eno could sail to Europe; to do so would aid in Eno's reformation, Sherman assured Arthur, so that "I honestly believe [the secretary's] conscience will acquit him and he will sleep the sounder in years to come." Neither Arthur nor Frelinghuysen agreed, one result of which was that John Eno remained in legal limbo in Canada until 1893.[38]

For all her determination, Mary Eno Pinchot's money could go only so far; what she had, she made available for her brother's protracted defense. Among other things, this meant reordering her own nuclear family's financial arrangements. In the mid-1880s she asked her husband to return her dowry, and he complied, selling some Manhattan real estate and taking out a mortgage for the remainder, acknowledging that "you should do as you wish with your own."

Her wish was to underwrite a new initiative aimed at either securing a presidential pardon for her brother or, failing that, convincing federal prosecutors to write off the case as *nolle prosequi*. This led to yet another round of court hearings and interviews with government officials, all the while relying on General Sherman's advice and contacts. The impact of her appeal to President Harrison, Sherman noted in 1891, "will be influenced by the effects [on votes] of granting nolle prosequi to John without doing the same for all the parties who have gone to Canada to avoid arrest and extradition." That political reality was matched by another: she needed to be careful to address her concerns to the appropriate official, since "jealousies among Cabinet officers in Washington [are] proverbial." He thus urged her to focus not on Secretary of State Blaine, who "I know . . . would like to do you and your father an act of kindness," but on the Attorney General. In time, this approach prevailed. In 1894, the government agreed not to prosecute.[39]

John Eno's name could never be cleared, a consequence of his manifest guilt. But that stain was no reflection on the aggressive campaign his sister had mounted on his behalf. At its commencement, Sherman had lauded her "heroic qualities," and at its conclusion in 1893 her twenty-eight-year-old son Gifford praised her for having "done all that was possible to help [John Eno] get clear, and then to make a man of himself," a compliment that would have deep resonance for Gifford, who at that moment was attempting to launch his career as a forester. For all that Mary Eno Pinchot had done for her brother, she would do even more for her son, as Theodore Roosevelt would discover.[40]

Rising Son

J AMES AND MARY PINCHOT knew how to plan a soiree and give it a
rich symbolic cast, and the summer tea party they hosted in honor of
son Gifford's twenty-first birthday on August 11, 1886, was no exception. Although the invitation list was short (only members of the extended
family attended), their numbers filled the billiard room of the Pinchots'
now-completed summer home, Grey Towers. In her diary, Mary Pinchot
recorded that all "had a fine time" toasting "G's health" and "taking our
first meal in the house" under "beautiful moonlight." The celebration of
Gifford's coming of age had been paired with the christening of this stately
mansion, itself a reflection of the family's social ambitions.[1]

One of those ambitions was revealed in the gift they purchased for Gifford and that Amos, Gifford's younger brother, presented to him: an 1882
edition of George Perkins Marsh's *The Earth as Modified by Human Action*.
Originally published twenty years earlier, Marsh's profoundly important
book on the devastation that humanity had already inflicted on the planet
had deeply impressed itself upon the American imagination. Drawing on
his extensive study of the rise and fall of ancient Mediterranean empires
facilitated by his years in the region as a diplomat, the Vermont-born Marsh
concluded that environmental despoliation had been central to the collapse
of these once-powerful civilizations. By clearing their forests, for instance,
they had unleashed a series of interlocking and escalating problems such as

erosion, the silting up of streams and rivers, and the loss of soil fertility. With watersheds damaged beyond repair and agriculture faltering, the economic orders and social structures that had depended on productive landscapes were everywhere compromised. Marsh's grim tale of past woes was of contemporary significance. Attentive readers in the 1860s and 1870s did not miss its potent American parallels as this New World society entered an industrial age in which natural resources were being consumed with astonishing celerity. Like the Greeks and Romans, we were poised to destroy ourselves.

All was not lost, however, Marsh argued. Human restoration of savaged terrain, the conservative management of forests, arable land, and waterways, and a sharper appreciation of nature's limitations should allow the new republic to escape the old threat of catastrophic decline. Paired with his apocalyptic rhetoric was Marsh's more beguiling language of optimism and hope.

The senior Pinchots were among those who found in *Man and Nature* a set of fascinating possibilities for the United States. They did so in part because Marsh's arguments confirmed those of two of James Pinchot's French heroes, Colbert and Bernard Palissy. Colbert, Louis XIV's minister, had much earlier asserted the direct "relation between forests and national welfare," as did eighteenth-century naturalist Palissy, and apparently James Pinchot delighted in quoting Palissy's belief that neglecting forests was "not merely a blunder but a calamity and a curse for France."[2]

Given this intellectual affinity, it is little wonder that the Pinchots took to heart Marsh's declaration that "we have now felled forest enough everywhere" and embraced his resolute call to "restore this one element of material life" so that Americans would become "more emphatically, a well-ordered and stable commonwealth, and, not less conspicuously, a people of progress." Their initial contribution to this revival would be to transform the stark, treeless hillside on which Grey Towers had been erected; as Gifford observed in April 1886, "[T]here are already enough trees planted on the place to take away any feeling of bleakness." Surely all the celebrants at the young man's birthday party had observed these initial reforestation efforts and had heard of the family's larger goal of reforesting hundreds of bare acres that lay above and below their chateau.[3]

It is just as certain that Gifford's grandmother, aunts, uncles, and assorted kin knew that these restorative designs were of a piece with his career aspirations. One year earlier, shortly before he had entered Yale College as a member of the class of 1889, his father had reportedly popped a question that would change his life: "How would you like to be a forester?" This was, Gifford would remember, "an amazing question for that day and generation—how amazing I didn't begin to understand at the time." He did not because, George Perkins Marsh's influential book notwithstanding, no American had yet accepted its practical consequence—making forestry a career.

Intrigued by the prospects James Pinchot had outlined for him, Gifford quickly became conscious of the implications of his father's question; he relentlessly talked about this profession with every member of his family. Once at Yale, he boasted to incredulous peers that forestry would become his lifework, and he pestered members of the Yale faculty for more information about the as yet undeveloped field of study. When William H. Brewer, a professor of agriculture at Yale's Sheffield Scientific School, assured him that no American university curriculum included forestry and that its science therefore was untaught and unknown, Gifford hastened to inform his parents of his good fortune. "I shall have not only no competitors, but even a science to found," he wrote gleefully. "This surely is as good an opening as a man could have."[4]

The Pinchots concurred with Gifford's belief that his maturation and prospective career were bound up together. That is what they had long encouraged and had reinforced to him that day he reached the legal age of majority. When James and Mary Pinchot gave Marsh's seminal text to Gifford as a guide for the next stage of his life, an offering set within their plans to repair this broken land, they expected their familial concerns to engender national consequences.

MANCHILD

Gifford's childhood and adolescence were as managed as was his birthday party. It is not that his parents knew from their son's birth that he would become a forester, but they were convinced that his could be a brilliant and eminent career, whatever its focus. They would spare no expense to ensure this outcome.

What their money bought initially was a peripatetic existence. Born in his maternal grandparents' sprawling home in Simsbury, Connecticut, on August 11, 1865, young Gifford shuttled between this estate, mostly visited during the summers, and other Eno residences in New York City, including the Fifth Avenue Hotel. In the early 1870s the Pinchot family went abroad for three years, touring England, Germany, Italy, and France, a grand tour that they would partly recapitulate in the early 1880s. While these lengthy journeys disrupted Gifford's formal education, his parents supplemented the invaluable cultural exposure that travel offered by hiring tutors or enrolling their children in local schools; wherever the family settled down, Gifford and his younger siblings, Antoinette (known as Nettie) and Amos, studied French, dance, art, and the rudiments of mathematics and literature. He was no scientist in the making.[5]

Then again, the natural world was a consistent frame of reference in the family's discussions. Whether he was slopping through tidal rock formations along the coast of Normandy or setting down his thoughts about the life cycle of honeybees, Gifford seemed drawn to the biotic realm. His parents at once modeled and encouraged his budding fascination. Their travel diaries reveal eyes keenly attuned to the landscape or, more precisely, to a Romantic aesthetic of the relationship between humanity and the world it inhabited. What made the English countryside so "lovely," Mary Pinchot wrote in her Memo Book of 1880, was its "green hedges, well-kept lawns, parks, [and] cottages with gay flower beds." This land "seems so cared for as if it had been so for generations," she observed; here, "the hand of man appeals to our humanity, and gives an added charm to even the most beautiful of Nature's works." That cultivated sensibility found its parallel in James Pinchot's musings, jotted down while traveling by rail to Manchester, England. "I never saw Nature more inviting, with her green fields & trees—the hedges, the ivy green and the animals scattered about here and there completed the picture," a picture that was as sublime as it was divine. "I never felt more sensibly the goodness of God than at that time."

To see the Lord's handiwork was to hate the devil's. As his train pushed into the great manufacturing city of the Midlands, James predictably

recoiled from the industrial purgatory, with its "tall black chimneys looking like lofty towers from which immense volumes of smoke are issuing."
When, during his 1880 stay in England, fifteen-year-old Gifford voiced his
delight in roaming its bucolic landscape and fishing on its quiet ponds, and
then uttered his disdain for London's chaos and filth, he suggested just how
well he had been schooled in the nuances of his parents' pastoral perspective.[6]

Educating Gifford became a central preoccupation when he began to
spend considerable time away from his family. The first such instance
occurred during the fall of 1880. While the senior Pinchots, Antoinette, and
Amos traveled on the Continent, fifteen-year-old Gifford spent several
months boarding with the family of Canon Leslie Angelsmith of Canterbury Cathedral. Gifford's studies were canonical; he made selected forays
into British literature, delved into mathematics, and toured the requisite
architectural landmarks of the British past.

His real lessons came in the mail, however. Three or four letters a
week—sometimes more—crossed the Channel, each bearing a set of
reminders, encouragements, or sharp reproofs. From his father, Gifford
learned that young gentlemen needed to be independent and self-reliant;
James charged him with the responsibility for "money matters" while in
Canterbury, because "Leslie [Angelsmith] is not as careful as I would like."
When the young man in turn was careless, he was reminded how to behave;
when he neglected to get his shoes repaired or his coat mended, his father
told him how to go about the task, and how much to pay for the work. And
if he failed to obey familial demands—most especially those concerned
with maintaining his correspondence—James Pinchot could be witheringly direct. "Your mother has just received another letter *without a date*.
Your carelessness and inattention to our wishes is painful." More painful
were Gifford's apparently dilatory responses to his parents' steady stream
of communications: "If you will not write or if will not regularly," James
reprimanded, "I shall feel obligated to ask you to leave the Canterbury and
come over here." Gifford was on a short chain.[7]

Mary Pinchot's link to her absent son was forged of different material.
She focused more on his inner beliefs than his external behavior, believing
that his spiritual growth would determine the course and quality of his life.

Glad that he valued his freedom, she reminded him of the importance of relying upon God. Pleased that he felt so comfortable with the Angel-smiths, she assumed that that was because they were "conscientious, God-fearing people," which was "the best thing that can be said of anyone." Delighted that he was exploring the contours of his commitment to Christianity, she sought to steer his inquiries toward the figure in whom she had the most faith: St. Paul. "The closer you can get in knowledge of him and in following him—the nobler and broader your life will be," she advised. Because there was "no human character in secular or religious history which should so much be held up as a model for boys," because this role model had counseled his followers to "stand fast in the faith," so did Mary Pinchot press her son to take a stand. In doing so, she counseled, he would "be true to God . . . and shall fulfill to the utmost his mission in placing us here."[8]

Yet spiritual contemplation alone would not unveil Gifford's precise mission. For the Pinchots, this important question also would be resolved through active discussion and considered action, which, by the time the family had returned to the United States, led to the decision that the young man's "decidedly helter-skelter" education must be regularized. Accordingly, they enrolled him in New Hampshire's Phillips Exeter Academy in the autumn of 1881.[9]

THIS BOY'S LIFE

The school was in a state of chaos when Gifford arrived. Founded a century earlier, when its instructors had been empowered to "regulate the tempers, to enlarge the minds, and form the morals of the youth committed to their care," Phillips Exeter now struggled to meet any of those pedagogical aspirations. That was in good part because the school's mission was confused—it was part college preparatory, part high school—and its faculty and principal were at war with one another. Enrollment, moreover, was in sharp decline, and not many of those who chose to attend stayed the course; their academic indifference can be gauged by the fact that in the decade before Gifford arrived, 40 percent of the students had gone on to college; by the following decade, that figure had plummeted to less than 20 percent. It would not be until after Pinchot's years there that the school would undergo a startling reformation, becoming one of the nation's most prestigious secondary schools.[10]

Despite the academy's many problems, despite the fact that it was in this unsettled environment that Gifford spent his first, most sustained period of time away from his parents, the young man thrived. He appeared to come into his own, his family agreed, most obviously in his almost-professional fascination with the sciences, leading his mother to encourage an acquaintance of hers, A. H. Gesner, to correspond with her son about the prospects of a scientific career.

Gesner had suspected that the recipient of his October 1883 missive, now in his second year at Phillips Exeter, would not remember him—"it is so long since we met"—but when he learned that Mary Pinchot's son was "just as fond of Natural History as ever," a fondness Gesner shared, he hastened to write, as one scientist to another.[11]

Actually, he wrote to warn the eighteen-year-old student about a dangerous flaw he found in many of those who took up scientific study. Over the years he had been dumbstruck by *the number of men who fail to see God in nature,* men who "persuade themselves that all the *nice,* the *fine,* the delicate adjustments and arrangements of beasts, birds, and flowers, came of themselves or were a spontaneous or developed form." Although Gesner hoped Gifford had "not met with them yet," he would in time, if only because there were so many scientists "who do not believe in God at all." He prayed that it would combat "this progress of unbelief in . . . those who are given to the study of Nature." More to the point, he hoped fervently that young Pinchot would "prepare his mind to defend the truth and be a Champion for God in Nature," leading the way out of perfidy and into the light. What "we want," he concluded, "was *Christian* scientific men."[12]

That Gesner presumed to speak for what he perceived to be an embattled minority of believers set against a cavalcade of atheists, and yet simultaneously could envision no contradiction in the very conception of a "Christian scientist," placed him among the mainstream of his nineteenth-century countrymen; for them, historian Charles Rosenberg has argued, "the study of God's works never implied skepticism towards their Author"; for them, "moral and scientific progress did not seem contradictory but . . .

inevitably parallel and complementary." Gesner could at once trumpet the Bible as the source of all revealed truth and admit that it "is not a scientific book nor is it written in scientific language"; and in these distinctions he saw a harmonic convergence. He was not alone, which is why he and his peers "could move fluidly from one intellectual and emotional realm to another" and be at peace.[13]

So was Gifford Pinchot. Phillips Exeter provided him with ample opportunities to shift from one branch of knowledge to the other. Many Sabbaths found him engrossed in F. W. Farrar's massive two-volume *The Life and Work of St. Paul* (1879), which his mother had given him—"I like [it] very much and I do not confine myself to reading it on Sunday"—and then just as enthralled by tromping through the meadows, probing the bogs, and exploring the forests that lay in and around the town of Exeter. He spent long hours conferring with the school's chaplain about consecrating his life to Christ, and even more time chasing butterflies and trapping bugs to add to his natural history collections. The world that God created offered unlimited possibilities for a young man who, as a family friend noted, seemed a "confirmed naturalist."[14]

This world also offered an amazing number of distractions. His parents worried about the deleterious impact that the school's extracurricular activities were having on Gifford's studies, and well they might. His letters teemed with news of his participation in a daunting array of sports and organizations. Depending on the season, he played lacrosse, football, or tennis and reveled in the school's athletic camaraderie, in being among the "jubilant multitude" that surged through campus following victory. This sense of brotherhood was enhanced in other ways—through regular attendance at Bible study classes and participation in the Gideon Lane Soule Literary Society and other clubs whose meetings packed his daily calendar. The swirl of activity left him puzzled. "When I first came here I got the impression from the boys that this was one of the dullest places on the face of the earth," he confided to his mother in 1882, but "I have certainly been to more entertainments this winter than if I had stayed at home."[15]

That revelation left James Pinchot sputtering. Parties were not supposed to be "the object of your winter," he wrote. "Study is the thing now." When Gifford learned how to learn, which was why he had been sent to Exeter, when "I hear that you are doing all your lessons easily and well," then might he re-engage in the social round. As for Gifford's election as captain of the lacrosse club, his father offered no support. "It seems to me that you cannot hold this position of responsibility . . . and still attend to your lessons." Trying to accomplish both would lead to failure: "It is a case of attempting to serve two masters." The young Pinchot capitulated and cut back on his activism, deferring to his father's analysis. "It is very hard to keep my manners and bearing what they should be when there is no one to caution me when I go wrong."[16]

A dearth of cautionary words was the last thing Gifford needed to worry about. His parents continued to offer an unceasing flow of advice on his eating habits, exercise regimen, and general health. They quibbled with how he held his pen, demanded that he write with greater regularity—"you are to write your letters twice a week on the days mentioned, and no excuses"—and with greater care. Their justification for this barrage linked character with action. If Gifford was "never to have any backbone or resolution even in the little matters," how would he have any in larger affairs? Managing his life required a sense of control and discipline the elder Pinchot did not yet sense in his teenaged son. "Do not I beg of you attempt any spasmodic effort . . . [but] go straight along evenly and carefully and you will get on well enough." Avoid intemperate action, conserve energy, make efficient use of time—this future leader of the American conservation movement could not have been better prepared to embrace its rhetorical emphasis on rationality, order, and control. Within this language, he would feel right at home.[17]

Concerns about Gifford's health would ultimately lead the Pinchots to withdraw him from Exeter in the winter of 1883–84. Throughout the fall term he had complained of a "weakness" of the eyes and believed that this condition might delay his matriculation at Yale, a diagnosis his parents shared. Their prescription for the return of his health and academic prospects was to pack him off to the Adirondack Mountains—accompanied by his tutor Mr. Strickland, his sister Nettie, and her governess—where he was to seek restoration through a wilderness cure.

This nostrum was much touted in the circles in which the Pinchots moved. Breathing the clean air of the mountains and drinking their pristine waters, invigorating the body through sustained exercise, and exercising the soul through high country contemplation were established remedies in late-nineteenth-century medical literature and cultural discourse. The Saranac Lake region, to which Gifford repaired for several months, was the rehabilitation zone of choice for members of the New York elite, whether the illnesses to be treated were relatively mild, such as the perceived need for Gifford to recover his strength, or life-threatening, such as tuberculosis. For many physicians, such as Dr. Edward L. Trudeau, whose famed local sanatorium and rest cure drew great notice and with whom Gifford would become quite friendly, time in the woods was the antidote for each and every malady.[18]

With this form of medication, young Pinchot had nary a complaint. Getting off the train at Plattsburgh in early January 1884, he plunked down $7 for a snappy sealskin hat to ward off the intense cold—"that was the cheapest good looking cap I could find"—and rarely took it off during his three months in the northern woods. That is because he spent the vast bulk of his time hiking and snowshoeing across a frozen landscape. "I find that I can with perfect ease stand a day in the woods, even with the mercury very near zero," he boasted to his father. "Yesterday, I was on my feet for eight hours consecutively without sitting down, and with but a small lunch, but without getting at all exhausted and without experiencing a single bad result. Not even stiffness." His renewed flexibility and enhanced stamina were "evidence of how successful I have been doing just what I came up here for, namely, to get strong."[19]

When it came to boosting his academic skills, another goal of his residence in Saranac, he was not quite as successful. Under the tutelage of Mr. Strickland, each morning Gifford read Cicero and Plutarch and tried to refine his mathematical skills in preparation for the Yale entrance examinations. The work was hard, he hated the confinement it imposed, and he wearily advised his parents that "time will not be profitable so far as progress in my studies is concerned." He might have to go to Yale with "conditions," deficits in his scholarship that he would be compelled to work off before he gained full admittance to the college.[20]

Not that he was overly concerned. Indeed, he urged his parents to look on the bright side. "It is well to make the best of what we have got," and

Even at the age of five, Gifford Pinchot was fascinated by the trappings of the outdoorsman.
Grey Towers NHL

what he had gotten had been a useful dose of close instruction in "wood-craft and also [in] how to shoot." The latter was especially important, he felt; day after day he traversed the rugged, hilly land hunting for rabbits and other wildlife, and each day he became more of a crack shot. After one such outing, he proudly informed his parents that "I killed the largest number of rabbits Mr. Evans [a local guide] ever knew of one person's killing in a day, seven." Another guide had said that Gifford "shot better than any sportsman he had been with, except Dr. Trudeau, who is the best shot about here." That claim induced a bit of swagger. "I am going to be a combination of Davey Crockett and John L. Sullivan by the time I see you again."

Gifford's adolescent embrace of the cult of true manhood was framed within the culture's increasing emphasis on masculinity and muscularity. That is why he touted himself as another Sullivan and Crockett, and why he eagerly anticipated that spring's "glass ball shooting" contests in these words: "I expect to make records not unworthy of . . . Buffalo Bill." Consistent with his newfound prowess—physical and psychological—were Gifford's persistent concerns about Nettie's governess, Miss Miller. "She has too little natural dignity," he informed his mother, "and tries to have more girlish action and expression at times than is compatible with her age, position, and size. With your approval I will speak to her about this." As he sought to reprove her, he also resisted her dominance, reporting that she sought "to run me, and . . . is sometimes rather childish in the way she goes to work to attain these ends."[21]

Growth Spurt

James Pinchot was forced to acknowledge that his son had become a man when, in mid-November 1885, he ventured into Gifford's dormitory room at Yale. As he gazed at the artwork his son had hung—pictures of family friends General William Tecumseh Sherman and of the undergraduate's namesake, Sanford Gifford, as well as an etching by Eastman Johnson—he recognized in his son a grown-up sense of identification—a sense that was confirmed when the senior Pinchot made the mistake of calling Gifford's classmates "boys," for which he received a swift reminder that twenty-year-old males were in fact adults. Mary Pinchot shared her husband's recognition of and confusion over the transition that was then occurring. "How dear and good that boy is!" she wrote her husband following the Christmas vacation. "It sometimes makes me sad to think that our children are so old and that we will soon . . . make up to them only a small part of their world."[22]

The college experience facilitated the process of separation and differentiation. While at Yale, especially during the tenure of Noah Porter, who was president during Gifford Pinchot's freshman year, students were compelled to take on adultlike roles and responsibilities in their scholastic and extracurricular activities so as to build active minds and strong characters. This was the best and, some on the Yale faculty believed, the only way "of introducing young men to their modern world, and to themselves." Doing so, Porter admitted, entailed weaning his charges from "the public opinion of the little community which has hitherto formed [the student's] aspirations and his hopes," that is to say, his family. For Porter, college was the "fusing crucible."[23]

The construct of that crucible, however, was up for debate. Toward the

close of Porter's tenure, some of the faculty pressed him to open the curriculum to electives and ease up on the number of required courses, reforms
then sweeping through American higher education. Many students shared
their teachers' discontent, were no less pleased with Porter's resistance, and,
like Gifford Pinchot, applauded when he resigned in May 1886. Pinchot's
support for the new president, Timothy Dwight, was immediate. "I believe
[his] election is pretty satisfactory to all hands."[24]

They should have been satisfied. Dwight oversaw the subsequent reno-
vation and expansion of the physical plant, encouraged a steady increase in
the student body, and generated the infusion of new capital into endow-
ments; these transformations, when combined with a slow refurbishing of
the curriculum and significant changes in the administrative structure,
produced a new Yale. No longer what one contemporary critic had disdained as "a colonial divinity school," it had become a modern university.[25]

Gifford Pinchot benefited from this modernist urge. That it was now
possible to study French over four years was a boon to this grandson of
émigrés; in his junior year, he won the college's French language prize.
Dwight's reforms also helped make it possible for Gifford to study the sciences—his classes in meteorology, geology, and astronomy may not have
been directly helpful to his subsequent career as a forester, but that he was
able even to incorporate these subjects into his studies was due in large
measure to the introduction of elective courses that Dwight had promoted.[26]

But Pinchot, for all his talents, had no intention of becoming a scholar.
From the moment he stepped on campus, he threw himself into the intense
social life of the Yale undergraduate. This tall, thin, handsome young
man, whose striking visage was made all the more riveting by a luxurious
mustache, made certain to be in the front rank of the infamous freshman-
sophomore "rush," in which all members of the two classes lined up in a
"solid column five or six men wide and twenty or twenty-five men deep";
each row locked arms and then surged against the other class, straining to
move it from its ground. "There was a good deal of a squeeze for a minute
& then the Sophs. went back, and as they went, or rather were driven, there
first two or three ranks fell and of course ours went down on top of them."
The "sharp struggle" continued with a wrestling match and then a bare-
knuckle brawl for control of a sidewalk; once more at the front, Gifford

reported that he had borne the brunt of a charge "and was lifted off my feet and carried quite a distance." During the subsequent half-hour-long melee, some "of the fellows were stripped to the waist," Gifford recounted to his stunned parents, "but I lost nothing except a few buttons and the integrity of my trousers."

There were other high jinks to report—he wrote home of smuggling dogs and cats into chapel services, learning the intricacies of dormitory fire fights (which involved flinging lit matches at one another), and, when released for vacation, jamming together with forty other freshmen into a railroad car headed for New York City and turning the journey into a "stormy time" for the other passengers by singing, shouting, and cheering. In subsequent years, he became involved in campus literary productions and was tapped for the most prestigious and secretive society, Skull and Bones, becoming every inch the devoted college man.[27]

He would later regret some of his intense devotion to the groups and clubs to which he had belonged, and in whose exclusive spheres he remained for much of his four years in New Haven. After attending his forty-fifth reunion in 1934, he admitted to his sister Nettie that his "class was full of cliques and animosities when we were in college." Happily, those adolescent rivalries had diminished with time, "and I was almost as glad to see men for whom I had no use forty-five years ago as those who are my best friends. Of course that isn't true as I have written it, but it gives you something of an idea of the way in which we got together."[28]

This retrospective reconciliation only added to his wealth of appreciation for and vivid identification with Yale. Throughout his long life, he worked closely with innumerable sons of Eli (many of whom were also members of Skull and Bones), and while in government service he frequently championed those who shared his collegiate connections. "You will notice this is again a Yale man," a bemused Pinchot wrote President (and Harvard grad) Theodore Roosevelt in 1904 when he recommended a candidate for the federal judiciary, "but that is almost the only kind I know." Given this admission of his deep and parochial attachment to the New Haven college, both men might have appreciated the fact that the *New York Times,* in its 1946 obituary for Pinchot, reported that he had received his undergraduate degree from Roosevelt's alma mater.[29]

Gifford Pinchot (third from left) *was an enthusiastic Yale man and maintained close relationships with many former classmates for the rest of his life.*
Grey Towers NHL

James and Mary Pinchot did not share their son's enthusiasm for all things Yale. They protested his many nonacademic activities, but Gifford responded that they misjudged the nature of collegiate life. He was no more moved when they pleaded with their skinny child not to play football, and rebuffed a family physician who wrote seconding his parents' fears that the brutal game—which contemporary William James had called the moral equivalent of war—put him in great peril. He tried out for the freshman team, made it, and subsequently played as a reserve on the great Walter Camp teams of the 1880s.

Gifford's penchant for pranks and sports did little to diminish his religious devotions. Quite the contrary. They helped reinforce his commitment to, because they were emblematic of, muscular Christianity, a faith fueled by a masculine ethos; gridiron-hardened men could best shoulder the cross. It was around such peers that he built his social life; when he helped establish an eating club, he made certain to select a goodly number of "evangelical Christian" men as members. An active participant in Bible study classes, he was also deeply involved in various campus-based activities of the Young Men's Christian Association (YMCA) and was an engaged volunteer in one of its outreach projects, the Grand Street Mission in New Haven. "I am getting more and more interested [in] and identified with the work of the church," he advised his mother, an identification that led his peers to select him as a deacon of the Class of '89; for four years, along with his good friend and future forester Henry S. Graves, he helped lead week-day and weekend religious services and also taught in the Yale Sunday School.

So thorough was his involvement that for a time he pondered becoming a missionary. His mentor, James B. Reynolds, Yale '84, who later was a driving force in the international movement of the YMCA, urged Gifford to take up the cross, believing it would "call forth all your powers." Although he would not follow that precise path, Pinchot would credit Reynolds with broadening his political outlook and sensitizing him to the plight of the poor; following college, Reynolds encouraged Pinchot to become active in the University Settlement house on Delancey Street on New York's Lower East Side. "There I came into operating contact with the other half and learned something of how it lived and thought and why, whereby my conservative opinions were greatly changed, to my very marked advantage."[30]

The disadvantages of a life of explicit Christian service, however much that life would have offered a meaningful outlet for Pinchot's considerable energy and faith, became clear only when another good friend, J. E. Donnelley, himself began to cool to the idea. After attending the 1888 annual summer ingathering of collegiate evangelicals in Northfield, Massachusetts, Donnelley reported that professional Christianity appeared "an unnatural, strained sort of life"; it was deficient in the very qualities of "divine help and motive power" that he and Pinchot had thought had defined its mission. The denouement for Pinchot came in early October of his senior year, when he announced to his mother that he had made a crucial decision: "I have finally taken my courage in both hands and broken away from Bethany," the center of religious fervor at Yale. "This is a great relief and satisfaction."[31]

No less satisfying was his latest enthusiasm, he advised his parents, a research internship with botanist Daniel Eaton. "I have gotten well started with [him] on the trees of New Haven, and the work promises to be extraordinarily interesting. I only wish I had more time to give to it. As it is I shall spend all my leisure in the woods after specimens." From Eaton, he also collected supportive advice. The professor suggested that Pinchot stick to his original purpose of studying forestry, a suggestion with which his student thoroughly agreed. "I do not see that I can be more useful in any other way, or so successful and happy."[32]

Success and happiness were not what other advisors predicted for him if he pursued what they considered to be the chimera of forestry. Dr. George Loring, former secretary of the Department of Agriculture, whom Pinchot had visited in January 1889, assured the young man that "there was little chance for work" in his proposed field. European conceptions of the science of forestry and forest management would not be transplanted across the Atlantic because of the sharply divergent political and physical landscapes in the United States; here there was "no centralized, monarchical power" that could compel forestry's implementation and, in any event, there would be little need, due to the "vastness of the country and [the] rapid second growth" of its forests. Concurring with this gloomy assessment was Bernhard Fernow, the first professional forester with whom Pinchot had ever spoken, who headed the agriculture department's tiny forestry division. During an interview in Washington and in later correspondence, he sought to dissuade Pinchot from taking up the profession as a full-time occupation. "The wiser plan would be to so direct your studies that they will be useful in other directions also," he wrote. "The study of the sciences underlying forestry will also fit you for landscape gardening, nursery business, botanist's work, etc."[33]

But forestry for Pinchot was an end unto itself, as it was to his parents, who counseled their son "to keep at the subject." Still, he had his doubts. As his final semester at Yale drew to a close, and as he wrestled with how to pursue what at times seemed a nebulous dream, he weighed an offer to work for the YMCA at Yale. This apparent about-face startled James Pinchot, who could not understand Gifford's ambivalence or hesitation, and who expected him to pursue the study of scientific forestry in Europe following graduation. But his son the deacon, well versed in the cycles of religious conversion, might well have recognized that his belated misgivings, like the wavering of a born-again Christian, were a matter of testing the depths of his commitment.[34]

That he pondered hard his prospects as a missionary or forester is important in another respect. However different the two professions were, that for him they were equivalents reinforces historian Charles Rosenberg's insight into the shared character of religious and scientific careers in the late nineteenth century. "Science, like religion," he observes in *No Other Gods,* "offered an ideal of selflessness, of truth, of the possibility of spiritual devotion—emotions which in their elevating purity could inspire and motivate, could legitimate the needs of particular individuals to achieve and control— but in a context seemingly far-removed from the sordid compromise implied by most other careers." Only the form of professional purity Gifford would pursue was open to debate.

He announced his final commitment at commencement in 1889. As the winner of that year's Townsend Prize for debate, he was called upon to speak at graduation exercises. "I had carefully prepared myself to talk, not on Forestry but on some subject long since forgotten," he would write in his autobiography. "But on the spur of the moment I dropped it, my future profession welled up inside of me and took its place, and I made to the exalted graduates of Yale . . . my first public statement on the importance of Forestry to the United States—and my first public declaration that I had chosen it as my lifework." Pinchot, ever "eager to bear witness to my faith," a faith that demanded passionate self-sacrifice, testified that his calling would be to minister to the American forests.[35]

Such feelings of civic responsibility were part of his patrimony, he asserted later that summer. On August 28, two weeks after his twenty-fourth birthday, he rose before the citizens of Milford at a celebration marking the centennial of the U.S. Constitution and spoke of the obligations of citizenship. "We are trustees of a coming world," the young Yale graduate announced, but "we are first of all . . . citizens of Pike County, Pennsylvania, and it is here that we are to realize, if at all, the blessings of the great birthright which has descended to us from the courage, perseverance, and energy of our forefathers." The only way for the citizenry to merit that blessing was to feel, "every man of us, not only that we have a share in the commonwealth, but that the commonwealth has a share in us." When he concluded that the state thereby had "a right to our service, to our thought, and action," he spoke in the language of noblesse oblige and republican virtue, the twin political inheritances intertwined in his family's transatlantic past.

One of those who picked up on this familial echo in Pinchot's words was William Bross, who like his contemporary James Pinchot had left Milford for the wider world. Writing from his *Chicago Tribune* offices, Bross extolled the young man's commitments but was not surprised by them. "Knowing so much of your ancestry, all of who were intelligent, honest & enterprising people, I shall lose faith in the doctrines of heredity if your success in life is not marked and commanding."[36]

Part Two

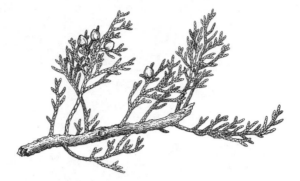

A YOUNG STAND

An American in Nancy

RESUMÉS ARE a fascinating form of self-promotion, documents that can obscure as much as they reveal; they offer not only the means by which to brandish one's exploits and accomplishments but an opportunity to remain silent about less than triumphant activities.

Gifford Pinchot knew all about this subtle interplay between the facts and fictions of a well-publicized life, learning early from his parents that the appearance of success, if touted consistently, might just translate into its reality. About and from the young Pinchot, especially where it concerned the importance of his fledgling career in forestry, Americans would hear a good deal. Well before 1898, when he became the fourth chief of the Division of Forestry in the Department of Agriculture and thus acquired an official claim on civic consciousness, he deftly presented himself before that public in such a manner and with such regularity that his selection as the nation's forester would occasion little surprise. He became what he and the larger audience had expected he would become.

To realize that expectation, however, required an extended promotional campaign, the fruits of which were originally pasted in the innumerable binders of his voluminous clippings file and which now fill twenty-six reels of microfilm. Scrolling through these faded reams of newsprint makes it clear that the campaign hinged on a much-repeated assertion about his precocious commitment to and his mature knowledge of the American woods. "Since boyhood he has been interested in trees," one such account from the 1890s asserted, and from that early fascination flowered a pioneering professional, the first scientifically trained American forester. This precise claim made it safe to assert another, less restrained one. "[F]ew, if any, men in this country know more about trees than he." However accurate that assertion was—and it was not particularly so—it nonetheless spoke evocatively to an age increasingly bedazzled by the cult of scientific expertise, and quite willing to follow the lead of its high priests. Pinchot forever played to and off that need, gaining as a consequence influence and notoriety for himself and the movement he came to represent, a status that was recapitulated much later in the title and text of his autobiography, *Breaking New Ground;* driven by a Whiggish plot, its narrative is of progress hard won through Pinchot's single-minded (and at times single-handed) conversion of a hesitant nation to the cause of forestry and conservation.[1]

GRAND TOUR

Pinchot brimmed with no such confidence when in early October 1889 he boarded the SS *Elbe* for passage to Europe, where he hoped to assemble an ample library of forestry texts, perhaps meet with some of their authors, and seek their advice about how he might proceed to establish his career in the New World. While in Paris he also anticipated touring an important, related exhibit, *Eaux et Forêt,* held at the World Exposition of 1889. The trip's purpose, then, was to bolster his scant knowledge about a profession to which he expected to commit his life.

That this situation troubled the ambitious American, that he knew what he did not know, became evident as the *Elbe* pushed back from its pier, slowly pivoted south, and headed down the Hudson. "I must admit that I felt rather lonely at parting and on my solitary way down the bay," Pinchot noted in his diary, a solitariness that intensified as he steamed "past the splendid Statue of Liberty, which I now saw for the first time, and through the narrows out to sea." Unlike steerage immigrants from Europe, however, for whom the sight of the "Lady" was a beacon of arrival, for Pinchot its sighting marked an anxious departure—he was on his own, and beginning to realize that he might be out of his depth. This meditation came to an abrupt halt when the harbor pilot ran the *Elbe* on a mud bank in the Narrows. Shaken, Pinchot was soon relieved to report that "we got off speedily, which was lucky, for the tide was at full flood."[2]

As the vessel resumed its course across the Atlantic and Pinchot began to stroll among his fellow passengers, his earlier anxiety seemed to wash away, like the mud on the *Elbe*'s hull. Although his worries would resurface at various points during his eighteen-month stay in Europe, he generally managed to control them, relying on his well-cultivated sense of confidence to pull him through moments of doubt. His bearing in this respect was evident throughout the eight-day passage across the North Atlantic, during which he filled his diary with close analyses of the other travelers, their personalities and quirks. From the stuttering British accountant Herman Lescher, an incredulous soul who asked Pinchot if he "did not hear the rattlesnakes [move] about our house at night," to Isaac Hills, a déclassé American youth who was "conceited, ill bred, affected and generally disagreeable," to Mr. Haas, a corpulent "self-satisfied, impertinent, ridiculous, good natured German Jew, Jew, Jew"—Pinchot's Waspish commentary reflected the values of his class and provided him with a self-administered measure of assurance. The voyage had not cut him loose from familiar moorings.[3]

After landing in Southhampton, England, Pinchot traveled to London, visited friends in Oxford, and then returned to that nation's capital to pursue queries about a career in forestry. Unfazed that he had no connections, he started out, as he put it, "to see what good gall would do for me at the Forest Department of the India Office." That office was a logical choice for someone seeking entrée. It had been through its colonial control of the vast south Asian subcontinent that Britain had there established a model forest service and forest reserves. To furnish trained foresters, the British had created Cooper's Hill, a school staffed by some of the world's preeminent foresters. It was with these men that Pinchot hoped to speak, and within minutes of his arrival at the India Office, after securing an introduction to Sir Charles Bernard, then head of the Indian Forestry office, and an offer of an indefinite loan of relevant books, he wangled letters of introduction to two German-born foresters who would shape his early development as a

forester—Dr. William Schlich, director of Cooper's Hill, and, most important, Dr. Dietrich Brandis, "once head and always founder of the Indian
Forest Service." Pinchot could not believe his good fortune. "I have never
met such disinterested kindness to a total stranger before. It was altogether
delightful, and will be the greatest use to me, I think."[4]

The dividends of "good gall" were many. While arranging a visit to
Cooper's Hill in late October, he began to work through the varied forestry
texts he had been lent, the first sustained reading in what would become his
life's work. Included in his burgeoning library was Schlich's *Manual of
Forestry,* the field's leading primer. It was Schlich himself who took Pinchot
on a tour of the Cooper's Hill campus and its facilities, brought him to one
of his lectures on how to develop a forest management plan, and then
escorted him through an "experimental plantation of his of scotch pines," a
full day that concluded with a several-hours-long excursion through the
park of Windsor Castle. "I have never seen a more beautiful drive," Pinchot
gushed, amazed at the landscape's noble tranquillity, with herds of "red
deer . . . grazing under the magnificent oak and beech trees," one of which
"was very likely the oldest [beech] in the world (1000 or more years)." The
antiquity and managed character of the terrain astounded the visitor from
the New World, who now better understood what forestry could offer his
native and rough land. "The beautiful shape of the trees, the arrangement
of them, the turf, the whole together was simply ideal."[5]

This harmonious and pruned environment would not be easily replicated, Schlich cautioned, any more than the British system of forestry could
be simply and wholly imported to the United States. He urged his young
guest to hedge his bets, to study chemistry and botany in addition to forestry,
advice that Pinchot had heard from American mentors. It was advice that
also fostered an inner conflict. "As I learn more of Forestry," he wrote after
his visit to Cooper's Hill, "I see more the need of it in the U.S. and the great
difficulty of carrying it into effect." By framing the conflict in this manner,
especially in highlighting how challenging would be forestry's political
implementation, Pinchot identified the arena in which he would spend so
much of his professional energy; politics, not science, would be his métier.[6]

His political bent would emerge during his European travels, influencing the rigor with which he would pursue the requisite scientific knowl-

edge that his European mentors, including Schlich, believed he needed. With them, Pinchot recognized that such study was essential if he were to make a credible case for the introduction of forestry to the American landscape. But there was a limit to how much time he would devote to the study of forestry, for he and his parents were convinced that an extended stay would undermine his opportunity to pursue what he called his "Washington scheme"—becoming the head of the Division of Forestry in the Department of Agriculture, the only post from which he thought he could advocate forestry's cause to good effect.[7]

For the moment, studying forestry took precedence over such political scheming. Two days after his visit to Cooper's Hill, he packed up and left England for France, carrying another sheaf of letters of recommendation from Professor Schlich—one to Sir Brandis in Bonn, whom Pinchot expected to visit, and others to his colleagues at L'Ecole Nationale Forestière in Nancy, where Pinchot proposed to begin his formal professional studies. Just how necessary that study was struck him when he walked through the Exposition Universelle in Paris.

This world's fair, like others in the nineteenth century, was designed to display French genius, political power, and cultural prestige through an intimately planned landscape of grand boulevards, massive edifices, and stunning exhibits of encyclopedic breadth. Of the 1889 fair's breathtaking quality, nothing was more emblematic than the Eiffel Tower, that soaring if controversial signifier of French industrial might. Unlike other visitors, one of whom denounced the tower as a "gigantic and hideous skeleton . . . reared by Cyclops," Pinchot had a muted reaction after ambling underneath it. "I was of course immensely impressed by its size, but the lack of any standard to test it by makes it hard to define to oneself how big it really is." Smaller in size but much more overwhelming was the exhibit he next toured, *Eaux et Forêt*. Located in the commodious horticultural hall, it offered a complex survey of all that contemporary hydrologists and foresters knew about their respective subjects, as well as their vital interactions. Much like the forestry exhibit in the previous world's fair in Paris in 1878, *Eaux et Forêt* stressed the rational management of the landscape, boosting the degree to which French expertise had triumphed over natural forces. The exhibit's depiction of that victory evoked in Pinchot an odd set of reactions. "I was impressed and bewildered and discouraged," he confessed in his diary. "The exhibit is magnificent and so complete that at first I despaired of making any adequate description of it." As he wandered its halls, jostled by the great crowds that roamed through the exhibit, he lingered only so long as "to get the general plan well in my head." Then he slipped away into a sculpture garden, the statuary of which he understood more immediately than the complicated environmental relationship between water and forests. Pinchot's lack of knowledge, and need of a thorough education, had been exposed.[8]

Paris offered Pinchot another kind of opportunity as well: to explore his covert fascination with the erotic. Along with Yale comrade James Reynolds, who had expressed a desire "to see one of the tough shows as a sample," and "feeling the same way myself," Pinchot spent an evening at the Folies Bergère, testing himself against the cabaret's explicit sexuality. By his standards, he passed: the ballet *Les Baigneuses* was "the most carefully arranged bit of indecency that I ever saw," he jotted in his diary; later, when one of the Folies' "tough looking maidens . . . put her arm around me as we were going downstairs and invited me to a game of 'billard Anglais,'" Pinchot offered a stiff rejection of this "bagatelle": "I kept my face closed."[9]

He was more open to the intellectual allure of the stout, imposing, and learned Prussian forester Dietrich Brandis, whom he visited in Bonn in early November. After strongly seconding Schlich's recommendation that Pinchot go to Nancy, Brandis freely dispensed his insights into the status of contemporary forestry. Over the next several days, Pinchot absorbed as much as he could, emerging from his lengthy talks with Brandis with "a clearer idea of forestry than I ever came near to having before." One of those ideas concerned the introduction of the science to the United States, the difficulties with which Brandis had some experience, given his pioneering work in India. For this reason, Pinchot informed his father, Brandis was "the most useful man I could see for he knows all about the conditions of a new country."

Schlich knew something about the Old World, too, and advised the impressionable American to learn the French system of forestry thoroughly because it was "so much larger and more important than the English."

Doing so would also open doors that otherwise would be closed to him. Because of their scientific and cultural significance, French foresters would not "care to be bothered with a greenhorn" such as he, Pinchot wrote his father in an effort to convince him that enrolling at Nancy was the logical next step; gaining at least a rudimentary education in the field would facilitate his access to "the powers that be," an opportunity that "must be taken now or lost for good." The senior Pinchots, although longing for their son's return, quickly assented to his plan of study; they had been the first to teach him how critical it was to make the proper connections.[10]

A L'Ecole

Nancy enabled him to connect forestry as taught in the classroom with its reality on the ground. Its facts were many, its science complex, and at the heart of the school's curriculum was an intense focus on silviculture, the means by which foresters produced and cared for forests. Because a forest's productivity was largely determined through an economic evaluation of its woods, students at Nancy also were introduced to specialized information on such related topics as land rent, interest rates, and forest capital, as well as the most efficient methods for sustaining a forest's yield of wood, and thus its financial value. Without such knowledge, foresters would be able to calculate neither when to harvest timber for maximum profit nor when to time reforestation to ensure a new cycle of growth.

This monetary emphasis fit within another, more intellectual and political conception of the wooded landscape. L'Ecole Nationale Forestière, established in 1824, was one of the Grandes Ecoles of France devoted to the creation of a professional and technologically trained elite who would devise efficient and rational means by which to extract and conserve the nation's resources during the post-Revolution era. Its students were molded to function within a series of forest laws defined through the Code Napoleon, laws that delineated the central government's control of the environment and that signaled the establishment of a new relationship between the people and the forests. No longer emblems of aristocratic privilege, trees would be actively managed in Bonaparte's France, pacified for the benefit of the state.[11]

The intense management extended to Nancy's curriculum, which Pinchot, a good and diligent student, discovered was governed by tedious routine and filled with minutiae. He chafed under its rigidity, complaining to
his mother and Brandis that the courses on French forest law, for instance,
were "pretty useless." He was impatient, too, with what he considered a
claustrophobic and inimical student-teacher relationship—a result, he
observed, of "this miserable baby system of shutting the students up and the
resultant feeling of the teacher that all students are inferior beings." There
were exceptions, among them the school's assistant director and professor
of silviculture, Lucien Boppe. "Short, stocky, with immense vitality and a
great contempt for mere professors," Boppe had learned "in the woods
what he taught in the lecture room," a practical quality that Pinchot prized;
his illuminating lectures "made Forestry visible," a sharp contrast to others
on the faculty who left the American groping in the dark.[12]

For his fellow students he carried no torch. These indolent, benighted
souls drove the upright Pinchot to distraction. He was flabbergasted that
few, if any, seemed to respect their chosen profession, denigrating it as
fumisterie (claptrap), dismissing its claims to progress, and doubting that
that there is "any really scientific or exact or necessary work for a man to do
in it." These were all things the ever-optimistic Pinchot, who was banking
on forestry's prospects to transform his native land (and himself), deeply
valued. He could make sense of this baffling pessimism only by indulging
in a bit of character assassination. "It appears that this sort of ass is very
common among French students, and seems a logical result of their imbe-
cile system of education," he noted in his diary. "A youth whose experience
has been gained chiefly within the four walls of the Lycee and Ecole F., and
in holes like the Eden Theatre, is about fixed to think he knows it all."[13]

Pinchot's ignorance was no less astounding, and in an effort to increase
his working knowledge about forestry and escape Nancy's deadening environment, he regularly fled the school compound to hike through nearby
woods, making notes and sketches of the conditions he observed, compar-
ing what he witnessed on the ground with what he had absorbed in the
stuffy classrooms. It was then that he gained his "first concrete understanding of the forest as a crop": by working on a rotational system, in much the
same way a farmer might plant, harvest, and replant corn, trees could be
cut, the land reforested, and the trees cut again. In this way, the French

system of forests could maintain "a permanent population of trained men" and "permanent forest industries, supported and guaranteed by a fixed and annual supply of trees ready for the axe."[14]

Pinchot readily absorbed many of the guiding principles of this business. Its stress on efficiency and rational planning captivated the imagination of the young man whose father had been so dismayed by the irregularity and untidiness of the American countryside. The son in turn was struck by the manner in which French forests "were divided at regular intervals by perfectly straight paths and roads at right angles to each other," a forceful demonstration of scientific management and governmental authority, of nature controlled through human stricture and structure. It was emblematic of "fiscal forestry," a concept that found its origins in mid-eighteenth-century experiments in Prussia and Saxony. This pursuit of an ordered and legible landscape, James C. Scott has observed, contained a remarkable ambition to tear down and rebuild the forest. "[T]he actual tree with its vast number of possible uses was replaced by an abstract tree representing a volume of lumber or firewood." In other words, a nation used "forest science and geometry . . . to transform the real, diverse, and chaotic old-growth forest into a new, more uniform forest that closely resembled the administrative grid of its techniques." To Pinchot and his classmates at L'Ecole Nationale Forestière was this knowledge imparted; they were being trained to see and to think like a state.[15]

For all its attractiveness, Pinchot recognized that this Gallic precision could never be transplanted to American soil; its autocratic perspective would wither in republican terrain. "With us," he advised his mother, "the painstaking minuteness that prevails here is impossible, and [it] may be that a general knowledge of methods here, just enough to suggest lines of action at home, would be enough. I see no reason why our Forestry system should not be as unlike and as superior in the end as our agricultural methods are." Although he recognized the limitations of European forestry, he was enthusiastic enough about its capacity to bring order to the land and the human use of it that his friend James Reynolds was led to exult. "Go on, brave heart, and elaborate that system of forestry for the U.S. I expect that some day you will have reduced our forests to such a degree of subjection that not a half will rustle without the express permission of the autocratic G.P."[16]

However overblown, Reynolds's assessment dovetailed with Pinchot's struggle to locate a balance in the relationship between the forester and the forest, a struggle that was of considerable concern for one who saw in his chosen profession a missionary's pulpit. While locked in his studies in a grim urban landscape, he yearned for the ministering of the forests. "I felt like being in real woods again," he wrote his parents in January 1890 after he had struck off into the Vosges Mountains south of Nancy. His hike filled a pronounced aesthetic need, "to walk again under the tall straight firs on a ground covered literally ankle deep with beautiful green moss. . . . " This lush arboreal landscape, with its mix of fir, beech, and pine, offered much-needed solace and a much-missed and clean-lined vista. Once more he was able to "see off through the woods, as the coppice shoots prevent you from doing in the plains" around Nancy. It was on these reverent, solitary forays into the French countryside that the young American professed to be the happiest; he was most at home alone.[17]

He was happy as well when, in April 1890, at Brandis's insistence—he "is very much persuaded that practical work is better than book knowledge, and I think he is very much right"—Pinchot took a six-week holiday from school, journeying to Zurich, Switzerland, to work with Forstmeister Ulrich Meister of the Sihlwald. This municipal forest, which stretched "for some five miles along the narrow valley of the Sihl," had been under human management "since before Columbus discovered America," Pinchot was humbled to learn. Working closely with Meister, he gained important lessons in the "organization of a normally stocked forest" and its object of "first importance," the cutting "each year of an amount of timber equal to the total annual increase over the whole area, and no more." Because it was "desirable in any long settled community that the forests be so managed as to yield a measurable constant return in material," the Sihlwald was structured so that "areas of equal productive capacity are covered" by trees of every age, "from last year's seedling to the mature tree. . . . " Over time, this mixed-age forest would be thinned, allowing seedlings to flourish and through the regular harvest reap a steady profit. In 1889, the Sihlwald "yielded to the city a net revenue of more than eight dollars an acre," a magnificent return that startled Pinchot and underscored this point "so often lost sight of"—that the "protection of the forests is not an end, but a means, and that the whole question of forestry has a very definite and important

The Brandis Expedition, 1890. Gifford Pinchot (rear, center)
with, on his right, forester Dietrich Brandis, who pioneered
forest management in India and was a tremendous influence
on the development of Pinchot's career. Grey Towers NHL

financial bearing." Shortly after his return to Nancy, Pinchot recounted these insights in a series of articles for Charles Sargent's *Garden and Forest,* an American publication in the forefront of conservation thought of its day, and in doing so put his young nation on notice; it had a long way to go before it would duplicate the success of European forestry. [18]

The gap between Europe and the United States in the care of forests became even more obvious when later that summer Pinchot spent four months with Brandis and a group of British forestry students touring a select series of northern European forests. The students he could have done without; they were a "fresh and wearisome crowd," he wrote his family, young men whose behavior was "infantile," but their ignorance of German was advantageous—he boasted that his language skills won him a coveted seat in Brandis's carriage. Friend Reynolds mocked such self-importance. "I am properly impressed with your position as sub-grand worthy chief of the party and will forebear any question as to what must be the sum total of knowledge of German in the crowd if the gentleman whom you mention knows more than the rest." Pinchot did not mind being the butt of Reynolds's jest. At Brandis's side, he was introduced to and listened in on the conversations between Brandis and other influential German foresters who joined the party at various points.

To this dialogue, Pinchot had little professional knowledge to offer, but he had brought along a set of enlarged photographs of North American forests that he had asked his parents to specially make for him to show to his traveling companions; he anticipated that these illustrations would "bring me at once into good relations with the German foresters." The strategy worked, for as the Europeans pored over the photographic enlargements of Pacific, Adirondack, and Appalachian forests, commenting all the while, Pinchot garnered considerable insight into the way professionals assessed a landscape and evaluated its timber stands. He learned better how to see as they did, through what Professor Boppe had called "le coup d'oeil forestier," the forester's eye. Knowledge was a matter of give and take.[19]

HOMEWARD BOUND

At the conclusion of the Brandis excursion in October 1890, essentially one year after Pinchot had arrived in Europe, the young American student was ready to return home, despite the objections of virtually every forester with whom he had spoken during his European studies and travels; they concluded that he must remain for at least two more years, pursue a Ph.D. at a German university, preferably Munich, and only then sail for his native land. Anything less, they determined, and Pinchot would fail to establish professional forestry in a land that knew it not.

The most vigorous proponent of this educational prescription was Brandis himself. Early in their relationship, he had decided that Pinchot's greatest flaws were his impatience and his willingness to be deflected from the task at hand as Brandis had defined it. Yet knowing just how powerful Pinchot's hasty impulses were, Brandis hoped to cram as much information into him before he decamped for the United States. Brandis's perspective accounts for the tenor of his extensive correspondence with Pinchot while he was at Nancy. The German forester required his charge to read certain texts or to evaluate particular scientific concepts, and then send essays that evaluated their importance; Pinchot's responses were to be written on what Brandis described as a "half margin. On the blank half I will then send you my remarks and return your essays to you," a system for long-distance tutorials that enabled the German to gauge the depth of Pinchot's understanding. The only praise he would offer was couched in such a way as to goad Pinchot to greater efforts, to extend his studies. "If you return to North America as a *well-trained forester,*" Brandis cautioned in April 1890, "you have a splendid career before you, not otherwise."[20]

The ambitious American threw caution to the wind, however, reading Brandis's comment for the praise he wanted it to contain. "That is the first time I have heard the Dr. say anything of the kind"—a reference to the possibility of a "splendid career"—and "while he still insists on the long stay, yet the rest of it is good enough to more than make it up," he wrote his mother. "Consequently I feel very proud and haughty today." Headstrong, too. He had concluded as early as the spring of 1890 that he should not delay launching his future as a forester in America. He had reached that conclusion in part because another mentor, the Swiss forester Meister, shared Pinchot's view that an extended residence and continued study in Europe were unnecessary.[21]

That Meister told Pinchot what he longed to hear was part of the attraction. "[H]e advised me to go home and get to work after finishing the summer's tour with Dr. Brandis (which was exactly what I wanted to do)," Pinchot later admitted, "so of course I was sure he was right." Yet he was attracted to Meister's perspective for another reason, one that was more social and political in origin. Pinchot was beginning to recognize that extended training in German forestry practices might actually be counterproductive, based as it was on a "painstaking minuteness" and cultural system alien to democracy. Brandis had trained and worked within an autocracy, Pinchot reasoned, a world in which the *Oberfoerster* dominated the landscape through a rigid hierarchy and an inflexible social structure. The implications of this culture emerged in a story Pinchot would recount about his one-month stay in Prussia in November 1890. "I shall never forget the old peasant who rose to his feet from his stone breaking, as the Oberfoerster came striding along, and stood silent, head bent, cap in both hands, while that official stalked by without the slightest sign that he knew the peasant was on earth," a disdain that cut against the American grain. "What went in America wasn't somebody's say-so," he would assert, but an ingrained belief in the power of a democratic culture to respond only to "the wide-spread, slow-moving pressure of public opinion," a situation that Brandis was constitutionally incapable of understanding. Meister, on the other hand, "a citizen of the most democratic country in Europe," and someone who "brought together all the qualities a pioneer public forester must have to succeed in a country like ours—practical skill in the woods, business common sense, close touch with public opinion," proved to be the individual "who best understood how to get things done" as Pinchot wanted to do them. Despite all that Brandis had done for him, then, Pinchot was acting on Meister's advice when in December 1890 he strode aboard the *Darnia,* a German freighter anchored in Le Havre and bound for New York. As he settled into his room, he knew that he was but "half trained," yet was ready enough, and "willing to try with what knowledge I have now."[22]

Competitive Edge

Pinchot's lack of sustained formal training would come to haunt his future work as a forester, but what he lacked in education he hoped to make up in ambition and drive. This very energy was what impelled him to hustle home. Throughout his European sojourn he had been in constant fear that someone, anyone, might get the jump on him, might introduce the princi-ples of forestry to North America, robbing Pinchot of what he believed would be his special contribution to the republic. Imagine the spasm of anx-iety he felt when Brandis informed him that Heinrich Mayer, a German-trained forester who had already written a "strong book on American Forests," and whose professional skill and knowledge Brandis urged Pin-chot to try to emulate, had just "lost his place in Japan" and consequently may "speculate upon an appointment in America." Brandis, who appar-ently thought that floating Mayer's name and aspirations might induce Pin-chot to continue his European tutelage, could not have been more mis-taken; it was precisely such perceived threats that sharpened Pinchot's desire to light out for America. That is why, too, in the rush of correspon-dence between Gifford and his parents that explored the many possible paths his career might take, one concern was uppermost in the young man's mind. "[A]ll I want to do is find the best and quickest way to get started and known as a forester."[23]

One of the people he raced to overtake was Bernhard Fernow, sometime mentor, always competitor. Or so Pinchot had imagined their relationship while studying in Europe, an understandable reverie given that he had designs on Fernow's job as head of the nation's Division of Forestry. How Gifford would succeed the much more experienced forester had occupied the family's thoughts even before Pinchot had left the United States in the summer of 1889; meeting with Fernow early that January while he was still a senior at Yale, Pinchot had offered to enter the division as an unpaid assistant, thereby to learn more about the work, his superior, and his own prospects for advancement. Although this tantalizing possibility was put on hold while Pinchot studied in Europe, it was never far from his mind; he and his parents freely speculated on the son's chances to supplant the nation's forester.

In July 1890, Fernow only further fueled the family's speculations when he wrote Gifford in Europe and offered him the post of assistant forester; this opportunity carried with it, he noted, "heirship to the Chief place." When this offer was coupled with Fernow's repeated hints that he might retire and return to Europe, Pinchot quickly cabled his acceptance, wrote his father that he hoped he shared his son's delight, and concluded that the "chance to make a name is now open, but I wish I had a little more preparation."[24]

Pinchot was entirely unprepared for what then happened. First Charles S. Sargent of Harvard's Arnold Arboretum, another of the young forester's well-placed advisors, wrote Pinchot denigrating Fernow's attainments, abilities, and reputation, and urging him to refrain from associating with someone whom Sargent "did not like at all." Then James Pinchot weighed in with an even more alarming assessment. Fernow "seems to me always posing and insincere," he wrote; there "is after all a certain amount of claptrap in Fernow's ways of doing things that should put you completely on your guard." Stunned, Gifford, who had already written Fernow that he wished to defer his appointment until December, prayed that the requested delay would serve as "a large hole to crawl out" so he could save face and "keep on good terms with Fernow, which may be important." Satisfying his hunger for public acclaim and office, Pinchot was learning, would be more complicated than he had anticipated.[25]

What was uncomplicated was his growing certitude that Fernow was unfit to lead the forestry movement in America. Appropriately modest about his own scientific studies—"a year is altogether insufficient to make a forester"—Pinchot nonetheless felt confident that the brevity of his European studies superseded Fernow's academic accomplishments and practical training. German foresters with whom he had been working had comforted him in this regard, assuring him that "Fernow has never had to do with the practical management of forests." That explained, Pinchot wrote his parents, why Fernow did not seem "at all anxious to have his division spread into the great center of national forest management that he says it ought to be." Forestry's future as a respected profession was dim indeed if it continued to be led by an older bureaucrat who lacked "force," who was "not master of the situation."[26]

To become what it appeared Fernow was not, Pinchot went public, representing himself as a young man of new ideas, an active and fresh voice, an *American* forester. The first of these forays appeared as a collection of articles Pinchot wrote on various aspects of European forestry, which was slated for publication in Charles Sargent's *Garden and Forest,* a national periodical trumpeting the virtues of forestry on private and public land. The magazine, which was published between 1887 and 1897, never gained wide circulation, but its readers were influential and included government and university scientists, national political figures, and civic leaders. To be published in its pages was to be introduced to the right audience, a lure Sargent dangled before Pinchot when he encouraged him to contribute regularly to the periodical. "Such a series . . . would have the effect of bringing you to the notice of people in this country interested in forests and forest management, and so pave the way for something for you in the future." Present in Sargent's generous offer lay a small risk of alienating *Garden and Forest*'s august audience with an ill-chosen word or thought, but, Pinchot reasoned in a letter to his parents, if he made no "rash statements, and [gave] as few opinions as possible," if he restricted his contributions to "mere statements of fact, there [would] be little or no chance to make any important or even slight mistake bearing on my career at home." Of greatest value was that with the articles' publication, "I shall get a good deal of free advertising."[27]

Pinchot's instincts about the power of the press bore fruit. Even before the articles appeared in late July 1890, commencing with a three-part discussion of the Sihlwald Forest (fittingly, the prose was dry and unexcited), his early professional attainments were the source of some discussion in the United States, or so his proud father reported to his mother after dining with select company in New York City. "Everyone here seems interested in him, and all seem of the opinion that he has chosen wisely to make forestry his profession," he informed his wife. "Even Genl. Sherman at his table last evening said Gifford would have a great deal to do in the near future." It was that kind of inner sanctum to which Pinchot knew he had to appeal. Dr. Brandis had said as much, warning that should he depart Europe before completing the full course of forestry studies, he could only succeed as a forester by relying upon his family's extensive social network and political contacts. Pinchot concurred, writing his mother: " . . . it seems to me as tho' the influence you and Papa have with the leaders of the Republican Party, and chiefly with . . . General [Sherman, is] my strongest hold at present." The senior Pinchots' pull, when combined with Gifford's continued journalistic output, would compensate for his truncated education—which had left Pinchot, in Brandis's disappointed words, as but a "better informed amateur."[28]

An amateur he may have been, but within two weeks of disembarking in New York in mid-December 1890, he made his professional debut by delivering a talk on "Governmental Forestry Abroad" to a joint session of the annual American Economic Association and American Forestry Association meetings held that year in Washington, D.C. Fernow had arranged the session and, because he "always took a special interest" in Pinchot and looked upon him "somewhat as my charge," invited him to participate. He even suggested his topic, writing that should he accept the challenge of writing about the "*policy* that other Governments pursue toward forestry interests," he would need to demonstrate his grasp of "the leading thought in the various governments with reference to this interest, and comparatively and clearly present the subject." Doing so, Fernow concluded, would allow the session to serve as "a good introduction for you."[29]

This opportunity, Pinchot had immediately recognized, "was far too valuable to be lost." The session's object was "to make plain the duty of the government toward the forest in the hope of influencing legislation," a task that shaped how he presented the state of international forestry. At its base, he wrote, lay a critical principle—that the rational management of forests could not be successfully conducted without "the supervision of some imperishable guardian; or in other words, of the state." Only when this kind of control was asserted over the landscape would it be possible to establish scientific forestry on the ground, a science that depended on two related insights: that individual trees require many years to obtain what Pinchot called "merchantable size," and that "a forest crop"—cuttable timber— could not be harvested annually from the same tract of land. For forestry to work, its practitioners must be patient, and its political setting must be paternal.[30]

Those were among the most important lessons to be drawn from the European experience, Pinchot asserted after taking his audience on a quick tour of the history and practice of forestry in Germany, France, and Switzerland. But none of these states was governed the same, and it therefore followed that just as their practices were not monolithic, neither were their experiences uniform. Forestry was an elastic concept, stretching to meet the distinct social contexts, cultural matrices, and political environments in which it was introduced. That was an essential point for his American listeners, Pinchot thought, for although he disputed the prevalent suspicion that German methods were "exaggeratedly artificial and complicated" and driven by an "iron clad formality," he was quick to acknowledge that those "methods could not be transported unchanged into our forests without entailing discouragement and failure." Forestry was not a Prussian preserve.[31]

American forest management, in fact, "must be worked out along lines which the conditions of our life will prescribe," a prescription best exemplified in the more flexible Swiss approach. Their "republican" standpoint rejected the Germans' steady focus on a forest's "minutest detail," Pinchot argued, and instead compelled foresters "to reach the best result which is possible at the moment by an intelligent application of the general principles of forestry through the medium of forest organization, 'which is imperfect and incomplete.'" This methodology, at once pragmatic and fluid, and which recognized the limitations of an inexact science, better fit the American temperament.[32]

It dovetailed with Pinchot's political calculations, too. For him, Switzerland served as a middle ground between German precision and orderliness and American cut-and-run, just as Ulrich Meister mediated between Dietrich Brandis and the American lumber barons who had ripped their way through vast virgin stands of ancient New World forests. Pinchot thought he had found in Swiss forestry a means by which to meld the profit motive with aesthetic appreciation, cutting the forest in such a way as to maintain its arboreal beauty. After his visits to Zurich's Sihlwald, for instance, he recognized that it could serve as a model for New York's vast Adirondack forests, sections of which were state-owned and whose future were under sharp debate during his residence in Europe. Preservationists, including large private landowners whose properties abutted the state lands and who hoped to maintain the mountainous region's forested landscape, were opposed by sawmill operators and railroad interests, who wanted free rein to exploit its extensive timber holdings. Pinchot vowed to mesh both groups' needs. "I believe I have found the right method of treatment for the Adirondacks," he wrote to his father in light of his inspections of the Sihlwald, "one under which they will be as picturesque as though left wholly alone, and which will bring a respectable income at the same time." Such a blend of perspectives "will be nec[essary] to conciliate the doctors, the sportsmen and practical men who look to the money return." In Zurich he had seen the future, and it worked.[33]

It would also work for him. He was well aware of the manifold professional possibilities that might come from his first public appearance as a forester. His talk in Washington offered "the chance to get a standing among the people interested in forestry," perhaps even snagging there an offer to manage a forested estate, and maybe even trumping his competition. "What I want," he confided to his mother as he drafted "Government Forestry Abroad," was "to be distinctly ahead of Fernow. . . ." Talking about matters abroad would advance his career at home, a thought that had left him praying for a smooth passage across the north Atlantic. "I hope most sincerely I shall not be much sea-sick, for every minute will be needed"

to rewrite and practice his presentation; "I can't afford to fail in the introduction of G.P. to the forest lovers of the U.S."[34]

All this preparation and anxiety for a fifteen-minute talk, all this stress
on an event that, when it was over, Pinchot used but two words to describe:
"Pleasant time." That was more than one could say about the days in and
around the conference, during which the frenetic young man traveled by
train up and down the eastern seaboard making contact with and sounding
out those whom he felt had important roles to play in the development of
the American forestry movement. On December 20, 1890, he spent a day in
Boston with Charles Sargent, who schooled him in the political obstacles
and personality conflicts that marred then-current efforts, and came away
with a sense that the nation's greatest expert on trees had little to offer. "S.
sees needs and difficulties, both most vividly, but will do nothing himself,"
Pinchot observed, which was a good thing, for he believed that Sargent was
"not thoroughly up to the situation nor in touch [with] the movement."

If pleased that the Bostonian chose to sit on the sidelines, Pinchot learned
the next day that the field was not exactly replete with opportunities. Back
in New York, while lunching at the Union League Club, he met by chance
with Abner L. Train, secretary of the Adirondack Commission. After listening to Pinchot pour out his ideas about practicing forestry on lands
under the commission's control, Train responded that the political situation
militated against hiring a forester for the foreseeable future. Nationally, the
prospects were no more bright, a message that General Sherman delivered
to Gifford the following evening after dinner, and that former Secretary of
the Interior Carl Shurz seconded over lunch with him a mere eighteen
hours later. Their disappointing insights were confirmed time and again
the next week while he was in Washington, during which he conducted
interviews with well-placed members of the Departments of Agriculture
and Interior; from them, Pinchot learned that his grand "schemes for
immediate work on legislators," through which he had hoped to promote
his profession, were "busted."[35]

Still intact, however, was his ambition to supplant Bernard Fernow, and
that had only been encouraged by what he had learned about the German
forester during his first hectic weeks back in the States. From the editor of
Garden and Forest, W. A. Stiles, Pinchot learned of the animosity between

Sargent and Fernow. Sargent, infuriated by Fernow's lackadaisical role as secretary of the American Forestry Association, pondered the development of an alternative organization that would more forcefully press forestry's case before the public and in the political arena; he even would encourage Pinchot to initiate this effort.

Of Fernow's political hesitation and professional caution, Pinchot would gain firsthand experience when listening to the opening words of the forestry chief's talk in Washington on the "Practicability of an American Forest Administration." Fernow did not think it was practicable, arguing instead that a more accurate title for his disquisition would be "'the difficulties attending the introduction of forest management to the United States,' for the negative elements of the problem are still so numerous as to make a positive result, at first sight, at least, doubtful." Its prospects remained in doubt, he concluded, after considerable reflection upon what he labeled "the tremendous momentum of bad habits, unfair usage, and personal politics, that must be overcome to make a rational forest policy possible." It would take, Fernow mused, "a giant, or rather two giants combined, strengthened by the courage of conviction that this is an urgent matter to be acted upon, to carry through . . . any measure involving radical changes in the existing land policy."[36]

Fernow may have believed that together he and Pinchot would redirect federal land management policies, but Pinchot entertained no such illusions. After observing Fernow at his Division of Forestry offices, and then spending the night at his home in Washington, Pinchot concluded that the German forester was not equipped to take the necessary (and large) steps to ensure the future of forestry in the United States. Although impressed by "Fernow's personal history," a narrative that convinced Pinchot that Fernow was a "man of sterling worth" and a "fair man, as far as his intentions go," he nonetheless worried in 1890 about Fernow's psychological fitness. Because he was "unhealthily apt to take up any real or imaginary slight or offense," Pinchot surmised that the touchy forestry chief was not "a man to make a cause popular." The twenty-five-year-old knew he could do better.[37]

The Damaged Fabric

A SELF-DESCRIBED tenderfoot, Pinchot was overwhelmed by his first encounter with the vastness of western land and sky. His travels through the region in the spring of 1891 were part of a grand continental circuit that would take him by rail throughout the South and Southwest, and then swing north along the Pacific coast, before returning to New York via the Canadian Pacific Railroad, a three-month jaunt that was part professional in orientation, part personal in exploration; although he had been hired to report on the prospects for forestry on some of holdings of Phelps Dodge & Company in Arizona and California, he was also free to roam the West. He took great advantage of this opportunity, too, exploring the Grand Canyon and Yosemite and hiking in the Sierra and Cascades. Before he had departed, General Sherman had urged young Pinchot to get to know the United States "before I began to give it free advice," a suggestion the eager forester was only too happy to act upon. What he found was a landscape of bewildering differences.

Especially in the Southwest, a rough terrain filled with "[s]agebrush, prairie dogs, flat-topped buttes, hills covered with Piñon and Cedar," little was what it seemed. In the clear western light, gaining proper perspective was tricky: towering "mountains that looked as if you could almost throw a stone and hit them . . . were miles away." This illusion was nonetheless as palpable as the "log cabins, corrals, and the bones of cattle along the track." Jumbled together, these impressions, Pinchot confessed, "helped make up my first picture of the West."[1]

Just how different this region was from that of the East became strikingly obvious when in April he trekked into the Grand Canyon. Just getting there nearly killed him. During the first leg of his journey, from Phoenix to Flagstaff, he rode shotgun on a stagecoach along the infamous Black Canyon Road—infamous because it was more rut than road. At one point the stage slammed into a gully, pitching Pinchot from his seat. "I lit sprawling on the side of a cut," he would write, "which was lucky, for much of the road skirted a precipice." Transport on the second stage, from Flagstaff into the canyon, was safer but more frustrating. It was all the fault of the mule, whose obstinacy gave new meaning to the word. Unwilling to move at a steady pace or direction despite its lanky rider's frequent use of a homemade switch, it tarried such that Pinchot and his companion, unable to locate nearby water in the dark, had to make dry camp every night on the trail. Adding to the journey's charm, and to Pinchot's sense of himself as a comic dude, was the awkward fit of his six-foot-two frame astride this low-slung beast of burden.[2]

All was forgiven when at last he stood on the edge of the southern rim. He could scarcely believe his eyes. "The Cañon cannot be adequately described," he confided in his diary. "It is a vast hole full of air and mountains." For the next four days he struggled to come to terms with its overwhelming spatial dimensions; at more than 270 miles long and up to twelve miles wide, carved by the coiling Colorado River, it "was without parallel or comparison. I could only strive to find a reference point, some way of measuring it," but that proved impossible, for "language cannot even shadow forth what it is." Descending into the mile-deep chasm, dropping through its four climatic zones, and then standing by the "vast dark river" brought Pinchot no closer to understanding the power of the place; undammed, the Colorado's black surge "was tremendous and appalling in the gloom of a gathering storm." Climbing back up to the distant south rim, he bought himself time by stopping to smell the flowers, only to be disoriented anew when he regained the top: he was wrapped in a blinding snowstorm. Pinchot did not know on what or where to focus. "A man can only wonder," he commented in his diary. "At sunset it is magnificently beautiful and by moonlight magnificently terrible."3

In search of a stable middle ground, he gained perspective through religious metaphors that helped frame the troubling landscape. The canyon's "great power" lay in its "serenity," he finally decided. "It is absolute peace." A peace that was divine, he felt, a sign of the immanence of the Lord: "God's hand is there most wonderfully and I thought and sang the doxology."4

He sang a less reverential tune when he discovered that his mule, which he had hobbled and let stray while he had ranged throughout the canyon's floor, had headed back to Flagstaff without him. This animal, like the extraordinary terrain that so transfixed the tall easterner, was beyond human control.

That he would be overwhelmed by nature was not what he had thought when he had set out west some weeks before. After all, on this trip he was working for Phelps Dodge & Company, a powerful resource extraction corporation that "owned mines and timberlands from New Jersey to Georgia and Michigan to Arizona," whose purpose readily demonstrated the human ambition to dominate the natural world. Pinchot was no stranger to that conceit, due to his training in scientific forestry, and his skills apparently meshed with the company's ambitions. In January 1891 it had hired Pinchot to report on some of its forested lands in Pennsylvania and, pleased with the results, later that spring had asked him to evaluate its holdings in the Sulphur Spring Valley of southern Arizona, "with a view to planting trees." Although the offer contained no salary, the company's board, whose members Pinchot described as men who were "heirs to a long tradition of wealth, respectability, and good works," voted to pay his expenses; it did not hurt, though Pinchot did not mention it in his diary or in *Breaking New Ground,* that some of these worthy souls were his maternal cousins in the Phelps family.5

Good connections, in this instance at least, made for a bad idea. Pinchot would soon discover that Phelps Dodge & Company's afforestation plans were not well conceived; what had seemed to make sense in the cozy company headquarters in New York City would melt in the Arizona heat. Once on the ground, and after quickly taking into account the region's fierce weather, slight annual rainfall, and enormous evaporation that sus-

tained but a "desert vegetation of mesquite and sagebrush," Pinchot realized that the transplantation of trees suitable for logging would be "a hard
proposition." He scouted out other sources of timber, in hopes of locating
something that could withstand the valley's temperature extremes and arid
conditions—he hiked into the nearby Huachuca Mountains to evaluate its
woods for clues to what would survive, and later contemplated trying to
duplicate the successful planting of eucalyptus in southern California—but
nothing panned out. Admitting in his report to Phelps Dodge that "my
own scanty acquirements in Forestry [make] my judgement of small
account," he was, at the beginning of his career, confronted with the possibility that there were limitations to what foresters and forestry could
accomplish.[6]

GROUNDWORK

Such limitations had been less immediately obvious in the lush and green
mountainscape of western North Carolina. A month before he had traveled to Arizona, on the tail end of a trip he had taken with Fernow to investigate the hardwood forests of Arkansas, Pinchot had swung through
Asheville to examine George W. Vanderbilt's massive estate, Biltmore,
then under construction. There he ran into a substance he would not
encounter in Sulphur Spring Valley—mud. It was the worst he had ever
slogged through, but the compensation was that the ample rains needed to
create the gooey muck did wonders for forest growth. He could barely contain his enthusiasm: Vanderbilt's extensive property was "just right for forest management on a rather intensive plan, and the reproduction of both
conifers and deciduous trees [is] excellent." Here nature put up no clear
barriers to cultivation, to the human impress. It is no surprise that here Pinchot would ultimately launch his career.[7]

Making an impression was one of the reasons Pinchot had stopped off in
Asheville. Dietrich Brandis had long counseled him to find a wealthy
patron with forested lands who would allow the neophyte to practice his
craft; Vanderbilt, an heir to one of America's greatest fortunes, and Biltmore, into which he was pouring a considerable portion of his inheritance,
fit the bill admirably. It helped too that the architect of the stunning edifice,

Richard Morris Hunt, and its landscape architect, Frederick Law Olmsted, were good friends of, and had even worked for, the Eno and Pinchot families, but Pinchot did not want to presume too much on these ties. During a November 1891 meeting in New York City with Olmsted about Biltmore, he had "kept my tongue still on the subject of doing a working plan, not wishing to seem eager or pushing." Although securing this new job was not simply a matter of knowing the right people—his professional qualifications and good social sense were surely why Olmsted recommended that Vanderbilt hire him—as with the timber surveys Pinchot had run for Phelps Dodge, it did not hurt that the young man enjoyed rich family connections.[8]

Joining Vanderbilt's staff full-time—he began work in late January 1892—Pinchot was quickly enmeshed in a large-scale aesthetic experiment intended to reconcile nature and culture, the wild and the civilized—qualities that his experiences in Arizona in 1891 had suggested were irreconcilable. No one was better positioned to attempt this reconciliation, nor contributed more to its articulation, than Frederick Law Olmsted. In his design work for Central Park in New York City and Boston's Fens, in his rearticulation of space on a grand scale at Yosemite and Niagara Falls, he demonstrated how to manage landscapes, urban and wild, in such a way as to mask their managed character. As he wrote of the Ramble in Central Park: this district, "which can only be entered on foot, consists of a series of walks carried, in constantly changing grades and directions, through 80 acres of ground of very diversified character, the aspect of natural arrangement being everywhere maintained, while the richness of cultivation is added."

An artful blend of the natural and the cultivated was what Olmsted sought to produce at Biltmore, too. There he wished to give the surrounding forests a primeval gloss to make them appear old (much as architect Hunt used wood paneling throughout Biltmore's interior to give the new mansion an antique feel). It would not be easy. The soil was "extremely poor and intractable," and the nearby woodlands were in miserable condition, "all the good trees having again and again been culled out and only runts left." Because, in Olmsted's estimation, there was "not a single circumstance that can be turned to account in gaining any desirable local character, picturesqueness, for instance or geniality," the only possible solution was to fabricate a new environment "out of whole cloth." Olmsted's aim was to blur the distinction between wildness and cultivation to demonstrate the essential harmony of human space and natural cover, so that when Vanderbilt or guests rode in carriages up the proposed thickly wooded and winding three-mile drive, they would have the "sensation of passing through the remote depths of a natural forest." His recognition that all "landscapes are constructed," that all are "phenomena of nature *and* products of culture," had important consequences, historian Anne Whiston Spirn observes. At Biltmore, he and his protégé Gifford Pinchot would advance an American culture *of* nature.[9]

A critical step in this process had occurred during the early stages of construction. In 1889 Olmsted had persuaded George Vanderbilt to reforest even the surrounding mountains and valleys. Through farming and grazing as well as fires, the land had been battered and abused. Restoring it would be an immense task, he confirmed, yet "far more interesting to a poetic temperament than any of those commonly considered appropriate to a country-seat life." Whatever Vanderbilt's temperament, Olmsted was convinced that such poetics would have an enduring, practical outcome as well: introducing forestry to this vast domain would be of "inestimable service" to the United States, he advised Vanderbilt, an emblem of a new, more rational form of land management for a nation already better known for its rapid and unrestrained exploitation of natural resources than its sustainable development. Biltmore, despite its architectural excesses, would serve as an antidote to the Gilded Age.[10]

But Olmsted's hopes for Biltmore's instructive qualities—what he called its "semi-public" potential—lay not in its ostentatious architecture, in its "granite pile," but in its surrounding terrain. And of that there was a great deal; Biltmore would eventually encompass more than 125,000 acres. In Olmsted's mind, these lands would serve as a beacon for the rest of the country; what he imagined was at stake was nothing less grand than the American national landscape itself," argues historian Frederick Gutheim, "to be inspired and taught by the Biltmore demonstration."[11]

What underlay this demonstration was Olmsted's firm belief that human beings required an orderly landscape within which to live, even when they found themselves within wilderness. He was frankly less interested in designing naturalistic vistas close to and around Vanderbilt's mansion than he was in extending the lines of a rational and perceptible order out onto the acres far distant from that imposing edifice. He thus urged his twenty-six-year-old employer to lay out only "a small park into which to look from your house . . . and make the rest a forest, improving the existing woods and planting the old fields." Vanderbilt essentially agreed with this plan, and Olmsted commenced his work with an extensive topographical survey of the estate's initial 5,000 acres and an evaluation of the lands to be replanted. It was while this project had begun to unfold that he suggested to Vanderbilt that he hire Gifford Pinchot to oversee the final implementation of the Olmstedian landscape vision. The working out of this vision and the establishment of forestry on the grounds was, one architectural historian has concluded, "the most successful and significant of Olmsted's contributions to Biltmore."[12]

That conclusion may baffle those for whom Biltmore stands as Pinchot's first triumph, for it runs contrary to most primary and secondary accounts of the impact the Biltmore forestry experiments had on the development of the profession in the United States. These traditional renderings rely heavily on Pinchot's version of events as depicted in his *Biltmore Forest* (1893) and elaborated on in *Breaking New Ground.* Harold Pinkett, one of Pinchot's biographers, reconfirmed his subject's original argument that it was on Vanderbilt's estate that forestry first made its mark on the American forest. Biltmore, he asserted, provided a "unique" opportunity for Pinchot to develop "a management plan without any precedent."[13]

Pinchot's new standards of American forest management began with a topographical survey of the estate, drawing up a plan by which to manage existing forest cover through selective harvesting of its woods, and establishing the profitability of forestry; it branched off into later experiments in the reproduction of forests and silvicultural techniques designed to promote tree growth and increase lumber production. In each of these developments, or so the argument runs, Pinchot stood as the central actor who thereby gained insight into the profession's glittering potential in (and for) the United States. If the "Biltmore forest is a success," Pinchot confided in a letter to Dietrich Brandis, "I need not fear to undertake the management of any piece of forest land that I have seen in the United States." Whether as prospect or in retrospect, his labors in Asheville apparently laid the foundation for the creation of American forestry; at Biltmore, he laid the foundation for the Forest Service.[14]

Perhaps. But Pinchot's accomplishments were not his alone, nor was his confidence derived from his own efforts, despite the implication of his use of the first-person singular in his letter to his German mentor. Olmsted, after all, had created the intellectual and cultural context for the younger man's work on the estate; it was he who launched the topographical survey of the estate that Pinchot would extend, and it was he "who was responsible for the plan to make Biltmore Estate the nest egg for practical forestry in America," as Pinchot acknowledged.

There had been older precedents as well, idiosyncratic attempts to introduce forestry to the New World, beginning with European colonial settlement. By the late seventeenth century, the ancient stands of eastern hard- and softwoods were being rapidly harvested to heat homes, open up fields for agriculture and grazing, and provide lumber for all forms of construction; the astonishingly swift consumption of wood impelled some towns and colonial governments, as well as the British government, to enact legislation to slow down the wholesale assault. The British navy, for example, wanted to protect its rights to mast-sized pines (a claim that was much contested), and communities needing firewood moved to restrain local deforestation.[15]

Those ad hoc efforts had escalated in number and seriousness in the two decades immediately prior to the Biltmore experiments of the late nineteenth century. Among them was a forestry project conducted on a 12,000-acre hunting preserve known as Blooming Grove Park, located near the Pinchot family home in Milford, Pennsylvania. Its owners, influenced by the same European ideas that Gifford Pinchot would encounter some twenty years later, modeled their 1870s timber-cutting practices after those practiced in France and Germany, notably in "the grand forests of Fontainbleau and the Grand Duchy of Baden." They did so, argued one of the owners, Charles Hallock, a future editor of *Forest and Stream,* because only "the cultivation of forests . . . and the selling of timber and surplus game of all kind" would compensate "in some degree for the frightful waste which is annually devastating our forests and exterminating our game."[16]

It was such pioneer efforts and arguments that would lead Pinchot's colleague and good friend Henry S. Graves to acknowledge that although he and Pinchot were "the first Americans to take up forestry as a profession . . . we often are given too much credit for initiating the national forestry movement." As Graves recognized, "the swift advance in forestry in the nineties . . . would not have been possible if there had not been the background of activities by scientists, educators and other public spirited citizens over a period of 20 or 25 years before we came on the ground."[17]

Pinchot may not have always been so generous, though he too knew how much his work depended on that of others. He knew because one of his predecessors would not let him forget it. Bernard Fernow took great delight in reminding Pinchot of those, including himself, who had helped clear the trail that Pinchot ultimately would hike down. A longtime advocate of the application of forestry principles to land management in this country, Fernow was one of Pinchot's favorite sparring partners; for most of their long and distinguished careers the two foresters denigrated one another's work and professional accomplishments. Their correspondence in the early 1890s established the ground rules for what would develop into a long-standing feud. The rules were simple: no holds barred.

Some of the tension between the two men derived from Pinchot's acceptance of Vanderbilt's offer of employment. Because Fernow had offered Pinchot the position of assistant forester in Washington while the young man had been training in Europe, he believed he had had first claim to Pinchot's services; Fernow was dismayed when Pinchot denied that they had had any such agreement. "A greater disappointment could hardly have been prepared for me, than your sudden determination to drop the plan, which I had cherished for more than a year," Fernow wrote. "I have suffered not inconsiderably from my waiting to realize your appearance here, having kept the position virtually open and doing two men's work meanwhile." Pinchot denied that he was under either a legal or moral obligation to Fernow, but he apologized "that the course I have taken has entailed any trouble for you." Hardly placated, in a February 1892 letter the nation's chief forester discounted Pinchot's ability to know what was best for his career or the cause of forestry, and dismissed the Biltmore experiments as but an "impracticable fad."[18]

His dismissal worried Pinchot, so much so that in the summer of 1893 the younger man wrote Fernow wondering if his work at Biltmore was unique. In his reply, Fernow happily toyed with the young forester's insecurities. He conceded that Pinchot was innovative in his application of French, German, and Swiss forest management practices, and thus allowed Pinchot to stake his claim. In the same letter, however, Fernow undercut this concession by noting that he was nonetheless familiar with "several [earlier] attempts to thin out judiciously and advance the crop" in the United States, experiments that employed methodologies similar to Pinchot's. The unkindest cut of all then followed. Biltmore in the end could not claim precedence, Fernow observed, for the "proposition and first steps taken toward bringing a large forest area under management belong historically . . . to the Adirondack League Club," an announcement designed to blunt some of Pinchot's quest for glory. The club, he pointed out, which controlled more than 180,000 mountainous acres in northern New York, had hired him in the 1880s to develop a forest management plan for its wooded lands, which he had done; that plan, another contemporary observed, "was to put into practice the system of rational forestry prevailing on the continent of Europe, which reconciles the preservation and continual reproduction of forest areas with a continual and increasing income." Pinchot was not the first on the ground.[19]

This was not news to Frederick Law Olmsted, to whose groundbreaking work at Biltmore Pinchot quickly adapted. A close examination of some of Pinchot's formative experiences suggests why he so readily implemented Olmsted's landscape design, adopted many of its architectonic assumptions, and shared his mentor's conviction that forestry was both an art and a science, just as the landscape was at once a cultural and a natural artifact.

BRUSH STROKES

Pinchot's recognition of the aesthetics of forestry was long-standing and born of his privileged childhood. His father, James Pinchot, was an avid collector of American landscape art, especially of the second generation of the Hudson River school of artists. Surely it is not a coincidence that James Pinchot, who grew up in the Delaware River valley at a time when human labor and energy had wrestled a good living from a fertile land, was drawn to canvases that spoke eloquently of this complex environmental transformation. Some of his purchases, such as Worthington Whittredge's *The Old Hunting Ground* (1864) and Sanford Gifford's *Indian Summer on Claverack Creek* (1868), were wistful elegies to a time in which human activities were presumed to be in concert with the surrounding terrain. That America was the Garden of Eden, and that Americans were participants, however necessary, in its defilement—critical themes in Hudson River iconography—gained more explicit articulation in what was arguably Pinchot's most important acquisition, Gifford's *Hunter Mountain, Twilight* (1866). Its foreground, a sagging, heavily logged-over slope, with a thin stream running toward a farmhouse cast in shadow, rises up to meet the somber mountain, a "melancholy tenor" accentuated by the "sickle moon and an evening star" barely visible in the sunset sky.[20]

The painting's potent claims were ones that both its creator and his patron understood intuitively. Sanford Gifford had grown up near Hunter Mountain, whose 4,000-foot elevation dominated the southern Catskills in New York's Greene County, and his grandfather had been employed in the region's once-ubiquitous tanning industry. The artist was no doubt aware that tanners such as his grandfather had slashed through thick stands of hemlock so as to extract the tannin in its bark, environmental depredation that was evoked in the painting's stump-littered canvas. James Pinchot knew all about stumps, too, for his family had also prospered through the wholesale destruction of a once-sylvan land. The axe, a symbol of economic progress and cultural poverty, of conquest and death, was double-edged.[21]

Its symbolic impact may have cut across generations, too, for *Hunter Mountain, Twilight,* when it was not on tour to American or European exhibitions, was hung prominently in the Pinchot family homesteads in

James and Mary Pinchot built Grey Towers, their "summer castle," on a hillside overlooking Milford, Pennsylvania, and they and their children reforested the cutover lands. Grey Towers NHL

which Gifford Pinchot would come of age, first in the Pinchots' townhouse in New York's Gramercy Park, and later still in a family home in Washington, D.C. There a young Gifford, for whom the artist already served as godfather and namesake, and who would inherit the work upon his father's death, may well have meditated on the painting's disturbing set of meanings, pondering exactly what implications these held for him. The conjunction between the family's artistic interests and son Gifford's ambition to regulate the ravages of intensive logging caught the eye of one of New York's major art dealers, Samuel Avery; he wrote to James Pinchot that Gifford's early forestry reports—"noble reports of a noble work"—did honor to the young man's "combined names."[22]

That this was so, that in the Pinchots *Hunter Mountain, Twilight* could not have had, as an art historian has noted, "two owners better attuned to its terrible beauty," takes on an additional significance. Gifford Pinchot has long been accused of practicing a kind of dry-goods forestry, a denunciation of the profession's supposed exclusive utilitarian origin and commercial orientation. But Pinchot may well have built his later studies in forestry's scientific language upon an already established aesthetic vocabulary; in his hands, the forester's tools could become a paintbrush.[23]

From his parents Gifford would learn how to touch up the land, too. In the 1880s, the senior Pinchots began construction of their Richard Morris Hunt–designed "summer castle." Grey Towers was to be perched atop a denuded landscape that the family would repair when they laid down gardens, reestablished meadows, and replanted the forests on the surrounding hills; it would become a blooming testament to the family's—and humanity's—ability to restore what it had once destroyed.[24]

These elegant grounds were not wholly gentrified. To the south and east of the imposing chateau, past the formal gardens and through a line of trees—a mixed stand of Canadian hemlock, white pine and oak, and sugar maple—lies the Sawkill River, an unchecked rush of water that the family left untouched. Their deliberate restraint had its point. The Sawkill, most noisily in the spring when it roars down a series of cataracts, gave the estate a surge of wildness. There, along its glistening slate and shale banks, civilization found its counterpoise *in* nature.[25]

It was only natural that Olmsted would have hired someone who, like Gifford Pinchot, understood the landscape architect's desires to make an aesthetic claim through the reclamation of Vanderbilt's sprawling, once-wooded estate.[26]

STUMPED

That did not mean Pinchot knew what to do. His confusion was understandable. He was a mere twenty-six years old when he arrived at Biltmore, and his youth was compounded by his professional inexperience. He had had but a sketchy undergraduate course in science at Yale, and had had no more than a year of training at L'Ecole Nationale Forestière in France before arriving in North Carolina. He now admitted to Dietrich Brandis, who had once counseled Pinchot to remain in Europe until he was more fully trained, that "the time has come, as you foretold it would, when I begin to feel the scantiness of my preparation."

To fill out his deficient scientific education, he spent "anxious hours over my French and German textbooks" and fired off correspondence across the

Atlantic to his former forestry professors in France, to colleagues in Germany and Switzerland, and to sympathetic Americans, seeking information about silvicultural practices as well as eliciting much-needed support and encouragement. The latter was a great help, but his studies and correspondence actually deepened his frustrations. Most of the scientific texts, as well as the foresters with whom he consulted, were European in fact or in orientation; these books described, and his correspondents worked within, arboreal landscapes already well tended, fully reduced to human control. Such was hardly the case with the indigenous forests of western North Carolina, and thus the insights of Pinchot's mentors were of little help in deciphering the environment in which he was supposed to practice his new craft. It was "hard to get much light," he would later observe, "from the writings of men who had never seen a forest as I had to handle." Pinchot knew he was as green as they came.[27]

If only the land itself had been as verdant. Its deforested condition contributed greatly to Pinchot's professional dilemmas. Vanderbilt's properties were "far from rich, with a disproportionate amount of young wood," he noted in *Biltmore Forest*. Where not heavily cut, tree growth had been stunted by fire; other sections contained badly eroded slopes, markers of poor agricultural practices. These deleterious conditions clearly hindered his reclamation efforts. How bad the situation was became clear when in 1894 Bernhard Fernow made an unannounced visit to Biltmore, found Pinchot off-site, and tried to inspect the young forester's handiwork; the chief of the Division of Forestry later wrote Pinchot that he had been unable to determine where the young forester had cut timber to improve forest health or had planted trees to enhance forest growth.[28]

That was embarrassing, but equally so was the fact that if Pinchot could not refurbish the land, then it would be that much more difficult to turn a profit, thereby undermining his chance to demonstrate practical forestry's money-making capacity to a skeptical American audience. As he announced in *Garden and Forest* in March 1892, his experiments at Biltmore "should do much to remove forestry from the anomalous and often illogical position into which the mistaken zeal of some of its friends have forced it, and to ground its roots in the solid Earth of business common sense." His work in North Carolina, he declared, "asserts a proposition which must ultimately lie at the base of forest preservation in this country: namely, that it is not necessary to destroy a forest to make it pay." Proving the truth of that principle was more difficult than he realized, a difficulty he initially resolved by a bit of creative bookkeeping. When he tabulated the ledgers after his first year of work at Biltmore, and published his financial accounts in *Biltmore Forest,* a pamphlet he prepared for and distributed as part of Biltmore's exhibit at the 1893 Chicago World's Fair, he claimed to have turned a profit. Alas, much of the income stream was the result of the estate buying its own wood products, and Pinchot failed to include his salary in his calculation of expenses. Had he followed better accounting procedures, his project would have been in the red.[29]

These sleights of hand might have fooled an uninitiated public, but not well-trained foresters of the likes of Fernow and Brandis. Both spotted Pinchot's flawed bookkeeping and recognized its significance. "You will remember . . . that I expressed my grave doubts as to your ability under the conditions then existing . . . to establish the profitableness of forestry," Fernow wrote after reading *Biltmore Forest.* "I have seen no reason for changing my position in that respect and agree with Mr. Brandis when he called the experiment 'verfehlt' [a failure]—from that point of view [profitableness] only!" Biltmore had in effect offered up America's first below-cost timber sale, a financial outcome Pinchot would regularly reproduce during his years as the nation's chief forester.[30]

Biltmore was also the site, in 1895, of the first extensive episode of lumbering managed according to the principles of scientific forestry, a cut that would raise questions about the environmental impact of this new form of land management in the minds of the two most responsible for it, Gifford Pinchot and German forester Carl Schenck.

With a glowing recommendation from Brandis, Vanderbilt had hired Schenck in 1895 to replace Pinchot as Biltmore's resident forester when the American decided to open up an office as a consulting forester in New York City. As early as 1893, Pinchot had, in his words, been "growing impatient for fresh fields and pastures new," so while he continued to supervise the Biltmore operations, Schenck was placed in charge of the day-to-day activities. From the start the two men, born of different cultures, found much that troubled them in each other. For Schenck, his American counterpart seemed less than committed to forestry management at Biltmore; Pinchot had met him in New York when he first arrived in the United States, and had given him an extended tour of the city. "Queerly, the task awaiting me at Biltmore was scarcely touched upon in our conversations," Schenck recalled, conversations "which were restricted rather to discussions of hunting and fishing." Pinchot, in turn, was put off by what he would regard as the Prussian's disdain for the Appalachian people; "he had far less understanding of the mountaineers than he had for the mountains," Pinchot later observed. "He thought of them as peasants. They thought of themselves as independent American citizens—and they were right."[31]

Mutually wary, their minds were not at one about the importance of the intensive logging that would occur amid an ancient forest of yellow poplar along Big Creek, located in the 80,000 acre Pisgah Forest near Asheville, which Vanderbilt had recently purchased. In August 1892, he had sent Pinchot to scout out the property under the pseudonym of "Mr. Gifford," and with the charge to "avoid all towns and [to] keep away from houses as much as possible." Apparently Vanderbilt, one of the nation's richest men, feared that if it were known he was considering buying the lands, it "would have been fatal to our scheme," Pinchot noted. Uncomfortable with the duplicity, Pinchot swore that that was "a thing I shall never do again. It is not that there was any chance of discovery." But what he had come upon took his breath away. "Bounded by water courses and high crests of mountains," he wrote his parents of Pisgah, "there is probably less than a square mile of cleared land on the whole tract, and that chiefly along to the streams. The forest is exceedingly fine . . . the streams are as beautiful as any I have ever seen, except for our Sawkill." Wandering through the rough, isolated terrain, transfixed by the magnificent sunsets, Pinchot worked his way up and down the "sharp ridges, steep slopes, and narrow valleys" that were studded with chestnut, red and white oak, and yellow poplar; everywhere he spotted signs of deer, bear, and turkey, and once discovered a fallen tulip tree (yellow poplar) that he calculated to have been "thirty-three feet in circumference, breast high, while it stood." His wilderness tramp, Pinchot laughed to a friend vacationing in stylish Bar Harbor, Maine, had been transformative. "I have had no use for money recently, having been out in the wild, wild woods, sleeping on the ground, conversing with moonshiners, and feeding on warmed-up dough." The language of his report to Vanderbilt was only slightly less giddy. "To say that I am delighted with the whole area is to put it mildly."[32]

It was the poplar in the Pisgah that Pinchot felt should be logged first. It was not only about this particular decision that he and Schenck, who would supervise cutting, disagreed; they also reached contrary conclusions about the operation's significance, revealing their differing convictions about the prospects of American forestry.[33]

Of the two narratives of events, Schenck's, composed more than fifty years after the fact, is the most troubled and troubling. He had arrived at Biltmore in the spring of 1895 to replace Pinchot, and had come with high praise from Brandis. Shortly after his arrival, the two men rode into the Pisgah, tethered their horses on a ridge overlooking the Big Creek valley, and descended through its wooded beauty. "In the valley were the most beautiful trees I had ever seen," Schenck recalled, "towering tulip [poplar] trees, with gigantic chestnuts, red oaks, basswoods, and ash trees at their feet." He learned from his American guide that this "glorious primeval forest," once inaccessible, now would supply millions of board feet to a Vanderbilt-owned mill in Asheville, with the lumber to be sold on the open market. Big Creek would demonstrate once and for all that scientific forestry could be profitable.[34]

Pinchot's plans for how to transport the felled timber to Asheville included the construction of a splash dam, so called because foresters used such temporary structures to build up a reservoir of water that then would be released to flush logs down an otherwise less-powerful tributary. On Big Creek, a splash dam would push piles of timber down to the deeper and swifter waters of the Mills River, a tributary of the French Broad River, which would then carry them into Asheville. This proposal reportedly worried Schenck. Although he did not voice his worries at the time, he would have preferred to have constructed permanent logging roads rather than rely on the vagaries of riparian transport. Neither was he as convinced as Pinchot that the logging would clear the way for the natural regeneration of the poplar. Before the cut, for instance, he and a visiting forester—the renowned Baron von Ribbentrop, who, like Brandis, had been an important figure in the development of forestry in British India—searched for evidence of potential stock from which to regenerate the forest; "we could not find . . . one seedling of a tulip [poplar], and not one tree of pole size." When Ribbentrop therefore objected "to the removal, under Pinchot's plan, of all the tulip trees except the hollow ones," when he observed that the plan was "sure to extinguish forever our most valuable species of tree," Schenck professed to being caught in an impossible situation. "Should I have boycotted the Pinchot plan? Impossible! Pinchot was my friend and I was unwilling to betray him." Schenck was ready to sacrifice his "good name" even though he was convinced that the Big Creek cutover would be a financial debacle and a silvicultural disaster.[35]

Schenck's worries appeared justified when in October 1895 the timber harvesting began in earnest. He quickly realized that the initial splash dam would not work as Pinchot had projected because a drought had so sub stantially diminished stream flow. The German forester then ordered the construction of a second dam on the north fork of the Big Creek, timed the release of the two dams' waters so that their "waves" would converge simultaneously "at the confluence of the two creeks," and waited for "rains and freshets to augment the flow." They did more than augment it. After a hard and steady rain, the dams' waters were released, and the logs shot down Big Creek and crashed into Mills River, where they catapulted over its banks, plowing into farmers' fields and tearing up nearby bridges. The debacle provoked an enraged populace to file "a very rattail of lawsuits." These legal skirmishes were the least of Schenck's worries. Refloating the beached timber and the logs stranded along flats in the French Broad River delayed milling for six months; this hiatus appeared to wipe out whatever profit the logging of two million board feet was to have generated.[36]

It was the devastation to the Big Creek ecosystem, however, that compelled Schenck to question forestry's future in the United States. "The bed of Big Creek, arched with Rhododendrons, green with moss-covered rocks, and replete with brook trout," he lamented, "was made a ruined run, a veritable arroyo of torn shores and skimmed stones." America seemed destined to follow the European lead, for "where has it not been true that forestry, superimposed upon the primeval, has destroyed nature's gorgeous beauty at the first stroke of the ax?"[37]

Gifford Pinchot shared some of the German's concerns. His narration of the Big Creek logging, first laid down in his diary and later recapitulated in his autobiography, revealed an initial hesitancy about his decision to log. After "much searching of our souls," though, the loggers carefully selected "the Poplar trees to be felled," and they were "thrown with much care not to smash the long smooth trunks or destroy the young poplars already on the ground." Despite this caution, Pinchot reported considerable damage to the terrain; he qualified his disappointment with a nod to "the difficulties of working with new men, the size of the timber, and the necessity of getting every tree down without breaking it." Although not perfect, the beginning phase of the Big Creek logging operation, he felt, was nonetheless a "good job."[38]

Nothing else about the operation seems to have given him pause. Unlike Schenck, he was convinced that the cut would generate natural reproduction, and reported, in stark contrast to his Biltmore associate, that Ribbentrop had thoroughly supported Pinchot's ideas and plans. The baron had written the young American that the Big Creek operation would be "a wonderful good operation—a perfect piece of work," an assessment that gratified the American neophyte. "It was of immense satisfaction to me to know that one of the most experienced foresters in the world, whose bailiwick had extended from equatorial ugles to timber line on the highest mountains on earth, thought we were doing the right thing." Neither did Pinchot evince qualms about the splash dams or the log drive—when "we were ready for the drive, the drive went through." This interpretation neatly blended with his assertion that when the Asheville mill had completed its work, cutting three million board feet in contrast to the two million Schenck had calculated, the Biltmore estate had netted a profit. All this led Pinchot to conclude that "Big Creek was the first successful attempt in America to secure the natural reproduction of a particular tree by commercial lumbering under forest management."[39]

How could two foresters reach such different conclusions about the Big Creek logging? Each man's future helped shape his recapitulation of that past. Schenck's subsequent experiences at Biltmore would not be unalloyed triumphs. Vanderbilt fired him in 1907, and the school of forestry he had established there was effectively eclipsed when Fernow and Pinchot set up competing schools at Cornell and Yale; furthermore, most of his best students became Pinchot devotees. In the years following his return to Germany to fight in its army during World War I, he remained in his homeland, largely out of contact with the people and events that dominated the development of the profession in America. The account of Big Creek reflects his sense of disappointment, just as his memoir, *Birth of Forestry in America,* strikes a discouraged note.[40]

American forestry did not have an easy delivery, Pinchot conceded, and he had made plenty of mistakes tending the profession's cradle. One year after arriving in North Carolina, he had acknowledged that he was "just a beginner," having "done little in the work of my profession." It was a becoming modesty that, if not entirely accurate, nonetheless captures the sense of incompleteness that he too felt about his tenure in North Carolina. But Pinchot would come to see these setbacks as having heuristic value; they taught him invaluable lessons, he would conclude, because of the remarkable set of accomplishments that lay ahead in the next decade. Within ten years of the Big Creek cut, and especially between 1900 and 1905, he helped define forestry's place within American culture. It was during those years that he helped establish its professional organization (the Society of American Foresters); created, underwrote, and taught in its premier graduate school (the Yale School of Forestry); and oversaw the creation of the Forest Service, serving as its first chief. Biltmore had been a crucial first step in Pinchot's career, and its importance was symbolically acknowledged years later when some of the estate's acreage was incorporated into the professional world he had created: in the 1930s, Pinchot would help persuade the Vanderbilt heirs to sell the Pisgah to the federal government, turning it into a national forest. What better testament could there be to the value of the work he had done there?[41]

He had an answer for that, too, and found it in the consequences of the regeneration experiment he and Schenck had conducted on Big Creek. Unlike his German colleague, who in his memoir admitted that he did not know what had happened to the forest, in the mid-1930s Pinchot returned to Asheville to evaluate the impact of the intensive harvesting forty years earlier. "I tramped down from Pisgah Ridge through the old Big Creek operation," he wrote, and found the "[p]oplar reproduction we had tried for was there in great abundance. I was profoundly delighted, as I had a right to be, with the stand of young Poplar that dated from our marking and cutting. It proved that our method was right." It was proof as well that Big Creek was where he had first attempted to locate the balance between the nature of the forest and the culture of forestry. To achieve that balance required accepting the axe as double-edged, a tool that could both destroy and revitalize. Pinchot did. He assured readers of *Breaking New Ground* that he shared their antipathy for the cutting down of trees, but "you can't practice Forestry without it."[42]

A Political Two-Step

T HERE IS a self-conscious, though not unique, choreography to environmental politics. Contending organizations, and just as often contentious individuals, play to and off one another to gain advantage and to secure a hearing. This reciprocal sparring, this subtle interplay between allies and opponents, first emerged in the late nineteenth century, part of the birthright of the then-nascent conservation movement. Its originators, John Muir and Gifford Pinchot, recognized that politics was a form of dramatic art. Not only did their tangled relationship—they were alternately good friends and tempestuous rivals—reinforce that understanding, but out of their fraught interactions, and what was made of them, emerged a dramatic narrative that set the movement's interpretive agenda for years to come.

STORYLINE

The narrative kicks off with a theatrical exchange between Muir and Pinchot over the then-heated question of whether sheep grazing should be allowed on public lands in the Cascade Mountains of the Pacific Northwest. Grazing was responsible for a good portion of the West's agricultural wealth, but it was also the source of considerable environmental devastation. Wool may have been a renewable resource, but the same was not always true for the mountain meadows through which sheep moved, and grasslands had a difficult time regenerating after being chewed up and trampled down. The vast herds' damaging presence on public lands, according to Linnie Marsh Wolfe, a Pulitzer Prize–winning biographer of Muir, was the key to a significant clash between Muir and Pinchot in the crowded lobby of the Rainier Grand Hotel in Seattle.

Although Wolfe failed to specify when the confrontation occurred, the two men's travel records indicate that their paths crossed there in early September 1897. Pinchot, then a recently appointed special forest agent for the federal government, had arrived in Seattle on an extended tour of the newly created forest reserves in the West, the creation of which had greatly angered ranchers and farmers, mine operators, and lumber owners. They were infuriated that President Grover Cleveland, in setting aside 21 million acres, had locked away resources that they had hoped to exploit. So hostile and powerful were these forces that through their representatives in Congress they had managed to suspend Cleveland's action, pending congressional hearings. Hired as an agent of the Interior Department in June 1897, Pinchot had been charged with evaluating the quality and character of the forest reserves, measuring the depths of western hostility to their creation, and, where possible, building support for Cleveland's action.[1]

His was no easy task. He encountered the expected stiff opposition, though he also managed to secure some favorable reports, notably in Spokane's *Spokesman-Review* and the *Seattle Post-Intelligencer*. He would brag that the latter's editor, after a lengthy interview, "came to the right view" and demonstrated his newfound knowledge in a strong editorial supporting Pinchot's position. But these victories may have come at a cost, engendering a hostile reaction from an unexpected quarter—John Muir.[2]

Muir had stopped in Seattle on his way from Alaska to his home in California. He and Pinchot were well acquainted, having traveled together as members of the National Forest Commission during the summer of 1896. The commission, sponsored by the National Academy of Sciences, had been established to evaluate the possibility of carving national forests and parks out of public lands in the West; in its final report it had concluded that it was indeed both possible and desirable to reserve landscapes for their resources and beauty, a recommendation that had been the impetus for Cleveland's "set-aside" order, an executive action that had so riled western-ers. It was in this context that Muir and Pinchot reconnected in Seattle on September 5, 1897. The younger Pinchot, who felt a strong affinity for the famed naturalist, was "much delighted" to see him again and spent the better portion of that day and night with the man whom he considered to be "a storyteller in a million."[3]

Such admiration did not protect Pinchot from Muir's wrath when, the next morning, he allegedly read Pinchot's interview in the *Post-Intelligencer*. Muir was astonished that the special forest agent could both champion the need for the reserves and assure his audience that he did not believe that sheep grazing would unduly damage them. Muir accosted Pinchot in the hotel lobby and demanded to know whether he had been correctly quoted on the matter of sheep. Pinchot acknowledged that he had been (after all, he had dictated the interview to the newspaper's stenographer), whereupon Muir snapped: "In that case, I don't want anything more to do with you. When we were in the Cascades last summer, you yourself stated that the sheep did a great deal of harm." The wool, it seems, had not been pulled over his eyes.[4]

Muir's biographers have not been fooled either. Linnie Marsh Wolfe, among others, believed this incident unmasked Pinchot's penchant for hypocrisy. That he now would accept grazing in the reserves, she affirmed, was a cheap political gambit designed to curry favor with the powerful wool growers' associations in the Pacific Northwest. Pinchot's "little appease-ment policy," Wolfe observed, provoked Muir's righteous indignation, so much so that with "his eyes flashing blue flames," he renounced his friend-ship with Pinchot. Political ramifications were unavoidable, she concluded: "[A] rift opened that swiftly widened" between the two men—one that, by extension, split the conservation movement in two. Pinchot had come to represent those who favored utilitarian conservation, a policy that reflected humanity's overt management of the environment. Muir stood for those who disdained such management, who advocated the preservation of wilderness lands. This deplorable difference, Wolfe concluded, set back the movement considerably, and the responsibility for this tragedy lay with Gifford Pinchot.[5]

Wolfe's is a compelling interpretation, bringing no small comfort to those who embrace Muir's perception of the proper relationship between humanity and nature, and who perforce dismiss Pinchot as morally bereft, a political hack. There are, however, several problems with this anecdote and the conclusions that have been drawn from it. First of all, the artful scene that Wolfe set in Seattle may not have occurred. Her sole source is an unrecorded conversation between Muir and William E. Colby, a close friend and the secretary of the Sierra Club. True, Pinchot's diary records that the two met in the lobby on the afternoon of September 5, 1897, but theirs was apparently a most cordial meeting:

> Lunch with [J. A.] Holmes [of the U.S. Geological Survey] at the Rainier Grand and after met John Muir in the lobby. Spent the afternoon with these two. Much delighted to see Mr. Muir again. Dinner with them. . . . Church in the eve with Holmes and then dictated interview for the Post Intelligencer . . . then more later with Muir and Holmes.

Pinchot, then, had not provided the *Seattle Post-Intelligencer* with his views on grazing in the reserves, published the next day, until later that evening; when Muir and Pinchot met in the Rainier Grand lobby on September 5, there could not have been the fiery interchange Wolfe recounted in her biography.[6]

What of the next morning, September 6? That day's *Post-Intelligencer* carried an extensive "interview" with Pinchot, only one line of which mentioned sheep: "Pasturage may also be permitted by the secretary under suitable rules and regulations." Whether Muir would have been enraged by Pinchot's qualified statement in support of regulated grazing is less intriguing than the question of whether Muir actually saw (and read) it and, if so, whether he would have had an opportunity to confront Pinchot about its supposed implications. According to the shipping records published in the local newspaper, Muir was aboard the SS *Puebla* when it set sail from Seattle at 8:00 A.M. on September 6, the morning on which Pinchot's words first appeared in print. Surely, given the constraints of nineteenth-century ocean travel, the "eminent scientist" would have boarded the vessel some hours earlier, which narrows the time frame when Muir and Pinchot could have encountered one another. Did they cross paths at, say, 6:00 A.M.? Would a knot of reporters—whom Wolfe indicates witnessed the fascinating and historic moment—have gathered there at such an early hour and, if so, why did they not report this drama?[7]

The tentative character of Wolfe's data is further qualified by the fact that Muir and Pinchot continued to correspond after Muir's alleged severing of their association. In this correspondence, moreover, they did not shy away from discussing the very issue that allegedly had driven them apart— sheep grazing. Writing to "My dear Pinchot" three months later, in December 1897, Muir evinced his delight in hearing from the young forester: "I was very glad to get your cheery hopeful forest letter in which you say you are not only confident of maintaining the present reservations but full of hope that we shall be able to protect them in the future and increase their area." Muir's enthusiasm, however, did not extend to the Department of the Interior's management of the contested public lands. In particular, he was "rather discouraged" that General Land Office Commissioner Binger Hermann "should have thrown open the Oregon Reserves to sheepmen and sheep." In casting blame on Hermann, Muir indicated that he understood the differences between Hermann's decision to "throw open" the reserves and Pinchot's advocacy of regulated grazing therein. These policy distinctions enabled Muir to advocate a stronger alliance with Pinchot. Hermann, Muir asserted, was one of those "blundering plundering money making officials" whom, together, they must fight to protect the reserves, a point he returned to in a postscript: "I shall be glad to hear how you succeed in your forest plans. I look with little [hope] with Bliss and Herman[n]." Sheep, it appears, had not trampled on their relationship.[8]

Muir and Pinchot disagreed about whether sheep should *ever* be allowed to graze in the forest reserves, a disagreement that may have surfaced during their tour with the Forest Commission. But Pinchot was a staunch opponent of intensive grazing. No toady of the wool growers' associations, he later proposed strong regulations governing the precise extent and nature of grazing allowable on federal lands, believing he did so in response to the teachings of John Muir.

In May 1900, for instance, he went to Arizona with Frederick V. Coville, botanist for the Department of Agriculture, to investigate what Pinchot called the "ticklish question" of grazing: ticklish, for grazing was "the most important use that had yet been made of the Forest Reserves, and the center of the bitterest controversy." Into that controversy Pinchot and Coville plunged, and after three weeks of riding through the territory's northern tier of mountains and southern river valleys, the two reached a not-so-startling conclusion. "The trip established what I was sure of already," Pinchot wrote, "that overgrazing of sheep does destroy the forest. Not only do sheep eat young seedlings, as I proved to my full satisfaction by finding plenty of them bitten off, contrary to the sheepmen's contention, but their innumerable hoofs also break and trample seedlings into the ground." He also found that overgrazing by sheep stripped the Arizona watersheds of their ground cover, contributing to soil erosion and silted rivers. "John Muir called them hoofed locusts," Pinchot later would declare, "and he was right." This hardly sounds like a man who had been scorched by the naturalist's "flaming blue eyes."[9]

If the two men's relations were not as strained as the apocryphal Seattle hotel incident would seem to suggest, if their differences over the question of grazing were not so pronounced, why do most of Muir's biographers persist in casting Pinchot as the black sheep? Why set the devil Pinchot against the angel Muir? Why, in turn, have the majority of Pinchot's biographers responded in kind, elevating their subject to heavenly heights, thereby demoting Muir and frequently writing him out of the history of the American conservation movement?[10]

The answer lies in the interplay between historiography and environmental politics. Both sets of historians have used their subjects to reconstruct the past along certain lines to reaffirm present-day perspectives and values. The focus of Michael Cohen's *The Pathless Way* was not just on the great naturalist and founder of the Sierra Club, but on "my own thinking; and not only my own thinking but the thinking of a whole community, of my generation," a generation in whose heart Muir "has always had a special place. . . ."[11]

Pinchot has warmed the hearts of his biographers, too. Many of these have used "the Chief" as a lens through which to write an institutional history of the Forest Service, thereby projecting (and protecting) his reputation down through time. The purpose of this quest for a usable past is obvious, even if not always conscious. By denying a central place to one's subject's opponent in the past, one can undermine his successors' legitimacy. Ramifications of this emerge in the long-standing and often bitter struggles that have marked relations between the Forest Service and the Sierra Club, organizations that Pinchot and Muir, respectively, helped establish.[12]

Neither Muir nor Pinchot would be much surprised by the way their respective biographers have treated the other, or by the way their institutional legacies have repeatedly clashed, for they are in large part responsible for sparking these ongoing disputes. Both men were immensely skilled at generating the kind of favorable public relations that, by its very nature, ignores the competing claims of the opposition and casts one's opponent's actions or beliefs in the most unfavorable of lights. What makes this acrimony so intriguing is that the relationship of Muir and Pinchot once was so benign.[13]

HIGH GROUND

John Muir was particular about where he met people. If he hoped to convert them to his beliefs about the need for the preservation of wilderness, he preferred to meet them in the mountains themselves. That was where his politics were carried out, Cohen has noted, for "mountain thinking was different, and so consequently was mountain society." Such heights were the only proper setting for a conversion to wilderness values, and if only that conversion "could be made strong enough, it would be carried back down to the lowlands and change cities."[14]

That said, the setting for what appears to have been the first meeting between Muir and Pinchot in October 1892 could not have been more appropriate. True, they met not in the sunlit valleys of Yosemite, in which Muir cultivated the friendship and support of so many of the luminaries of the early conservation movement, but in the flatter and greener hills of New York's Adirondacks. They were introduced at some point while Pinchot and Fritz-Greene Halleck, whom he described as "a close friend of mine and a fine woodsman," tramped through and evaluated "a superb tract of 40,000 acres" that Vanderbilt's brother-in-law Dr. W. Seward Webb owned and on which he hoped to practice forestry. On this extensive prop-

John Muir, the famed naturalist and founder of the Sierra Club, was a close advisor and mentor to Gifford Pinchot until the two men clashed over construction of a dam in California's Hetch Hetchy Valley.
Forest History Society

erty in upstate Hamilton County, called Ne-Ha-Sa-Ne Park, Pinchot and Muir spent several days hiking together on what Pinchot later told Halleck was "the pleasantest trip I have ever had in the woods." To seal that memory and to make a claim on Muir's affections, Pinchot, upon his return to Biltmore, sent a large hunting knife to Halleck to give to Muir. "As I shall never forget the trip myself I do not want them to forget that I spent a few days with them either."[15]

Muir and Pinchot met next in the urban (and darker) canyons of New York City in June 1893. More precisely, they shared a meal at a dinner party in the elegant Gramercy Park home of James and Mary Eno Pinchot, where, Muir wrote his wife, he was entertained in "grand style."[16]

Although his hosts had not met him before, they collected intriguing dinner guests as avidly as any big-game hunter stalked trophies, so when they learned that the celebrated John Muir was in the city prior to sailing for Europe, they immediately invited him to dinner. And why not? By then, Muir had become quite well known within literate circles. A prolific essayist whose evocative descriptions of rugged western landscapes, from

Yosemite to Alaska, regularly appeared in leading eastern periodicals such as the *Century Magazine* and *Harper's Weekly,* he had recently used his renown to good advantage. A year earlier he had helped found the Sierra Club, whose goal was to protect the eponymous range of mountains in California that his words had done so much to bring to the American public's notice (he had dubbed them the "Range of Light," regarding them as a sacred space). Muir's celebrity thus brought him to the Pinchots' attention and home, and in its richly appointed interior he played his part as the amiable raconteur of the American Wild West, albeit one in full dinner dress.[17]

Mountain thinking could be expected to make little headway in such a civilized environment, but perhaps it did, for it helped forge Muir's close friendship with Gifford Pinchot, who, he advised his wife, was "studying forestry." Although Pinchot left no written impression of that evening, surely he was as swept up then as he would later be by the famed guest's capacity to spin a good yarn. At the Pinchots', as elsewhere in Muir's travels, "I had to tell the story of the minister's dog," a reference to his much-lauded Alaskan tale entitled "The Stickeen." All those at the Pinchots' table seemed "to think it wonderful for the views it gives of the terrible crevasses of the glaciers as well as for the recognition of danger and fear and joy of the dog." But the invited guests were not his only audience: "[I]t is curious to see how eagerly the liveried servants listen from behind screens, half-closed doors, etc."[18]

The night had been so successful that the senior Pinchots followed it up with a series of invitations to Muir to spend several evenings at their home in New York and at Grey Towers; Muir, without irony, called the bluestone manor overlooking the Delaware River valley a "cottage in the hills." Pinchot's parents hoped that these meetings, however infrequent, would help further their twenty-eight-year-old son's fledgling career as a forester. Surely Muir, the great spokesman for America's wild lands, would be a valuable person for Gifford to know.[19]

They were quite right. Early correspondence between the two men suggests that Muir gladly took up the role of mentor and guide. "Nothing in all my trip gave me greater pleasure than finding you a Young Man devoting yourself to the study of World Forestry amid the whirl of commerce," Muir declared in a letter upon his return from Europe, at once flattering Pinchot and encouraging his devotion to his career. That his fascination with forestry was based in part on a rejection of commercial enterprise—and was thus in concert with Muir's mountain thinking—was accurate to a point. The contemporary press had been abuzz with reports of the Yale graduate's selfless pursuit of a career in public service: "Handsome Gifford Pinchot has set an honorable example" for his generation, a columnist of the *Boston Herald* had written in 1891, for those "certain young men in Gotham who flatten their noses against Club windows in the morning, and soften their brains with gossip, champagne, and unmentionables at other periods of the day and night." His maternal grandfather Eno was not quite so impressed, and would neither accept nor understand his grandson's choice of career; repeatedly he had sought to lure him into his lucrative businesses, but he failed to change Gifford's mind. This failure did not mean, as Muir had implied, that the idealist had rejected commercial enterprise. How could he have done so? His taking up a career in forestry, for which he would earn precious little money, depended on his family's having achieved the very financial success he appeared to spurn.[20]

Pinchot was grateful for more than Muir's praise. He treasured the older man's advice to learn forestry through living in American forests. Muir had called the experience "getting rich," an ironic redefinition of the phrase, and Pinchot worked hard to cultivate this form of wealth. In the spring of 1894, he advised Muir that he had been "trying to live up" to his expectations. That May, while working on a forestry plan for George Vanderbilt's North Carolina estate, Biltmore, he had put his words to action. "In a very small way I have tried your plan of going alone, and was off for four days by myself," Pinchot informed his mentor. "They were as pleasant days as I have ever passed in the woods, and I am only waiting for the chance to do more . . . [for] I am perfectly satisfied that I can learn more and get more out of the woods than when there is anyone else along. . . ." Meeting Muir's expectations did not mean he thought he could eclipse them. "I am afraid that I shall never be able to do the amount of hard work that you have done, or get along on such slender rations," Pinchot acknowledged, but he hoped that by following Muir's path he might "be able to get more into the life of the forest than I have ever done before."[21]

Muir applauded Pinchot's efforts to follow in his steps. "You are choosing the right way into the woods," Muir responded. "Happy man. You will never regret a single day spent thus." Muir then urged his new protégé to press on with his work in the woods. "Go ahead. Yours must be not merely a successful but glorious life." Indeed, he challenged Pinchot to give his ambition free rein. "Radiate radiate radiate far and wide as the lines of latitude and longitude on a globe," he wrote in Whitmanesque exultation; "you have," he confided, "a grand future and a grand present." That exultation he would live to regret when, in the early twentieth century, Pinchot radiated well beyond Muir's orbit and thus out of his control. But that lay in the future. For now, Pinchot's career seemed assured and in tandem with Muir's own vision. The older man's only regret now was "that I cannot join you on your walks."[22]

His regret lasted until the summer and fall of 1896, when they were fellow travelers on the National Forest Commission's extended tour of the American West, during which the two men shared many a hike—and through such incredible terrain! In mid-July, the commissioners gathered in Montana, and together and individually explored the Bitterroot Valley and western stretches of that state. They later journeyed along the Willamette, Rogue, and Umpqua Valleys of Oregon, and visited Klamath and Crater Lakes; next up were the Sierra, San Bernardino, and San Jacinto mountain ranges of central and southern California. As the late-summer temperatures rose, the group headed into Arizona, toured the Grand Canyon, moved on to New Mexico, and concluded with a visit to Pike's Peak ("we rode to the top," Pinchot remembered with some chagrin, "in a stage, which seemed a scurvy thing to do to that great mountain") and excursions to portions of five pre-existing forest reserves in Colorado. By October, their trip concluded, the commissioners headed back to Washington to deliberate and write their final report.

For Pinchot, there were innumerable high points on the three-month trip; halfway through the western tour, for instance, he made a successful and solitary climb up Mount Dana, from whose heights he "saw the glorious chain of the Sierras tumbling like granite waves from south to north, and wearing about its middle a girdle of green trees." But reuniting with John Muir in Belton, Montana, at the trip's start was also a peak experience. "You may imagine my delight to find John Muir with the party," he wrote home. "He and I have been talking vigorously a good deal of the time ever since. We had a capital time fishing together at the lake [Kalispell], and saw two wonderful evenings on the water. The scenery was grand, gloomy, and peculiar, and in one way nearly as fine as the Yosemite." Hoping to build on this companionable moment, he invited Muir to join him on a trip down the lake via steamer, an open-air conveyance he thought preferable to traveling its length by freight train, as the others were scheduled to do. "Muir wanted to go with me," and apparently with good reason. He "had been eating good trout with me at my camp while the others had them fried to a crisp at the hotel," but the head of the commission, Charles Sprague Sargent, dissuaded the naturalist from following his stomach. Pinchot felt a close affinity for Muir, and felt it was reciprocated.[23]

That they talked and sauntered together did not necessarily mean Pinchot and Muir thought alike, however. Their positions relative to the commission were quite differently conceived, a reflection of the different calculations each man made about his ability to contribute to the group's deliberations. Muir was not actually a member. He refused to accept an appointment to the commission, participating only as an observer because he believed that in this manner he could retain his independent voice and maintain his credibility while influencing the commission's findings. Pinchot, by contrast, adopted a strategy in which holding the post of secretary to the commission was crucial. Working from within was the one way that he, as the youngest member of the commission—younger by a full generation in some cases—could gain access to the centers of power in which the final report would be written.[24]

These differing approaches to the commission's work provide insight into the two men's basic political and personal styles. Muir was uncomfortable as a joiner, while Pinchot would in time prove to be the consummate organization man. These contrasting traits lay at the heart of the ideological disputes that later arose between them. It was during the mid-1890s that they began to sense that their interpretation of conservation was not the same, that when they looked at trees they did so with different eyes. Muir confirmed this indirectly when, in a letter to his wife, he commented that of all the members of the commission only its head, Charles Sprague Sargent,

Harvard botanist and director of the Arnold Arboretum, "knew & loved trees as I loved them."

What Muir intended by that affirmation is unclear, for his subsequent writings on American forests portrayed them as majestic examples of botanic growth, a position he shared with Sargent, and as rich repositories of timber the federal government should protect and manage, a perspective he shared with Pinchot. For his part, Pinchot was not at all ambiguous about his growing, deep differences with Sargent.

Their disagreements had emerged even before the tour, during preliminary discussions of the commission held in New York City in mid-May. Pinchot reported to Brandis that Sargent seemed unwilling to entertain in-depth explorations of the current or proposed forest reserves, planning an itinerary that allowed visits to only those whose "borders [were] within easy reach of the railroad." Nor was the chairman interested in "any forest work," or in opening up a dialogue on issues "which require for their proper discussion the training of a forester." Pinchot predicted that if Sargent's agenda remained firm, "which I shall do my level best to prevent," any subsequent report the commission might offer to the public "will sink to the same level of insignificance with other discussions of the subject which have preceded it."[25]

Brandis's reply only reinforced Pinchot's worries. Sargent "labors under the delusion so common among Botanists in England, that Forestry is Botany," the German forester determined. "He does not apparently realize that Forestry is a profession, like Medicine or Engineering." This fundamental misunderstanding framed Brandis's reactions to Pinchot's concerns and shaped his perceptions of the commission's raison d'être. "Sargent is king in the U.S. as regards Arboriculture. Owing to his marvelous knowledge of American trees he is looked upon as a Demi God, and it is natural, that he should view Forestry from that point of view, that he should desire to make the labors of the Forest Commission subsistent to this one great end." In this context, pressing forestry's case would be difficult at best.[26]

Pinchot pushed nonetheless, with little result. Sargent, he advised his parents in mid-July, was "curiously deficient in ability to see things about a forest. He sees only the individual trees, and the possibility of seeing more does not occur to him. He is chary of accepting my conclusions because he says he could not have reached them in the same space of time," to which Pinchot responded that that "was quite natural, for he hadn't been trained in that line." Aware that his parents would be worried that he had been overly aggressive in pursuing his beliefs, Pinchot reported that he had "been wholly polite and absolutely good natured." He was optimistic, moreover, that Sargent would "gradually accept our opinions and promulgate them as incontrovertible." That would not occur, as Pinchot sensed by late August. After yet another lengthy discussion with Sargent about national forest policy, Pinchot wrote that "Sargent [was] utterly wrong on all points as usual." One ramification of this widening intellectual rift between the two men was that John Muir, whom they both admired, would be compelled to choose between them. About Sargent, it would turn out, Muir and Pinchot were not kindred spirits.[27]

It is tempting to infuse this difference of opinion with all the weight and force of those that would come in the future, to suggest that they had *never* been kindred spirits. But in so doing one would turn a complicated relationship into a rather simplistic one. And these were anything but simple men. As their letters and diary entries indicate, they delighted in each other's company during the commission's tour, so much so that when in late July Muir decided to break away from the commission for a quick trip to Alaska, he invited Pinchot along. The younger man accepted with alacrity, despite his father's caution that he might lose more than he would gain. "[Y]ou will never in all probability have another opportunity like this one to hear the West discussed by such a body of trained men"; in the end, due to a conflict with a commission-sponsored inspection trip of the Bitterroot Mountains, Pinchot had to pass on Muir's tantalizing offer. "You will know, without any words from me, how sorry I am that matters turned out in this way. I had already written home that I was going with you, and I know how sorry my people will be when I tell them ... that the plan is changed." He was clearly and unabashedly proud of the connection he and Muir had fashioned that summer.[28]

That link was forged not only in their shared concern over the deplorable state of the American forest but in lighter ways as well, most visibly in the adolescent bravado with which they displayed their common enthusiasms. One evening in Oregon, when their colleagues chose to sleep in cabins, Muir and Pinchot bedded down under the stars in an "alfalfa mow." Several days later Muir, Pinchot, Sargent, and a fourth member of the commission, Arnold Hague of the U.S. Geological Survey, rowed across fabled Crater Lake, seeking to inspect the island that rises at its center, only to be forced back to shore when a violent thunderstorm overtook them and whitecaps began to pour into the overloaded boat. When the sodden crew regained land, Muir and Pinchot cut off on their own and scampered up a steep hillside, reaching a rocky ledge about one hundred feet above the lake where they built a fire to dry out their clothing. That night, Muir noted in his diary, Pinchot stood out in another way. He alone slept outdoors in a driving rain, an act that could only have endeared him to his mentor. "That was the sort of behavior," Michael Cohen notes dryly, "which would go a long way toward making Muir forget other indiscretions." By their actions and affectations, Muir and Pinchot were equally boys among men.[29]

They thought of themselves as brother truants, too. This was evident during their visit to the Grand Canyon in October 1896. During their stay they set off on what turned out to be a day-long tramp along its southern rim, exploring its many crevices, exchanging observations about its geology, flora, and fauna, and doing handstands to better perceive the canyon's muted hues, the "reds, grays, ashy greens of varied limestones and sandstones, lavender, and tones nameless and numberless." Pinchot mostly listened as Muir spoke, enthralled by his knowledge, caught up in his stories. The pair did not return to their hotel that night, choosing instead to sleep among the cedars and pines, resting on piles of juniper boughs at the canyon's edge. They did not get much sleep, for Muir regaled the younger man with his adventure stories, including "The Stickeen," the telling of which lasted well into the night. When at 4:30 A.M. the sky began to lighten, they returned to the hotel, sneaking back "like a pair of schoolboys," Pinchot remembered, "well knowing that we must reckon with the other members of the Commission, who probably imagined that we had fallen over a cliff."[30]

Muir shared Pinchot's fond memories of schoolboy high jinks. He wrote Pinchot later that fall about how he "looked back with pure pleasure to . . . our own big day of sunshine and starshine along the verge of the tremendous and divine Colorado Canon," where, he reminded his protégé, they had so recently stood "with heads level + hearts level + eyes upside down." They were, it seems, at one, and for the rest of the decade they constantly made reference to their Grand Canyon excursion, drawing upon its reservoir of goodwill and intense feeling to sustain cordial relations. Camping was a powerful metaphor for a special kind of male bonding.[31]

That bond was easy to maintain when differences of opinion over forest policy did not loom large. In July 1897, Muir wrote Pinchot to congratulate him on his appointment as special forest agent for the Department of the Interior, urging him to do "grand work for Yourself and for all of us." In supporting Pinchot's decision to take this position, part of the responsibility of which was to reevaluate and redraw the forest reserve boundaries on public lands, Muir reacted differently than had Charles Sargent. The Harvard scientist had denounced Pinchot's decision in a scathing letter to another of the younger man's advisors, Sir Dietrich Brandis: "When I made him secretary . . . I did so with the expectation that he would eventually be able to take a prominent place in National Forestry." That expectation was now shattered. "He has gone over now to the politicians," Sargent asserted, "and his usefulness, I fear, is nearly at an end." Muir disagreed. By working from the inside, by accepting this "most responsible position especially under present conditions," Pinchot could effectively preserve the size and character of the threatened reserves, Muir believed. "In running the new boundaries of the new reservations no doubt small changes should be made," but for "every acre you cut off, fail not I charge you to add a hundred or a thousand."[32]

Pinchot shared Muir's extravagant hopes for the public good he might accomplish as an agent for the Department of the Interior. After meeting with Charles D. Walcott, director of the U.S. Geological Survey, he wrote his father of what he termed the "newest piece of luck." Interior Secretary Bliss "has referred the whole matter of the forest reserve boundaries to Walcott, and Walcott in turn to me." What that transfer of authority meant was "in all probability the addition of a good deal more than a million acres" to the system. A sign of Pinchot's confidence was his December 1897 request to Muir to suggest which lands in the Sierra ought to be incorporated into current reserves, to which Muir sweepingly replied that the "region around Lake Tahoe southward to the Stanislaus River should I think be reserved," as well as "the Shasta region though sadly devastated." Muir suspected the younger man was in the right place at the right time, and he was correct; much of the lands Muir suggested were incorporated into the forest reserves.[33]

Muir underscored his approval of Pinchot's work by inviting him to join one of his treks that summer: "I shall hope to meet you somewhere in the Rockies. Possibly we may go to Alaska." In any event, Muir continued, keep "me advised of your movements—I shall be delighted to meet you again in as charming a region as Lake McDonald." Pinchot could think of nothing better than to travel with Muir. "You know that my appetite for being in the woods with you has grown vastly by what it fed on" the previous summer. For them both, walking together had a number of meanings.[34]

Even when their paths diverged at the beginning of the twentieth century, and Muir became more sharply critical of Pinchot's perspective on conservation, they continued to recall past hikes and plan future ones. In August 1899 they spent five days together in northern California, during which Muir and C. Hart Merriam, future head of the Biology Division of the Department of Agriculture, "told stories all the way"; Pinchot scribbled in his diary that these were "two wonderful men to travel with." Their travels took them on a brief tour of the Calaveras Grove of sequoias, then threatened with lumbering, and they plotted ways by which to save the giant trees. It was like old times. "That trip, short as it was," Pinchot later wrote Muir, "is one of the brightest spots in my year," adding that to "make a trip with you on foot, with my pack on my back, has been one of my keenest hopes since the summer of the National Commission."

Such a tramp in the woods would be a tonic, Pinchot wrote, "where a man could go and work and get the wrinkles in his mind smoothed out." His were in need of smoothing. "I have to get into the woods, clear in, sometime this fall," he admitted, "or winter's work will not amount to anything. And the prospects for useful work are too good to be wasted for lack of forest-made snap." Pinchot's prescription for good health and increased productivity was no less genuine for its calculated appeal to Muir's oft-declared belief in the medicinal qualities of arboreal retreats. Two could play the game of mountain politics.[35]

Family Squabbles

The reciprocal cordiality of these letters, and the shared love of the natural world they unveil, are impressive in and of themselves. But they are all the more remarkable when one realizes that these two men had reached a point in their thinking and careers in which such reciprocity was increasingly difficult to manage. The bonds of language and affection could stretch only so far, and by the late 1890s the limit had been reached. At that time a new stage in their private correspondence and public relationship emerged, one in which the previous roles of mentor and student were no longer applicable or acceptable. In their place, a more discordant, hostile tone set in, a tone that would characterize their interactions until Muir died in 1914.

The break between them did not come with a rush, and its evolutionary character is perhaps best analyzed on two levels—one political and the other personal—each of which infused the other, intensifying the conflict.

The potential for political disagreement was first manifest during the discussions of the National Forest Commission over the nature of its final report. In the group's official deliberations and private conversations, it became clear that its members were divided roughly into two camps. Sargent, Muir, zoologist Alexander Agassiz of Harvard University (who attended only one meeting of the commission), and Henry Abbott of the U.S. Army Corps of Engineers believed that the only way to preserve the reserves was to close them to development, and that the best way to keep them inviolate was to deploy the U.S. Army to defend their boundaries. Pinchot and geologist Arnold Hague would have none of that. The forests were to be used, they argued, not closed off; the most effective force to ensure their regulated use and protection was the development of a professional civil service, a forest service, along the lines of those Pinchot had examined while studying forestry in Europe. This dispute posed a significant threat to the writing of the commission's final report. As Pinchot acknowledged to Muir just prior to the final series of meetings, "I am somewhat anxious to know just how the cat will jump. It is a rather critical time." Indeed. But the cat did not jump exactly as Pinchot hoped. The commission voted in favor of Sargent's proposals, urging President Cleveland to reconfirm the current reserves and add to their number; these new and extensive tracts of public lands would be closed to all development save mining and lumbering, and the army would be charged with their patrol. The preservationists seemed to have won the first round.[36]

The victory was hardly bloodless. Although in the end he did not do so, Pinchot threatened to write a critical, minority report; because the commission did not adopt a management plan for the reserves, nor issue what Pinchot believed essential—"a strong public statement, at the time when the new Reserves were created, that they were not to be taken out of circulation and locked up"—he worried (correctly) that political disaster loomed. Sargent felt no such foreboding, and instead was infuriated with what he perceived as Pinchot's threat even to the appearance of unanimity. In a letter to Muir, Sargent unloaded on Pinchot and Hague, criticizing their "strenuous demands" and adamant opposition to his position. "I was obliged to talk rather disagreeably with them," he wrote, and was only too "delighted that my official connection with them has come to an end. They have . . . done much harm in letting out the impression that the Commission was divided in its opinions." But it *was* divided, a division that did more than just forever set Sargent and Pinchot apart; it foreshadowed the impending split between Pinchot and Muir.[37]

That the break between them was not already overt was probably due to the simple fact that they liked one another, a liking that at this point took precedence over their philosophical and political differences. Besides, it was not clear how deep those differences ran. Muir had not yet fully resolved the question of whether preservation and conservation were incompatible. His essays in the *Century Magazine* during the period surrounding the Forest Commission's work made it clear that he, like Pinchot, supported the idea that national forests should be preserved and *used*. "It is impossible in the nature of things to stop at preservation," Muir declared in 1895. Forests, "like perennial fountains, may be made to yield a sure harvest of timber, while at the same time all their far-reaching uses may be maintained unimpaired." That balancing act was still evident in his 1897 essay on "The American Forests" in which he directly praised Pinchot's work. The young forester was not wrong in seeing Muir as an ally.[38]

Their alliance was strategic. For Muir, the principles of forestry, of the scientific management of the land, were a considerable advance over the slash-and-burn tactics that generations of Americans had employed in their conquest of the continent. Forestry seemed to promise the survival of trees, and thus of forests, and Muir was only too happy to join with those such as Pinchot who were its chief advocates. Muir's support of forestry was equally crucial for Pinchot. Without the former's eloquent voice and sharp pen raised on behalf of forests and forestry, the public's interest in them would not have been as great or as focused. Without that interest, as Pinchot knew better than most, there would be no legislation passed in support of the reserves or for the establishment of a forest service; and if there were no forest service, he would have failed to realize the goals he had set for himself and his profession.[39]

This web of mutuality would unravel under the pressure of new circumstances that called into question the two men's original alliance. In 1898, for example, Pinchot was appointed head of the Division of Forestry in the Department of Agriculture. He built it and its successor, the Forest Service, into one of the most potent bureaucracies in American political culture. Thereafter, he would have little use for the voluntarism that had characterized the Forest Commission's activities, or for the preservationist visions that came to dominate its proceedings. Pinchot was now a professional insider, a power broker whose source of strength lay in the political networks he constructed in Washington and nationwide, and in the managerial solutions he brought to bear on environmental matters. In this brave new world, utilitarian conservation was the primary philosophy.

Muir's speech had changed as well. Beginning in 1898, he began to believe that the practice of forestry and the preservation of wilderness were incompatible, a tentative conclusion that would harden into conviction in the first years of the new century. This shift had a direct impact on his relationship with Pinchot. They were now firmly on opposite sides of the fence, with the head of the forestry bureau now more easily lumped in with those plundering lumber barons, long the recipients of Muir's disdain.

The ties between the two men withered further in the heat generated by the battle over the damming of the Hetch Hetchy Valley. This spectacular valley, carved out of the Sierras by glaciers and the Tuolumne River, had become part of Yosemite National Park in 1890 and been designated a "wilderness preserve," a status for which *Century Magazine* editor Robert

Underwood Johnson, Muir, and others had fought hard. But as early as the 1880s, San Francisco's water board and politicians had discussed the possibility of constructing a dam at the narrow end of the Hetch Hetchy Valley, creating a much-needed reservoir. Those plans were revived early in the twentieth century, and in 1903 and 1905 the city applied to Interior Secretary Ethan A. Hitchcock, under whose jurisdiction the valley lay, for permission to build the dam. Hitchcock denied these early requests, indicating that they violated the spirit of the national park, but not before requesting that Pinchot, as head of the Forest Service, examine the question. Pinchot assured the secretary that the dam would not "injure the National Park or detract from its beauties or natural grandeur," an assurance that amazed Muir. "I cannot believe Pinchot, if he really knows the valley, has made any such statements," he wrote Johnson, "for it would be just the same thing as saying that flooding Yosemite would do it no harm."[40]

He had made the statement, as Muir learned after writing directly to Pinchot, seeking confirmation of his views. The forester noted that for him "the extreme desirability of preserving the Hetch Hetchy in its original beauty" must be weighed against the water needs of "a great group of communities" in the Bay Area. Material benefits and public health in this case took precedence over the cause of wilderness preservation. Muir challenged Pinchot's vision: ignore the "benevolent out cry for pure water for the dear people," he urged, for the "scheme for securing these water rights is as full of graft as any of the lumber companies to obtain big blocks of the best timber lands." Besides, if the object was simply water, it could "be obtained below Hetch Hetchy, tho' at a greater cost. The idea that San Francisco must go dry unless Hetch Hetchy Yosemite is drowned is ridiculous. . . ." Written in May 1905, this was probably the last letter Muir sent Pinchot.[41]

Their clashes accelerated in force when in April 1906 an earthquake jolted San Francisco, bursting water and gas pipes and setting off a fire that incinerated much of the city's housing stock and industrial base. In the wake of this catastrophe, and hoping to capitalize on the wave of national sympathy for its plight, the city promptly reapplied for permission to dam Hetch Hetchy. Chief forester Pinchot was at the ready. "I was very glad to learn from your letter . . . that the earthquake had damaged neither your

activity nor your courage," he wrote Marsden Manson, the city engineer. "I
hope sincerely that in the regeneration of San Francisco its people may be
able to make provision for a water supply from the Yosemite National
Park. I will stand by to render any assistance which lies in my power." His
assistance, especially when combined with the support of a new secretary of
the interior, James Garfield, a close friend of Pinchot's, produced the desired
result. San Francisco received administrative approval to proceed with its
plans for the valley.[42]

Although Congress turned back this particular effort, due to a storm
of protest that Robert Underwood Johnson, Muir, and numerous others
unleashed, the issue would not go away. In 1907, Muir and Pinchot met for
a day in California to discuss Hetch Hetchy. Pinchot admitted he had never
seen the valley and, according to Muir, therefore "seemed surprised to learn
how important a part of the Yosemite Park the Hetch Hetchy really is."
Pinchot suggested that Muir write Secretary Garfield and request that he
"keep the matter open until [the Sierra Club] could be heard." In September, Muir fired off an extended description of the valley to Garfield. Less
than a month later, Pinchot wrote to President Theodore Roosevelt that
although he fully sympathized with Muir and Johnson's position, "I believe
that the highest possible use which could be made of [Hetch Hetchy] would
be to supply pure water to a great center of population."[43]

The Hetch Hetchy debate would not be resolved until 1913, after Pinchot and Roosevelt were both out of office. It would be under the administration of Woodrow Wilson, and through the efforts of his secretary of the
interior, Franklin Lane, former city attorney of San Francisco, that Hetch
Hetchy would become a reservoir. Once again, Pinchot came to the forefront as an important witness in the congressional hearings that summer.
Once again, he argued that the public welfare was of preeminent importance. "Injury to Hetch Hetchy by substituting a lake for the present
swampy shore of the valley . . . is altogether unimportant when compared
with the benefits to be derived from its use as a reservoir." To make this
claim, those benefits needed to be democratically distributed, and he believed that with the dam they would be. It was on this point that he sought
to turn the political tables on those such as Muir who set preservation of

beautiful wilderness before essential human use. Something was wrong with keeping the valley "untouched for the benefit of the very small number of comparatively well to do to whom it will be accessible," he declared. "The intermittent aesthetic enjoyment of less than one per cent is being balanced against the daily comfort and welfare of 99 per cent"—and the scales necessarily tilted in favor of the masses. Building the dam at Hetch Hetchy was a matter of equity.[44]

Muir and his supporters, on the other hand, were certain that the San Francisco project was not a democratic initiative. It would, in truth, benefit only powerful special interest groups. Capturing the dam's waterpower would drive the "political ambition" of former San Francisco mayor James D. Phelan, Muir complained to Johnson, while for sugar magnate Claus Spreckles that same power would run the city streetcars he longed to possess. That Pinchot could cozy up to these San Francisco capitalists was perverse, a far cry from the man Muir had once known. When Pinchot was dismissed from the Forest Service in 1910, Muir could only shake his head at what might have been. "I'm sorry to see poor Pinchot running amuck after doing so much good hopeful work—from sound conservation going pell-mell to destruction on the wings of crazy inordinate ambition." Nothing in the last days of the Hetch Hetchy debate made him change his opinion.[45]

Political disagreements and sharply contrasting visions of how natural resources should be used help explain the collapse of the friendship of Muir and Pinchot. But there was another, more psychological dimension to that collapse. Its timing is important. The separation came only after Pinchot's professional career was assured, after he had been named head of the Division of Forestry in 1898. It also came in conjunction with the ruptures in his relations with other mentors, including Bernhard Fernow and Charles Sargent.

Fernow, who claimed that it had been his idea that Pinchot pursue forestry studies in Europe, and whose support of the young man's early work struck James Pinchot as "posing and insincere," could be an irritable man to be around. That is what Gifford had decided in the late winter of 1891, when the two men traveled together through the piney woods of

Arkansas, and that was why Gifford ultimately declined to work under him. Fernow, he found, had a domineering personality, proved harshly critical of others in the profession, and sought sole credit for advances in forestry. No shrinking violet himself, Pinchot grew "pretty weary" of these traits, of Fernow's "running everybody down with tiresome uniformity," and realized that they could not work effectively together. When in late 1891 George Vanderbilt offered Pinchot the opportunity to demonstrate practical forestry on 5,000 acres of his land in North Carolina, he jumped at the chance. A miffed Fernow slapped out at his protégé when he suggested that in taking on Vanderbilt's job, the young forester had jeopardized his fledgling career.[46]

The two continued to bedevil one another for years to come. When Pinchot published a small tract on the white pine in 1896, Fernow wrote a devastating review of it in *Garden and Forest;* Muir counseled Pinchot not to write a rebuttal. "Never mind Fernow. Go ahead with your own work + very soon he will become polite and good," counsel that in this instance Pinchot heeded. But he in turn could be just as impolite. Granting that Fernow had a "remarkable native ability," Pinchot believed in his heart that the German-born forester was too cautious, his perception of the possibilities of forestry too limited, and his expertise exaggerated—this from a man who had but a year of formal training in forestry! Pinchot's critical evaluation of Fernow allowed him to circumvent his job offer in 1891, and then to happily succeed his former advisor as head of the division seven years later. Youth had triumphed.[47]

Pinchot's conflicted relations with Charles Sargent followed a similar path. Sargent, too, had encouraged Pinchot's desire to become a forester, repeatedly offered advice on the direction the younger man's career should take, and opened some doors to ease his way. Inviting Pinchot to join the National Forest Commission was the most important of these gestures; it was an extraordinary break for the thirty-one-year-old forester, who had learned how to rely on the kindness of older men.

Yet while making the most of these opportunities, Pinchot alienated his benefactor. That was not hard to do, for Sargent shared Fernow's touchy persona. He was opinionated, a man of great self-assurance and no small ego. When crossed, as he was when Pinchot challenged the recommendations of the final report of the Forest Commission, he lashed out at the ingrate. Pinchot clearly did not understand, Sargent complained in a letter to Dietrich Brandis, that being chosen for the commission was unprecedented, "as only members of the Academy serve on such Commissions"; never had a nonmember been tapped as a commission secretary. This honor alone should have guaranteed Pinchot's compliance and held his mouth in check.[48]

Relations between them deteriorated further when Pinchot accepted Interior Secretary Bliss's offer to act as a confidential forestry agent in 1897. Sargent accused Pinchot of dropping his friends for a political appointment, a sign to the Harvard professor that their standards of conduct were on different planes. Little wonder that he predicted the end of Pinchot's professional career when Pinchot took over Fernow's position in the Department of Agriculture. "This is a good place for him," Sargent counseled Muir. "He can do no harm there and after a very short time people will cease to pay any attention to what he says." That bit of wishful thinking would come back to haunt him in later years, so much so that Sargent took to calling Pinchot "that creature" and, later still, in the 1920s, rued the day he had helped advance Pinchot's career.[49]

The personality disputes between Fernow, Sargent, Muir, and Pinchot were cut from the same cloth. Each of these older men had much to teach the up-and-coming forester about American forests; each had sought to direct his manifold energies and talents in ways that would benefit their various and allied causes; and each saw in him a youthful reflection of themselves—strong shoulders that could help bear his elders' burdens. But these relationships contained within them, in the manner of those between parents and children, the seeds of separation; they were oedipal in complexity, if not in construct. These conflicts were later immortalized in the controversial invitation list that Pinchot drew up for the important 1908 Conference on the Conservation of Natural Resources. It was an impressive gathering. According to Pinchot biographer Nelson McGeary, never "in the history of the country had so many important government officials and scientific men been brought together" as at this White House conference designed to discuss conservation and the conservation movement. What McGeary failed to note, however, was who had not been invited:

Bernard Fernow, John Muir, and Charles Sargent led the list of those snubbed, an act of omission that was as psychologically charged as it was politically motivated.[50]

CREATIVE TENSIONS

However personally damaging, these men's internecine battles did not cripple the early conservation movement; they were essential to its development and success. The political discord, ideological differences, and psychological tension provided the crucial elements in a formative public dialogue between conservationists, preservationists, and the broader citizenry they hoped to serve and influence. In no other way could conservation so quickly have become a household word and an idea of considerable force in the politics of the Progressive Era.

Such combative interchanges are found in virtually all efforts to reform the American polity. This was as true for the abolitionists of the antebellum era as it would be for those advocating the civil rights of minorities in the twentieth century. In each case, the wars of rhetoric and ideals, intemperate as they often were, have served a broader purpose: each group gained by the other's presence. Radicals can make moderates look more conservative to those who fear reform, and as a result the moderates can often secure greater success. Moderates, on the other hand, pushed by the logic of confrontational politics, are often compelled to adopt elements of the radical agenda to maintain their standing in a particular movement. This is not to suggest that change is inevitable, that history is inherently progressive. Life is never so neat. But we should not be blind to the dynamism of such struggles. It was out of the tradition of brawling over environmental policies and politics that the national forest and park systems were born, and out of it too came the subsequent creation of wilderness areas in the national forests. In this respect, political conflict can be a subtle composition, as opposing factions, like partners in a dance, seek to take (or grab) the lead—and occasionally step on one another's toes. In the late nineteenth and early twentieth centuries, John Muir and Gifford Pinchot initiated just such a dance.

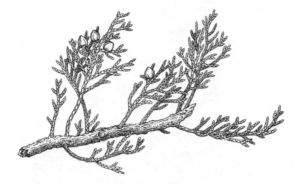

Part Three

MATURE
GROUNDS

Keeper of His Conscience?

THEODORE ROOSEVELT and Gifford Pinchot loved to play games, especially those in which they could flash their youthful vigor or test their manly prowess. They discovered their mutual delight in such things when, in February 1899, Pinchot first visited the then-governor of New York in Albany. "We arrived just as the Executive Mansion was under ferocious attack from a band of invisible Indians," he fondly recalled in his autobiography, "and the Governor of the Empire State was helping a handful of children escape by lowering them out of a second story window on a rope." That night the two men indulged in a few games of their own. The taller Pinchot used his long reach to good effect in a round of boxing: "I had the honor of knocking the future President of the United States off his very solid pins," he would boast. Bragging rights were not his alone. The smaller, albeit more powerfully built Roosevelt came back to overwhelm his lanky guest in a wrestling match.

Tales of derring-do rounded out the evening. Pinchot and Grant La-Farge, son of the painter John LaFarge, had stopped off to see Roosevelt on their way to examine a forested tract the Adirondack League Club owned in the North Woods. The club had requested help from the Division of Forestry in establishing a plan to manage the lands, and Pinchot and LaFarge hoped that making the trip would also help them sketch out their plans for co-authoring a book on the region (the volume was never written). But as they explained to the attentive governor, their real ambition was to make a winter ascent of Mount Marcy, which at 5,344 feet was the highest elevation in New York State. Their plan met with Roosevelt's hearty approval—"that was exactly in his line."[1]

Yet what sounded so bully in the warmth of the executive mansion turned brutal on the ground. After completing their work for the club, Pinchot and LaFarge, with two guides, snowshoed through glistening white woods, every tree of which "was a monument of snow." The temperature had fallen to well below zero—in his diary Pinchot guessed it was anywhere between twenty-five and forty degrees below—and the frigid air easily penetrated his light clothing: "I was wearing just what I wore in the woods in the summer, plus sweater, cap and mittens." The next morning, from their base camp in a cabin on Lake Colden, the foursome headed toward the peak, shoeing over twenty feet of snow, with more falling. Before they reached the timber line, the two guides turned back, and when Pinchot and LaFarge broke from the lee of the mountain for their final assault, they struggled against a furious blizzard, which, though they did not know it at the time, was battering the entire eastern seaboard; hundreds of miles to the south, more than thirty inches of snow fell on Washington, D.C. On Mount Marcy, the gale-force winds were so powerful that they forced the lighter LaFarge to stop. Meanwhile, Pinchot pressed on, crawling on his hands and knees, breaking handholds in the glare ice, "holding my head down in the squalls, and stopping every minute or two to rub my face against freezing." He stayed on the summit only long enough to snap photographs of the mountain's signal pole, and "thankfully crawled down again."[2]

Theirs had been a grueling, "foolish" ordeal. Pinchot's sealskin cap, which he had purchased as a young man on his first extended winter's stay in the Adirondacks, did little to prevent frostbite on his ears and neck, and his full mustache did not protect his upper lip; one of the guides had an even more severe case of frostbite, from which he was laid up for more than a year. The more lucky Pinchot, though, may have taken some pleasure in recounting the dangerous trek to one who had so applauded its ambitions; he and LaFarge, on their way back to New York City, spent the night in a

*Gifford Pinchot, with friend Henry Graves, investigated
forest conditions in the Adirondacks of New York in
1898. Whenever he could, and regardless of conditions,
Pinchot slept outdoors.* Grey Towers NHL

snow-snarled Albany and presumably regaled an envious Roosevelt with
the story of their mountaineering exploits.[3]

Pinchot's sharing of this adventure with an appreciative Roosevelt, like
their earlier and sweaty embrace in sport, was not just an example of male
bonding. It reflected, even as it helped to initiate, an intellectual closeness
between the forester and the future president that henceforth would characterize their personal relationship and public careers. Just how far did this
meeting of body and soul go? No little distance, it seems. Their friendship
only deepened during Roosevelt's years as president, when Pinchot served
first as head of the Division of Forestry and later as chief of the new Forest
Service, founded in 1905. More than a kept bureaucrat, Pinchot became a
significant figure in the president's so-called Tennis Cabinet—not for these

hale fellows the domestic, feminine, and interior implications of a "Kitchen Cabinet."

The great outdoors continued to be the context for the evolving relationship between Pinchot and Roosevelt. Together they would chop wood for exercise, set off on extended tramps through Washington's Rock Creek Park, ride horses, and swim the Potomac River in late fall. These moments of exercise had been important to Roosevelt. Just before leaving the White House in March 1909, he wrote Pinchot that "for seven and a half years we have worked together, and now and then played together—and have been altogether better able to work because we have played." These interactions were no less significant for Pinchot; it was by sharing in this strenuous life that he had become one of the president's "faithful bodyguard."[4]

Pinchot was one of the faithful in another sense. He and the president seemed of like minds, especially on matters of federal conservation policy. As with many of their generation, they were appalled by the human destruction of nature everywhere visible in early-twentieth-century America. The solution, they believed, lay in federal regulation of the public lands and, where appropriate, scientific management of these lands' natural resources; only this approach, guided by appropriate experts, would ensure the lands' survival. So parallel ran their thoughts that Roosevelt reportedly assured Robert Underwood Johnson, editor of *Century Magazine,* that on questions of conservation the chief forester was in truth the keeper of his conscience.[5]

What Roosevelt meant by his declaration, if he voiced it, is not clear. Nor is it immediately obvious what his words might have meant with respect to public policy for the nation. How much leeway did Pinchot have to craft the federal conservation agenda during the Roosevelt years? Were the decisions he reached his own or were they reflections of an administrative consensus that Roosevelt determined? There is no better way to come to terms with answers to these queries, and thus with Pinchot's place within the movement for which his name is synonymous, than by monitoring these two men's responses to two of the most important conservation issues to emerge during Roosevelt's tenure in the White House—the effort to impose federal legal authority over what would become the national forests and the decision to dam the Hetch Hetchy Valley in California.[6]

HOOFED POLITICS

One of the central issues confronting the intermountain West in the post–Civil War era was the impact on the landscape not of the region's tiny human population but of its domesticated animals, specifically the massive herds of sheep and cattle that then grazed on public lands. The size of these herds is astonishing. In Colorado in the 1890s, a state with a human population totaling a bit more than 400,000, there were approximately 1.7 million head of sheep and more than one million head of cattle. The competition for land that such numbers induced, Joseph Nimmo (then chief statistician for the Treasury Department's Bureau of Statistics) observed dryly, was "subject to frictional resistances and embarrassments," a bureaucratically coy way of saying that the pitched battles fought over this terrain were vicious and violent, a fierce set of range wars between cattle drovers and sheepherders that dominated land-use patterns. The boundaries they finally agreed upon, the "dead lines," were quite literally named for their determination of where each form of grazing could occur: a cow or sheep that strayed across the line was at risk of being gunned down.[7]

Vigilante justice, by its very definition, suggests that there was then little federal or local authority exercised over the uses to which public land were put; seemingly the only restraints on the movement of herds throughout this intermountain landscape were those imposed by the limits of forage and water. Indeed, by the late 1800s, the concept of "free use" or "free grass" had become a crucial element in the presumed stability of the regional economy. Unfettered access to the millions of acres in the public domain in the West, the argument ran, was a citizen's undisputed right and a social good, an argument vigorously touted through a political culture that bound together cattle and wool growers' associations, newspaper publishers, and officeholders at all levels and partisan persuasions. Together, these actors forged a potent consensus that shaped a national commitment to the maintenance and expansion of this form of agricultural production.

In his seminal report on the region's economic prospects, Nimmo freely acknowledged that "the range and ranch cattle business . . . is one of the most attractive and important commercial and industrial enterprises of the present day." It was so, he argued, because the "occupancy of the public lands throughout the central and northern portions of the great dry area for range cattle purposes" had "subdued and utilized such lands for the production of a cheap and nutritious article of food." Although there were aspects of the industry that he critiqued—particularly its desire to secure long-term leases that would effectively limit human settlement and establish land monopolies—Nimmo accepted intense grazing on public lands as a given, sanctioned as a matter of social utility. He had no beef with an industry of this magnitude and consequence, and for which "preservation" of the land was an utterly foreign concept; "use" was all.[8]

The consequences of unrestrained development, and the vicious cycle of economic greed and environmental despoliation it set in motion, were escalating toward the close of the nineteenth century. With improved rail transport to the burgeoning eastern urban markets, rails that also brought a surge of migrants into western states, the pressure on this region's lands intensified. Seeking the quick profits that grazing on the public lands could produce, ranchers drove ever-larger numbers of cattle and sheep onto the range. This overstocking and the boost in cattle shipped to market dropped prices, and that consequently led to the release of still more herds into mountainous pastures, as ranchers tried to recover their losses. By the early twentieth century, the national forests provided forage for more than 6 million sheep and 1.5 million horses and cattle. These numbers overwhelmed the carrying capacity of the land, noted Albert Potter, who had been a rancher in Arizona before he became the first head of the Forest Service's Grazing Section: "[V]egetation was cropped by hungry animals before it had a chance to reproduce; valuable forage plants gave way to worthless weeds." This observation could apply equally to Colorado or California, Washington or New Mexico; in each "the highest and most inaccessible slopes and alpine meadows" were under siege. Stripping these lands forced an increased demand for newer, more distant, and greener range to maintain herd size, sustain income, and protect market share.[9]

Reining in this form of uncontrolled growth in the mid-nineteenth century was unthinkable largely because a vocabulary of restraint did not yet exist. A new rhetoric had to be created that would, through a set of scientific, economic, and political principles, establish a different relationship between humans and the land on which they lived. By the late nineteenth century, the broad outlines of this new perspective had begun to emerge. Its central thrust rested on the conviction that the nation's natural resources and agricultural production were interwoven parts of a whole. Those who developed this nascent ecological vision believed, for example, that the massive herds of free-ranging sheep in the valleys, foothills, and slopes posed an interrelated series of dangers: not only did they decimate grasses and plants, but their pounding hooves damaged stream beds and increased erosion and silt, polluting innumerable watersheds. Another consequence of overgrazing was that "young tree growth is stamped down or eaten off," leaving the soil "bare and unprotected" and compromising forest health. These devastating conditions by themselves increased the threat of forest fires, but more responsible still was the livestock owner's penchant for setting fire to the range to regenerate the grasses and, by burning forest undergrowth, extend available pasturage; one report on Colorado in 1900, for example, indicated that irresponsible grazing played a role in the devastating conflagrations that torched more than 758 square miles that year. "Free grass" was anything but cheap.[10]

The same conclusions could be drawn about other forms of unrestrained resource exploitation in the Rockies—lumbering and mining among them. Their combined devastation of the landscape is what impelled a growing demand for some federal controls, and those local and national figures who demanded such regulation came to call themselves conservationists. It was an old term, but an apt one: drawing on European romanticism and antebellum worries about the initial onslaught of the industrial revolution on a once-bountiful landscape, and indebted in part to European land-management principles, some Americans began to argue that conservation was necessary to slow national consumption of resources, regulating demand so that the nation might have a continuous supply of them well into the future. The "central thing for which Conservation stands," Pinchot argued in 1910, "is to make this country the best possible place to live in, both for us and our descendants."[11]

Although he knew the term's many foreign and domestic antecedents, if only because he had read George Perkins Marsh's *Man and Nature* and had been trained in Europe in some of these intellectual constructs, Pinchot nonetheless would claim to have invented the concept of conservationism.

The idea came to him in February 1907, he affirmed in *Breaking New Ground,* while on a horseback ride along Ridge Road in Washington, D.C.'s Rock Creek Park. Founded by an act of Congress in 1890, Rock Creek is one of the largest forested urban parks in the United States, containing more than 1,750 acres with paths and roadways that meander along the picturesque stream valley in the northern part of the city. Pinchot often rode through this thickly wooded terrain astride his trusty steed, Jim, as a way to shake off the day's concerns; exercising in this picturesque landscape invariably left him refreshed and reinvigorated.[12]

On this particular winter afternoon, however, he had taken "his problems with him . . . when he meant to leave them behind." At issue was a vexing public policy conundrum: how best to coordinate and manage the nation's public lands and the people's use of them. Oversight responsibility was badly fragmented, Pinchot mused, as individual departments jostled for power within a bureaucratic maze. "To put it in a sentence, there were three separate Government organizations which dealt with mineral resources, four or five concerned with streams, half a dozen with authority over forests, and a dozen or so with supervision over wild life, soils, soil erosion, and other questions of the land." As he wrestled with what might be the common ground that would tie these many, great, and jealous interests together, he had an epiphany: "Suddenly it flashed through my head that there was a unity in this complication—that the relation of one resource to another was not the end of the story" but its inauguration. What wrought order out of chaos was a belief in the power of conservation to transform human activity. "When the use of all the natural resources for the general good is seen to be a common policy with a common purpose," Pinchot wrote, "the chance for the wise use of each of them becomes infinitely greater than it had ever been before." With this new perspective, he came to believe that the "[c]onservation of natural resources is the key to the future," and more grandly predicted it would also be "the key to the safety and prosperity of the American people, and all the people of the world, for all time to come."

His sense of the encompassing character of his vision would unfold over time. "There was too much of it for me to take it all in at once," he admitted. "As always my mind worked slowly" and that "day in Rock Creek

Park I was far from grasping the full reach and swing of the new idea." Only after extensive conversations with his colleagues in the Forest Service and other government scientists—most notably W J McGee, head of the Bureau of American Ethnology, whom Pinchot credited with distilling his idea to its essence—did he recognize its full implications. The goal of conservationism, he would write in language borrowed from McGee and British philosopher Jeremy Bentham, was to produce "the greatest good, for the greatest number, for the longest run."[13]

Even as only an adaptation, this definition of conservation was significant in two respects. The addition of "the longest run" to the phrase committed conservationists to the creation of sustainable economies and ecosystems, a potentially important notion in a society so wedded to profligacy and waste. Pinchot's definition of conservation also made a more narrow, albeit valuable contribution to resolving the question of how competing federal land-management agencies might better interact and cooperate.

This conceptualization of conservation also posed problems, however. Who defines what the greatest good is, and on what basis? How to measure its production and equitable distribution or, more trickily, how to weigh humanity's material needs against environmental conditions over time? And would it be possible for succeeding generations to redefine the greatest good? About the resolution of these issues, Pinchot was less voluble. What he was convinced of—and spoke most often about—was that only a rigorous pursuit of conservation would enable this democratic society to provide a steady stream of goods and services to bolster the citizenry's standard of living and to deliver on its social promise. Opposed to material inequalities, respectful of the land, and determined to account for the needs of subsequent generations, Pinchot's notion of conservation seemed to promise the resolution of some of the most pressing problems confronting an industrializing America.[14]

Yet there was no mechanism by which to implement the principles of conservation on the public lands. This was partly a result of a bureaucratic jumble in which the nation's publicly owned forest reserves were under the jurisdiction of the Interior Department, while the Division of Forestry, which Pinchot had headed since 1898, was situated in the Department of Agriculture. The division's foresters controlled no forests and had no public lands under their jurisdiction on which to directly practice their ideas of conservative forestry; Pinchot would broker a deal with Interior so that his foresters could work on the national reserves, and would offer their services as well to state governments and private landowners. These first steps notwithstanding, even if Agriculture or Interior had wanted to implement large-scale forest management on these lands—and in the late nineteenth century, that was not then their commitment to do so—neither had the authority to police activities on them. The sheep and cattle could roam at will, and lumber companies could harvest wood with little restraint.[15]

That situation changed markedly during the first decade of the twentieth century. When Teddy Roosevelt replaced the assassinated William McKinley in 1901, Pinchot found in the new president a powerful friend who not only appreciated the need to transfer the nation's forests to agriculture, but who, by 1905, would help line up the necessary congressional votes to secure that end, a political victory that Pinchot had longed for since 1898. For this transfer to succeed, however, required that the newly created Forest Service be a considerably stronger agency than its departmental predecessor. Gaining that strength would depend in part on a sustained growth in its personnel, an increase in its budget, and a heightened public awareness of its work and the importance of its mission. That these needs were largely fulfilled during Pinchot's relatively brief tenure as head of the service (he was its chief for five years) testifies to his administrative flair and bureaucratic ambition.

It helped that since 1898, Pinchot and his talented staff had been preparing for the possible transfer of the nation's forests and the corresponding and vast increase in their responsibilities. Inheriting a staff of sixty when he succeeded Bernhard Fernow, by 1905 Pinchot had expanded the workforce to five hundred. That number did not include the hundreds of summer hires: students drawn from the nation's emerging forestry schools who gained experience working on public and private lands at little cost to the taxpayer. Making a mere $25 a month and working in the rough backcountry, they "[got] the Harvard rubbed off [of them] before they came into contact with the loggers," forester E. T. Allen observed. After graduation, many of these young men eagerly sought full-time employment with the agency. Building up such a core of well-trained and committed fledgling foresters had been the goal of the summer program; they would serve a future Forest Service as staff for its widening domain. And every one of them would be needed by 1907, when the national forests swelled to approximately 150 million acres.[16]

The solution to managing this sprawling land base, and the many people hired to protect and regulate its use, Pinchot believed, was intertwined with whom the agency employed and on what basis. Trained in the European model of foresters as civil servants, and appalled by what he considered the corrupt system of political patronage that had hitherto shaped the employment practices of many governmental agencies, the chief was determined to take on only those who merited their positions. Passing a civil service examination, after undergraduate and perhaps graduate study, would reinforce the professional ethos that he expected to dominate the service's actions.[17]

But these certified foresters, especially those in the field, had to be given considerable latitude, he felt. Professionals required autonomy—which, when combined with the nature of their outdoor labor and the need to develop local acceptance, meant that they must be responsible for the decisions they made on the ground. This principle took on added importance with the transfer of the forests to Agriculture, leading Pinchot and his staff to devise a more decentralized administrative structure. It consisted first of three regional districts, which were later redivided into six; each had a supervising officer, to whom reported individual forest supervisors, who in turn oversaw the work of district rangers. Located exclusively in the West (the Weeks Law of 1911 established the funding mechanism for the establishment of national forests in the East), geographically dispersed, and at great remove from the nation's capital, these districts and the new flowchart that defined their internal working relationships made structural sense.[18]

It was also supposed to increase the service's efficiency. This was aided by the adoption of a series of innovative strategies for managing the flow of paper. Clerical staff received rigorous preparation. "I am really at a loss to know how to describe the training each new appointee received before being given a definite assignment," Agnes Scannell wrote Pinchot thirty years after she had first reported for duty in January 1907. "No detail was

A gifted administrator, Gifford Pinchot helped to create a remarkably efficient, rational work environment during his tenure as the nation's chief forester. Forest History Society

overlooked; and when one passed through that training, he or she might *forevermore* measure up to the highest standard of secretarial efficiency." Adding additional order to the office environment was the early adoption of the vertical filing system by the Forest Service, the first federal bureau to do so. Pinchot demanded close and quick attention to inquiries from the public and Congress as well; staff was required to respond to all correspondence within thirty-six hours. To reinforce this edict, so one agency legend has it, he had desk drawers nailed shut.[19]

The more decentralized structure had political implications, too. By distributing these varied offices throughout the West, tying them to local communities and their economies, and shrewdly deciding to deposit forest receipts in the region's banks, Pinchot sought to encourage broad social and political support for the agency and its actions.[20]

To curry further favor, the media-savvy chief pressed his district rangers and forest supervisors to follow his lead and "[u]se the press first, last, and all the time if you want to reach the public." None could match his energetic pursuit of favorable publicity. The Forest Service set up an in-house press bureau and made great use of a new technological marvel: a mailing-label machine that could rapidly crank out the 670,000 addresses of groups and individuals targeted by the service to receive its reports and releases. Pinchot would argue that this activity was a legitimate expense, advising one skeptical congressman that such publicity was "the only defensible pol-icy for any Government organization, any part of whose purpose is to col-lect and disseminate facts." But many congressional representatives were convinced that the extraordinary flow of information that poured out of the Forest Service constituted a misapplication of the public fisc; in 1909, Con-gress prohibited the spending of federal funds for the preparation or publi-cation of news material of any kind (a prohibition that did not extend to its franking privileges).[21]

This crackdown—which was roundly criticized by the media—only underscored the perception that Pinchot and the agency he led were har-bingers of the emerging modern and dynamic state. Reaching a similar conclusion was a later observer who was well versed in the evolution of fed-eral bureaucratic culture. In his seminal text *The Quiet Crisis* (1963), Stew-art Udall, secretary of the interior under Presidents John F. Kennedy and Lyndon B. Johnson, hailed Pinchot as a "magnificent bureaucrat" whose animating, progressive vision made the Forest Service "in his time the most exciting organization in Washington."[22]

Better evidence still of the Forest Service's formidable presence was its successful pursuit of the requisite legal authority to arrest trespassers on and regulate use of the national forests. Roosevelt agreed that such power was necessary, but the livestock owners and other western resource special interest groups did not. When the Forest Service began to levy fees for graz-ing privileges, regulate the presence and movement of herds, and charge lumber companies for the right to harvest timber in the national forests, its actions sparked a series of court challenges to the agency's then-unprece-dented behavior. Which is exactly what the agency hoped would happen. Only judicial proceedings, reasoned Pinchot and his legal team—led first by George P. Woodruff and then by Philip P. Wells, both Yale classmates of Pinchot's—would provide the necessary sanction for the Forest Service's regulatory agenda.

A close friend of Gifford Pinchot's at Yale, George Woodruff headed up the Forest Service's legal team. Later, he provided legal support to another of Pinchot's projects, the National Conservation Association, and served as attorney general of Pennsylvania when Pinchot was governor in the mid-1920s.

Grey Towers NHL

The Forest Service lawyers were as nimble as they were creative. In Woodruff, Wells later observed, the agency had a sterling advocate, a man of "courageous logic." The legal team forced "its way from indisputable principles to meritable conclusions with small regard for precedents to mark the intermediate path." Happily, the agency's "legal problems were new, and the precedent markers had not yet made a wise solution difficult or impossible."[23]

Two such precedent-setting and critical challenges to the Forest Service's regulatory authority occurred in 1906. In California, Pierre Grimaud was charged with illegally running a herd of sheep on the Sierra South National Forest, while Coloradan cattleman Fred Light was caught turning out 500 head onto the Holy Cross Forest Reserve without a permit and in defiance of a district court injunction. So eager was the Colorado legislature to blunt the Forest Service's authority that it voted to underwrite Light's legal challenge.

Both cases worked their way through federal district courts and were appealed to the U.S. Supreme Court. In the end, the challengers failed to make their case. In 1911, in *U.S. v. Grimaud* and *U.S. v. Light,* the Supreme Court upheld the forest management acts of 1891 and 1897, which combined to give the secretary of agriculture the ability "to regulate the occupancy and use of and to preserve the forests from destruction." The federal government could now control access to public lands.[24]

The policy implications of these legal triumphs were immense. Henceforth, the Forest Service could administer the public domain by issuing restrictions on grazing to improve soil fertility and the stability of watersheds, implement badly needed scientific studies to determine how to preserve and use western lands, and develop reforestation and revegetation programs designed to repair stripped-over terrain. Through human stewardship, and in the interest of the public good, western lands could be redeemed.[25]

The same notion of stewardship might also regenerate human life out beyond the 100th meridian, which bisects the Plains States from North Dakota to Texas—or so Hamlin Garland asserted in *Cavanagh: Forest Ranger,* a 1910 novel with a preface by Pinchot. The newly empowered forest rangers and the federal agency they represented, Garland believed, would become symbols of a long-overdue cultural revolution in the intermountain region, "constituting in my opinion the most significant movement in the West at this moment." Speaking through Forest Supervisor Redfield, one of his protagonists, Garland lashed out at the frontier rough-and-tumble: "From the very first the public lands of this state have been a refuge for the criminal—a lawless no man's land; but now, thanks to Roosevelt and the chief forester, we at least have a force of men on the spot to see that some semblance of law and order is maintained." By enforcing "ultimate peace and order over all the public lands," Garland confidently predicted, the Forest Service would usher in a new, more "civilized west," replacing its "picturesque" and antiquated counterpart, "the free-range stockman and his cowboy cohorts." It was "the forest ranger, riding his solitary trail," who was "the vidette [scout] of the real civilization which is to bring in "the 'real West,'" the ranger who "represents the future and not the present, the Federal not the local spirit." Gifford Pinchot could not have said it any better.[26]

He did not even try. Instead, in his preface, the forester happily applauded the novelist's "sympathetic understanding of the problems which confronted the Forest Service before the Western people understood it." That someone outside the agency recognized and appreciated its struggles was heartening and might, he hoped, facilitate the forest rangers' introduction of federal sovereignty, the "new order," to the West.

Talk Shows

By itself, Garland's fictional depiction of the social struggle that erupted throughout Colorado and other western states accurately captures the actual resistance that the administration's conservation principles engendered. Those miners, ranchers, and lumbermen who opposed the implementation of federal conservationism did so in ways both subtle and blunt, an opposition that was most fully displayed in a series of raucous public meetings throughout the intermountain West to which Pinchot was regularly invited and which he usually attended. During these boisterous assemblies, westerners shored up their political support, championed states' rights as the only means to blunt an aggressive executive branch, and sought to alternately browbeat and sweet-talk the nation's forester into altering governmental policies. He never yielded, but then he had no authority to do so: he may have been the focal point of discontent, with the administration's enforcement of regulations branded "Pinchotism," but in truth he was merely a glorified spokesman, albeit an effective one.

He gloried in his role, too. His commanding height, together with the dark mane and moustache that framed a striking face and intense eyes, heightened the dramatic, if ritual-like, tension of these many encounters, which were often (and aptly) held in the opera houses or theaters of Denver or Salt Lake City, Boise, Wallace, or Cheyenne. That they became ritualistic is important: these meetings served as middle grounds, zones in which each side of the debate could stake its claims, establish the legitimacy of its

position, and seek to moderate or maybe even come to a grudging appreciation of the opposition's perspectives. For the most part, civic peace was
maintained through civil dialogue.

Civility did not mean a dearth of disagreement, however. Each of these
gatherings had its share of verbal fireworks and tense confrontations, none
more so than the Denver Public Lands Convention, held in mid-June 1907,
which attracted an estimated 4,000 delegates from the western states. The
conference was called by the Colorado legislature "for the purpose of discussing the relation of the states to public lands, and, if possible, [to] agree
upon some policy in regards these lands to be urged upon the general government," and its timing reflected an upsurge in western frustration with
the implementation of Rooseveltian conservationism.

During the preceding six months, congressional representatives from
the West had beaten back attempts to institute grazing regulations on the
public domain, and had vigorously attacked but failed to derail increases in
the Forest Service's budgetary appropriations as well as in Pinchot's salary.
They seemed to hit pay dirt when, through the Fulton amendment, named
for Charles Fulton of Oregon, the anticonservationists were able to amend
the appropriations section of the Agricultural Bill of 1907; the amendment
included language prohibiting the president from creating or expanding forest reserves within Oregon, Washington, Montana, Colorado, and
Wyoming. Against what many in Congress once had felt was an unstop-
pable federal conservation juggernaut, the legislative branch had finally
flexed its muscles.[27]

Only to be flattened in turn: Roosevelt, who needed these funds to operate the government, knew he had to sign the bill by March 4, 1907, a week
after it passed through Congress. Before so doing, however, he encouraged
the Forest Service to prepare the necessary paperwork authorizing him to
withdraw more than 16 million acres of public land, some to augment old
national forests, the bulk establishing twenty-one new forests in six western
states. With the president's "enthusiastic support," Pinchot and his staff in
the field and in the capital pulled together data on which timber and grazing lands to enclose. Working around the clock, they drafted the necessary
proclamations to ensure the transfer of these public lands into the national
reserves, and thus under federal regulatory control. As each was completed,

Pinchot himself ferried it to the White House; only after signing all the proclamations and ensuring, in Pinchot's words, that these 16 million acres "were rescued from passing into the hands of private corporations," did the president put his signature on the Agricultural Bill.[28]

When Roosevelt announced the creation of the so-called "midnight reserves," his opponents were livid and, in his felicitous phrase, "turned handsprings in their wrath." However dire their threats, the chief executive believed they "could not be carried out, and were really only a tribute to the efficiency of our action." When he and Pinchot then met with a delegation of aggrieved western representatives, the president let them see, Pinchot later reported, that the "joke was on them. It was their kind of joke, and the meeting ended in a highly temporary era of good feelings."[29]

"Temporary" meant two weeks—for that is how short a time it took for state legislators in Colorado to assemble and agree to issue a call for the Denver meetings. The gathering was billed as a showdown with the federal government; the initial announcement, later toned down, rebuked Washington for having usurped "the rights of the states and its citizens to develop and acquire title to these public lands and to utilize [the] resources." At Denver, then, the question of whose lands these were would be thoroughly ventilated. It was a question of considerable constitutional concern: at stake was whether the states or the federal government had ultimate sovereignty over public lands.

The idea that the Roosevelt administration expected to establish any boundaries at all provoked an intense hostility that led some to charge the federal government with waging war on its citizens, pursuing what one Colorado newspaper lambasted as a "Russian policy" of arbitrary and authoritarian rule on the range. "Very few of the autocratic monarchs of the world," the *Steamboat Pilot* trumpeted, "would so dare to set aside the will of the people this way." Another, more playfully, mocked the administrative pose of omnipotence:

> Wise old guy this Baron Pinchot
> Seeks to fence in all the earth,
> While we sit here and watch his doings
> In a manner full of mirth. . . .

Many in the West strongly opposed the federal government's new regulatory role, particularly the Forest Service's power to regulate behavior in the national forests.

Courtesy Denver Public Library, Conservation Collection, Western and Genealogy Department

But while you're building fences
Of barbed wire and the like,
Remember that the cowboys
May decide to go out on strike.
Maybe when they're through with you
And you their wrath have felt,
Your pet scheme will be blasted,
And your scalp hang from their belt.

Lurking beneath this bold rebuke, however, and evident in the poet's use of the word *maybe,* was the fear that the insurgency would falter before an aggressive federal government. That fearful reality was most vividly cap-

tured in a cartoon that appeared in the *Rocky Mountain News*. Sitting upon
a regal throne and wearing a bejeweled crown, a severe-looking Gifford
Pinchot holds in his right hand a mace, a symbol of monarchical power.
Arrayed behind him, mounted on powerful steeds, are six forest rangers,
their right arms raised above, brandishing whips, markers of unchecked
authority. In the foreground kneel abject westerners, hats in hand; defer-
ential and impotent, the stockman, the irrigationist and miner, the new set-
tler and pioneer, were no longer masters of their own fates. As one of the
cartoon's captions alleged, even "wild game is of more importance than
prospectors and settlers." The chief forester ruled with an iron hand.[30]

Defusing that charged atmosphere was one of the reasons Roosevelt had
sent Pinchot to the 1907 Public Lands Convention; Pinchot also was asked
to plumb the depth of the opposition and calculate the political damage that
would come from continued implementation of federal regulation. To
judge from the conference's first two days, his work in Denver was complicated. Each speaker seemed to feed off his predecessor's animosity, as
speech after speech excoriated the Roosevelt administration and Pinchot in
particular. Senator Henry Teller of Colorado was among those who blasted
the concept of federal sovereignty: "We cannot remain barbarians to save
timber. I do not contend that the government has the right to seize land, but
I do contend that we have the right to put it to the use that Almighty God
intended." Such blunt and contentious language emboldened the audience
so that when, on the afternoon of the convention's third day, Pinchot finally
strode across the stage of Denver's Brown Theater, he was met with a storm
of catcalls and jeers.[31]

There was no place he would rather have been. "If you fellows can stand
me," he laughed when he finally gained the crowd's attention, "I can stand
you," a light retort that quieted the hecklers. Pinchot then launched into his
standard spiel about the critical relationship among national forests, conservation practices, economic growth, and political equity. Creating the
vast national forests had had a series of beneficial effects, he declared.
"[G]overnment-regulated timber auctions prevented monopoly and the
consequent excessive price of lumber," stabilized markets, and ensured that
there was "no question of favoritism or graft." As the federal presence
helped regularize life in the intermountain region, so did it serve the public

in other, no less complicated but positive ways. For those who inhabited an often-arid region, Pinchot was at pains to emphasize what he considered to be a critical connection between woods and water—forested lands protected "watersheds of streams used for irrigation, for domestic water and manufacturing supply, and for transportation." For these reasons alone, he asserted, "the protection of irrigation throughout the west would justify the president's forest policy." Rather than resist Roosevelt's conservation policies, western insurgents should embrace them.[32]

Some of his listeners must have absorbed his message, for when Pinchot concluded his address, he was reportedly cheered "lustfully." Not all were seduced. Succeeding speakers tore into the federal government's flaunting of its regulatory powers. Yet these more intransigent delegates apparently were shocked when, following Pinchot's speech, the Public Lands Convention's resolutions were announced. Although the platform called for an end to federal intervention in western affairs, and asked for a reevaluation of national forest legislation and regulatory activism, these resolutions were temperate, quite unlike the blustery sloganeering that had characterized the public speeches and back-room discussions. The resolutions sent the delegates packing, one newspaper editorial concluded, "roaring as mildly as a suckling dove."[33]

Part of the credit for the apparently pro-conservation victory lay with behind-the-scenes maneuvering on the resolution committee, which inexplicably had been stacked with a goodly number of the government's supporters. Pinchot's presence itself was influential—that he confronted his detractors face to face, and stated his position forcefully, helped his cause. That cause was aided too by his assertion that conservation played a definitive role in the government's decision-making process. The interlocking relationship between the people and the land on which they lived, all set within a web of trees, water, and soil, of high country and lowlands, not only defined the paramount problem facing the West but also was its inspired solution. Each human context and need was important, Pinchot had observed; each legitimate interest must be acknowledged and fulfilled where possible. After all, as he regularly explained to western audiences largely convinced that federal control abrogated local access to and ignored local knowledge of the reserves, grazing "is primarily a local issue and

should always be dealt with on local grounds. Wise administration of grazing in the reserves is impossible under general rules based upon theoretical
considerations." Being sensitive to different landscapes meant that "[l]ocal
rules must be framed to meet local conditions, and they must be modified
from time to time as local needs may require."[34]

Federal power was further restrained by citizen participation in defining
the mission of the national reserves. In "The Use of the National Forests,"
a Department of Agriculture pamphlet released in June 1907 to coincide
with the Denver meetings, he pointed out that these public lands "exist today because the people want them. To make them accomplish the most
good the people themselves must make clear how they want them run."
But no interest, individual or combined, could or would be allowed to dominate Forest Service policy on public lands. "There are many great interests
on the National Forests," and of necessity these "sometimes will conflict a
little." To secure the consensus necessary to ensure a rational use of the land,
it "is often necessary for one man to give way a little here, another a little
there." In this new Rooseveltian age, there "must be hearty cooperation
from everyone."[35]

They must cooperate, most of all, because nature would compel them to
do so; the carrying capacity of the land was the first (and final) arbiter of
how and when a landscape would be utilized. "The protection of the forest
and the protection of the range by wise use," Pinchot had reminded his
Denver audience, "are two divisions of a problem vastly larger and more
important than either." This is "the problem of the conservation of all our
natural resources," a matter that required careful consideration. "If we
destroy them, no amount of success in any other direction will keep us prosperous." His generation was confronted with a question, in short, that
spanned "both the present and the future." Private, short-term interests
must give way to public, long-term needs.[36]

The administration's strategy of conflict resolution helped transform the
often-vociferous debate over federal conservation policy. Its goal had been
to decenter the narrow, specific concerns of particular resource groups,
thereby forcing each to acknowledge the legitimate needs of the complex
collective, an approach that thrust the public good—federal conservationism, that is—into the forefront. It then became the basis for discussion,

muscling aside the demands for "free grass" or "free range," and quieting the once-dominant voice with which grazing interests spoke in the political arena. "Czar Pinchot" proved to be a most effective weapon in the Roosevelt arsenal.

WATER FIGHT

That persona would be just as effective during the bitter battle over the building of a dam in the Hetch Hetchy Valley to create a stable water supply for San Francisco. As we have seen, in the now-standard narration of the controversy John Muir and Gifford Pinchot determined its tempo and impulse, beginning with their private correspondence and personal negotiations in the first years of the century, and escalating later in the public confrontations and verbal sparring during the early teens. Suggestive of this emphasis is the original title of a 1989 documentary about Hetch Hetchy—*The Wilderness Idea. John Muir, Gifford Pinchot and the First Great Battle for Wilderness*.[37]

Yet these two men's certitude and mutual animosity were not solely responsible for the timing and character of the debate. Without minimizing the influence of the thousands of men and women who were directly engaged with this national discussion, there was one other major figure who had as much to do with shaping its contours as did Muir and Pinchot—President Theodore Roosevelt.

Roosevelt's contributions to the debate are of a different order than theirs. As the president of the United States, and the first professed conservationist to hold that august office, he pushed Congress to enact a wealth of legislation that at the time (and in retrospect) is remarkable. Among other noteworthy accomplishments, Roosevelt created innumerable wildlife sanctuaries, national parks, and national monuments, as well as adding 150 million acres to the national forest system under the aegis of the new Forest Service. Complicating an understanding of these achievements is that his conservationist philosophy seems to have neatly balanced the beliefs of Muir and Pinchot. Roosevelt drew upon the preservationist and utilitarian ideals of conservation for which they are considered the leading exponents, but was not doctrinaire in his application of either set of principles. This did not make his decision concerning Hetch Hetchy any easier. Indeed, it made it all the more tension-filled: Roosevelt could be of two minds. His ability to accept such ambiguity, even to foster it, not only was crucial to the evolution of the whole affair but also reflected something of vital consequence. The president was his own man.[38]

He demonstrated his independence throughout the Hetch Hetchy controversy. In 1903, just as the debate was heating up, Roosevelt went camping with Muir throughout Yosemite. In asking Muir to serve as his guide for the trip, the president had promised "to drop politics absolutely for four days and just be out in the open with you." He kept part of that promise, at least. The president remembered those four days with great delight, most vividly the valley's extraordinary natural landscape, "the solemn temple of the giant sequoias" where the men first camped, and their final site "fronting the stupendous rocky mass of El Capitan, with the falls thundering in the distance on either hand." In a letter to naturalist John Burroughs, Roosevelt noted he "was a little surprised that [Muir] knew nothing about any of the birds save a few of the most conspicuous, but he knows so much about rocks, trees, glaciers, flowers, etc., that it is simply captious to complain."[39]

He had no complaint that theirs proved more than just a sightseeing tour; neither man was about to forgo politics. Instead they engaged in extended discussions of the political future of the conservation movement generally, and more specifically contemplated ways to protect Muir's beloved Sierras, discourse that bore fruit. Shortly after leaving Yosemite, Roosevelt urged the secretary of the interior to make the northern Sierras a part of the national forest reserves. It is no wonder that later Muir would gush that "I never before had met so interesting, hearty, and manly a companion. I fairly fell in love with him."[40]

That love, and influence, only went so far. When two years later a question arose as to how much federal control would be exerted in Yosemite, a question linked to San Francisco's petition to build the dam in Hetch Hetchy, Muir attempted to exploit his earlier visit with Roosevelt. He wrote the president suggesting that he had made a promise to protect the national park from commercial development. Roosevelt brushed aside Muir's claim, dismissing as "too vague" his and the Sierra Club's denunciation of the proposed dam. On these and other matters, the president wrote Muir's close friend Robert Underwood Johnson, caution was essential: "My own belief is that California will resent anything like interference on my part." Roosevelt was not about to be stampeded into accepting Muir's perspective.[41]

His favorite forester could not buffalo him either. In the summer of 1907, for instance, as Pinchot and the new interior secretary, James R. Garfield, were preparing to release yet another report in favor of a reservoir in Hetch Hetchy, Roosevelt suggested that they think again about alternative sites; he delegated Pinchot to visit Muir in California to solicit his views. Muir argued pointedly that Hetch Hetchy must be saved from destruction, and followed this verbal report with a lengthy written one to Garfield. In the end, Muir's brief did not fully persuade Garfield or Pinchot, and they informed the president that Hetch Hetchy probably remained the best site for a reservoir. In forcing his staff to reexamine their beliefs, Roosevelt gave shape to his own. It was only after this administrative reevaluation that he decided to accept their recommendation; with Roosevelt, policy-making was an intense event designed to build firm consensus.[42]

The president deliberately made the process all the more intense when, in September of that year, he wrote a letter to Muir that laid out his assessment of the political situation surrounding Hetch Hetchy and suggested ways Muir could challenge the very findings embedded within Roosevelt's subordinates' report. He admitted that "Pinchot and Garfield are rather favorable to the Hetch Hetchy plan, but not definitely so." Roosevelt then asserted that he would do everything in his power "to protect not only Yosemite . . . but other similar great beauties of this country"—an assertion that must have been music to Muir's ears.

But Roosevelt was acutely aware of the dilemma in which he thereby found himself. If the preservation of these lands was "used so as to interfere with the permanent material development of the State . . . the result will be bad." This economic constraint reinforced a political one. "You must remember," he wrote, "that it is out of the question permanently to protect [these beauties] unless we have a certain degree of friendliness toward them on the part of the people of the State in which they are situated." Such political support for the preservation of the Hetch Hetchy Valley had not yet been manifest. Rather, the reverse was true. Everyone seemed in favor of the dam, "and I have been in the disagreeable position of seeming to inter-fere with the development of the State for the sake of keeping a valley, which apparently hardly anyone wanted to have kept."[43]

Encouraging others to act as he would not was another matter. He made it quite plain that Hetch Hetchy's salvation lay in the creation of a ground-swell of popular support, something it presently did not have. Were this political liability overcome, the administration's position might well change to meet new political conditions. As Roosevelt declared, "I would not have any difficulty at all [in supporting your position] if, as you say, nine tenths of the citizens took ground against the Hetch Hetchy project."[44]

Muir took full advantage of the president's political insights. It was only after receiving this letter that Muir, along with the Sierra Club and its allies, swung into action, sparking intense publicity and increasingly favorable press for their cause. This close scrutiny could not have materialized until after Garfield and Pinchot's report had circulated within the administra-tion, a report that conceded Hetch Hetchy's beauty but concluded that the need for the reservoir was too pressing to ignore. Public scrutiny intensified too only after the secretary of the interior granted San Francisco's applica-tion. The pressure that Muir and his compatriots generated in 1908 and 1909 did not dissuade the administration from its support of the Hetch Hetchy dam, but this pressure was quite effective in the realm of electoral politics. Congress, confronted with rising public opposition, refused to act on the measure. Hetch Hetchy, for the time being, was safe, and it would not be inundated during Roosevelt's watch.[45]

Muir's success at this stage of the debate was not without its share of irony: Roosevelt must be given partial credit for defeating his own admin-istration's proposal. This suggests again the independence and complexity of his posture, characteristics also of his final message to Congress in December 1908. Here he touted the pressing need to preserve wilderness for its own sake, most notably in Yellowstone and Yosemite National Parks. "In both, all wild things should be protected and the scenery kept wholly unmarred," the president declared, a declaration that historian Rod-erick Nash believes repudiated Pinchot's stance on Hetch Hetchy. A more careful reading of Roosevelt's message indicates, however, that his support for preservation was—as always—conditional. In this case, it was coupled with an equally vigorous championing of the utilitarian perspective Pinchot espoused. That is what accounts for the president's argument that those national parks adjacent to national forests, including Yellowstone and Yosemite, must "be placed under the control of the forest service of the Agriculture Department, instead of leaving them as they are now, under the Interior Department and policed by the army." A transfer of authority of this kind would have seriously challenged the capacity of preservationists to influence the management of these public lands. In this particular blending of claims for both the utilization and preservation of public lands, Roosevelt once again demonstrated that his conscience was his own.[46]

INSULATION

If this was so, why then suggest otherwise, as Roosevelt reportedly did in a conversation with Robert Underwood Johnson at the height of the Hetch Hetchy debate? In part, Roosevelt did so because Pinchot *was* an important influence on his conservation politics and policies. The president concurred with the forester's insistence upon the advantages of conservation and his emphasis on the political equality and economic benefits that it could produce. If he had not, Roosevelt would not have allowed Pinchot to draft many of his speeches relating to forestry and conservation while governor of New York, and later as president. These contributions, among myriad others, earned the Rough Rider's deep appreciation of and high praise for Pinchot's "tireless energy and activity, his fearlessness, his complete disinterestedness, and single-minded devotion to the interests of the plain people. . . ."[47]

That presidential approbation translated into administrative influence is beyond doubt. Yet the nature of that influence, and the constraints the president placed on it, are better understood by assessing one of the rationales Roosevelt offered for his decision to permit San Francisco to build a dam in Hetch Hetchy. It appeared in a letter he wrote to Robert Underwood Johnson, in which the president commented offhandedly that as "for the Hetch Hetchy matter, it was just one of those cases where I was extremely doubtful." But he finally set those doubts aside and "came to the conclusion that I ought to stand by Garfield and Pinchot's judgement in the matter." To judge from this text alone, his subordinates' certitude had won out over presidential ambivalence.[48]

Yet Roosevelt's words also reveal an important dimension of the political relationship between the president and his forester. In establishing Pinchot (and Garfield) as the dam's chief advocates within the administration, in indicating that he ought to "stand by" them despite his hesitancy, Roosevelt underscored the manner in which Pinchot functioned as Roosevelt's lightning rod. Pinchot did not simply articulate governmental policy but was also to act as if it were his policy, thereby catching the thunderbolts the opposition would subsequently hurl. In this he would spare his superior no little heat.

One of those whose opposition was so deflected was John Muir. In the final stages of the debate over Hetch Hetchy in 1913, he was infuriated by Pinchot's forceful advocacy of the dam and believed that Roosevelt would have preempted Pinchot's activism had he still been president. After all, it "was Roosevelt who [in 1905] tried to save the valley, at least for a generation or two, by compelling San Francisco to first develop the Lake Eleanor and Cherry River to the utmost." Muir's memory was playing tricks with him. It had been Pinchot who had written and signed the administration's letter to the Sierra Club about the plan to enact a long-term, multi-reservoir option for San Francisco. That Muir had forgotten about his now-archrival's role in these confidential discussions testifies to how effectively Pinchot protected Roosevelt from criticism, protection that enabled the president's reputation to remain intact, and, retrospectively, to flourish.[49]

Clear political gains flowed from this symbiotic relationship, but its design depended as well on both men's willingness to invest in it. There is no question that Pinchot's investment was as personal as it was political. Like many of the other younger men pulled into Roosevelt's circle, he was in awe of the chief executive, and he displayed his fierce adoration by hurling himself into his work for each of the more than seven years Roosevelt held office. All this struck Pinchot's parents as excessive, and they blamed Roosevelt for so abusing their son. One of the family's well-placed friends, the senior Pinchots wrote their son, had spoken to them of "the way you are sacrificing yourself" for a president who apparently "did not care for anyone's health or comfort." This source also had advised "that you were being

President Roosevelt and forester Pinchot on the Mississippi River. The two men forged a close personal and political relationship that grew during their years together in Washington, D.C., and later during the 1912 presidential campaign.
Grey Towers NHL

exhausted by [Roosevelt] and his ways," an observation that, James Pinchot acknowledged, "tallies with what I think and your mother thinks."[50]

Mostly they thought Gifford's career was in jeopardy. He would "soon be a used up man—old and worn out," a forty-two-year-old without a future, his father predicted in 1907. "If you are to have [one] of any kind you must begin to prepare for it," something he was incapable of doing so long as he remained in his present state of adoration. "The time has come when you should take a stand and save your self while you can." This was no easy task, the Pinchots understood, for Roosevelt was a "vampire."[51]

Certainly the president sucked in the energy of his subordinates and, in Pinchot's case, made shrewd use of the forester's devotion and drive. Roosevelt revealed how he had handled Pinchot in a 1910 letter to Henry Cabot Lodge, a close friend and advisor. Then on a hunting expedition in Africa, the former president had just learned that his successor, President William Howard Taft, had fired Pinchot for insubordination during the Ballinger-Pinchot furor. The former president confided that he was "very sorry about Pinchot. He was one of our most valuable public servants," valuable particularly for his enthusiasms: "He loved to spend his whole strength, with lavish indifference to any effect on himself, in battling for a high ideal."[52]

But for the zealous Pinchot to be kept in his place, Roosevelt noted, his energies had to be carefully harnessed, something Taft had apparently not understood. "Not to keep him thus employed rendered it possible that his great energy would expend itself in fighting the men who seemed to him not to be going far enough forward." Other contemporaries reached similar conclusions: Pinchot "is an enthusiast, and like all of that kidney he sometimes requires a master hand to tighten the reins at the proper time," an observer commented. "When Gifford Pinchot needed the hand of the master [during the Ballinger controversy], there was none to whom he could turn. . . ." Like the land itself, Pinchot had to be managed.[53]

This strategy did not include giving Pinchot free rein over the president's conscience. On the contrary, Roosevelt's letter to Lodge reminds us exactly whose administration it had been, and who, by extension, bore ultimate responsibility for the decisions it had reached concerning the politics and management of the national forests. Always there was an important and precise distinction between Roosevelt's and Pinchot's duties and roles, between those of the chief executive and the chief forester, a distinction between superior and subordinate that shaped the conception, articulation, and, ultimately, the course of federal conservation policies in the Progressive Era.

Family Affairs

URING AN enjoyable late June weekend in 1913, while staying at Grey Towers, Gifford Pinchot scrawled an odd observation in his journal, odd only because there is no similar entry in the many other diaries he kept throughout his life. That weekend's guests, Margaret and Aleck Morgan, the notation read, were "the most ideal couple I ever saw. Just wonderful." Why did this forty-eight-year-old bachelor take note of and then bother to write about what he perceived to be a happily matched and married couple?[1]

The reason became clear as the Morgans motored away from Grey Towers on Sunday afternoon and, shortly thereafter, Cornelia Bryce arrived to spend the night. Sixteen years younger than Gifford Pinchot, and active in the women's suffrage movement and the Progressive Party, Cornelia was a favorite of Theodore Roosevelt, who was a close family friend—the Bryces and Roosevelts lived near one another on Long Island. Cornelia, like Pinchot, could lay claim to a lineage replete with material accomplishments and political engagement. Peter Cooper, her great-grandfather, had accumulated a substantial fortune as a manufacturer and inventor in New York City, a portion of which he had used to found the Cooper Institute for indigent students. A political reformer as well, Cooper had served on the board of aldermen, fought Tammany Hall corruption, and stood—however reluctantly—as the Greenback Party's candidate for president in 1876. His son Edward, Cornelia's grandfather, also had been a successful industrialist and inventor and had shared his father's reform energies; challenging Tammany's tight grip on the city's political machinery, he had managed to capture the mayor's office in 1878. Such interests seem to have marked the life of Cornelia's father, Lloyd Stephens Bryce, as well. He briefly represented Long Island's Seventh District in the House of Representatives (one of his daughter's earliest memories was of handing out leaflets during that campaign), became publisher and editor of the *North American Review,* and later was William Howard Taft's choice to serve as U.S. minister to the Netherlands. That Cornelia would be a three-time candidate for the U.S. Congress in the 1920s and 1930s suggests how well she learned that running for office was the familial form of exercise.[2]

One of the perks of being in on the political chase, she would later remember, was the occasional dinner "with an ex-President who took me into the smoking room to talk politics with the men after the women had left the table." Although Cornelia Bryce would profess that Theodore Roosevelt's invitations "never struck [her as] in any way unusual," she admitted to feeling flattered when, after one such evening, he proclaimed that she possessed the "best political mind of any woman of his acquaintance." It may have been this same magnetic politician, in whose orbit she and Pinchot regularly moved, who introduced her to the man she traveled to visit in Milford on a late summer afternoon in 1913.[3]

Their first sustained connection probably came during Roosevelt's Bull Moose campaign of 1912, for which Pinchot served as a strategist, speechwriter, and fundraiser. It was in this latter capacity that Pinchot had interviewed Cornelia Bryce that spring "about taking part in the Progressive movement." In what could also be read as a kind of self-description, Pinchot reported to fellow campaigner Frances A. Kellor that "Miss Bryce has a great deal of money, is greatly interested in . . . modern advance of all kinds, and I think could be gotten to take a vivid and productive interest in the work of the Progressive Service."[4]

Bryce's and Pinchot's joint concern with public affairs had its private dimension. The two began seeing a good deal of one another throughout

Wealthy, politically sophisticated, and active in a host of progressive causes, Cornelia Bryce Pinchot (1881–1960), shown here marching in a 1917 suffragette parade, ran for Congress three times and was an ardent supporter of her husband's political career, as he was of hers. Grey Towers NHL

the fall and the next spring, principally at social events and dinner parties in New York and Washington. It was her first visit to the Pinchot estate in Pennsylvania, however, that signaled a dramatic intensification of their courtship. That is when this vivacious and charming redhead clumped into Gifford Pinchot's heart. On Monday morning the two went fishing along the Sawkill, a stream with spectacular waterfalls that ran from west to south through the family's lands surrounding Grey Towers, and the environment in which Gifford most loved to fish. Miss Bryce, he did not fail to observe as they hiked through the woods on the way down to the stream, "wore a kind of Blouse and rubber boots." His interest in her attire was of a piece with evidence of his growing fascination with her. When they reached the Sawkill, the two were disappointed to find its waters low and flat. Despite the poor conditions, the inveterate angler Pinchot hooked a twelve-inch German brown trout; he urged his guest to reel it in, but she didn't rise to his bait.[5]

They continued to troll for one another's affections, and sometime during the spring of 1914, less than a year after he had mused about the perfection of the Morgans' marriage, Gifford Pinchot proposed to Cornelia Bryce. She had not given her final assent when, on July 31, 1914, the couple made a pilgrimage to her parents' homes. In Roslyn, on the northern shore of Long Island, Pinchot spoke of his intentions to her mother, Edith Cooper Bryce. Her blessing bestowed, the couple then caught a ferry across Long Island Sound to Saugatuck, Connecticut, where Pinchot similarly conferred with her father. The fifth of August, Pinchot exulted in his diary, was "the day of the final yes," and less than a fortnight later, in a small ceremony in the Bryce family home in Roslyn, with brother Amos Pinchot serving as best man and Theodore Roosevelt in attendance, Gifford Pinchot and Cornelia Bryce became husband and wife.[6]

The bride and groom were not especially young; Gifford was forty-nine, and Cornelia was thirty-three. Cornelia had apparently delayed marriage in good measure because she had felt smothered at home. Despite the Bryce family's liberal political posture, Cornelia's parents believed that active, public lives were reserved for its male members. That accounted for her sporadic schooling: "my family held to the idea so common a couple of generations ago that the female of the species needs no education," she told a convention of women college administrators in the early 1920s. Resentful of this denial of opportunity, a self-described "misfit in what is called 'society,'" she rejected what she described as the "butterfly existence my parents wanted for me." Her rebellions may have been small, but they were critical to her emerging sense of self. Throughout her teens and twenties, Bryce became a much-decorated rider on the eastern seaboard's equestrian circuit, a sport she pursued because women "rarely competed" in it, it had a "reputation for danger," and it afforded "a most gratifying opportunity to score against hard-boiled masculine competition."

Cornelia had considerably less interest in men as potential spouses. She refused to "come out" in the rarefied New York society in which her parents were ensconced and rebuffed any number of high-society suitors. Later her parents were stunned when their twentysomething daughter announced that she and a friend were going on a tour of the nation, with neither pearls nor maids. "I made up my mind to shed my present and my past," she would later recount, and although the journey from Maine to California and back may not have been a revolutionary act, she felt that it opened up a larger world, that her travels had been essential to her "declaration of independence." Only when she perceived herself to be independent would she begin to hunt for a mate of her standing and temperament, as the language she employed to describe her courtship with Pinchot suggests. "Some years ago," she wrote in 1927, "I marked down, pursued, and captured one of the few really big men I have ever known—'one who never turned his back but marched breast forward'—and lived happily and gloriously ever after."[7]

This "big man" had been targeted before. Well-off and strikingly handsome—at Yale his nickname had been Apollo—and the oldest child of a socially prominent family, Gifford Pinchot must have been an alluring prospect. There indeed were a number of young women who expressed a strong interest in him, and his correspondence tracks the waxing and waning of these romantic attachments. Of a young woman named Maria, there was much to discuss. In January 1891, sister Antoinette, then twenty-three, reported seeing "lots of Maria" while Gifford was out of town, and teased: she "is certainly a most attractive object, and as she was quite wild to hear about little Gifford we gave her no peace until she told us every word you had ever said to her." Her physical attractiveness was one of the things that had caught Gifford's eye and led him to ponder the possibility of marriage. Or so he must have informed Horace Walker, a Yale classmate and fellow member of Skull and Bones, who quickly responded with a cautionary epistle. "You ought to be very careful if you really feel towards her as you said. You do not want for a wife a girl that appeals simply to one side of your nature—a 'kissable girl'—as you express it." Confessing that he "may be wrong," and fearful of giving offense, Walker nevertheless voiced his concerns. It "does not seem to me to be *true* love that appeals to that side of a man. . . . You want a *woman* and above all one that you can respect." Maria did not appear to have the requisite qualifications: "[I]t has struck me more than once," Walker continued, "that she does not draw the best out of you."[8]

In time Gifford would concur, breaking off the relationship later that year. But his reasoning—that any deepening of their connection would inhibit his forestry career—puzzled his friend Walker. If, as Walker had earlier proposed, Maria was not the right girl, or if Gifford had "doubts" about her, then ending the relationship made sense. But why "your work prevents you from having a C.B. [Connubial Bliss, in Skull and Bones slang] and forces you to 'kill it' is worse than Greek to me. I can easily see that it delays matters two, three or four years but if it really means that you can't marry the girl you love and who loves you . . . then all I can say is that you've struck a damned poor job."[9]

Another woman whose love for Pinchot went unrequited better understood the complications his passion for forestry imposed on affairs of the heart. Florence Adele Stone, George Vanderbilt's favorite niece, met Pinchot at Biltmore and developed a crush on him. Although only eighteen years old when their paths crossed in Asheville, she correctly perceived that the way to the twenty-six-year-old forester's affections was through his professional sensibilities. Her chatty letters brimmed with wistful evocations of their time together riding through the North Carolina mountains, of the landscapes through which she subsequently moved—from Bar Harbor to Newport to the Colorado Rockies—and of her scientific observations; one dated March 1892 was to have been a "short epistle of dry facts" about clouds but carried on for pages, an effort her biographer concludes was designed "to impress him with how much she had 'boned up' on scientific matters."[10]

Impressive too, Miss Stone hoped, was her hunger for vivid experience outside the boundaries of the luxurious world within which she had been raised. "[R]eal things are what I want now," she wrote while "looking idly out on the ocean, and counting the stars" from her upstairs bedroom in her uncle Frederick's Newport cottage, Rough Point. "I often think how I would like to go off all by myself, under a different name, as a poor governess, only not really be poor, nor live with anyone, just have people think so. Then I would travel, go everywhere, see what poverty, sickness and sorrow really were, what misery and crime meant. I have lived and seen only one side of life, and merely read and imagined the other. And it is difficult to understand and sympathize with what I know so little about."

Her eagerness to connect with what mattered, and build her character in the process—so like Pinchot's ambitions to find meaning in vigorous public service—did not in the end bind them together. About this loss, she expressed much regret when they next met at the Chicago World's Fair in the summer of 1893. Busy with the Biltmore exhibition, Pinchot had little time to engage in conversation, but as brief as their interaction was, it reminded Stone why one of her current suitors could not measure up to the engaging forester. Gifford Pinchot "has everything a man ought to have, at least the things the man I dreamed of had, and the other—well, the other has a great many things: a perfect love, a very unselfish nature, and he is so considerate and thoughtful. But that is not enough; I want so much more."[11]

That Pinchot's occupation was his preoccupation—"he told me how busy he was going to be this summer," she noted in June 1893, "how he never had so much to do and so little time to do it"—added to his luster, and to her ultimate frustration. Yearning to reconnect with him ("I will never see him! I can't stand it, since he knows how I feel"), yet conscious that he stayed away because he did not reciprocate her feelings, she plotted to remain for the winter of 1893–94 in New York City, where she knew Pinchot intended to set up as a consulting forester. "I am sure it will be a horrible winter for me, always in a fear of excitement at a dance, always wondering if he will talk to me. And how often he will hurt me through and through! I believe the more he hurts me, the more I will love him."[12]

Pinchot's beguiling, maddening elusiveness also caught the eye of newspaper gossip columnists. From his arrival in Washington in the late 1890s as the nation's chief forester, the local press corps dubbed him "the most eligible of Washington beaux"; speculation about why he remained a bachelor developed into a parlor game. Although one interviewer drew back from asking directly why he had not married, coyly concluding that "there are some limits to newspaper investigation," others printed titillating accounts of his singular status. Asserting that Pinchot "cares nothing for women," the *Washington Star* assured its readers that his indifference was attributable to his physique and demeanor: "tall, thin, almost to emaciation," Pinchot had the "looks and habits of an ascetic." His parsimony was as fiscal as it was physical, *Current Literature* mused in 1910, and this trait had implications for his love life. "The reputed possessor of several millions, it is said that he probably does not spend even the sum of $5,000 paid to him as a salary from the government"; such a man "has been too devoted to his work to find a help-mate or perhaps to feel the need for one." The conservationist, whose job it was to rein in the nation's accelerating lust for natural resources, seemingly had learned to bank his own fires.[13]

The curious journalists were correct that Pinchot seemed married to his work. Less accurate were their guesses as to why he had chosen to wed his public career and private life. They would surely have been startled to learn that Pinchot did not consider himself to have been a bachelor before he and Cornelia tied the knot in 1914, though in a legal sense he had had no previous wife.

THE CONSERVATION OF DESIRE

True, Laura Houghteling had been dead since 1894, but that did not stop Pinchot from remaining her devoted soulmate. The two had met occasionally in the late 1880s and had attended the same Asheville social gatherings in the early winter of 1892. With some jealousy, Florence Stone fantasized that these soirees continued after her departure for New York City: "I went to church with George [Vanderbilt] yesterday," she wrote Pinchot in late March, "and we walked home afterward and reminisced on Biltmore. . . . We both imagined you in a blissful frame of mind dining at Miss Houghteling's—the very name sends shivers down my back—but no, honestly, I think she is perfectly lovely and so pretty."[14]

It was amid the wooded terrain surrounding George Vanderbilt's Biltmore manse later that spring that Pinchot and Laura Houghteling had what he considered their most significant early encounter. As Pinchot rode his horse one April afternoon down along the lower ford of the French

In 1892, while working on George Vanderbilt's estate, Biltmore, Gifford Pinchot fell in love with Laura Houghteling. She would die of tuberculosis within two years.

Grey Towers NHL

Broad River, evaluating the progress of his early forestry efforts, his attention was diverted by Miss Houghteling, riding through the Biltmore nursery. Off he shot in full pursuit, just managing to catch her before she crossed an iron bridge that led across the river and off the estate. Out of breath yet enchanted, Gifford was embarrassed on two counts: it was the first time he had summoned up the courage to call her by her first name, and as he did so, he felt a blush spread across his face. He flushed anew when they parted company—she to return to Strawberry Hill, the home in which she was convalescing from tuberculosis, he to his outdoor endeavors—for she misspoke his name. "[M]y dearest called me Peter as we separated."[15]

Her confusion did not last. Over the next eighteen months, their acquaintance deepened into love. Pinchot visited her as frequently as his work allowed—at night and on weekends—during which times they read poetry together and spoke fervently of their dreams and aspirations; they became inseparable. One who witnessed their growing infatuation was Julia Sullivan, Laura's nurse. She later recalled in a letter to Gifford how startled she had been to come upon them in full embrace in the parlor of Strawberry Hill. "I was so frightened I came near dropping the tray and came as very near saying 'Excuse me' or something like that. She told me all about it that night after we went upstairs to bed and said that if I ever had said 'excuse me' she would never have forgiven me." Bursting with happiness, wanting "to get well so badly," Laura, Sullivan noted, would "stay in bed and rest and then imagine that rest was all she needed to make her well."[16]

By October 1892, Pinchot's close circle of Yale friends also knew that his relationship with Laura had entered a more profound phase; that is when he declared to Laura that she was his "C.B." She made an impression on his friends as well. "I was delighted to meet your C.B.," college chum Pat Corbin wrote a year later. "She seemed like a *very* attractive girl, and with enough attractions in reserve to make her one who would grow always upon further acquaintance," an analysis of her virtues that other friends had shared after meeting her. Laura Houghteling fit the code, as one correspondent put it, of being "a true fine girl," someone to love in full "and better still have her give you her love."[17]

Laura's ability to give was limited by her illness. Since being diagnosed with tuberculosis in the late 1880s, she had been traveling to Asheville from her family's home in Chicago, seeking in the mountains of western North Carolina the recuperative powers of a high country climate that Laura's physician in Asheville, S. Westry Battle, like other nineteenth-century practitioners, believed might cure those afflicted with the dread disease. Gifford knew all about her tuberculosis—and also knew something about the proposed cure and her possible prognosis; this knowledge seemed only to enhance his commitment to her. Laura's tragic state was fuel to his devotion, a responsiveness his friends encouraged. "I only hope that you can help to make happy, for such a girl as she must be, what remains to her of life," Horace Walker wrote.[18]

"It must take a load off your mind to have things go as smoothly as far as your family are concerned. You'll have trouble enough without that," commented Walker on what he presumed was James and Mary Pinchot's support of their son's passion. There he had it wrong, for Gifford had yet to share the extent of his feelings for Laura with his parents; they would be the last to know. At the same time that he had confided his amorous feelings to his peers, for instance, he had sent his mother a thumbnail sketch of "Miss Houghteling" that disguised his infatuation and her affliction. "She is in great repute with all of us [at Biltmore]. I have seldom met so sane and straight-forward a girl, or one with so little foolishness about her," he wrote in March 1893. "We discuss the state of the universe from time to time, and arrange its details, and have very jolly times together." From this bantering tone, Gifford's parents could not have guessed either that he had lost his heart to her, or that she was losing her life.[19]

Seven months later, when he finally told them of his feelings and her illness, they were shocked and felt betrayed. Even then, he did not tell them in person, but wrote them a letter in October 1893 while in Chicago overseeing the Biltmore forestry exhibition at that year's world's fair. While in the Windy City, Gifford frequently visited the woman he had come to love. How he chose to communicate his affection for her to his parents was as hurtful as the fact that he had previously hidden it from them, his mother responded when she received his news; she wondered why he had chosen to write about this significant news rather than share it in face-to-face conversation. James Pinchot was less measured in his disapproval, letting loose a series of broadsides that criticized his son's behavior, demanding an accounting of Laura's family and their social standing, and questioning his twenty-nine-year-old son's continuing commitment to his family and his career.[20]

He had not meant to be deceptive, Gifford replied. "I did not know before I left Milford [that summer] how I felt . . . or I would have told you both about it," he assured his mother. "Of all the things in my life it is that upon which I would most like to consult with you, and for which I want your fullest and most heartfelt approval." He neglected to mention his much earlier consultations about Laura with his friends; their advice was more welcome because he knew in advance that it would be more supportive than his parents' would be. His insight in this regard had been forged through experience—his sister's. Just two years earlier, in 1891, Nettie Pin-chot had met and fallen in love with Alan Johnstone, then an aide to the British ambassador to the United States. James and Mary Pinchot had done everything they could to quash the budding romance. In the end, they failed to halt what they initially believed was a disastrous match.[21]

Gifford, who had witnessed the intensity with which his parents had intervened in their daughter's affair of the heart, and who shared a Yale friend's disdain for "the idea of other people picking out a C.B. for you," wanted to avoid another protracted in-house struggle. His subterfuge about Laura had given him the requisite breathing space, allowing him to become "altogether sure of [him]self." Once certain of his sentiments, only then did he feel able to inform his parents. When the senior Pinchots came to know Laura as he had, Gifford felt sure, they would understand and accept his love for her, "just as now you agree with Nettie's choice of Alan." In what constituted perhaps the only serious challenge he ever offered to his parents' authority, Gifford controlled the timing and context of his courtship.[22]

It was more complicated assuaging his parents' other anxieties about the future of his relationship with Laura. Knowing how sensitized they were to the nuances that determined the hierarchy of the late-nineteenth-century American elite, he spoke not of the Houghtelings' wealth but of their respectable associations. "It is not beyond or beside the truth that the . . . most refined people in Chicago are [Laura's] best friends, and many of them her relatives," he noted. Relating the Houghtelings to members of his extended family was also part of his attempt to address his parents' worries that he had formed a connection to a family of uncertain provenance. Laura's mother, Marcia Stockbridge Houghteling, "is very much like [Aunt] Antoinette Phelps, but far more intellectual & more quiet"; her father, William, a manufacturer, reminded Gifford of his maternal grand-father, Amos F. Eno, but was, he conceded, "a much less able man." Still, there "is no one in the family to drag anyone down, nor concerning whom I have heard a word amiss." If not quite of the Pinchots' level, the Hough-telings at least were good people.[23]

To Gifford, their daughter was goodness incarnate and a boon to his out-look on life. That was a point his sister drove home. "It's rather hard luck that Miss Houghteling has had health problems," she wrote her mother, "but there is nothing like happiness to cure" any ailment—including the mood of a previously morose brother: "It's a blessing to see [Gifford] so entirely recovered from the melancholy young person of last summer and I must say that I feel as if Laura Houghteling had let us have back the old cheery Gifford." As had his supportive sibling, Gifford described to his parents Laura's virtue, character, and refinement, and with the same intention—to ease his parents' greatest fear, that a woman in his life would damage his prospects. "You are not in the least more anxious that I should make a name than she is, or more willing or eager to help me," he advised his parents. "My feeling for Laura has raised my conception of my life and duty, has made me purer and better, and has brought me very much nearer all the good things and influences that have so far been the best part of my life. I believe just as wholly that my life work will be far better because of her, and my chance to help fellowmen and do God's work in the world very much wider and better."[24]

That Laura made him whole, Gifford promised, would make his work as a forester all the more important. It "is as dear to me today as it has ever been, and . . . it holds first place more firmly than ever, because I value my duty higher, thanks to Laura's full sympathy with it." His commitment would remain firm, too, because "I should know of no quicker way of sacrificing her respect and affection than by losing my place as a working factor in the world of active men." Private affection would not deflect his public aspirations nor weaken his familial ties. "I am going straight along according to the plans that we have made together," that is, the ones he and his parents had long before devised. "You may be very sure that my chance of amounting to something as a forester has not suffered, and will not if I know it, by any step that I may take in the future, or have taken in speaking to Laura." Then he wrote the words James and Mary Pinchot perhaps most longed to hear. "There is no question of an engagement between Laura and me at present. She very wisely says that there will be time enough for that when she is stronger. . . ."[25]

Four months after he had written so optimistically to his parents, Laura's struggle with tuberculosis ended. Devastated as her health degenerated during January 1894, Gifford developed a pallor that came to reflect her own; unable to sleep, he kept a constant vigil by her bedside. Yet for all his despair and for all the pain she was in, the two evinced a calm that other members of their families did not feel. Disbelief and denial partly explain Gifford's equanimity. "There is no real cause for encouragement, as I greatly fear," he confessed to his father after a visit with Laura in Washington, D.C., where she had been moved to spend her final days in the home of her uncle, Senator Frank Stockbridge of Michigan. Still, "I am feeling more hopeful about her," a feeling Laura knew was as sweet as it was misplaced. When in early January her physicians had informed her there was no chance of recovery, she worried about how to break the news to Gifford. Her nurse and confidant, Julia Sullivan, later described their conversation to Pinchot: "She said she knew you would not believe it, but it had to be. She had felt it for a long time." They did not have long to wait, either; whatever faith Gifford may have placed in a miraculous recovery died with Laura on February 7, 1894.[26]

DIVINE GRIEF

Rocked by Laura's death, Gifford put up what his family thought was a brave front. "Poor Gifford!!" sighed brother-in-law Alan Johnstone. "He is so plucky and patient—it will be sad work for him for long I fear." But there was this saving grace: "[H]e is happy in as much as he knows that their parting is not forever, and the blow that would harden and injure many men's characters will only serve to bring out the good points in him. I have never seen anyone who inspired me with so much respect and esteem as he has this week."

Johnstone's wife, Gifford's sister, had worried before Laura's demise that there "seems nothing one can do for him as he doesn't talk of [Laura's declining condition] and we don't like to ask him questions as it makes it harder for him to keep his self control." Now, she wrote younger brother Amos, she was impressed with how their elder sibling was dealing with his crushing loss. "He is taking his sorrow most wonderfully. He is so brave and quiet about it, but I think he will never be the same cheery old Gifford again." Yet she felt he would recover in the long run, a confidence her mother shared. "I have no doubt that in the end it will come out right,"

Mary Pinchot assured nineteen-year-old Amos, then at Yale. "Things always do when faith and hope with high mind lead the way. Gifford has all of these, though for the moment they seem to be almost veiled by his sorrow ... [B]ut there is no doubt that since God so let it be, that it is right." Heavenly sanction aside, she had one deep concern about her much-loved son's bereavement. "I believe that Gifford has a high and noble mission to fulfill and I believe he will do it—but I don't want to see him narrowing himself down to one thought," she wrote. "It is not right in this world to live in the past or with the dead."[27]

Gifford did not share his mother's unease because his faith in another dimension granted him serenity. A month earlier, even as he expressed hope that Laura would recover, he drew consolation from a prospect of life everlasting: "[B]oth Laura and I have ... talked it fully over and are not afraid because we know [her passing] can be nothing more than a temporary separation, short for her, however long it may be for me." This perception, he explained to his father, was why Laura's impending demise "is all much less terrible than it must seem to you and indeed to anyone but ourselves. I have not been able to tell this to anyone as yet, so I am glad to write it and especially have you and Mamee [Mary Pinchot] know just how we feel for I am sure you will sympathize with us entirely."[28]

Gifford's confidence that there was life after death was reinforced within weeks of Laura Houghteling's funeral. By day, he worked assiduously to extend his forestry initiatives at Biltmore; from North Carolina he also commuted to New York City, where he was busily establishing his career as a consulting forester. By night, he cultivated his memories of the woman he had lost. Spending time "looking over my Lady's books and sketches" made him "very happy," he noted in his diary for March 17, 1894; a month later, he spent a full Sunday in her former room at Strawberry Hill, "marking after her copies of *Selections from Browning* and *Sonnets from the Portuguese*." Holding the books they had read together, remembering the lines of poetry that had defined their love, kept her close. "I have lost no ground. My Lady is nearer and dearer than when she died," he observed. That Sunday in April had been a "wonderfully happy day, full of her presence and peace."[29]

For him, Laura's presence was no mere figure of speech. He marked her passing, and continued significance to him, by the clothes he wore. For at least two years he was "clad in black, from neck to foot," as when he and his replacement at Biltmore, Carl Schenck, first met in April 1895. "Apparently he was in mourning," the German forester learned, "but his cheery eyes were in strict contrast to his mourning attire."

Pinchot had much to be cheerful about, for Laura inhabited his dreams as much as his waking life. So thoroughly were the two states of consciousness woven together that he was not always certain which he was in. Rattling along in a train to Frankfurt, Germany, in May 1895, he "was blessed with the wonderful nearness of my Dearest. . . . I could hardly help expecting to see her with my own eyes." A year earlier, while staying at Grey Towers, he had taken a walk through the wooded grounds and settled down in the summer house to "read forestry" when "this beautiful thing" happened. "[M]y Lady was nearer than ever this afternoon," he wrote, even using the first-person plural when he set the scene for his diary: "[W]e looked from the summer house together."[30]

Pinchot was convinced that such visitations were possible and that they regularly occurred. He and Laura had devoured the literature on spiritualists and spiritualism, mystics and mediums, which was vastly popular at the time. Their reading list ranged from biblical texts—*Revelation* and *The Gospel of John*—to the religious ruminations of Emanuel Swedenborg and the revelatory poetry of Ralph Waldo Emerson; they scoured too the otherworldly novels of James Lane Allen and, especially, Elizabeth Stuart Phelps's *The Gate Ajar* and *Beyond the Gates,* sentimental fiction about communing with the dead that Mark Twain took great delight in skewering in *Extracts from Captain Stormfield's Visit to Heaven.*

Nor were they alone in their beliefs. Many of their contemporaries found considerable comfort in the notion that the earthbound might part the veil and communicate with deceased family, friends, or lovers. That idea had taken on added (and understandable) appeal in the years following the bloody Civil War, and only slowly diminished as a force within the American imagination with the dawning of the twentieth century. Pinchot's generation had been captivated by the scientific trappings of this insistent search for meaning in poltergeists and strange rapping sounds in the night. "Spiritualism became a self-conscious movement precisely at the time that it disassociated itself from occult traditions of secrecy," historian R. Laurence Moore has asserted. "It appealed not to the inward illumination of mystic experience, but to the observable and verifiable objects of empirical science." This was as true of the Society for the Diffusion of Spiritual Knowledge, founded in 1854, as it would be of the organization that psychologist William James established in 1885, the American Society for Psychical Research (ASPR), whose members included such luminaries as Charles Eliot Norton, Josiah Royce, Charles Sanders Pierce, and Theodore Roosevelt. Like them, Pinchot embraced the scientific enterprise, even in matters of the supernatural.[31]

Such an embrace did not squeeze out Pinchot's sense of the divine. A careful observer, for twenty years he kept a meticulous log of his innumerable interactions with Laura; most days, he recorded in his diary, were either "clear" or "cloudy," "bright" or "blind." These were not meteorological observations but rather indications of the clarity of his encounters with the dearly departed. Yet this record-keeping had an important spiritual end. It brought him to an intimate sense of and a mystical appreciation for an omnipresent God. Laura, who "was one with God," served as Gifford's guide to holiness and peace. "One beautiful moment" with her presence in May 1896 reinforced his belief (and hope) "that the natural body is not raised" after death, "but a wholly different spiritual body." In this new state would Laura also become his bride; they were joined together during a "beautiful evening, following a good day. My Lady and I are one in the sight of God," he confirmed in August 1894. More direct was his diary entry for April 22, 1896: after a late evening sojourn outside of what he called "our house," the Washington abode in which Laura had died, he commented that "in God's sight, my Lady and I are husband and wife."[32]

Why did such a robust and energetic young man fall madly in love with an invalid? Why did he choose to link himself with a beautiful young woman who would soon die, and then nurse his intense affection for her for so long after her death? The benefits of this richly imagined matrimony were at once personal and professional. Gifford had argued forcefully with his skeptical parents that a healthy Laura would be a helpmate, not a hindrance to his career. So she proved to be in the afterlife. Convinced that she guided him through complex negotiations with Congress, he believed too that she steadied his voice when he delivered important speeches. Behind this most successful man hovered a remarkable female consciousness, a fact he slipped into the public record in 1910 when he dedicated his book *The Fight for Conservation* to 𝕃𝕙, the font of which was appropriately funereal. Her tragic demise had had a silver lining. Gifford could at once freely and fully adore Laura and ardently pursue his parents' and his own great expectations. His and Laura's was thus also a marriage of convenience, for the challenge of finding a woman his parents would accept was too overwhelming; he would not marry until his father had died and his mother was on her deathbed.[33]

MIDLIFE CRISIS

James and Mary Pinchot's final years marked a period of transition in the extended Pinchot family. In the weeks before his father's death in February 1908—James had been struck with the grippe in late December—Gifford stayed close to home, attending to his dying father's needs, distracting his mother by going on long drives in the family's electric car, and arranging the impending funeral; on January 26, with his father feeling "very comfortable," Gifford slipped over to the White House, Mary Pinchot wrote in her diary, for the "first time in weeks."[34]

Following James Pinchot's death on February 6, Gifford's disengagement increased. He admitted to a friend that "things became a good deal disorganized with me." Small wonder. Since Gifford's birth, his father had been an omnipresent guide, advisor, and occasional scold. He had made extensive use of his thick network of social ties and political contacts to open doors for his son that would have been closed to other, less well-connected petitioners. For many of the same reasons, as he drew on the affection of well-placed family members and close friends, and tapped into the good offices of Republican Party stalwarts and former Union generals to give Gifford a leg up, so James and his wife built a sumptuous home at 1615 Rhode Island Avenue in Washington, D.C., as a domicile for them and their bachelor son. In its ballroom and parlors the senior Pinchots entertained and courted the city's power brokers and social elite, leaving little to chance in their desire to advance Gifford's prospects.[35]

The richly appointed, book-lined library in the family's Washington, D.C., home on Rhode Island Avenue was a favorite workplace for Gifford Pinchot. Grey Towers NHL

If James Pinchot could not control something, he worried about it, and so regularly posted cautionary missives even to his adult son. As twenty-five-year-old Gifford prepared to head south in 1891 for a "long trip through the pine country alone," for example, he learned from his father about the dangers that awaited the venturesome. Head not "where you do not know all about the region you are about to explore," his father stressed. "The falling of a horse or an accident among the negroes and ignorant whites might be serious." He felt compelled to give this advice even though he recognized that it often fell on deaf ears. "I know you think I am always too alert about dangers but you cannot be too careful."[36]

To protect Gifford was also to promote his professional ambitions. When James urged his son, fresh from his year-long study of European forestry, to establish his name by writing the first American primer on the subject, he insisted that Gifford not let his competition know anything about his authorial ambitions. The key threat was Bernhard Fernow. "Remember that you cannot be too cautious in saying things to Fernow or to [German forester Ribbentrop] that Fernow will hear. If you decide to tell R. about the book be sure to commit him to secrecy."[37]

Besting Gifford's rivals was also the secret ambition behind the family's munificent gift to Yale in 1900, to establish there a school of forestry; this school, the family hoped, would outstrip the school that Fernow had established at Cornell and the one Carl Schenck directed at Biltmore. In hoping to eclipse these earlier educational ventures—and both would close shortly after Yale opened—the Pinchots promoted a nativist desire to liberate forestry in the United States from foreign influences. "We had small confidence in the leadership of Dr. Fernow or Dr. Schenck," Gifford Pinchot later wrote combatively. "We distrusted them and their German lack of faith in American Forestry. What we wanted was American foresters trained by Americans in American ways for the work ahead in American forests." Spoken like his father's son.[38]

And what better way for Gifford to honor this extraordinary paternal activism on his behalf than to ensure that his father had a prominent place from which to observe the fulfillment of one of Gifford's greatest successes? In 1905, he appointed James Pinchot the first vice president of that year's American Forest Congress, for which Theodore Roosevelt was honorary president and Secretary of Agriculture James Wilson was president. This convention, which the younger Pinchot had organized, was called to pressure the U.S. Congress into finally passing legislation that would transfer the nation's forest reserves from the Department of the Interior to the Agriculture Department. The maneuvering had begun under Bernhard Fernow in 1897, and intensified when Pinchot succeeded him as chief of the Division of Forestry in 1898. Convincing the Department of the Interior to relinquish the lands was as challenging as swaying western representatives and senators; no bureaucracy easily gives up assets such as the 63 million acres of public land that were to be transferred. The constituencies that exploited the resources those lands contained also understandably resisted a change in their status. Even the powerful Speaker of the House, Joe Cannon, was dead set against the transfer; without his support, no such legislation would pass the House.[39]

By 1903, however, a group of forces came together that gave Pinchot optimism that the transfer was in the offing. In response to steady lobbying by the American Forestry Association and the acknowledgment by Interior's Ethan A. Hitchcock that a transfer would produce "better administrative results," as well as President Roosevelt's public declaration of support, which Pinchot believed helped change Cannon's mind, congressional opposition began to melt. Two years later, in January 1905, the American Forest Congress passed a resolution calling for the transfer; less than a month later, on February 1, Roosevelt signed a bill that turned the forests over to the Bureau of Forestry (formerly the Division of Forestry and soon to be renamed the Forest Service), with Gifford Pinchot at its head. "What I had been hoping for and working for, from the moment I came into the old Forestry Division seven long years before, had finally arrived," the new chief forester wrote with enthusiasm, a sentiment his now-ill father most certainly shared.[40]

James Pinchot knew even better than his son just how long it had taken to reach this triumphant moment. After all, it had been he who, twenty years earlier, had urged Gifford to consider a career in forestry, and who now could witness from a front-row seat the much-anticipated, long-deferred marriage of American foresters and the nation's forests. In recognition of the intensity with which James Pinchot had oriented Gifford's now-realized aspirations, the son with sweet loyalty later would offer this eulogy. "My Father's foresight and tenacity were responsible, in the last analysis, for bringing Forestry to this continent. That being true, he was and is fairly entitled to be called the Father of Forestry in America."[41]

Mary Pinchot, whom Gifford would help bury six years later in 1914, never received such a public encomium. Yet her fixation on him, often at the expense of her younger children Antoinette and Amos, was every bit as intense as her husband's. Nicknamed "the mouse"—a generally affectionate term her children would use in their correspondence about her—she never hesitated to roar in her favorite son's defense. Speaking to a *Detroit News* reporter in January 1910 shortly after President Taft had fired Gifford, she asserted her faith in her son's abilities and touted her role in their development. "I record as the paramount blessing of my life that I am Gifford Pinchot's mother." As one "who helped to form his ideals," she affirmed that she had "always ardently sympathized with all that he hoped to do." In fact, she had gone beyond sympathizing by offering a piece of shrewd advice to Gifford that for the rest of his life he sought to follow. To successfully promote forestry, she written him in 1890, he must "help make a public opinion which will force the Government to do what ought to be done."[42]

Her decided preference for her eldest put Gifford's siblings in his shadow; Mary and James Pinchot's close identification with and large ambitions for their oldest child colored relationships not only within the Pinchot household but between the Pinchot children and those with whom they formed attachments.

Tall like her older brother, and an "angular beauty," Antoinette, who was born in 1868, was not in direct competition with Gifford. Her parents, like the broader culture, had no expectation that a young woman of wealth would pursue a career in the public eye. But it cannot be a coincidence that she married a diplomat—and an English one at that—whose career would take them abroad, and thus beyond her parents' reach and outside Gifford's radiant sphere. After being stationed in Denmark and The Hague, she and her husband would finally settle in England, with a retreat in the south of France, and from these distant posts she would maintain affectionate relations with her nuclear family via correspondence.[43]

Her strategy was effective as long as the other Pinchots stayed on their side of the Atlantic. But when in 1900 Nettie met up with twenty-eight-year-old Amos and his bride, Gertrude Minturn, who were then on an extended European honeymoon, and was later joined by James Pinchot, Mary Pinchot sensed there might be trouble. She cautioned her husband before he sailed from New York: "Don't worry about her, or worry her—she is an independent being and has a right to do as she thinks best. We have got to give them up sometime, and we might as well begin to do so by degrees. I [will] not wait until they [have] broken with us."[44]

Mary was right to worry. No sooner had the Pinchots reunited on the continent than the air grew thick with accusations, recriminations, and bruised feelings, with James Pinchot leading the charge. "Father insists on fighting with Nettie whenever the occasion offers," Amos wrote to Gifford, and their sister, used to running her own life, did not back down: "I

*Strong-willed like
her brother Gifford,
Antoinette ("Nettie")
Eno Pinchot (1869–1934)
married an English diplo-
mat, spent her adult life in
Europe, and groomed her
only child, Harcourt, for a
career in English politics.*
Grey Towers NHL

intend to speak to Nettie about it for she is absolutely pugnacious, unreasonable, and incapable of seeing two sides to anything." Her unwillingness
to compromise—hardly unusual in this family of strong wills—was finally
attributable, Amos thought, to her frail health; she "is in bad shape in my
opinion and that is why she is so sensitive to opposition and so silly in her
tenets on various subjects." Silly or not, she made certain thereafter to steer
clear of her father.[45]

Nettie found release in charting her own course in her adopted land.
There she was active in campaigns for women's rights and threw open her
English home to Allied soldiers suffering from the aftershocks of World
War I; a magnetic woman, she gathered round her a large coterie of friends
and acquaintances. These social causes sustained her until the very end.
"Those who called on her when she was ill, with some hope of amusing
her," the *London Times* reported shortly after her death on July 1, 1934,

"soon found that the wit, the humor, the incisive phrase and pungent criticism, the ordered knowledge and force in argument were all coming from the exhausted invalid."[46]

Every bit her mother's daughter, while healthy she had devoted this same inexhaustible energy and expansive list of contacts to guide her only child—Harcourt Johnstone, known as "Crinks"—in his political career in the Liberal Party. After his defeat in the 1927 election for the House of Commons from West Wilts, for instance, Crinks wrote in praise of her activism to his uncle Gifford. "We had a close fight—and a long one as English elections go—and Ma displayed a really remarkable power of speaking + still more—of making herself beloved by the people." Commiserating with his nephew about his loss—"I have been licked so many times in so many different ways that I have become sort of immune to it"—Gifford was delighted to learn "how large a part your Mother had in the fight." His sister Nettie may have run away from home, but she carried with her the Pinchot political acumen.[47]

Amos was not so lucky, never finding a niche of his own; he suffered from (and by) comparisons to his dynamic brother for most of his life. This was particularly manifest as he came into adulthood. No sooner had Amos set foot on the Yale campus in 1893 than Gifford came to New Haven to introduce him to favored faculty, friends, and haunts, a fraternal generosity that Mary Pinchot much praised. "You are indeed most happy to have been introduced by your Brother—and such a one—who has the warm respect and regard of all who know him." This only served to double the pressure on Amos. "You will have his reputation to live up to and also your own—for we all have such confidence in you that we feel that your own standard will keep you up, let alone his."[48]

Yet Amos could not be his brother's better, the family made clear in the choices it thought were open to him in the years following his graduation from Yale. Knowing Amos's fascination with the outdoors—he was an avid hunter and angler—Gifford hoped to bring his brother in under his wing; the fledgling forestry movement could use his sharp mind. First at Biltmore, and later while serving the Department of the Interior as a consulting forester in the summer and fall of 1897, Gifford had induced Amos to spend time with him in the woods; whether running surveys in the

Appalachians or in the mountainous West, they always found time to break away. Amos loved these opportunities to go deep into the backcountry, where they could hunt deer along the wooded ravines of western North Carolina, or stalk mountain goat in the Cascades, or fish along Montana's pristine rivers.

As much as he reveled in these moments with his brother, though, bedding down each night amid arboreal splendor, Amos was overwhelmed by Gifford's full-throttled approach. "You make hard work out of everything you do—even loafing and doing things for fun!" Amos joked truthfully after spending time at Biltmore in 1893. "For the sake of the family I hope to become a shiftless bummer and be able to take it easy sometimes without busting any gut or getting too small for my clothes. It would even things up and redress, from a 'point of diminishing returns' to a normal point, the family expenditure of energy." His gentle reproof, repeated over the years— "I know that it is harder for you than for most people to be lazy," he wrote three years later, "but I wish you would be sometimes"—made it clear that however enticing the physical landscape through which Gifford moved, forestry as his brother practiced it was not for him.[49]

Nor was the law. Amos's legal studies at Columbia, which he began in 1897, were "as uninteresting as the deuce," he confessed to Gifford, and when war with Spain broke out the next year, he abandoned his moldering law books for the thrill of combat. Although he never saw fighting, the succeeding months were not dull. If nothing else, his ever-anxious parents were thrown into a panic, especially by the thought that their son had enlisted in the U.S. Army as a private. While Amos trained at a base in Hempstead, Long Island, James Pinchot came up with a plan to elevate his son's rank and keep him out of the war, using his political pull to secure an officer's commission. Gifford, whom his parents had deputized to visit Amos, doubted that such interference was the best strategy: "With the small chance that there seems to be that the Troop will be sent away I am not sure that it would be a good plan for Amos to get a commission." Besides, he added, "there seems to be no chance of his staying a private." That was in part due to Amos's abilities, his unwillingness to leave his comrades, and a diminished tolerance for life at the bottom. "I can see that the routine of a private's life is beginning to wear on him a little," Gifford observed in July.

Later that month, Private Pinchot shipped off for Puerto Rico on the S.S. *Massachusetts,* where a string of misfortunes befell him. Riding a mule on maneuvers, he tumbled over a cliff and the mule landed on him, permanently damaging his hip; then, recovering in a hospital, he contracted typhoid fever. Gifford was dispatched to bring Amos back to New York and then enrolled him in the New York School of Law, from which he graduated the following year. What Secretary of State John Hay had dubbed a "Splendid Little War," for Amos had been anything but.[50]

A sense of frustration colored much of Amos's subsequent life, too. In 1900, he married "well" but unhappily. His career prospects would prove as exasperating. While Amos and his bride, Gertrude, were on a Grand Tour of Europe for their honeymoon, he capitulated to his mother's wishes that upon his return to the United States he become the family's lawyer and financial advisor. "I am willing and anxious to come home and take the best care of things I can *at once (I mean by this not attempting to invent and do things on my own),*" he confirmed to Mary Pinchot in April 1901, "but merely . . . to collect rents, deposit coupons and inspect the real estate we own." Amos understood that this labor would free his father from these thankless tasks and would enable Gifford to pursue his career unburdened by such quotidian responsibilities; his older brother, Amos accepted, had been the one raised "to do something important."[51]

There were moments of significance for Amos, however. At his brother's side, he became a stalwart in the progressive wing of the Republican Party, and emerged as an intimate member of Theodore Roosevelt's inner circle, particularly during the excited run-up to the 1912 election. He would later break with the Rough Rider, join the Democratic Party, and, after voting for Wilson in 1916, find himself in a curious situation: "It is hard for me to get used to the idea of your victory," he wrote the reelected president, "for I have hardly ever been on the winning side." By the 1930s, fearful of the growth in executive authority under Franklin Roosevelt, Amos Pinchot moved sharply to the political right; he always felt most comfortable on the margins.[52]

It was while an activist in the Progressive movement that Amos first claimed his own ground, using his words and money to advocate political change through his writings for and financial donations to a variety of jour-

Amos Richard Eno Pinchot (1873–1944), third child of James and Mary Pinchot, was a talented but troubled polemicist. A staunch progressive in the early twentieth century, by the 1930s he had migrated to the political right—in contrast to his brother's continuing radicalization.
Grey Towers NHL

nals, among them *The Masses, The New Republic,* and *The Nation.* His first major publication, entitled "Two Revolts Against Oligarchy," detailed the rise of insurgent parties in American history in response to corrupt imbalances of power. Its appearance in the muckraking *McClure's Magazine* in 1911 won Amos considerable notice, an excited Gifford wrote home. "Men like Governor [George C.] Pardee [of California] tell me they have read it two or three times, and everyone is agreed that it is beyond question the article of the month. It has given Amos an important position at one stroke."[53]

Emboldened, Amos soon set aside his pen for the hustings. Announcing his campaign on the Progressive Party ticket for the New York state senate in 1914, he promised to offer a radical alternative to contemporary stand-pat politics. It was not his advocacy of collective bargaining and the need to recognize labor unions that prematurely ended Amos's aggressive bid for office, however, but an unassailable claim on his familial allegiance. When that year Gifford became the Washington (Progressive) Party candidate for the U.S. Senate from Pennsylvania, a fatally ill Mary Pinchot asked Amos to stand aside. He complied. "[O]f course I should not think of going into the primary for the Senate if it would hurt Gifford's chances," he assured his mother. "I'm glad enough for any excuse not to have to go in and fight."[54]

That he would not stand up for his rights in this instance, however understandable given his mother's failing health, was part of a larger pattern of deference, a poignant marker of which was his decision to name his first-born son after his brother. Yet if Amos thought this would gain for the newest Gifford something of his namesake's prestige within the family, here too he would be mistaken; in 1915, the elder Gifford would reclaim his name upon the birth of his own son, Gifford Bryce Pinchot.[55]

As with his siblings, Gifford struggled to come to terms with his life as an adult, especially during the six years between his parents' deaths. A telling signal that he had begun to detach himself from the emotional moorings that had bound up his youthful world was that Laura Houghteling began to fade from his diary after his father died; the daily notations became less frequent, and the once-detailed commentary on his dreams and meditations about her nearly disappeared. There were still moments of mystical contact—in January 1911 he noted that he had had a vivid dream "of my Dearest"—but they are most notable for their absence. The growing importance of the most vital Cornelia Bryce was yet another sign of the changes in Pinchot's psychological orientation. It was only appropriate, for example, that the July 30, 1914, entry in his diary indicated that it was "not a clear day," code for his inability to "see" his beloved Laura. That was perhaps the last time he would employ this deeply resonant phrase. Now he yearned for a woman of this world, and he finally felt able to link his life with hers. The next day he would speak to Lloyd and Edith Cooper Bryce about his matrimonial intentions and his love for their daughter.[56]

Gifford Bryce Pinchot (1915–1989), Gifford and Cornelia's only surviving child, was raised in a loving and emotionally stable household, but he had no interest in replicating his parents' often turbulent public careers.
Grey Towers NHI.

This temporal soul helped him in ways the ephemeral Laura never could. Within hours of their marriage, Gifford and Cornelia Bryce Pinchot hopped a ferry across Long Island Sound to visit his terminally ill mother, and to share their happiness with her as she lay dying. They then headed to Pennsylvania to kick off Gifford's whirlwind (if ultimately unsuccessful) campaign to unseat two-term incumbent Republican senator Boies Penrose. Within days—nine to be precise—Gifford and Cornelia put this electoral bid on hold, to bury and then mourn Mary Pinchot. Eighteen months later, Cornelia gave birth to what would ultimately prove to be the Pinchots' only surviving child, Gifford Bryce. A son no more, fifty-year-old Gifford Pinchot would finally find immense compensation in his new, compelling, and challenging roles as husband and father; his was a belated but fecund coming of age.

A Political Natural

T HEY CALLED it a "coal party." In early May 1911, several hundred citizens of Cordova, Alaska, led by a former mayor, members of the city council, and the chamber of commerce, stormed the wharves on which the Copper River and Northwest Railroad stored tons of imported Canadian anthracite. They dumped as much as they could into the deep waters of Controller Bay, claiming historical sanction for their protest; like the participants in the Boston Tea Party of the 1770s, the Cordovans were striking back at a distant colonial government. Then they put the torch to their own King George III, burning an effigy of Gifford Pinchot, denounced by *The Alaska-Yukon Magazine* as a man who "thinks more of trees than people."[1]

Demonstrations flared in other port towns. Along the docks of Seward and Valdez, signs were tacked up that decried a 1908 order from President Roosevelt that had withdrawn coal deposits on public land in Alaska from lease or sale, and thus from mining. Others lambasted Pinchot's presumed role in support of Roosevelt's order. As one placard declaimed:

PINCHOT : MY POLICY

No patents to coal; All timber to forest reserves; Bottle Up Alaska; Put
Alaska in forest reserves; Save Alaska for all time to come.

In the village of Katalla, the citizenry first incinerated a copy of Roosevelt's order and then ignited the by-now requisite representation of the
forester Alaskans most loved to hate.[2]

As dramatic as these ritualized slayings may have been, they were of
comparatively little moment to the bloody—if still mock—executions that
had been under way in Washington, D.C., for the preceding twenty-four
months. Among those who lost (or would lose) their place as a consequence
of the brawl known as the Ballinger-Pinchot controversy were Gifford
Pinchot, Richard Achilles Ballinger, secretary of the Department of the
Interior, and President Roosevelt's successor, William Howard Taft. The
root cause of their individual and collective political demise was differing
conceptions of the authority of the executive branch to enact and enforce
the kind of conservation legislation that had so riled Alaska. Pinchot and
the Forest Service had hugely benefited from Theodore Roosevelt's conservationist ethos and his liberal interpretation of the executive's capacity to
legislate on behalf of that ethic. But when Roosevelt left office in March
1909, his successor did not share his assumption about the extent and range
of executive power; as strict constructionists, Taft and Ballinger were also
wary of challenging congressional authority.

Their political perspective, Pinchot would come to believe, smacked of
a reactionary urge to undercut the gains the conservation movement had
made under Roosevelt's more forceful and aggressive presidency. But
through late May 1909 he was willing to give the new president the benefit
of the doubt. Responding to a correspondent who questioned Taft's fidelity
to the cause, Pinchot praised the president's steadfastness. "I am sure you do
injustice to President Taft's sincerity and strength of purpose. His stand has
been definitely taken for the defense of the interests of the country in the
entire field of conservation." At the very least, he counseled, "suspend judgment until there has been time for the situation to become clear."[3]

He was less charitable toward Ballinger, with whom he had clashed
repeatedly over the regulation of public lands and the management of their
resources. When the secretary revoked the Roosevelt administration's earlier decision to not sell or lease potential waterpower sites for development,
for example, Pinchot sought to outflank his rival by impressing on Taft in a
private meeting the need to keep the sites under public control. After two

such visits in late April, Taft brought Ballinger to heel, reported Pinchot to good friend James Garfield, under whose watch as Roosevelt's secretary of the interior these sites had been withdrawn. As a result, in Pinchot's words, Ballinger is "now giving out that he is all for conservation, that being Taft's policy." This was apparently but a short-term success, for in July Pinchot decided that Ballinger's formal goal was "to stop the conservation movement," a marker of which was his continued willingness to "turn over government lands to the water power trust."[4]

Within months of Taft's inaugural in March 1909, then, these growing differences of opinion had begun to harden, and the personal animosities became more vivid. "I think the whole problem in the present situation," observed Oscar Lawler, legal counsel for Ballinger's Department of the Interior, "is the apparent inability of Messrs. Pinchot and [F. H.] Newell [the soon-to-be-fired director of the Reclamation Service] to realize that an opinion that certain action is not legally justifiable does not of necessity involve the conclusion that the persons so opining are enemies of their plans." But enemies both sets of players felt the other to be, leading Ballinger and Pinchot (and staff in Interior and the Forest Service) to engage in open warfare that crippled the capacity of the Taft administration to govern. By November, relations had so deteriorated that some Republican Party operatives argued publicly that the only way to stop the political bloodbath was by "lopping off the head of Gifford Pinchot."[5]

Two months later, he was axed. In the resultant furor, which was driven by a press-feeding frenzy new to twentieth-century politics, and a closely followed congressional investigation whose records when published ran to thirteen volumes, Richard Ballinger himself became a liability. Calls for his resignation had surfaced in the summer of 1909, and their numbers surged following Pinchot's firing. He first tendered his resignation in January 1911, but Taft persuaded him to stay on, only to accept a second resignation offered that March as the damage to Taft's electoral prospects mounted. In the end, even the president could not escape the consequences of the Ballinger-Pinchot controversy. The Republican Party splintered in the months before the 1912 elections, with progressives such as Pinchot rallying to the Bull Moose candidacy of Theodore Roosevelt, a schism that allowed Democrat Woodrow Wilson to capture the White House. Taft polled a

scant eight electoral votes; his ignominious defeat reinforced his earlier conclusion that while Ballinger had been the target of one of the "most
unscrupulous conspiracies for the defamation of character that history can
show," he had been "the ultimate object of the attack." Like the aggrieved
Alaskans who had wreaked havoc on Pinchot's likeness, Taft knew whom
to blame for his bitter loss.[6]

POWER STRUGGLES

The reasons that Taft had cashiered Pinchot had been many, his options
few. Certainly differing political philosophies help explain the intellectual
context surrounding the president's decision to remove the chief forester.
But it was also grounded in a specific set of circumstances that, as the protesters in Valdez and Cordova had understood, revolved around conflict-
ing interpretations of coal claims near Katalla, Alaska. They were known
as the "Cunningham claims," so called because prospector Clarence Cunningham had first located them on lands that would become part of the
Chugach National Forest. Their legitimacy had been under investigation
since 1905. Rumors had circulated that the original claimants, each of whom
by law was restricted to 160 acres and each of whom had to demonstrate
that he was working his stake before securing title to the land, by prior
agreement had actually signed over their individual rights to the Morgan-
Guggenheim syndicate, a powerful resource extraction cartel.

With funding from financier J. P. Morgan and the Guggenheim-domi-
nated American Smelting and Refining Co., the organization was, in Pinchot's opinion, "one of the most powerful combinations of capital in America." If collusion between the original claimants and the syndicate could be
proven, this would have amounted to an illegal transfer of land title and of
subsurface mineral deposits. By federal law, when claimants applied for a
patent to public coal lands from the General Land Office (GLO) of the
Interior Department, they had to confirm that they were applying for title
"for my own benefit, and not directly or indirectly, in whole or in part, in
behalf of any person or persons whatsoever." Cunningham had so sworn,
but investigators for the GLO were suspicious that he had in fact followed
a well-established pattern of land fraud in the American West in which

conniving resource-extractive industries employed dummy claimants to secure control of public lands.[7]

One of those whose suspicions were aroused was Louis R. Glavis, chief of the GLO's investigative unit in Portland, Oregon. Believing he had uncovered evidence of fraud when he located a July 1907 land option agreement between Cunningham and representatives of the Morgan-Guggenheim syndicate, Glavis had objected to the opening of the claims. His superior, Seattle attorney Richard A. Ballinger, then head of the GLO, rejected Glavis's findings of fraud and removed him from the investigations. Ironically, GLO officials had already concluded on technical grounds that the Cunningham claims could not be patented because the claimants had missed a filing deadline; Ballinger's rejection of Glavis's arguments, however, allowed the controversy to simmer for another two years.[8]

That is when a frustrated Glavis turned to the Forest Service for help. Why he contacted the agency is not entirely clear. According to James Penick, whose *Progressive Politics and Conservation* (1968) remains the most complete and compelling analysis of the Ballinger-Pinchot imbroglio, Glavis surely knew that the GLO would turn back the claims. But he wanted to continue the investigation so that criminal proceedings could be brought against the Cunningham group, Penick argued. Since the GLO evidently had no desire to bring charges—Ballinger's removal of Glavis from the case indicated as much—Glavis sent a telegram to Alexander C. Shaw, a Forest Service law officer, suggesting that that agency might want to assess the current status of the Cunningham claims. His was not a random contact. President Roosevelt, on his last day in office, had expanded by executive order the size of the Chugach National Forest, bringing under its jurisdiction four of the contested claims. Yet the GLO had failed to notify the Forest Service that it was conducting public hearings on these claims, a failure Glavis's telegram rectified, and with spectacular consequences.[9]

The Forest Service rapidly responded to Glavis's information, immediately contacting the GLO for permission to examine all the relevant documentation of the claims and requesting that any hearings associated with the lands be delayed pending its analysis of the situation. Its swift reaction had much to do with its long-standing distrust of what it believed was the GLO's dubious record of protecting the public lands under its control.

The GLO took umbrage at these suggestions of its laxity or corruption. "The department of the interior has charge of all public lands," Ballinger vented in the *Seattle Post-Intelligencer,* "and does not intend that the forestry bureau, a part of another department, shall run the department of the interior." Roiling the waters further was the history of rocky relations Ballinger and Pinchot had had during Roosevelt's first term, a personal animus in part born of the bureaucratic politics associated with the transfer of the nation's forest reserves from the GLO in Interior to the newly created Forest Service in Agriculture. A sign of just how fraught their relationship had become was Pinchot's growing conviction that Ballinger—who in 1908 had left the GLO and served as attorney for the Cunningham claimants, only to return to government service as Taft's secretary of the interior—was a decided opponent of conservationism. If Galvis was correct that the Ballinger-led Interior Department was squelching a potential criminal investigation into land fraud in Alaska, it seemed only to confirm Pinchot's suspicions.[10]

To bring these complicated, internecine matters to a head, Pinchot set up an interview between President Taft and Glavis, to be held in early August 1909 at the president's summer retreat in Beverly, Massachusetts. Its purpose was to enable the GLO investigator to share his findings and concerns directly with the chief executive, and to explain his perceptions of Ballinger's perfidy. In a letter to Taft in which he introduced Glavis, Pinchot stressed that the "issues are large and can be handled by no one but yourself," an argument that placed Taft in a predicament. Were Taft persuaded by Glavis's brief, then Ballinger's position would be compromised, as would his standing within the administration. If Glavis was unable to convince the president of the validity of his charges, then the internal administrative struggle would undoubtedly spin out of control. "[P]arts of Glavis's story are so much known," Pinchot warned the president, "that I believe it will be impossible to prevent its becoming public, in part at least, and before very long."[11]

High-level employees of the Forest Service, including Shaw and assistant director Overton Price, helped Glavis prepare his case for delivery to the president, and within days of the Beverly meeting these men had leaked copies of documents pertaining to the GLO's handling of the Cunningham claims to the national press. Pinchot kept his distance from these backdoor operations, advising a friend that he had "said nothing about the Ballinger controversy to the newspapers, and I shall not unless, which I do not anticipate, the necessity for a complete exposure of the whole thing should arise in the somewhat distant future." The pressures to comment on the case were great, but "I shall try to keep in such a position that no one can lay any indiscretion at my door. This fight has only just begun, and I do not want to make any mistake, at least in this part of the proceedings." That he anticipated the "fight" would proceed in a certain manner suggested that he and his staff believed that the battle with Ballinger would force the president's hand. This "controversy has been very helpful in many ways," Pinchot concluded. "It ought to be a good deal more so before we get through with it."[12]

When in response to Forest Service tactics the equally adept GLO staff fed sympathetic reporters their version of events, the public spectacle was well launched. It grew larger in mid-September, when the president exonerated Ballinger of all charges leveled against him and authorized him to remove Glavis from office. This implicated the president—or so Pinchot assumed—in the whole sordid affair, a reaction that Taft anticipated. He urged Ballinger and his subordinates to expunge from their accounts "any references to Pinchot or the part he took in bringing Glavis's report to my attention" to maintain at least the appearance of administrative unity, and to turn down the heat the controversy had begun to generate. Of Pinchot, the president asked for greater circumspection. "I should consider it one of the greatest losses that my administration could sustain if you were to leave it," Taft wrote the chief forester, and then asked for his help in bringing "public discussion between departments and bureaus to an end."[13]

The only figure who seemed to relish the building controversy was Pinchot. He received what he would describe as the president's "most considerate and friendly letter" while fishing off the waters around San Clemente Island, the southernmost of the Santa Barbara Islands of California. He had gone there to recover from a hectic tour of the West, during which he had delivered a series of stirring speeches urging the president to remain true to Roosevelt's conservationist agenda. Pinchot also had held to a rigorous schedule of site inspections of forest ranger stations throughout the coastal states. Trolling for Pacific marlin on "a late, still afternoon," riding "the glassy heave on the ocean as the great Pacific rollers came in around the end of San Clemente Island," was thus a welcome tonic. More rejuvenating still was his epic battle, lasting two and a half hours, to land a 186-pound marlin one dusk: "High out of water sprang this splendid creature, then lunged with his lance along the surface, his big eye staring as he rose, till the impression of beauty and lithe power was enough to make a man's heart sing within him. It was a moment to be remembered for a lifetime."[14]

When Pinchot recounted this episode in essay form, the simply titled "Marlin at San Clemente" offered a discursive tale about a middle-aged man and the sea. As night descended, and with "Mexican Joe," his powerful oarsman, unable to brake the marlin's seaward surge, Pinchot found himself pitted against a worthy rival in a contest of will and strength that left him exhausted. Laboring to reel in the hooked marlin, he doubted "whether the stimulus of self-respect and the dread of failure were as strong in the fish as they were in me." Finally, more than seven miles offshore, Pinchot and his companion, "with a strong heave slid the great and beautiful creature in the boat."

Exhilarated at having landed what was thought to be the largest marlin yet captured in the cold Pacific waters, Pinchot also laughed at his triumph. The essay is accompanied by a photograph of him ashore, dressed in a suit and straw boater and standing stiffly next to the now-vertical marlin; the caption queries: "Don't you think both man and fish look stuffed?" He also minimized his record-setting accomplishment by admitting that it did not—because it could not—trump all other moments with rod and reel. "A good many men have asked me whether the gentler kinds of angling still hold their charm after such big sea fishing," he noted. "My answer is, Emphatically, yes. I have taken also tarpon, kingfish, yellowtail, the Eastern jewfish, and the Western black sea bass, the albacore, and many kinds of sharks, but in spite of it all I can still watch a float in a pond with the same pleasure, if not the same thrill, as when I was a boy."[15]

Contemporaries drew more-political conclusions from what a newspaper headline asserted was "Pinchot's Battle in Dark with Dangerous Swordfish"; its superhead read: "He Got Him." Who he got was left for readers to extrapolate. But to the horde of mainland reporters who sailed out to the island seeking interviews with Pinchot and his guests, among whom numbered former governor of California George Pardee and one of the state's current senators, Frank P. Flint, it was clear this was not just a story about man and fish. Pinchot would not talk with the press, having come to San Clemente for the solitude of open air and sea, but that did not stop another guest, C. F. Holder, from making the connection that the journalists hungered to publicize.

In stark contrast to the smoke-filled rooms in which Taft and Ballinger wheeled and dealed, and from which its minions issued backstabbing releases to a gullible press, Holden painted Pinchot in heroic hues. "Some time ago the *Argonaut* published an article describing Gifford Pinchot as a 'pink tea hero.' I wish I could have had the author of that article in my launch, as I followed Pinchot that dark night as he played that ten-foot fish in a heavy sea." Had the *Argonaut* reporter been there, Holden said, he would have swiftly revised his portrayal of the forester as an effete dandy: "[H]e would have seen the real Pinchot as I know him, a second Roosevelt in his manly qualities, a trained physical and mental athlete, a great big manly man, who fights in the open." A principled sportsman, he was a model citizen. "If I were asked to select an ideal type of the virile young American today, I would name Gifford Pinchot," for he was "the great and dominant personality in our national evolution."[16]

Holden's gushing words—and their implicit criticism of hothouse politics in the nation's capital—were widely disseminated, as was his advice that reporters had best "keep your eye on him." They did, helping to generate the rising chorus of praise that enveloped Pinchot at the conclusion of his two-week vacation. Everywhere he went he received a warm reception. In San Diego he was feted by such powerful figures as former secretary of the treasury Lyman Gage, sugar magnate John Spreckles, and newspaper titans E. W. Scripps and S. S. McClure; in Los Angeles he met with similarly well-placed power brokers. As Pinchot boasted to his mother, publicity surrounding the Ballinger affair had enhanced his renown. "Really, I seem to be getting to be a person." His growing prestige, when coupled with what he believed was a groundswell of support for the Forest Service and its conservation principles, gave him newfound protection. "I don't quite see how anyone can touch the Service or me."[17]

Pinchot carried that confidence with him into a hastily called series of meetings with President Taft in Salt Lake City on September 24–25. Before departing from Los Angeles, Pinchot issued what one newspaper called a "cautious" outline of "his stand in the recent controversy which has attracted national attention." The public lands must continue to be protected for reasons of economy and ethics, Pinchot asserted. "The forest is not alone useful for the timber we get from it; there are the streams, recreation grounds, shade and comfort, and fertile soil." This "first consideration" was superseded by another. "[W]ho is to get the benefit of conservation of the forests? That second question is not one of economics, it is greater, for it is primarily a question of morals." And how it was resolved would determine the nation's future. "The time fast approaches when we shall have to decide whether men or dollars control the country," and if the answer was that concentrated wealth would rule, then "we shall ourselves destroy the equality of opportunity," long an American birthright.[18]

Although Pinchot's tough words set the stage for a potentially dramatic encounter with Taft and Ballinger in Salt Lake, the secretary of the interior landed the first blow. Having arrived by train from Los Angeles just before the president's entourage pulled into the Denver & Rio Grande station, Pinchot remained on the platform to pay his respects to Taft and Ballinger. The latter, however, had no interest in being cordial. After stepping from the railcar, and with "a purpose plainly evident, Ballinger brushed sharply past Pinchot without a sign of recognition," a Salt Lake correspondent observed, "and shook hands heartily with [Senator] Borah [of Idaho]." An unfazed Pinchot, the reporter continued, then "turned to Taft and was greeted profusely, the President stopping several seconds with his hand in that of the chief forester. That the fight between the forester and the secretary of interior has gone so far as to involve personal animosities was indicated by Ballinger's treatment of Pinchot," not an auspicious beginning to Taft's campaign to reconcile these formidable rivals.[19]

The line between them was even more deeply etched in Pinchot's subsequent sessions with the president, according to the blunt, detailed record that Pinchot jotted down after his initial meeting with the chief executive. Having reassured the president that he would not resign (to which Taft "said he was greatly relieved, and said it with emphasis"), Pinchot did not promise to stop attacking Ballinger. On that issue, the two apparently were quite frank. "I explained fully that I have no confidence in Ballinger. [Taft] said my zeal was so great I tended to think any man who differed as to method was corrupt. I denied it and said I had not accused Ballinger of being corrupt." Pinchot then ended his chronicle with this critical declaration. "I said I would not make trouble if I could avoid it, but might be forced to, and he might be forced to fire me."[20]

It would come to that four months later. In early January 1910 Pinchot complied with a request from the chairman of the Committee on Agriculture, Senator J. P. Dolliver, for a letter detailing all he knew about the Cunningham claims, specifically the role that Overton Price and Alexander Shaw had played in orchestrating the agency's activities. After securing what Pinchot believed was Agriculture Secretary Wilson's permission to answer Dolliver's request, as was required by a recent Taft directive prohibiting officials from responding to congressional inquiries without their superior's permission, Pinchot sent his report to the senator. In it, he stoutly defended his subordinates' decision to make public key pieces of information about the Cunningham claims, for these were "properly within the knowledge of the Forest Service." While legal, their behavior was also morally derived: "Information had come to them which convinced them that the public interests in a matter within the line of their official duties were in grave danger at the hands of fraudulent claimants to these coal lands," Pinchot confirmed. Acting from a "high and unselfish sense of public duty," Shaw and Price "deliberately chose to risk their official positions rather than permit what they believed to be the wrongful loss of public property."

A powerful show of support for his colleagues, Pinchot's letter to Dolliver was also a barely disguised attack on the motivations and character of Ballinger and Taft; no one could miss the import of his defiant judgment that "[a]ction through the usual official channels, and finally even an appeal to the President, had resulted (because of what I believe to have been a mistaken impression of the facts) in eliminating from the government service, in the person of Glavis, the most vigorous defender of the people's interest." When the senator read these charged words on the chamber floor on January 6 and had Pinchot's letter published in the *Congressional Record,* the chief forester's fate was sealed.[21]

A Happy Solution of a Vexed Problem

*The Ballinger-Pinchot
controversy provided
cartoonists with an endless
series of opportunities to
poke fun at the central
protagonists*
Forest History Society

So was Taft's. After a lengthy and tense set of Cabinet meetings the next evening, the weary president put his signature on a letter notifying Pinchot that he had been removed from office. In so doing, Taft added new impetus to this seemingly interminable controversy, setting the stage for his political mentor to charge back into the center of the political arena, a charge that would force Taft into early retirement. "I believe he loves Theodore Roosevelt," wrote Archie Butt, a Taft confidante, "and a possible break with him or the possible charge of ingratitude is writhing him now."[22]

Pinchot, who also loved the former president, felt no such anxieties, and instead welcomed his future with open arms. Meeting the White House messenger at the door to his Washington home, he tore open Taft's envelope, "found the letter I half expected," and waved it at his mother, saying "I'm fired!" Her exultant response—"[m]y mother's eyes flashed, she threw back her head, flung one hand high above it, and answered with one word: 'Hurrah!'"—matched his own. Being sacked was a badge of honor.[23]

AFTERSHOCKS

It hurt nonetheless. "I am free for the larger fight" to establish an effective and durable national conservation movement, he wrote fellow forester George P. Ahern, but it "is hard to be out of the Service, I must admit." Without its founder, the agency itself was reeling, a response Pinchot had foreseen and sought to head off during ceremonies marking his last morning in office, January 8, 1910. The situation was delicate, requiring a restrained and sensitive response.

First meeting with the agency's leadership, Pinchot later joined a large, boisterous gathering of the full staff of the Forest Service's Washington office. Crowded together, the *Washington Post* reported, were "white and colored, men and women, varying in rank from charwoman to assistant chiefs." As he entered the general forum, he was greeted with a thunderous ovation, "as demonstrative as it was possible for three hundred persons to make," according to one account; the roar penetrated to the street below, leading a passerby to remark that "the whole service was insubordinate." Encouraging further unrest was not on Pinchot's mind; rather, he urged his fervent supporters to demonstrate their loyalty to him by sticking with the Forest Service. According to the *Washington Star,* he confirmed that "the work of conservation, to which they were devoting their lives, was greater than any one man or any administration, and should be carried on despite all obstacles." He might have been fired, but they must keep the faith.[24]

He had no intention of disappearing from the scene, however. "We are still in the same work—different parts of it, but always the same work," he noted of his ongoing commitment to their shared ideals, a congruence that he reinforced when he urged his now-former subordinates "to call on him whenever perplexing problems vexed them"; he assured them that the door to his palatial home at 1615 Rhode Island Avenue "would always be open to them." No longer the nation's forester, Pinchot nonetheless was positioning himself as a power behind the throne, a puissance that the far-distant citizens of Cordova, Alaska, acknowledged a year and a half later when they set a match to his likeness.[25]

Pinchot's veiled authority had been immediately reflected in what the press believed to be Taft's fortuitous selection of Henry S. Graves, then dean of the School of Forestry at Yale, to be the second chief of the Forest Service. Actually, there was nothing fortuitous about his choice of one of Pinchot's oldest friends and closest colleagues—the disgraced chief had helped arrange it.

Even as he had bid an emotional farewell to the assembled throng at the Forest Service's headquarters, he and his associates, most especially Herbert A. Smith, the agency's director of public relations, maneuvered to ensure a smooth transition in Forest Service leadership—smooth in the sense that the new chief would be someone who, while not currently employed in the agency, shared Pinchot's sense of its professional mission and political perspective. This was essential, Pinchot believed, for whomever "guided the future of the Forest Service . . . would have no small influence on the future of the great cause [of conservation] the Service had embodied and led."[26]

Worried that the president would select someone whom *he* could control and whose commitment to conservation would be muted, and hearing rumors that A. P. Davis of the Reclamation Bureau was under serious consideration as Pinchot's replacement, Pinchot and Smith embarked on what they considered a "benevolent conspiracy" to change the president's mind. Believing Davis "a first-rate man but without training in forestry," they quietly sought to scuttle his candidacy. Smith took the public lead, firing off a series of telegrams. One went to Graves in New Haven, urging him to consider the appointment (if offered). Another went to Lee McClung, then Taft's secretary of the treasury but formerly treasurer of Yale University; he was requested to persuade Anson Stokes Phelps, Yale's current secretary, to slip Graves's name before Taft, yet another son of Eli.

This complicated series of contacts within an old-boy network produced the outcome Pinchot and Smith desired: Davis never interviewed with Taft; A. F. Potter, the acting chief of the Forest Service, did but withdrew in favor of Graves. After Graves's session with Taft, on January 12—a mere five days after Pinchot had been dismissed—the dean of the school of forestry that the Pinchot family had established became the new chief of the Forest Service, the agency that Gifford Pinchot had created. Taft had unknowingly done Pinchot's bidding, one good reason why Graves's appointment gave the fired forester such a sense of "keen satisfaction."[27]

This quiet, behind-the-scenes activity was a bellwether for the complex relationship that would unfold between Pinchot and the Graves-led agency. Pinchot, for instance, never indicated why he did not support Potter's ascension, but his long-standing friendship with and considerable professional respect for Graves were probably not the sole reasons for preferring the Yale dean. Though he had once worked as Pinchot's second-in-command in the Division of Forestry, Graves, by coming in from the outside, could be counted on to operate with greater independence of President Taft than could Potter; without Graves's steadying hand, Pinchot's subordinates, stunned when their chief was fired, may not have been capable of resisting presidential mandates that ran counter to their perception of the agency's conservationist agenda.

Graves had another advantage. Like forest understory, over the years he had learned to thrive beneath Pinchot's overarching canopy. Their friendship had begun at Yale, and in 1893 Graves had begun a forestry apprenticeship under Pinchot's direction at Biltmore. He helped with Pinchot's forestry consultant work, and with financial help from the Pinchot family he had studied in Europe with Dietrich Brandis; in 1898, he had signed on as Pinchot's assistant director in the Division of Forestry. That Graves was used to being overshadowed would serve him well in the coming years when he would reflexively call upon Pinchot's well-developed capacity for political intrigue to protect the Forest Service from White House influence or congressional machinations.[28]

Taft was but the first of a long line of presidents who would discover just how effective this strategy could be. And Graves's selection, conversely, was the first sign of Pinchot's willingness to employ external forces to mold the agency's internal character, thereby securing some of the ends the former chief desired. He was still in the game, his presence at once clarifying and complicating the world in which the Forest Service, and its chiefs, operated.

Pinchot remained very much in play in the larger arena of national politics as well, despite Taft's having ejected him from office and, to some extent, because he had. Providing Pinchot with an ample platform on the national stage was the lengthy congressional investigation that would take testimony in forty-five sessions running from late January to mid-May. Planned before Pinchot was fired, its purpose, as the forester understood it in late December 1909, was to evaluate "the conduct of Secretary Ballinger, the Forest Service, and possibly the Reclamation Service and the Indian Office." At issue, he advised Roosevelt, then in Africa on a hunting expedition, was "whether Ballinger is guilty or not as charged by Glavis, and whether the Forest Service is responsible for the charges, but the chances are it will cover a much wider field."

Certainly Pinchot hoped the hearings would result in a more expansive inquiry, for that was the only way to penetrate what he believed was the core of the controversy. Under Taft, he told TR, "[w]e have fallen back down the hill you led us up, and there is a general belief that the special interests are once more substantially in full control of both Congress and the Administration." While not a bad man, Taft had turned out to be surprisingly weak and indecisive, Pinchot continued. "[H]is desire to act as a judge, dealing with issues only when they are brought to him," rendered him unpresidential; Roosevelt, by contrast, had demonstrated that the chief executive must be "the advocate and active guardian of the general welfare." Around this much larger political issue would the congressional hearings revolve, Pinchot predicted. "Unless Mr. Taft turns squarely about and promptly abandons his present direction and tendencies, I foresee a clearcut division between the Administration and the reactionaries on one side, and the progressives and the people on the other. The coming investigation must inevitably tend to make that division sharp and clear."[9]

Pinchot helped the inevitable come into being. Confronted with an investigative committee from the House and Senate whose pro-Ballinger majority he expected to exonerate the secretary of the interior, condemn Glavis, and find against the Forest Service, Pinchot and a coterie of advisors developed a strategy that sought to take advantage of these prejudicial circumstances. Out of lengthy discussions with his brother Amos, Louis D. Brandeis, who was Glavis's attorney, and Pinchot's legal representative, George W. Pepper, a coordinated plan emerged. Witnesses and attorneys would hammer away at Ballinger's credibility, tie him to the Morgan-Guggenheim syndicate, and make him appear, as Pinchot put it in his testimony, "unfaithful in his trust as a servant of the people and as a guardian of public property of enormous value." None of this would presumably carry much weight with a committee stacked in favor of the very man whose reputation

Pinchot and his allies hoped to tarnish. But then they never considered the congressional committee to be the court of last resort; rather, it was a means to reach a much more significant body of opinion, the American public.[30]

It was for the engaged citizenry that Pinchot and Glavis tailored their testimony. Both avoided calling Ballinger corrupt, and Pinchot almost downplayed the secretary's importance. "The imperative duty before this country is not merely to get rid of an unfaithful public servant," he testified, but "to bring about a fundamental change in the law and the practice toward conservation, to prevent for the future what has been in the past, the useless sacrifice of the public welfare, and to make possible hereafter the utilization of the natural resources and the natural advantages for the benefit of all the people instead of merely for the profit of a few." By brandishing a rhetoric that admitted little complexity and that reduced the debate to a Manichean struggle between good and evil, Pinchot hoped to facilitate its public consumption.

Pinchot was not certain he had accomplished that goal in his testimony when he finished it. In contrast to what he considered Glavis's brilliant presence of mind on the stand (Brandeis, too, thought the young man had been an "extraordinary witness. Have never seen his equal"), Pinchot lamented that his testimony over three days "was less impressively accurate than Glavis's"; at best, it was "reasonably effective." Public commentators gave the forester higher marks. One striking cartoon depicted him as a modern-day Hercules attacking a many-headed Hydra: standing in a snow-filled Alaskan forest, a muscular Pinchot swings an ax, whose handle is emblazoned "Testimony" and whose head reads "Publicity," at a writhing coil of rattlesnakes (dubbed "Land Grabbers"). Louis Brandeis confirmed that Pinchot effectively chopped through the opposition, calling the forester's testimony "simply perfect. It made a profound impression and was just what we needed."[31]

George Pepper, by contrast, was much less enthusiastic about his client's performance. A member of the Philadelphia elite, Pepper was, Pinchot wrote, "highly impressive in size and bearing—a big man, tall, broad shouldered, powerful. When he stood up, spread his legs apart, clasped his hands behind him, and began to speak, he seemed immovable." Yet for all his imposing stature, Pepper could not dissuade Pinchot from broadening his attacks on the administration beyond the issues the Cunningham claims

To Pinchot's supporters, his attack on Secretary of the Interior Richard A. Ballinger was a legitimate attempt to protect public control of federal lands in Alaska (and elsewhere). To opponents, Pinchot's actions were a form of insubordination and President Taft did the right thing when he fired the forester.
Grey Towers NHL

presented. Acknowledging that there was some justice to Pepper's concerns, Pinchot nonetheless replied that "[y]our point of view and mine necessarily differ because our principal objects differ also"; the lawyer wanted "to win before the Committee" and the forester "to win before the country."[32]

More fully attuned to Pinchot's perceptions was his brother, Amos. He offered Gifford invaluable legal support and political advice during the four months of hearings; he also took over the management of his legal team and hired additional lawyers, phasing out Pepper. He did so, he advised the Philadelphia lawyer, because it "seemed to me that your conception of the needs of the situation did not sufficiently embrace the necessity of giving the country a clear-cut outline of the methods which are being used against the people by members of the Administration who are too sympathetic to the special interests."[33]

Acting on this insight into the polemical demands of the hearings, Amos became an effective publicist for Gifford's cause. He was apparently the guiding force behind the production and distribution of a sophisticated summary of the testimony given through March 1910 that was mailed to newspaper offices around the country; this "well-organized selection complete with marginal summaries of page content," historian James Penick notes, was "a handy reference guide for busy editors who lacked the time to plow through the thousands of pages of testimony."[34]

Persuasive too was Amos's suggestion that Gifford leave the country after completing his testimony, reasoning that if he stayed too long in the limelight his reputation could be burned. In May he cabled Gifford, then in Ireland, that his absence had kept the focus on Ballinger, and to good effect. As a result, a rueful Pinchot wrote another European sojourner, Theodore Roosevelt, Amos "urges me strongly not to return at once." Indebted to Amos's sage counsel, Gifford later touted his younger brother as having been an "indispensable" force for good, who "was especially useful in getting the facts to the public before and after the hearings were over and the verdict rendered."[35]

The final verdict, announced in December 1910, "excited little interest and less surprise," in Pinchot's words. The committee, although split along partisan lines, exonerated Ballinger and rebuked his accusers. Yet, significantly, it indicated that the final disposition of the contested Cunningham claims should be determined in "the appropriate court of the United States"; that a change in venue was essential because "the nature and wide publication of the charges and imputations referred to in this report would inevitably impair the confidence, both of the claimants and the public, in the impartiality" of any decision the Interior Department might reach. The committee also accepted the contention that public lands must remain in public hands. "[I]t would be the height of unwisdom to permit these great coal fields to be monopolized, or gathered into the private ownership of a few for speculative purposes." To protect against such mismanagement, the committee recommended that Congress enact legislation that would prohibit the government from selling these lands and the valuable resources they contained.[36]

Pinchot relished the irony that after "the stand-pat majority had said what it had to say in defense of Mr. Ballinger, it proceeded to give vigorous support to the coal land policy which Mr. Ballinger attacked. It took the identical position which Price, Glavis, Garfield, and I have been defending from the start," he noted in a post-verdict press release. "There could be no stronger testimony to the essential soundness and justice of this policy than this emphatic support by the very men who have just done what they could to revive public respect for the most dangerous enemy the Conservation policies have yet had." With some justification, Pinchot could crow: "We had won the war—in spite of the fact that technically we had lost the verdict."[37]

The victory may have only leveled the playing field. "When this fight to save the natural resources began the coal in Alaska was about to be lost to the people," Pinchot claimed, and the "water power sites had been opened to entry, and the Conservation policy of the last Administration was being reversed." One result of the controversial congressional investigation, and the astonishing level of public scrutiny it had provoked, was to slow down the Taft counterrevolution. "Today, the fight for these resources is as likely to be won as it was then likely to be lost. I can see nothing but good in that."[38]

The Sierra Club echoed this view. Despite the then-current clash between some of its leadership, notably John Muir, and Pinchot over the proposed inundation of the Hetch Hetchy Valley, the organization rallied to Pinchot's side in the aftermath of the Ballinger affair. On May Day 1910, three hundred members of the club hiked into Muir Woods, a stunning 550 acre tract of coastal redwoods just north of San Francisco, the majority of which Congressman William Kent had donated to the federal government in 1905 (Muir had enthused that it was "the best tree lover's monument in all the forests in all the world"). After a lunch that Kent had provided, along with speeches by Kent, former California governor Pardee, and other luminaries, a Miss E. Mittell christened what the Sierra Club had determined was "the most perfect specimen in Muir Woods" as the "Pinchot Memorial Tree." On a nearby large rock, the club unveiled a bronze plaque that bore the following inscription:

This tree is dedicated to
GIFFORD PINCHOT
Friend of the Forest
Conserver of the common-wealth[39]

How Pinchot proposed to continue to conserve the commonwealth and uphold the common good was another matter. Since his firing, Pinchot and his allies inside and outside the Forest Service had been able to stabilize the agency; but its status would require consistent monitoring as congressional investigations into its budget and regulatory mission accelerated after 1910. And as much as Pinchot believed, and took pleasure in the belief, that he and the conservationist cause had trounced Taft and Ballinger in the public arena, their apparent success only set up a more prolonged and difficult battle—the resurrection of the Roosevelt conservation agenda, to be set within a reinvigorated executive branch. Figuring out how to restore the world that Roosevelt had constructed, now that Pinchot was no longer chief of the Forest Service, and by what means, now that the Republican Party seemed so fragmented, would consume the next years of the ex–bureau chief's life.

An Insurgent Agenda

To address these interwoven goals, Pinchot needed a platform. One was at hand. In a calculated move during the summer of 1909, Pinchot and James Garfield had called a meeting of like-minded conservationists, among them Charles W. Eliot, who had recently stepped down as president of Harvard; Walter L. Fisher, a close friend who would replace Ballinger at Interior in 1912; and Henry L. Stimson, another friend who was a lawyer and future Cabinet officer at the departments of State and War.

Hoping to stymie what they perceived to be the Taft administration's reactionary stance on federal regulatory control of natural resources, they agreed to establish a new Washington, D.C.–based organization, funded by private donations and staffed by professionals, the goal of which would be to educate the American people about the need for conservation and to lobby Congress to enact effective conservationist legislation. In its watchdog mission and methods, with a professional staff and a capital location, the National Conservation Association (NCA) would serve as a prototype for public-interest environmental pressure groups founded much later in the twentieth century. Like the NCA, the Wilderness Society (1935), the National Wildlife Federation (1936), and a coterie of post-1960 nongovernmental organizations such as the Natural Resources Defense Council (1970) would employ lobbying tactics and the threat of litigation to force a recalcitrant federal government and resistant corporations to heed environmental concerns.[40]

From its Washington headquarters, the NCA would tap into national discontent over the Ballinger affair, its founders predicted, and grow into a powerful lobby sustained by a dues-paying membership 50,000 strong. In fact, the organization never came close to meeting such lofty expectations (at its peak it had perhaps 2,000 adherents), and its glossy magazine, *American Conservation,* ceased publication after six issues. However, under the leadership of its first president, Charles Eliot, who would relinquish his post to Pinchot in January 1910, the NCA was composed of men with great ability and much experience. Many of them had been important Forest Service employees: Overton Price, after being released for his involvement in the Ballinger dispute, became NCA treasurer; George Woodruff and Philip Wells, Yale classmates of Pinchot's and onetime legal officers at the agency, signed on, as would James Garfield and Amos Pinchot; former newspaper reporters Thomas R. Shipp and later Harry Slattery served as the NCA's secretary, a position that held the day-to-day responsibility for the organization. Kept afloat until 1923 largely through Pinchot's munificence, the NCA closely tracked pending conservation legislation, from inception through committee hearings and subsequent votes; issued press releases that outlined its assessment of these legislative initiatives, and their costs and benefits; and distributed to a web of editors, journalists, and resource-oriented organizations—often to as many as 5,000 recipients—Pinchot's commentary on select bills.

Pinchot, naturally, had only praise for the NCA's work. In 1923, after he closed it down to concentrate on his new job as governor of Pennsylvania, he assured a friend that "no other organization in Washington has ever begun to approach its record of constructive service to the people of America." That may be an exaggerated claim, but the NCA was unique in its commitment to guard the nation's natural resources through a vigilant analysis of congressional legislation.

Take the Public Lands Withdrawal Bill of June 1910, for example. This otherwise commendable piece of legislation, which authorized the contin-

ued withdrawal of mineral lands from public sale and which the NCA felt
had a good chance for passage, contained what Pinchot characterized in a
press release as "one wholly indefensible provision." Section 2 provided
that "if certain minerals can be found upon [these lands], these sites can be
taken away from the people," he asserted. "Even if false claims are made
that mineral has been found, then the burden of proof is on the Government, which must go to the trouble and expense of defending the rights
which it is the object of the bill to secure."[41]

Fears of another assault on federal regulatory powers led the NCA to
swing into action less than a year later to attack an amendment to the 1911
Agricultural Appropriations Bill. The amendment, Pinchot charged in a
quickly scheduled speech to a National Wholesale Lumber Dealers Association meeting in Washington, was sponsored by Senator Weldon B. Heyburn of Idaho, "who for years has tried in every way he could to injure or
destroy the National Forests." Its language was as damning as its provenance. It "provides that all land upon which there is less than 4,000 feet of
merchantable timber, in contiguous areas of 160 acres, shall be excluded
from the National Forests." By Pinchot's calculation, this would exclude
"every mountain park, every watershed above timber line, every burned
over area coming back into bearing, in fact every tract of every kind that is
not covered with mature timber." To blunt this misguided assault, and like
a skilled lobbyist, he urged every "friend of conservation" to immediately
contact the conferees so that Heyburn could not succeed in breaking up
"the National Forests and so . . . injure the conservation interests of the
Western people." The lumber dealers were the first to respond to his plea,
sending a letter to President Taft urging him to veto the bill if it emerged
unchanged from conference; the NCA staff also fired off telegrams to con-
stituent groups throughout the country, and the conference committee
received a wave of protests. That evening the Heyburn amendment was
deleted—"like old times," noted Pinchot.[42]

New was the prospect of translating these close-quarter struggles with
legislators and lobbyists into popular language for a wider audience. That
is what Pinchot hoped to accomplish with the publication of his first public
treatise, *The Fight For Conservation* (1910). Rushed into publication at the
height of the Ballinger-Pinchot tussle, this collection of revised articles and
speeches touched on many of the same issues that had animated the clash

with the secretary of the interior. Although it was not a "systematic treatise upon the subject," Pinchot hoped the slim volume would "serve to show the rapid, virile evolution of the campaign for conservation of the nation's resources."

In spare, assertive language, a rhetoric designed to underscore the book's direct appeal, he wrote of the relationship between the "unexampled wealth and well-being" of the United States and the "superb natural resources of our country," an economic relationship that carried with it a compelling moral obligation. "We are prosperous because our forefathers bequeathed to us a land of marvellous *[sic]* resources still unexhausted. Shall we conserve these resources, and in turn transmit them, still unexhausted, to our descendants?" His generation had best answer in the affirmative, Pinchot argued, for unless "we do, those who come after us will have to pay the price of misery, degradation, and failure for the progress and prosperity of our day."[43]

The need to link present-day policy to future needs, a staple of conservationist argument since at least the writings of George Perkins Marsh in the mid-nineteenth century, informed Pinchot's categorical rejection of what he called a "stupidly false" term—inexhaustible resources. Neither coal, wood, soil, forage plants, nor water was infinite; each was at the mercy of unrestrained economic forces seeking short-term profit at the expense of long-term sustainability. Only strict regulation could alter these dangerous consumption patterns, he contended, an argument that was central to his abiding faith: "[T]he conservation of natural resources is the basis, and the only permanent basis, of national success."

As with Marsh, Pinchot's conception of success was as retrospective as it was prospective. "The vast possibilities of our great future will become realities only if we make ourselves, in a sense, responsible for that future." Part of that responsibility entailed dutifully planning for the conservative use of nature's abundance so that Americans would protect themselves "against the disasters that lack of foresight has in the past repeatedly brought down on nations since passed away." Avoiding the fate of ancient Greece and Rome, whose decline he assumed resulted partly from environmental despoliation, the United States could enjoy a rise to power predicated on careful husbandry.[44]

America's success depended as well on equitable access to, and distribution and consumption of, the nation's material wealth. This lifelong Republican, raised amid great luxury, advanced a democratic vision that tied conservation to the pursuit of communal responsibility and equal opportunity. "The man who really counts is the plain American citizen," Pinchot affirmed, and that is why he stood for "the Roosevelt policies because they set the common good of all of us above the private gain of some of us; because they recognize the livelihood of the small man as more important to the Nation than the profit of the big man." To ensure that "the plain American always and everywhere holds the first place," he concluded, Roosevelt's initiatives also "denounce monopoly and special privilege." In this creed, the scientific management of natural resources was in pursuit of an indisputable and fundamental democratic outcome: "The conservation of political liberty will take its proper place alongside the conservation of the means of living, and in both we shall look to the permanent welfare by the plain people as the supreme end."[45]

But for the nation to reclaim its political birthright ("the government our forefathers died for and gave us—government by men for human welfare and human progress"), it must "do away with government by money for profit." Fortunately, Pinchot argued, that day appeared to be in the offing. "Our people are like a hive of bees, full of agitation before taking flight to a better place," he wrote, and if they encounter opposition along their chosen path, "they are ready to sting."[46]

The conservationists' queen bee—however inaccurate the gender—was Theodore Roosevelt, and he was invoked throughout *The Fight for Conservation* (the only political figure named in its pages). The sanction his presence would provide, and the leadership he would bring to a revived conservation crusade, was incalculable. In this evaluation, Pinchot was not alone. James Garfield, Frederick Newell, and other former and current federal scientists and bureaucrats, who under Roosevelt had pressed hard for integrated management of public lands and resources, also recognized the galvanizing effect the Rough Rider would have were he once more to throw himself into the political arena.[47]

Roosevelt did not need much coaxing. Off gathering what he bragged was "the best scientific collection ever brought out of Africa," he still kept his ear close to the American ground. In September 1909, four months before Pinchot was fired, he had heard from Robert L. Bacon, ambassador to the Court of St. James, that Pinchot's place in the Forest Service might not be secure. "Is it possible that Gifford, good old Gifford, has to go too?" Bacon wondered. "I do hope the rumor cannot be true." TR asked Pinchot the same question shortly after hearing that the forester had been fired. From his camp in the Lado region of southern Sudan, Roosevelt wrote: "We have just heard by runner that you have been removed. I cannot believe it. I do not know any man in public life who has rendered quite the service you have rendered; and it seems to me absolutely impossible that there can be any truth in this statement. But of course it makes me very uneasy." Buoyed by his former boss's praise, Pinchot was also cheered by Roosevelt's request. "Do write me, care of the American embassy at Paris, just what the real situation is. I have only been able to follow things very imperfectly while out here." To Pinchot this could mean only one thing: Roosevelt was considering jumping back into the political whirl.[48]

Realizing that the former president had not yet received his lengthy December 31, 1909, epistle about the Ballinger controversy, a letter that Pinchot had closed by declaring his continued support for Taft "up to the point where my loyalty to the people of this country requires me to break with the Administration," he did not respond to Roosevelt's query. Within five weeks Roosevelt replied to the earlier letter. Writing from the Upper White Nile, he reasserted his unqualified praise ("you were the leader among all the men in public office—and the aggressive, hard-hitting leader—of all the forces struggling for conservation. . . . ") and hinted that he might return to the political fray. "It is a very ungracious thing for an ex-President to criticize his successor; and yet I cannot as an honest man cease to battle for the principles for which you and I and Jim [Garfield] and [Herbert Knox] Smith and [Attorney General William H.] Moody and the rest of our close associates stood." Before determining what his next steps would be, he wanted to rendezvous with Pinchot. "Is there any chance of your meeting me in Europe? If not, will you *meet me on* the steamer on my return? I wish to see you before I in even the smallest degree commit myself."[49]

The potential liability of such contact led Massachusetts senator Henry Cabot Lodge, an old and trusted friend of Roosevelt's, to advise the former president to steer clear of Pinchot. He should do so, Lodge wrote, because Taft had had to fire the forester. "No president could possibly have tolerated such a letter as Pinchot sent Dolliver. It seems almost as if Pinchot wished to compel Taft to remove him." The political explosion that followed his removal had badly shattered public confidence and created a false perception of political reality. "The general feeling in the country is that Pinchot represents the people and your policy of Conservation, which is true, and that Ballinger and the administration represent opposition to it, which is not true. But that is what the public thinks and you cannot get it out of the public mind."[50]

That being the case, Lodge warned his friend—then busily stalking African lion, elephant, rhinoceros, zebra, impala, and gazelle—that he ought to avoid darkest America. Among its dangers was Gifford Pinchot. Although Lodge admired him ("Pinchot is our friend. He has done great work, his policy is sound"), the coming months were not a propitious time for TR to reconnect with his gifted subordinate. "I have heard privately that Pinchot thinks of going abroad and means to meet you. I hope he will not, because the mere fact of his meeting you would at once produce misapprehension. I do not want to see you put in the apparent attitude of upholding Pinchot against the administration, because you are altogether too great and important to be connected in any way with a quarrel of individuals in the administration."[51]

Because Lodge was unaware of Roosevelt's warm invitation to Pinchot, his cautionary letter led TR in reply to bend the truth. "I don't agree with you about not seeing Pinchot. I am delighted to see him," he responded, and then covered his tracks: "The only person I invited to see me was [Senator Elihu] Root, and Root said he could not come; but when Pinchot said he wanted to see me I said I should be more than delighted." By not admitting that he had initiated contact with Pinchot, Roosevelt turned Pinchot into the courtier rather than the courted.[52]

Such distinctions probably would not have mattered to Pinchot; he understood the complications the proposed meeting held for TR, as well as its prospects, and decided that the latter were more important. Besides, the president had urged him to sail for Europe, and Pinchot rarely said no to his powerful mentor. He took precautions, however, to keep his departure out of the public eye; in late March he boarded the SS *President Grant* in New York, bound for Hamburg, Germany, under an assumed name, Gaylord Smith. After spending time with his sister Nettie and her husband, Alan Johnstone, a British diplomat then stationed in Copenhagen, he traveled to Bonn for a reunion with Dietrich Brandis's widow; by train, he then headed to Porto Mauritzo on the Italian Riviera, arriving on April 10, 1910. There, in a hotel, Pinchot had a lengthy reunion with Roosevelt. Their engaged and extended conversation was, Pinchot noted in his diary, "one of the best and most satisfactory talks with T.R. I have ever had. Lasted nearly all day, and till about 10:30 at night."[53]

What they discussed, neither man recorded explicitly. But Pinchot, in a letter to James Garfield, expressed his belief that the former president was with them in their struggles. "I found everything just exactly as you and I had foreseen. There was nothing changed, nothing unexpected." Except this. As a result of his analysis of the tense and troubling political situation in the United States, Pinchot believed that Roosevelt found himself "in a very embarrassing position, but that could not be helped."[54]

The root of this embarrassment, of this "very unpleasant situation," was William Howard Taft. Such was Roosevelt's observation in a long letter to Lodge, written on the same day he met with Pinchot. Taft had been "nominated solely on my assurance to the Western people especially, but almost as much to the people of the east, that he would carry out my work unbroken; not (as he has done) merely working for somewhat the same objects in a totally different spirit, and with a totally different result, but exactly along my lines with all his heart and strength." Taft's failure in this respect was compounded by the Republican Party's jettisoning of its commitment "to the needs of the country." The overall rejection of Roosevelt's principles made it difficult for the former president in good conscience to campaign on behalf of the current president and the party he led. Wanting to avoid a open break with his successor, Roosevelt could only "very earnestly hope that Taft will retrieve himself yet, and if, from whatever causes, the present condition of the party is hopeless, I must emphatically desire that I shall not be put in the position of having to run for the Presidency, staggering under a load which I cannot carry, and which has been put on my shoulders through no fault of my own."

For all his desires for a future unencumbered by vainglorious politick-ing, Roosevelt accepted, as did Pinchot, that the progressive spirit of the American electorate could not be denied; he accepted too, as surely Pinchot did, that he might have an important role to play in molding its expression. "I may add that it looks to me as if the people were bound to have certain policies carried out," Roosevelt informed Lodge, "and that if they do not get the right type of leadership—leadership which a cabinet of lawyers, or an Administration which is primarily a lawyers' Administration, is totally unfit to give—they will turn to the wrong kind of leadership. I might be able to *guide* this movement, but I should be wholly unable to *stop* it, even if I were to try."[55]

His words were prophetic. The disenchantment with the lawyerly Taft and the Republican Party grew rapidly after Roosevelt's return to the United States that summer; it increased when the Republican Party suf-fered some stinging defeats in the November off-year elections at the state and national levels. Even before those losses, speculation about Roosevelt's political ambition was rampant. During the summer and fall, a steady stream of progressives had flowed to Roosevelt's home in Oyster Bay on Long Island to sound him out and to test his insurgent resolve (and their own). Among the most frequent of visitors was Gifford Pinchot. As he had been after his meeting with Roosevelt in Porto Maurizio, Pinchot came away from these discussions convinced that TR would in time fully em-brace the progressive cause; when his attempt to reintegrate western insur-gents and the eastern Old Guard and to soothe pro- and anti-Taft forces failed, he would pick up the banner of reform and, like the Rough Rider of old, lead the charge to reclaim lost ground.

Pinchot had reason to feel optimistic. Joining the Roosevelt entourage as it swung through the West to generate support for western Republicans, a trip Roosevelt had looked forward to "with unalloyed horror," Pinchot observed the former president's remarkable drawing power. Some of the attention that Roosevelt drew had to do with the words Pinchot had writ-ten for him, such as the famed "New Nationalism" speech that TR deliv-ered in Osawatomie, Kansas, on August 31 to mark the birth of one of the most radical voices in the antebellum abolitionist cause, John Brown. Its first draft had come from the pen of Herbert Croly, founder and editor of the *New Republic* and author of *The Promise of American Life* (1909), a much-heralded progressive analysis that Roosevelt had read admiringly while in Africa. According to Senator Albert Beveridge, who had read Croly's draft and who relayed his misgivings about it to Amos and Gifford Pinchot, the proposed speech missed the mark. So it must have seemed to Roosevelt, who passed it on to the Pinchots for their comments; Amos believed it "a very un-Roosevelt-like document, not suggesting the Colonel in either literary style or point of view." TR agreed that Gifford should rewrite the entire text. Its final version, with which Roosevelt only tinkered, represented in Amos's mind an unbending declaration of faith in the Progressive spirit.[56]

That seemed clear enough in its implicit rebuke of Taft's faithlessness. "No man is worth his salt in public life who makes on the stump a pledge which he does not keep after election; and, if he does not keep it, hunt him out of public life." More explicit, and in keeping with Pinchot's assertions in *The Fight for Conservation*, was affirmation that "executive power |is| the steward of the public welfare." Only a powerful nation-state could simultaneously protect natural resources and promote human advancement. Of "all the questions which can come before this nation . . . there is none which compares in importance with the central task of leaving this land even a better land for our descendants than it is for us." This new nationalism tackled what Pinchot called the "central condition of progress," which is the "struggle to equalize opportunity, destroy privilege, and give to the life and citizenship of every individual the highest value to himself and to the commonwealth." Adopting this course, under Roosevelt's leadership, would allow the United States to experience an unparalleled material prosperity and civic renaissance, as well as a "permanent moral awakening."[57]

The Kansas audience, Pinchot reported to his mother, was deeply moved by Roosevelt's New Nationalism speech. "I've never seen a crowd that affected me as much as that one did. They listened to TR for nearly an hour in perfect silence." The resultant noise in the press was deafening, as the speech was praised and denounced with equal fervor. No citizen was more effusive than Amos Pinchot, who with fraternal pride thought the Osawatomie address an "exceedingly radical document." For his part, Gifford believed that in delivering it Roosevelt demonstrated "how his own Progressivism has grown steadily stronger."

At first the more conservative Senator Lodge agreed, having read but an excerpt of the talk in a newspaper. He reached a different conclusion after scanning the full text reprinted in *Outlook*, realizing then "how the newspaper reports, extracts and headlines had distorted and mutilated what you said, giving an extreme look to utterances which are carefully guarded in the article." The source of the extremist interpretations, Lodge assured the man he knew was no revolutionary, was "the Kansas crowd and the insurgents generally who have given the impression of extreme utterances when . . . [they were] only a presentation of the policies you have been advocating for some time."

However it was interpreted, the Osawatomie speech, and those Roosevelt delivered in St. Paul and Denver (which Pinchot also helped draft), firmly established the past president as the counterweight to the sitting president. Such was Pinchot's assumption when he gave voice to what he felt was a popular sentiment. "You are the leader to whom all look," he told Roosevelt. "You are progressive — Taft is not, and never has been or will be except under orders. The country is as progressive as you are. Wholly irrespective of whether you are to be President again or not, it wants you to lead it where in any event it is bound to go." In pressing his case for using TR's immense popularity to unseat Taft, a goal urged on Roosevelt by other insurgents as well, Pinchot helped launch a battle within the Republican Party over its short-term future.[58]

This was a power struggle Roosevelt initially resisted, and his resistance periodically led him to sigh regretfully over what he tagged as Pinchot's zealousness. To mutual friend Henry Stimson, who lost his 1910 race to become New York's governor, Roosevelt observed: "Gifford has in him great possibilities for usefulness, but if he travels much further along the road on which he has been recently traveling, he will relegate himself to the company of single taxers, prohibitionists and the like." Yet in the aftermath of the devastating losses that Republicans like Stimson endured, and in the buildup to the 1912 presidential election campaign, Pinchot's instincts proved more accurate than irrelevant. His prediction that an internecine brawl would doom the Republican Party, and his early call for and later organizing of a third national force, the Progressive Party, changed the face of early-twentieth-century political life. Even the critical Theodore Roosevelt admitted as much when in August 1912 he accepted the Progressive

Party's nomination for president. He also underscored his indebtedness to Pinchot when, as of old, the candidate made great use of Pinchot's polemics, readily tapped the forty-seven-year-old's still-boundless enthusiasm, and benefited from his financial contributions to the new party's coffers.[59]

The campaign was a glorious failure. With the Republican and Progressive Parties chasing after many of the same votes, a united Democratic ticket, under the leadership of Woodrow Wilson, swept to victory. About this defeat, Pinchot was sanguine. He believed Wilson an "admirable man," took some pleasure in Taft's miserable showing, and in any event had refused to gauge the new party's success by its showing at the polls. "I don't believe that victory this fall is an essential condition of the success of the movement by any means," he had advised Iowa progressive Henry Wallace that summer. "What is wanted mainly is a clear-cut fight for progressive principles, and whether we win or lose, I think there is no doubt that the average man will be better off."[60]

Elevated too were Pinchot's political aspirations, which were given a considerable boost due to his tireless campaigning and the public aura it generated for him. Within two years he would throw his hat into the ring as a candidate for the U.S. Senate from Pennsylvania. Under the banner of the Washington Party (as the Progressive Party was known in the Keystone State), and like Roosevelt before him, Pinchot would run against two powerful mainstream candidates—Republican incumbent senator Boies Penrose and Democratic challenger (and future attorney general of the United States) A. Mitchell Palmer.

Like Roosevelt, he would come in a distant second. But being on the stump would have its compensations. Bolstered by the presence of his energetic and savvy new wife, Cornelia, who talked herself hoarse in defense of her husband's advocacy of women's suffrage and public health, and benefiting from TR's two robust swings through the state, Pinchot fared better than most Progressives nationally; in state after state, the party suffered sharp reversals, a situation that nonetheless gave Pinchot hope. "We lost this battle, but we were not beaten," he assured campaign volunteers. "In the face of a landslide which swept every state in the union except California, the Washington party polled 270,000 votes in Pennsylvania and held its organization unbroken." Its spirit remained intact as well. "This is the kind of fight that can never be lost unless we quit fighting," he concluded. "I have been at it for fifteen years. I propose to keep on. . . . "[61]

Pinchot's measure of the length of his commitment to Progressive principles, dating it to when he first entered government service, contains an important corrective. When the *New York Times* had reviewed *The Fight for Conservation* (1910), for example, it suggested that the forester "stick to conservation and leave politics alone," as if the two operated in distinct spheres. The newspaper's suggestion was as influential as it was miscast: without exception, every subsequent biographical analysis of Pinchot's long career lays down a similar demarcation between his public service as a forester and his career as an elected official. The distinction is false, as is reflected in the actions of those Alaskan protesters, who in 1911 were so infuriated by the conservation policies Pinchot represented that they immolated his effigy. They intuited what Pinchot had long known. For him, politics was second nature.[62]

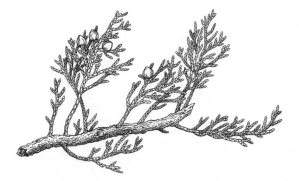

Part Four

OLD
GROWTH

Governing Ambitions

FROM THE grey snapper *(Lutenus griseus)*, Gifford Pinchot learned
much. In May 1913, he journeyed south to the Tortugas, a string of
islands that lie sixty miles "west from the southern extremity of Florida" and contain as "many little patches of sand as hurricanes choose to leave
above water." His destination was Loggerhead Key, site of a government
lighthouse and the Carnegie Institution's Marine Laboratory, where he was
the guest of the lab's director, Alfred G. Mayer. For the busy NCA lobbyist,
Loggerhead's perfections were many: "without a mangrove swamp to breed
mosquitoes," the island also lacked the human buzz of "a telephone, a telegraph, or a post office."[1]

Its blessed silence left Pinchot much time to roam through nearby Fort
Jefferson, an abandoned Civil War naval base, plunge into "the glorious
blood-warm water of the Gulf before breakfast," and explore the other
sand-spit islands. While Pinchot was touring the aptly named Bird Key,
home to a dense rookery of terns, in sailed famed behavioralist Dr. John
B. Watson, then running a Carnegie-sponsored research project on the
species' habits and habitat. "Attired in nothing whatever but a magnificent
coat of tan," Watson regaled Pinchot with the startling results of his experiments into the female tern's uncanny capacity to identify her egg when it
was set within a colony "of 10,000 eggs laid on the bare sand." After band-

ing a female and marking its egg, the scientist would turn the bird loose, move its egg several inches, and observe whether the mother would return to it. He then repeated his actions, each time moving the egg further away from its original resting place. When the distance reached fifteen inches, the returning mother ignored the egg, for it "was no longer within the purview of her maternity." Watson, whose later controversial studies into the psychological mechanisms of human behavior brought him as much scorn as renown, concluded from his work on the terns that their survival depended on what Pinchot described as "an impossibly keen sense of locality."[2]

Watson's insight would help the visiting angler unravel what for him had been an abiding mystery of the grey snapper. As Pinchot sailed among the low-lying islands and walked along their sun-baked beaches, he was riveted by his sightings of these "[d]eep, sturdy, knowing-looking fish" moving through the clear waters. They were especially to be spotted flitting among "the coral heads, great rocky mushrooms, a few of which still remain in the shallow water near the Laboratory." These underwater formations, "often fifteen feet in diameter, are divided by countless passages and crevices in which the yellowtail, the Grey Snappers, and many other fish literally swim," Pinchot later wrote in an essay entitled "Solomon in Scales." His frequent glimpses of the snapper only added to his amazed frustration. "Whenever I saw them I tried to catch them. And whenever I tried to catch them I failed. I had heard that the Snapper was the cunningest fish of the reef. Before long I was willing to swear to it."[3]

Their cunning was connected to their feeding cycle, which Pinchot discovered one evening while walking with his host down a moonlit beach on Loggerhead Key. Mayer had told his guest of a curious phenomenon, that when he strolled along the strand at night "an escort of Grey Snappers" often kept pace with him "in the very edge of the sea." Curious about the paired procession, Pinchot was startled when he realized the reason for the fish's seemingly odd conduct. "They had, it appeared, discovered that when a man walks the beach at night the little grey spirit crabs scatter ahead of him into the edge of the waves." Knowing that "spirit crabs are good to eat," Pinchot observed, the snappers "trailed along in the water, keeping abreast or just ahead of the walking humans, and harvested the wages of their wisdom as the crabs transferred themselves from our jurisdiction into theirs."[4]

Pinchot now understood why he had not been able to catch any snapper. "I had failed to make Grey Snappers take the hook by day—but at night they would take crabs. The bearing of this incident surely lay in the application of it." All he had to do was to think like a fish.[5]

The next day, Pinchot went digging for the equally elusive crustacean— "[t]he spirit crab lives in a hole in the sand, but when he is out of it, there is nothing swifter that travels the earth. . . . Greased lightning is leisurely by comparison"—but by nightfall he had corralled enough to begin his experiment. Using "the information the Snappers had given me," Pinchot baited the hook on his five-ounce Leonard fly rod with the crab, and the snappers bit as quickly as he could cast, fighting "like highly intelligent tigers against the spring of my little rod." Pinchot was certain that he was pursuing the "brainiest fish of them all," which added luster to the evening he spent "along the clean white beach, with the sweeping beam of the revolving light increasing rather than lessening the sense of happy solitude."[6]

The grey snapper had one more lesson to teach the contented, meditative angler. After cutting up a snapper for bait to lure larger fish closer to shore, Pinchot noticed that within fifteen minutes, "after a piece of dead Grey Snapper . . . had struck the water far outside of where we were fishing with crabs, not a single live Snapper was to be found where they swarmed before." He finally concluded that "the tide must have turned and taken the fish with it." He was wrong. Later, while walking back toward Mayer's home, Pinchot was escorted to his bed by a column of "wise little Grey Snappers, more numerous than ever, catching crabs ahead of me." These "self-educated fish," he mused, "knew that a walking man meant crabs" and that the vicinity of dead snapper "was no place for live ones." *Luteanus griseus,* he affirmed, "may have scales and a tail, but he knows more than many a man in pants."[7]

The same attentiveness was required to understand the broader natural and human environment, as Pinchot knew well. Since the early 1890s, when he had begun his career in forestry, he had become increasingly sensitive to the varied forces shaping the social and physical landscapes. The language of conservation was the means by which he understood both realms and the interplay between them. That was why it was as essential for a fisherman to know the distinguishing characteristics of a niche within a marine ecosystem as it was for a forester to act within the carrying capacity of the land. One could not succeed without such knowledge, any more than a politician could secure power without being attuned to changes in social structures, economic systems, and communal needs. As Pinchot did in his close observations of the grey snapper, one can learn a great deal by watching him as he sensed, absorbed, and adapted to alterations in the American polity.

A RECONFIGURED LANDSCAPE

Gifford Pinchot's world was changing, too. Indeed, 1914 marked a watershed in his life. With James and Mary Pinchot now deceased, the new husband and father also assumed the role of head of the extended family. His parents had made sure that Gifford was always first among equals with his siblings, and that fact now took on new meaning.

In one respect Gifford, Nettie, and Amos drew closer to one another. That was in part because of the twining of Gifford's and Amos's political activism; they had shared some of the stress of the Ballinger episode, and together they had labored hard to ensure the birth and development of the Progressive Party. Even their sister was drawn into the fray; though in Europe, she maintained a steady correspondence with her brothers, sharing vicariously in their political endeavors. In the United States for the climax of the 1912 campaign, she joined Gifford and Amos for a well-earned postelection vacation on the Texas Gulf Coast, a companionable ten days of sun and rain during which they hunted and fished in the bays and estuaries stretching north and south from Aransas Island; at their hotel they talked and read late into the evening.[8]

This familial equanimity was not always maintained. Friction between Amos and Gifford increased after 1914. Amos, whose ambitions for political office were never pronounced, began to demand of the Progressive Party, and thus of its standard bearer Theodore Roosevelt, a more radical response to current conditions; victory at the polls was less important than the maintenance of ideological purity. That was why he threw himself into the divisive debate that swirled around George W. Perkins, a onetime partner of financier J. P. Morgan. Both brothers had been vocal in their opposition to Perkins's dominant presence in fundraising for and defining the strategy of the Bull Moose campaign of 1912. So argumentative had they become—in public and private—that TR lashed out at them in letter to his son, Kermit. "The good Pinchots and their kind, the advanced radicals, want to fight Perkins and others, who as a matter of fact have been even more useful than the Pinchots in helping us in this fight. I think I shall be able to keep both sides together. But it is very weary work. . . . "9

The burdensome squabble carried on, and to such a degree that in 1915 Amos, who had less to lose in this battle than had his brother, broke with Roosevelt's "sane and tempered radicalism." It was a severing of ties that Gifford, because of his deep loyalty to the former president, could not and would not duplicate. "[W]hatever differences of judgment I may have with you," Gifford had written TR in late 1912, "they will not dim my affection for you, nor cloud the recollections of the good work we have done together," a sentiment that prevailed until TR's death in 1919.10

Maintaining affection for Amos was more complicated. The differences between the brothers accelerated with Amos's further shift to the political left. His vote for Wilson in 1916 might not have been terribly provocative, but within the family context it was, for no Pinchot had ever voted for a Democrat. Even in 1916, Gifford upheld this standard; he felt compelled to vote for the non-progressive (and Republican) Charles E. Hughes when TR refused the Progressive Party nomination, citing his antipathy for the Democratic candidate "who has played fast and loose with the safety, honor, and welfare of this country." Amos, by contrast, was certain that Gifford had cast his lot with the wrong man. "I agree with you that Gifford has made a vital mistake and wasted useful years following the oyster man—to nowhere," he confided to Representative William Kent. "I feel very sorry for the whole thing, for Gifford clung faithfully to the illusion that Teddy . . . would come out all right." Roosevelt did not, instead proving "himself only the captive balloon of undesirable citizens, who pull him down to earth or let him blow up in the air, according to the needs of the time."11

The Pinchot brothers sailed further apart in response to World War I. Amos, who had risked family opprobrium when he enlisted as a private in the expansionist war with Spain in 1898, now protested against American involvement in the bloody European conflict. His pacifism, evident in his early and strong support for Americans United Against Militarism, befuddled Gifford, who had never gone to war but was fervent in his demand that American soldiers bolster the Allied cause. "War is not the worst of evils," he told Senator Lodge in April 1917. "Self respect is a jewel beyond price, and righteousness and justice are the only foundations of an enduring peace," a principle that led Pinchot that same month to volunteer to work under Herbert Hoover in the war-related Food Administration. Three months later he resigned, as he and Hoover sharply disagreed over what Pinchot believed was the need to demand, if not require, that meat-packers guarantee hog producers a substantial return on their labor.[12]

As the war developed, the battle within the Pinchot family became more confusing and worrisome, a result of Amos's budding socialist sentiments, the deterioration of his marriage to Gertrude Minturn, and his adulterous relationship with the woman who would become his second wife, journalist Ruth Pickering. For Amos, coming into his own in good part meant not being his brother. Gifford appreciated this reality as well as the limitations it imposed; as he advised a friend about his brother's inexplicable support of the Democratic Party: "I wish that Amos were not taking the [Wilson] side but there isn't a thing I can do about it."[13]

Under different circumstances, the brothers' disagreements might not have been of great import. But the potential liability that Amos's radical opinions appeared to pose for Gifford's political future was the subject of continual familial anxiety. In 1914 Mary Pinchot, fearing that Amos would undercut his older brother's path to power, had pleaded successfully with him to withdraw from his senatorial campaign in New York. After Mary Pinchot's death, Cornelia Pinchot picked up where her mother-in-law had left off. Most strikingly, in the afterglow of her husband's 1922 victory in the Pennsylvania gubernatorial campaign, she plotted with Harry Slattery, secretary of the National Conservation Association, "to give out a story pointing out the differences between Gifford and Amos." What she had in mind was an article that stressed their political disagreements, "of how Amos always disliked T.R. and never lost an opportunity of attacking him, and how T.R. referred to him as 'one of the lunatic fringe'; how Amos was a pacifist during the war; voted for Wilson while Gifford was campaigning for Hughes, etc., etc." Knowing that to achieve maximum exposure the article would need a more salacious angle, Cornelia offered this tidbit: "I suppose it would be a rather dirty trick to talk about his admitted 'free love' theories because these might hurt Ruth, but it might be possible to refer to his divorce [from Gertrude Minturn in 1917] which is constantly saddled on Gifford." Although the article was apparently never written, and Gifford directly wrote his brother of his concerns—"be very careful to make it clear in anything that may appear in the papers as to which one of us is speaking"—Cornelia's intention to blacken her brother-in-law's reputation reveals the high level of competition for standing within the Pinchot family, and for the public eye.[14]

For all the familial rivalry, Amos helped frame the political environment through which Gifford moved in the late teens. So, too, did Theodore Roosevelt. Yet when Amos began to spin out to the margins of the political left, and Roosevelt retired from active political engagement after 1916, Gifford Pinchot responded by redefining his electoral prospects and ideological perspectives. Additional impetus for this reevaluation came with Roosevelt's death on January 6, 1919. Acutely affected, Pinchot grieved for the man who was his most significant mentor and *beau ideal*. Later, trying to capture the essence of Roosevelt's magnetic presence, Pinchot fastened on the Rough Rider's grand appetite for life: "[l]ife at its warmest, and fullest and freest, at its utmost in vigor, at its sanest in purpose, and its clearest and cleanest—life tremendous in volume, unbounded in scope, yet controlled and guided with a disciplined power that made him, as few men have ever been, the captain of his soul." The ramifications of Roosevelt's demise were at once personal and political; his death, Gifford wrote Amos, "may result in such control by the reactionaries as to put the policies you and I are interested in back many years."[15]

Pinchot had not lost the will to battle against what he considered retrograde politics, however. His lobbying work under the aegis of the National Conservation Association grew, and as such was a daily reminder of the continued need for vigilance in this shifting landscape. Fascinated with the powerful possibilities that radium posed for medical science and the treatment of cancer, for instance, Pinchot issued a series of warnings in early 1914 about deleterious changes to what had been critical legislation introduced "to reserve to the people of this country all radium bearing ore lands." Badly compromised in conference committee, the modified bill now allowed the continued monopolization of this precious ore, setting the "ruthlessness of commercial greed" against the "value of human life." Were it to pass, he cautioned, the "high cost of radium today—$100,000 a gram—[would make] radium solely a rich man's cure"; cancer would thus become "largely a poor man's disease."[16]

Questions of equity and access to other natural resources emerged as well in the NCA's close focus on the impact of preparations for World War I. The lobbying organization was attentive to legislative initiatives "masquerading as Conservation bills, whose passage would defeat the purpose of the conservation movement." Among the "iniquitous" initiatives Pinchot identified in press releases issued just after Wilson's reelection in 1916 were those dealing with the "perpetual" leasing of waterpower sites to private corporations, and proposals "to hand over to the Standard Oil Company and a few other interests the Navy's reserves of fuel oil." To fight these congressional proposals, the NCA distributed under Pinchot's name a stream of critiques of the pending legislation to thousands of local, regional, and national media, with the express hope that the newspapers would disseminate his arguments; others on the organization's lengthy mailing list received appeals to use their connections "in the Administration, or the Senate or the House, and to get others to do the same." This face-to-face lobbying would yield results, Pinchot assured his many correspondents. "All pulling together we can win, but we can't do it any other way."[17]

Although he took great pleasure in building up the NCA, and using its clout to oppose congressional actions he deemed subversive of democratic principles and counter to the conservationist ethos, Pinchot yearned for the more creative activism that came with direct governance. Old Guard Pennsylvania Republicans of the late teens, however, whose electoral clout derived from the notoriously corrupt political machines of Philadelphia and Pittsburgh, had little interest in the ambitious Progressive, whose name they happily mispronounced as "Pin-*shot*." Most vocal in his disdain was Senator Boies Penrose; five years after thrashing Pinchot in the 1914 Senate campaign, the senator snickered that his erstwhile opponent "seems to me about as important as a cheap side show outside the fence of a country fair, like the tattooed man or the cigarette fiend." Pinchot's situation was freakish. With no political ticket on which to run, and no coalition of voters on which to count, he could make little headway in the state, admitting to California Progressive George Pardee in October 1919 that while "I feel like fighting, . . . there is no use in butting your head against a stone wall."[18]

Although frustrated, hemmed in, and outflanked, Pinchot within a mere three years would accomplish the seemingly impossible; in November 1922 he was elected governor of the Keystone State, a smashing victory for reform-minded Pennsylvanians. Aided by the death in late 1921 of the sixty-year-old Penrose, whose loss helped break the urban machines' heretofore remarkable capacity to generate patronage and votes, Pinchot's victory was also the result of his earlier and shrewd adaptation to the state's closed political arena.

Seeking a position from which he could generate interest in his candidacy, he had wrangled an appointment to the Pennsylvania Forest Commission in 1920 and then engineered the dismissal of its chairman, Robert S. Conklin. Lacking training as a forester, and far too tentative an administrator for Pinchot's taste, Conklin found himself the target of the new commissioner's barbed attacks; in alliance with another member of the commission, Pinchot worked to discredit Conklin, in the end forcing Governor William C. Sproul to ask for the beleaguered man's resignation. Once it was tendered, the governor tapped Pinchot to serve as the new chair.[19]

The new appointee did not sit on his laurels. Demonstrating the negotiating skills, administrative instinct, and sheer enthusiasm for sustained work that had characterized his past career as the nation's chief forester, Pinchot swiftly moved the state's forestry department to center stage. He revamped its hiring practices so that professional foresters, not political appointees, served on the staff. Just as important was the speed with which the new commissioner secured rapid increases in the department's budgetary appropriations, decentralized its bureaucratic functions, expanded the range of the employees' responsibilities, and boosted their morale. When legislators balked at additional outlays to hire more foresters, Pinchot dug into "his own private purse," one colleague remembered, to bring them on board. Well funded, the department began to aggressively purchase abandoned lands, planted approximately one million trees to regenerate cutover terrain, and secured legislative sanction to purchase and plant another 20 million over the next decade. In his two years in office, Pinchot had done much to make Pennsylvania worthy of its arboreal name.[20]

That in this work the man Penrose once dismissed as the "Tree Doctor" had found the script for political success became clear in 1922 when Pinchot resigned his post to enter that spring's Republican gubernatorial primary. Boosting his campaign prospects was his high level of name recognition and growing reputation for honest administration. In this respect, even his detractors had to give credit where credit was due. J. Horace McFarland, president of the American Civic Association, who had a long-standing feud with Pinchot dating from the damming of Hetch Hetchy, assured another longtime Pinchot antagonist, Charles S. Sargent, that a Pinchot victory would benefit the state. "Now if you knew the situation in Pennsylvania you would, I think, swallow your disgust and be glad to have Pinchot as governor. I have no illusions about him . . . [but] he is of known capacity, he has done a fine piece of work in really organizing forestry in the state, he is a good administrator, and he could do good to this state for four years." That by constitutional mandate a governor could not be reelected was useful in this case, McFarland continued, for Pinchot "would be impossible long before the end of four years." Besides, if he were elected his ambitions would simultaneously frustrate machine politicians and destroy his career. "You are right in saying," McFarland concluded, "that if he is elected 'it will be the end of him politically,' for his swelled head will promptly take him out for President, and that will finish it."[21]

Gaining an inflated sense of self was a little difficult for Pinchot given his very narrow victory in the primary; he won a three-candidate race by a whisker-thin margin of 9,259 votes, amid evidence of fraudulent ballot stuffing on the part of the Philadelphia and Pittsburgh political organizations. Yet this preliminary triumph largely guaranteed a win in November because in Pennsylvania there were nearly three times as many registered Republicans as Democrats. This imbalance enabled Pinchot to sweep his Democratic challenger (a close friend, John A. McSparran, the head of the state Grange) by more than 250,000 votes. The difference in party registration was not alone responsible for the electoral outcome, the *Philadelphia Bulletin* asserted in its postelection analysis. Pinchot also benefited from what it described as a statewide revolt "against the associated county bosses who set up a claim of inheritance to the perquisites of state leadership upon the death of Senator Penrose."[22]

The new governor did more than take advantage of the state's turbulent politics and a timely demise. The groundbreaking coalition he put together also powered him into office, a coalition consisting of the marginalized (farm families), the ignored (industrial workers), and the recently enfranchised (women). He had been courting these constituencies since his first campaign in 1914. With his wife Cornelia, for example, he had become a charter member of the Raymondskill (Milford) chapter of the Grange. A secret society that Oliver Hudson Kelly founded in 1867 as the Patrons of Husbandry, its origins lay in Kelly's desire to ameliorate the bleak social conditions and declining economic status of rural communities, as well as to reassert agriculture's primacy in American life. That same set of ambitions continued to guide the organization in the 1910s when the Pinchots joined. As Cornelia Pinchot assured an appreciative audience at a Grange picnic in the early 1920s, the "men and women on the farms of America have been in the past, and are now, the greatest asset this Nation has. Our farm homes have developed a type of American manhood and womanhood that is to be looked up to with real pride as the bulwark of the nation." This political paean, like those her husband regularly delivered in his capacity as state chairman of the Grange's conservation committee, paid off. Among Gifford Pinchot's most consistent voters were those who lived in the isolated and impoverished farming communities dotting the rural counties of Pennsylvania.[23]

This portion of the electorate also rallied to his cause because of his staunch Prohibitionist beliefs. While he had had the occasional drink as a teenager, as an undergraduate at Yale, and while studying forestry in Europe, Pinchot reported being repelled by the sight and antics of those who drank deeply. "The incredible fact that I have never been drunk has led to my being considered as a sort of grossly inferior being entirely devoid of moral sense," he advised his father from Germany in 1890. "[T]he Germans seem to be still in that retrograde condition where a man's chief duty to society lies in the willingness to drink all he can get." For this devotee of self-control, drunkenness was anathema. He knew enough to know that not everyone shared his taste, however, and until the passage of the Eighteenth Amendment in 1919, he served alcohol to guests with some liberality; for a 1907 reception at the family home in Washington, D.C., he purchased ten cases of champagne.[24]

Once alcohol was constitutionally prohibited, Pinchot's "dryness" became a much-flogged political asset. "Years ago my work to conserve the natural resources for the benefit of all the people unavoidably directed my attention to the loss of human resources occasioned by traffic in strong drink," he told the *American Issue,* an Anti-Saloon League newspaper in Pennsylvania, before the spring 1922 primary. "I became a convinced opponent of that traffic when it was politically dangerous to do so." Following his election, in an interview with the editor of the New York–based journal *Review of Reviews,* he confirmed that he wanted "to see the saloon driven out of our State and Pennsylvania made unhealthy for bootleggers, both high and low," a pledge he would repeat at his January 1923 inauguration.

These declarations, for all their heartfeltness, also made strategic sense within the context of Pennsylvania politics. Rural and more socially conservative voters had flocked to the Prohibitionist bandwagon, and thus to Pinchot's platform. Moreover, his many and determined opponents within the Republican Party, ranging from Senator Penrose to the powerful Mellon family of Pittsburgh, a portion of whose fortune derived from the distillery business, were stoutly "wet." On this highly explosive issue had Pinchot's personal convictions and political instincts converged.[25]

That many members of his family flaunted federal and state laws to keep drinking threatened Gifford's public commitments. The threats were manifest stunningly close to home. Amos and Ruth, along with Cornelia Pinchot, made certain that guests at Grey Towers who wished to drink alcohol did not go without. That was possible by resorting to a simple subterfuge. Both brothers had homes on the grounds, so those who wished to imbibe were required to stash and consume their liquor at Amos and Ruth's house; in the midst of her husband's electioneering in 1922, Cornelia even apologized to Amos when some of her guests dipped into his whiskey supplies without permission.[26]

Cornelia was not always as sensitive to the dilemmas this arrangement posed. When she sent Amos a check for some whiskey, he refused to cash it for fear it might compromise his brother's anti-Prohibition stance. When she suggested moving liquor supplies to Grey Towers, he urged caution. "I wish you would talk over this matter with Gifford before you ask me to have the whiskey moved into your house. Gifford is likely to get into serious trouble if this is done. You cannot stand publicly for prohibition, stock your house with whiskey and have it found out, and not get into difficulties politically." Imagine the consequences, he urged his sister-in-law, "if it was discovered that there was a secret stock of booze on the premises. [Gifford] would have to do a lot of explaining that the liquor was yours and not his, and the more he explained the more people would laugh."[27]

Amos was right to fear that news of this illicit arrangement might filter out into the surrounding community. It is amazing that it did not. Equally surprising was that Gifford Pinchot apparently turned a blind eye to familial backsliding. The slightest hint that the "dry" governor was complicit in violating a constitutional amendment would have destroyed his political career. Just how private his private life was, the public never discovered.[28]

Less hidden was his perception of just how much he needed labor's backing to realize his electoral ambitions. In this most-industrialized state, labor's votes were an important factor on Election Day, a reality that Pinchot grasped early in his 1914 run for the Senate. That July, Robert D. Towne, editor of the *Scranton Daily News*, had watched the Progressive candidate do something "new and strange" for Pennsylvania politics; in response to the passage of the Seventeenth Amendment to the Constitution in 1913, which ensured the direct election of senators, Pinchot had kicked off a statewide, door-to-door, one-on-one campaign, a flavor of which Towne captured for his readers: "Pinchot stood in the middle of the road at Mayfield," he reported from that small coal-mining town in the northeastern part of the state, "talking with two men just out of the mines. He was telling them that if they voted for him for United States Senator they could trust him to stick to his principles." That the aspiring politician was "not down in Philadelphia hanging around the bosses," Towne wrote, "but up in the street in Mayfield talking to his political masters, two miners," marked the advent of a new creed: with Pinchot, the "people is now the boss."[29]

They were not as powerful as all that. But Pinchot continued to curry the favor of working men and women. As with his platform in 1914, all subsequent ones asserted his full support for the rights of labor to organize in unions and to compel government to establish minimum wages, regulate workplace safety, and enact workers' compensation and insurance programs. In insisting on these planks, he pushed well beyond what the Progressive Party had advocated in its 1912 program. His assertion that public health, child labor, and employment conditions mattered caught the attention of union leaders such as John L. Lewis and Philip Murray of the United Mine Workers of America (UMW) and resonated with the union membership. Pinchot secured solid support in the hard-coal regions of the state as well as in such gritty industrial towns as Bethlehem, Scranton, and Altoona. The energies he expended in campaigning on these issues redounded to his advantage in 1922.

Pinchot's success that year, a reporter for *The Nation* argued, was also predicated on the deliberate widening of his political support. When "he dug trenches extending from the general moral issues of the Progressive Party to the specific economic issues of the rising farm-labor group," Pinchot cleared the way to victory, one of the few Progressives who was able to make the transition into elective office in that more conservative age. "Farm support, labor support, plus the echoes of 'Onward Christian Soldiers' made Pinchot Governor of Pennsylvania."[30]

That was not the whole picture. He had also courted an all-important fourth element, without which he would not have won the gubernatorial election—women. That Pinchot shaped his 1922 campaign around female voters, for whom this was the first election for state office they could participate in, makes intuitive sense. What else would this son of a powerful mother, brother to an incisive sister, husband to an assertive wife do?

His reaching out to this new constituency reflected an important evolution in his beliefs. In 1906, for instance, he had uttered a strikingly insensitive assertion that quickly hit the wires and was reprinted throughout the nation; he allegedly "remarked to some of the [female] clerks of his department [the Forest Service] that he did not consider the services of any woman alive worth more than $50 per month." When these comments were leaked to the press, they sparked an uproar. In addition to a "scathing epistle" from May Wright Sewall, president of the Federation of Women's Clubs, Pinchot received a bristling rejoinder from feminist Hetty Green, who, the *Milford Dispatch* noted, "conveyed the impression that any man alive who made such a superficial statement was not worth 50 cents a year to the government or the nation." Commented the local reporter: "[I]t will be an unlucky day for Mr. Pinchot if he ever runs for elective office and the women of the country have a voice in the matter."[31]

Yet when women gained that voice, they voted for him with evident enthusiasm. That was in part because Pinchot knew how to make amends; he released to the newspapers much of the critical correspondence he received in 1906 as a way of taking himself down a peg, of doing penance. More profound was his sustained commitment to women's political rights. He was responsible for writing the plank in the Progressive Party's 1912 platform that called for suffrage for women, and argued that the party should commit itself to the creation of a new Department of Social Welfare. Many feminist reformers rallied around the idea, but Roosevelt and George W. Perkins rejected it because they perceived it to be too radical. These and other women-centered concerns helped define Pinchot's subsequent bids for office; he had come a long way.[32]

But not by himself, as one might suspect. Cornelia Pinchot, an active feminist, was tremendously influential in refining her husband's perceptions about the place of and possibilities for women in American political culture. Initially, she served as a model for what women could accomplish on the hustings before they achieved the right to vote and to run for elective position. Gifford's 1914 Senate campaign was a case in point. Cornelia was involved in all its aspects. She contributed money to campaign coffers, wrote letters, passed out literature, and proved a potent speaker. With her husband and on her own, she stumped the state, addressing women's organizations, church groups, and social clubs. Her dynamism, matching that of her tireless husband, broadened the campaign's focus, encouraging women to demand the expansion of the franchise and provoking a wider public discussion of feminist issues.[33]

Her aid was even more invaluable in 1922. Throughout Pennsylvania, women's groups had rapidly organized to take advantage of the adoption of the Nineteenth Amendment. As Democrats and Republicans, women began to pressure the once exclusively male parties to open up the organizations and to include women on the ballot. The Democrats proved more receptive than the Republicans; neither Boies Penrose nor the other powerful figures who dominated the GOP were particularly interested in pursuing women's issues or absorbing women into state and local committees. Republican women, for their part, were unimpressed with the males who controlled the party; the new interest groups they created, such as the Republican Women's Clubs of Pennsylvania, were effective in beating back the nomination of organizational candidates of whom they strongly disapproved. One who responded to their influence was Governor William Sproul. In early 1922, as he deliberated over who would fill the remainder of the late Senator Penrose's term in office, he ultimately selected George Wharton Pepper (Pinchot's lawyer during the Ballinger hearings) over the machines' objections. He acted as he had because Pepper was more acceptable to the state's newest Republicans.[34]

The power of the Republican women's clubs was amply demonstrated in the jockeying that took place for the Republican gubernatorial nomination. To secure the party's endorsement for his successor in advance of the primary, Governor Sproul, who by law could not run for a second term, announced his support for former lieutenant governor Edward E. Beidleman, but Beidelman did not pass muster with Republican women because of his continued opposition to their right to vote. They were no more impressed with Sproul's second choice, Attorney General George E. Alter, whose selection smacked of a smoke-filled back-room deal and who was opposed by Pinchot; before the League of Women Voters in Altoona, he denounced the choice. "A little group of contractor-politicians with a few friends went into a room in Philadelphia and closed the door," Pinchot told his audience, "and when they came out announced they had picked the next governor of Pennsylvania." Leading Republican women shared his opinion and began to announce their support for Pinchot himself. The Republican Women's Clubs of Pennsylvania was solidly in his camp, as was the vice chairman of the Republican State Committee, Mrs. Barclay Wharburton. "I have been determined to advocate for the nomination and election of Gifford Pinchot for Governor of this state," she told the *Philadelphia Record* in late March. She was confident that other women shared her feelings: "Every woman who reads his platform and knows his record will agree with me."[35]

Such declarations struck many male contemporaries as unusual, accustomed as they were to the singular power of patronage to shape electoral endorsements. "Spurning all overtures for an alliance which would have assured to them preferment in the party councils," the *Philadelphia North American* editorialized in May, "the women took their stand behind Gifford Pinchot, who was an independent candidate, who had no patronage at his command, and who was not in a position to confer upon a single one of them any political reward." That he was unbeholden to Republican bosses was precisely the source of his appeal to those women who also opposed machine politics, a theme that Cornelia Pinchot was instrumental in articulating on the campaign trail. After her husband's primary victory, she praised the idealism that women had brought to politics. "The women work entirely on principle," she informed the *Harrisburg Telegram*. "If they think the certain candidate the right one and a man who stands for proper ideals, they will spare nothing to make him successful." That included organizing door-to-door canvasses, using telephone surveys, and tapping into their social and religious networks to get out the vote. Their efforts not only made a difference in this particular race, she affirmed, but revealed how gender brought a new dimension to political activism: "The men cling to party and ties of friendship, but the women have proven by their wholehearted support that they believe in clean and honest government."[36]

For all its exaggeration—a gender gap in voting behavior was far more pronounced at the end of the twentieth century than it was in its second decade—Cornelia Pinchot's rhetorical jab was not without its merits. "If Pinchot is nominated, the women will have done it, not the men," harrumphed the *Pittsburgh Dispatch* in May. "The whole flood of oratory was directed to inciting resentment among women, and much of it was directed by women." One woman in particular was often touted as being responsible for Gifford Pinchot's defeat of George Alter, the hand-picked candidate of the machine—Cornelia Pinchot. "It was her work that licked up in the primary campaign," an Old Guard political operative admitted to the *New York Times* in August. "She spent hundreds of thousands of dollars to do it, and she did a d—— fine job."

Actually, Cornelia spent far less than that to achieve her goal; official records indicate she contributed approximately $30,000 to her husband's campaign (he donated more than $92,000). More than money, it was her "proved political generalship" that party regulars feared most, and that unnerved some rank-and-file Republicans enough to send anonymous hate mail to the candidate. With an attached photograph of Cornelia Pinchot came this scrawled warning: "Keep this off the stump if you have the interests of the Republican Party at heart."[37]

Not only were those interests apparently of little concern to Gifford Pinchot, he had no intention of keeping his wife bottled up; he knew even better than his opponents the profound impact she was having on the electorate. During the primary, he had written his sister Nettie that "Cornelia and I are having great fun in the campaign, to the success of which she is contributing fully as much as I am." He sounded the same refrain in a post-primary letter to Horace Plunkett, arguing that his triumph at the polls was due to his wife "and the women she organized, far more than any other single factor."[38]

That too was overstated; a badly splintered GOP had enabled him to win the Republican primary, and when the party swung behind his candidacy in the general election, he handily defeated his Democratic opponent. But that women, not least his wife, had been essential to Pinchot's success is nonetheless important, as was evident when the fifty-seven-year-old governor, with graying hair and a still-scraggly mustache, was sworn into office on January 16, 1923.

In his inaugural address, he proclaimed a mandate and announced that the "people of Pennsylvania have declared a new order in the government of their commonwealth," a new order "made concrete" by the platform on which he had run and which he now pledged to enact by using "every power of the Governorship" at his disposal. Among the many provisions he cited were a series that reflected the wishes of and were designed to appeal to the women who had expended so much energy on his campaigns—"to maintain and secure good laws for the protection of working children, women and men," "to give our children the best schools in America," and to "maintain the direct primary and protect the rights of women voters."

Of more immediate significance was the demographic composition of

Gifford Pinchot built an unusual alliance of conservative rural voters, labor unions, and women to drive his two successful gubernatorial campaigns in Pennsylvania. Grey Towers NHI.

his administration. When he promised in his inaugural to "appoint no one to public office whom I knew to be unfit," and then selected seventy-nine women to fill a variety of administrative posts—including the first woman Cabinet officer, Dr. Ellen C. Potter, who headed up the Department of Welfare—he was acknowledging an important change in his perspective. As chief forester, he had announced that women's labor was of limited value. As a new governor, he knew better.

THE BODY POLITIC

Tarred as a "multi-millionaire with socialistic ideas" and reviled as a "communistic" conservationist who would "sovietize" the state, Governor Pinchot was also heralded as a politician of "discretion and tact" who would govern "with firmness of purpose and strength of conviction." An adept public figure, he would give his opponents and supporters just enough evidence to sustain their decidedly mixed opinions of him. In its beginnings, though, his first administration was relatively uncontroversial. According to political scientist Paul Beers, reformer Pinchot "retained a strong streak of practicality for which he is seldom recognized. He held fast to his Republican credentials. After all, he had even supported Warren G. Harding."

As Pennsylvania's governor, Pinchot also observed the time-honored practices of dispensing patronage through county officials, and he focused on such critical but hardly polarizing issues as administrative reforms. The state had never had a published budget, its bureaucratic structure was a jumble of 107 departments and bureaus, and its services were poorly administered. During the first session of the legislature, Pinchot moved on all three fronts. He established a working budget that accurately reflected income and expenditures, and compelled state government to live within its budgetary limitations (how he had changed from his first creatively constructed budget at Biltmore in 1893!). Through enactment of a new administrative code, Pinchot was able to streamline governance and decentralize authority, much as he had done as head of the state forest commission. The savings from these reforms, with cuts in spending (including in his former preserve of forestry, and in his own salary), fundamentally altered Pennsylvania's fiscal status. By 1927, at the end of his four-year term, he had turned a $32 million deficit into a $6.7 million surplus, a feat that warmed the heart of his parsimonious Republican constituency.[39]

As justification for taking fairly conservative first steps, Pinchot noted that concentrating on a few realizable goals made political sense. "If you succumb to espousing every good cause, you keep building up the number of your enemies. Soon they reach such proportions that you cannot possibly be reelected." That he could not succeed himself as governor was beside the point. He hoped to run for the U.S. Senate in 1926, and expected to do so by campaigning on having stabilized the state's hitherto shaky finances. The economies he set in place, however, and the plaudits he garnered for having overhauled the Commonwealth's budget and administrative structures, did not provide the expected advantage when he entered the senatorial Republican primary in the spring of 1926.

Running against incumbent George Wharton Pepper and Congressman William Vare in what is considered one of the most fraudulent and bitter campaigns in Pennsylvania history, Pinchot was trounced. "I have just taken a very thorough licking, running a poor third in a three cornered race," he wrote his nephew, Harcourt Johnstone, a member of the British Labor Party. "The man who won [Vare] is a wet gangster who represents everything that is bad in Pennsylvania. The man who ran second [Pepper] was the candidate of the great special interests and the respectables who want to stand well with the powers that be."[40]

Vare outspent Pinchot by more than $700,000 and Pepper raised $1.6 million more than the governor, monies that later investigations revealed were poured into the outright buying of votes. So egregious was the fraud that the U.S. Senate, following the November election, which Vare also won, declined to seat the victor when Pinchot, as governor, refused to certify the final results. "I cannot so certify," he informed the president of the Senate, Vice President Charles G. Dawes, "because I do not believe that Mr. Vare has been chosen. On the contrary, I am convinced . . . that his nomination was partly bought and partly stolen, and that frauds committed in his interest have tainted both the primary and the general election."[41]

Yet the duplicitous actions of Pinchot's opponents were not the sole reasons for his defeat. His loss was tied as well to his role in three controversies that in different ways threatened the power of Old Guard Republicans in Pennsylvania and made it impossible for them to support him. Most dramatic was his declaration of war against the liquor lobby. The "present flagrant violation to enforce the Volstead Law is a blot on the good name of Pennsylvania and the United States," he declared at his inaugural. "If allowed to continue it will amount to a serious charge against the fitness of our people for genuine self-government." He then pledged fidelity to the law. "This administration will be dry. The Executive Mansion will be dry, and the personal practice of the Governor and his family will continue to be dry, in conformity with the spirit and letter of the Eighteenth Amendment."[42]

That some adult members of the Pinchot family—including the First Lady—did not accept or conform to the Eighteenth Amendment, and that the governor had every reason to know this, dramatically undercuts the power of his testimonial. But this failing did not stop him from vigorously enforcing state law throughout the Commonwealth (with the exception of Grey Towers). Between 1923 and 1927, after securing legislative authority and budgetary expenditures to enforce Prohibition (action that squeaked through the legislature following intense lobbying from the State Council of Republican Women), the state police were unleashed on the production and distribution of alcohol. In its annual report for 1924, the police reported intercepting more than 50,000 gallons of hard liquor and nearly one million gallons of beer, wine, and gin. In the next two years, the numbers declined— in part because of tighter enforcement, in part because the police began to target production facilities; by 1926, they had smashed over 1,000 stills and destroyed more than 58,000 gallons of alcohol, 35,000 gallons of moonshine, and nearly 50,000 barrels of beer.[43]

The hosannas those numbers generated from the Women's Christian Temperance Union were as predictable as the howls from the "wets." Pinchot knew the tumult that would come when he launched what he proclaimed to be a "New Birth of Political Righteousness." He understood, too, some of the political gains to be wrung from his administration's blunt attack on beer, wine, and spirits, not the least of which was the opportunity to attack Andrew Mellon, then secretary of the treasury under Calvin Coolidge.

Long allied with those who opposed Pinchot's many runs for office, Mellon held a tight grip on western Pennsylvania's Republican fortunes. A member of a powerful Pittsburgh family, he had been a major stockholder in the Overholt Distillery at the time of his appointment to Treasury (at which point he disposed of his shares). His political alliances and business investments, Pinchot believed, were the root cause of the secretary's unwillingness to use the federal enforcement powers at his disposal to aid states' efforts to enforce the Eighteenth Amendment; Pinchot lambasted Mellon's refusal to stamp out the "reign of terror."

In a 1923 speech before the Federated Council of Churches assembled in Washington, D.C., the governor went further, suggesting that the "federal enforcement service in Pennsylvania lost its soul through politics, and will never be worth its salt until it is wholly taken out of politics." Since Mellon appeared incapable of doing the job, Pinchot proposed that the president himself assume direct oversight responsibility for the enforcement of federal law. One year later, in a letter to Ralph Pulitzer—editor of the *New York World,* in whose pages Mellon had defended his actions and those of Treasury agents—Pinchot blasted back: "I do not know whether it is legal for a man who has been in the Whiskey business for forty years and who still has an interest in large quantities of whiskey, to be the head of the law enforcement, but I do know that it is wrong."[44]

Intemperate, Pinchot's condemnation was also calculated. Challenging Mellon's immense power over patronage in the state was only part of the calculation. The *Chicago Daily Tribune* was not alone in suspecting that this public battle over Prohibition was tied to larger aspirations. "Mr. Pinchot as a Republican [presidential] hopeful probably intends this smoke to fill the White House and bring President Coolidge out with a statement, wet, dry, moist, or for the majesty of all laws." Handing Coolidge "the rum question," it suggested, was a move to embarrass the president however he responded, and position Pennsylvania's governor as his possible replacement in the 1924 national elections.

Others felt similarly. Sympathetic political insiders in Washington and citizens across the country urged Pinchot to expand his efforts to secure congressional investigation of the Federal Enforcement Service in Treasury, understanding that this was a propitious moment to turn up the political heat. "Right now is the time for you to come out and throw your hat in the ring," a Virginia physician exhorted, "and capitalize [on] this controversy with Coolidge and Mellon by placing burden of blame for failure to enforce prohibition."[45]

For all Pinchot's efforts, Coolidge and Mellon were not dislodged, and his provocation did little to endear him to the party's elite or its broader membership. Payback came in many forms. Mellon and his supporters kept the governor from receiving the traditional post of delegate-at-large from Pennsylvania to the 1924 national Republican convention, a move that deprived Pinchot of an opportunity to stand before the convention as a "favorite son" candidate for the presidency. They closed ranks against him, too, in his failed bid for Senator Pepper's seat in 1926. In almost all other subsequent runs for office, Pinchot found himself arrayed against the formidable and hostile Mellon organization, cloaking his confrontations with them in the language of principled idealism. "I would infinitely rather be beaten as the enemy of liquor rather than win as its friend."[46]

He never struck such a pose with the labor movement. Although he and its organizers were on opposite sides of Prohibition, they built an enduring relationship. Little wonder: unions had never had such an ally in the governor's mansion, a fact that became quite clear in August 1923 when anthracite miners went out on strike for higher wages and improved working conditions. Before their contract expired, Pinchot had attempted to mediate between mine workers and operators, to no avail. In September, as the strike lengthened and pressure to resolve it built nationwide, Pinchot wrote President Coolidge to suggest that he step into the fray. Coolidge responded by giving Pinchot a stiff challenge; the president assured the nation that fuel would be available for the coming winter, and then invited Pinchot to act as his official mediator. Pinchot could hardly refuse, but Coolidge's dropping this difficult task in Pinchot's lap was widely believed to be one reason the governor simultaneously stepped up his attacks on what he perceived to be the administration's lax enforcement of the Eighteenth Amendment, a form of tit for tat.[47]

The new round of mediations went better than those of the summer. Through a set of adroitly negotiated compromises, Pinchot managed to secure a 10 percent pay increase for the miners, a shortened work day (to eight hours), union recognition, and the right to collective bargaining; in return, the United Mine Workers gave up their demands for a "check-off system" that would have allowed them to garnish their members' wages to underwrite union activities.[48]

Bringing the strike to such a successful close earned Pinchot much acclaim, one mark of which was a portrait on the cover of *Time* magazine. Newspaper editorials and columnists speculated about his national ambitions, a potential challenge that President Coolidge recognized and tried to co-opt; when he sent Pinchot his "heartiest congratulations," he stressed that his good work had been accomplished in "a very difficult situation in which I invited your cooperation." Pinchot loyalists quickly spun a different interpretation of the relationship between the governor's efforts and the president's disengagement. "[T]hey were 'amazed' that President Coolidge should have permitted the Governor to take the place as mediator that the

Gifford Pinchot, seen here in the 1925 presidential inaugural parade, hungered to run for the White House in the 1920s. But his troubled relations with the Republican Party leadership undercut his chances of becoming the party's standard-bearer. Grey Towers NHL

country assumed the President, because of his strike experiences in Boston, would reserve to himself," the *Harrisburg Telegram* reported. By making it plain "that he was acting solely on his own behalf and in the interest of the public," by letting it be "known he was not an ambassador of the White House, that he was receiving no instruction from Washington," Pinchot demonstrated his "Presidential timber."[49]

Whatever the future ramifications of the strike's settlement, Pinchot gained labor's immediate gratitude. With more than 400,000 members, the United Mine Workers was an important source of votes, many of which would swing into Pinchot's column in coming campaigns. But the governor's actions went well beyond those required to secure labor's approval. In this strike and later ones, he placed himself in opposition to those with

entrenched economic power. Past governors had sided with the mine operators and had used the state police and other constabulary forces to smash
picket lines and break up strike actions. Not Pinchot. He routinely charged
that work stoppages were a result of mine corporations' intransigence, and
he underscored his commitment to workers' rights by prohibiting the
dread Coal and Iron Police, a private force funded by operators, from inter-
ceding on the owners' behalf. So he acted in 1925 when another walkout
occurred. Although the 165-day strike was less successful as far as the
UMW was concerned, it secured provisions for arbitration that had eluded
the union for a quarter-century.

In thanking Pinchot for his steadfast support, union leaders indicated
they would rally the membership around his banner. "The time has come
to reward our friends, and punish our enemies," UMW leader Philip Murray announced in February 1926, an accounting that would soon come due
as "Governor Pinchot is expected to announce in a few days his candidacy
for the Senatorial nomination in the April primaries." His qualifications
were abundant; exemplifying "righteousness, justice, and equality," a subsequent UMW endorsement read, Pinchot was unique among the state's
governors because he had so "fearlessly advocated that justice be accorded
the mine workers." [50]

He had also championed the rights of consumers during this series of
strikes that had disrupted the flow of coal into the marketplace. Pinchot's
focus on their needs for heat to warm their homes and cook their meals was
part of his larger concern about economic inequities he believed were evident in the skewed access to and distribution of resources statewide. Those
inequalities and the monopolistic practices of mine owners were of a piece,
he argued, with the outcomes already evident in driving the rapid development of a new form of energy, electricity. The solution in both cases was
the same. Because coal and electric power were public utilities in Pinchot's
opinion, they should be carefully regulated as such.

To determine how this might be accomplished for electric power, Governor Pinchot requested funds from the legislature to study the problem
and to formulate remedies. The Great Power Survey, published in 1925,
was the work of a number of longtime Pinchot associates. George Woodruff and Philip Wells, both of whom had served as legal counsel for the

Forest Service, joined the new governor's staff; Woodruff was the state's attorney general, and Wells was his deputy. Robert Y. Stuart, who had replaced Pinchot at the state forest commission and would at decade's end become the chief of the Forest Service, was also on board. The mastermind behind the survey's work, though, was engineer Morris L. Cooke. A Pennsylvanian Progressive who came from a family as patrician as Pinchot's, he had the added advantage of being a deep admirer of Theodore Roosevelt. Cooke and the governor became fast friends, a friendship sparked by their shared commitment to develop a method for fair distribution of electricity. It must be found soon, Pinchot declared in a speech to the 1923 Conference of Governors that Cooke helped draft, for already the United States was on the cusp of "a new economic revolution." Strung together by the development of "[l]ong distance electric transmission" wires, this technology would "be the basis of the new economic and social order."[51]

That future was at hand, Pinchot argued, and urged his colleagues to waste no time in responding to it. He drew for them a historical analogy—the failure of the federal and state governments to understand the threats implicit in the rapid creation of nineteenth-century railroad cartels was a chilling reminder of the speed with which technological change could alter social arrangements. The same could and would be true of the electric power industry, he asserted. In fact, industry consolidation had been under way since the first years of the twentieth century, as corporations such as Westinghouse absorbed competitors or drove them out of business, elevated the price of power, and consolidated their operations in the burgeoning urban centers. Pinchot, Cooke, and other critics of the rapidly forming electric combines were not unalterably opposed to private enterprise, but they distrusted the corporations' interest in and capacity to produce and diffuse power equitably. The urban poor and rural farm communities were ignored in the race for economic dominance of the market; the Giant Power Survey estimated that "less than five per cent of the farms of Pennsylvania receive central station electric service," an appalling lack "at a time when electric light and power has become as essential to the home and the industry of the State as railroad transportation." Once more, the disadvantaged suffered disproportionately.[52]

Holding out little hope that market economics would correct this discriminatory consequence, Giant Power Survey advocates were just as skeptical about the proposals embodied in Secretary of Commerce Herbert Hoover's competing vision, Super Power. A frequent speaker before the National Electric Light Association (NELA), the national trade organization of the industry, Hoover invariably advocated maintaining the status quo. "Being one who believes that the progress of our nation can come only by preserving on one hand that vital initiative and enterprise of our people and on the other an equality of opportunity to all, I necessarily do not favor the strangulation of both by the hand of bureaucracy and politics." Unfettered, the member corporations of NELA would expand the generation of power, create a vast network of transmission lines and customers, and enhance the nation's prosperity, all without the need for new regulatory mechanisms.[53]

Cooke and Pinchot emphatically disagreed. They pounded away at what they considered the key differences between the Giant Power Survey and Super Power. Not only did Giant Power activists not assume, as Hoover did, "that the companies would integrate themselves in the course of years" without regulatory action, but they favored strict regulation to ensure standard rates for a wide range of customers. Such regulatory action would enable the broader distribution of this public utility, and would most benefit rural districts. Because Hoover failed to take these concerns into account, and so failed because he was in essence an industry spokesman, his model produced monopolistic behavior that in fact endangered what he believed was the nation's self-interest—the citizenry's "equality for opportunity."[54]

By contrast, the Giant Power Survey, which "proposes that electrical energy for all purposes shall be made available to everyone more cheaply than at present, and without unfair discrimination as to rates or service," was the wave of the future. To create this future required state action, for it was clear to Pinchot and Cooke that the federal government, dominated as it was by a conservative business elite and special interests, lacked the initiative to regulate the electric power industry. "Our federal leadership appears to be in the process of breaking down, if it has not already done so," Cooke lamented to Pinchot in March 1924. "If national authority is to be supported and national confidence in government reestablished it will in my opinion only come about through the more effective function of smaller

units." Fortunately, Governor Pinchot was perfectly situated to reinvig-
orate state government, "to sound a new note of state responsibility as
contrasted with states' rights," and give new birth to the "development of
American Sovereignty."[55]

It was just such a note that Pinchot struck in February 1925 when he
submitted the Giant Power Survey's final report to the legislature. If the
legislators acted on the report's findings, and promptly gave the state the
necessary regulatory authority to control what Pinchot described as a
"gigantic monopoly" and to extend electricity to every farm, hamlet, and
urban enclave, then it would strike a blow for freedom. "As Pennsylvania
and the nation deal with electric power so shall we and our descendants be
free men, master of our own destinies and our own souls." But if the delib-
erative body failed to act, "we shall be helpless servants of the most wide-
spread, far-reaching and penetrating monopoly ever known. Either we
must control electric power, or its masters and owners will control us."[56]

Ecstatic about the report's arguments, Pinchot applauded Cooke's work
as its director. "I do not believe if you live to be a hundred you will ever do
another piece of work, or that if I live to be a hundred I shall be associated
with another piece of work, of larger significance and importance to the
people of the United States, and indeed of the whole world than this which
was born in your head." Whether anyone else understood what was in
Cooke's mind was open to question. As Pinchot admitted, "the Legislature,
of course, has so far absorbed only the haziest idea of what it is all about."
He did not give the state's politicians enough credit. They knew, on a political level, exactly what the report contained. When business groups voiced
strong opposition, as engineering associations in the state rebutted some of
the report's technological assumptions, and when the industry's organ,
Electric World, bristled at the "communistic ideas of Morris L. Cooke,
director, and Governor Pinchot," the legislators backed away from acting
on the report; each of the nineteen bills the administration brought to the
floor for action died in committee. What Pinchot had described as Cooke's
"epoch-making" labors had come to naught.[57]

This was just one of the major defeats Pinchot would suffer in his last
two years as governor, reversals often tied to the time-bound tenure of a
one-term governor. In Pinchot's words, the "second session of a Governor

who can't be reelected is not exactly huckleberry pie." But as he told his sister Nettie, he was determined "to go out of office here with head up and tail over the dashboard, instead of oozing out of office as so many Governors have done." So it was with evident delight that he took the dais at the close of the legislative session in January 1927 and hammered the legislature one last time.[58]

The chamber was packed, for the "word had gone forth that Mr. Pinchot would deliver a sensational address," the *Philadelphia Public Ledger* reported. "Capitol Hill crowded into the lobbies and the aisles. Members of the Senate sat near the Speaker's desk," families and loved ones jammed into the hall, and even the surfaces of the members' desks overflowed, "gay with floral tributes from constituents and friends." As was traditional, Pinchot opened with a recitation of each department's activities that year, a listing that generated "some restless agitation," but the chamber quickly quieted down when the governor turned to political matters.[59]

After praising his supporters among women, labor, and the farm belt, Pinchot, "with a fine and vicious scorn in his voice," delivered a stinging denunciation of the corrupt character of contemporary politics. He slammed first the state's Public Service Commission, which, he thundered, "has done little to protect the rights of the people of Pennsylvania. It has done much to insure the welfare and the profits of the corporations." Its success in this regard was so great that "the plain people would be better off with no Public Service Commission at all than with a commission the majority of whose members are merely speaking tubes for the public utilities."

What followed these blunt charges "astounded the hardest-boiled politicians in the House," a reporter observed. "After four years in a position to learn the facts," Pinchot said, warming to his main topic, "I am going out of office with the most hearty contempt not only for the morals and intentions, but also for the minds of the gang politicians of Pennsylvania. Doubtless in the past there have been gang politicians of power and insight. But we look for them in vain today."

So degraded was this class of political gangsters, and so unquestioningly supported by indifferent or craven voters, that these thugs had had their way with the public treasury. "Gang control is a system under which the taxpayer is the goat at every turn in the road," consistently being fleeced because he or she knew no better. The stolen funds, when linked to trafficking in illicit activities, gave power brokers the capacity to fix elections and thus remain in control. "Hence any machine must include a body of the lowest politicians, such, for example, as the Mellon machine in Pittsburgh and the Mitten machine in Philadelphia, men who depend for their living and their power, on liquor, crime, vice."[60]

As he slapped out at the reputations of those seated before him, the audience grew tense. "When he mentioned the name of Mellon, Mr. Pinchot was forced to pause. Murmurs of disapproving anger, spasmodic bursts of applause and ripples of laughter—somewhat nervous laughter—spread through the House." Some representatives walked out, but Pinchot pressed his attack. Proud of his independence, and the political setbacks it of necessity produced, he was convinced that he had acted as he must. "From the beginning the most effective thing I could do to deceive the gang was to lay all my cards on the table and say precisely what I meant. They never got used to that."

Neither would they get comfortable with his final argument, a hopeful analysis of what he described as "a rebirth of Liberalism." Deflected by World War I, progressive forces were reemerging, ready to carry on the "fight for the rights, dignities and welfare of the American people." Soon, Pinchot predicted, millions of "patriotic men and women [will] take up the progressive movement where it was interrupted and carry it to its appointed and glorious conclusion."

No one doubted that Pinchot saw himself among their number, if not leading the charge. "Without a doubt the forester, who beat the organization four years ago, and spanked it today," the Philadelphia Public Ledger concluded, "is going out to do battle in new fields." Whether anyone would follow him was open to question, however. Having alienated almost every center of power within the state during his four-year term—and those he missed he had rebuked in his speech—it was not clear what further chance he would have to pursue elective office in Pennsylvania. Even Pinchot's allies might reject the "vehemence of expression and [the] bitter denunciation" of his final oration; the blistering language, a newspaper editorialized, "may tend to obscure in the public mind the sound achievements of his record."

Pinchot expressed no such reservations, reveling rather in the opportunity to speak without restraint, in a tone little used in public discourse. Sending a copy of his address to his sister in England, he remarked that he "really had a great time writing it, and even more fun delivering it. You ought to have seen the opposition squirm!" He felt most at home swimming against the tides.[61]

Chiefly Politics

HUNGRY FOR continued engagement and eager to remain relevant, the Pinchots returned to Washington, D.C., after their years in Harrisburg. Moving back into their "fine old mansion" on Rhode Island Avenue in January 1927, which James and Mary Pinchot had built at the beginning of the twentieth century as a staging ground for their oldest son's career as a forester, was Gifford and Cornelia's first step to reestablish their presence in the center of American politics. And to their impressive home, the couple invited the press for interviews and met with old political allies, making 1615 Rhode Island Avenue once more a political hub.

Even before her husband's term had ended in early January, Cornelia was laying down plans for the couple's role in influencing national legislation in the final months of that year's congressional session. "The governor's lady, ever since he married her in 1914, has been a primary factor in his public work and political crusades," the *Washington Star* declared. His "militant wife" would continue "to enact that role" during their residence in Washington, as indicated by the meeting to which she had invited members of Congress, "mainly old-time Republican Progressives" such as Nebraska senator George W. Norris. At that gathering, over which she presided because her husband had remained in Harrisburg to prepare for his final speech, Cornelia distributed an outline of the issues he hoped to contribute to when he returned to Washington.

Much of his agenda was related to the concerns that had framed his work in Pennsylvania. Gifford expected "to roll up his sleeves and punch the congressional bag most vigorously" on matters of electric development; he proposed to aid Senator Norris's fight to block the transfer of Muscle Shoals, a much-disputed federal dam project on the Tennessee River, to private enterprise. Likewise would he confront an old foe, the "electric overlords" who sought unregulated dominance over the nation's emerging power grid. As for the Keystone State itself, reporters learned that the former governor "does not dream of removing himself from the strenuous sphere" of its politics; to the contrary, he was planning a series of speaking engagements there and making himself available to testify in the impending U.S. Senate investigations into the electoral fraud that so marred Pennsylvania's 1926 senatorial contest. The sixty-one-year-old Gifford Pinchot was not about to retire.[1]

What had really motivated his return to the capital? Suspecting that "up his resourceful sleeve . . . a presidential ambition is concealed," journalists hustled out to the Pinchot manse when the governor arrived in town in mid-January. A Philadelphia reporter ushered into Pinchot's small library on the second floor found him sitting at a desk "heaped with unanswered mail, welcoming letters from old Washington friends and letters of regret from all parts of Pennsylvania that he had left the Keystone State," a staging that suggested the politician's continuing cachet. Happy as Pinchot was to be of enduring significance, he urged his visitor to reassure his readers of his continued interest in their welfare ("I shall keep in touch with Pennsylvania—please tell them that") and vowed to frequently return to the state: "[W]hen the trout season opens, I will give you one guess where to find me—yes, Milford."[2]

As he played to that distant electorate, Pinchot in his interview laid the groundwork for more national entanglements. It was a tree that provided his segue. Glancing out the library's window, Pinchot found his gaze arrested by the bare branches of a large mulberry tree "that almost scraped the top of the Pinchot mansion." Reflecting on its size and life span, he mused to the reporter: "I have seen that tree grow from a slip no longer than your arm. It was planted when this house was built back in 1900." The mulberry's age and durability were of no little import. "To me it has the character of the great cause of conservation—conservation in forestry, conservation in electric energy for the public, and conservation in good Government." Once planted, that movement had grown, but only because it had had stewards who carefully tended its development. Acting as a guardian for conservation, Pinchot declared, would take up most of his energy during the coming congressional session; in this work, he promised to "give such humble assistance . . . as I can as a private citizen working out from my past experiences in various offices."

The implication of this and other interviews was that Pinchot was planning to return to battlegrounds of yore. But although of still-youthful vigor ("as spry as a man 10 or 15 years his junior," one account praised), he had returned to old haunts that were much altered. "'I find new buildings and new faces on every side,' said the ex-Governor almost sadly," discovering even the venerable White House transformed. "'The tennis court where I occasionally played with Mr. Roosevelt is no more. It is covered with Executive Offices.'"3

Yet beneath the aura of nostalgia, some essential things remained unchanged. Once back in Washington, Pinchot reassembled his loyal staff. This decidedly familiar cast of characters included George Woodruff and Philip Wells; key functionaries in Pinchot's administration in Harrisburg, they returned with him to the capital where they had once worked in the Forest Service and the National Conservation Association. Henry Graves, still dean of the Yale School of Forestry, periodically joined the team. And one crucial figure who had not left Washington, Harry Slattery, former executive secretary of the NCA, also reunited with his old boss. While governor, Pinchot had kept Slattery on a retainer, for which the attorney wrote some of his speeches, acted as his national press agent, and kept him in touch with breaking legislation, the rise and fall of political alliances, and the scandals that were a plague on all houses, executive, legislative, and judicial.

As he had while head of the Forest Service, Pinchot relied on this cadre of close friends, many of whom had gone to Yale. The old-school connection endured, historian Brian Balogh has observed about those earlier years, because it was shaped by "deference built upon social ties and gratitude" and framed by Pinchot's "personal appeal, and the power of his message."[4]

These men's power over Pinchot's message, and its distribution, was just as significant. They made full use of Gifford Pinchot *as* Gifford Pinchot, knowing (as he did) that his influence emanated in part from his mere presence in the political arena. To introduce his interpretation of a particular crisis swung votes, crystallized support, provoked outrage. In June 1928, for example, Pinchot worked diligently with Senator Norris to scuttle attempts by utility investors to once more gain control of a proposed dam and generating station at Muscle Shoals; eight years earlier, with Slattery working behind the scenes, the two men had successfully blocked Henry Ford's bid to secure a 100-year lease to the site, and over the years Norris had been able to bottle up similar legislation as chair of the Agriculture and Forestry Committee.

A new effort to gain private control over the waterpower site emerged in 1928, with Pinchot yet again aiding Norris in the counterattack. Slattery wrote Pinchot that the utility companies had taken note of his contributions to this battle. "Am I really on the power blacklist?" Pinchot queried. "That is an honor I had not counted on." Slattery assured him that he was a marked man. "You've been identified . . . as someone spending millions to put over public ownership," a charge designed to enhance the utility lobby's coffers. "They wanted to shake the boys down evidently."[5]

The electricity industry was not alone in its use of Pinchot. Slattery's exchange with the conservationist demonstrated why he and the other members of what Walter Lippmann once described as the "Gifford Pinchot School of Crusaders" were so valuable to their leader. By his remarkable ability to ferret out salient gossip, Slattery revealed his status as a consummate insider, a broker of intrigue; his access to information helped Pinchot pick and focus in on his target just as the news Slattery conveyed also flattered Pinchot's self-image as gallant defender of the faith. Making certain that Gifford Pinchot remained the player he yearned to be kept Slattery and the rest of the crusaders in the game. Professional patronage was a reciprocal exchange.[6]

AGENCY OF CHANGE

On no organization's behalf were these veterans of the conservation wars more willing to fight than the Forest Service. Pinchot repeatedly explained to journalists in January 1927 that he and his colleagues were prepared to "blaze away on [its] behalf"; they would rally in its defense against what Pinchot expected would be "a determined drive" by the grazing industry and other special interests seeking to dismantle its authority and power. The old chief, now ex-governor, vowed "to wade into this particular fray 'up to the neck.'"7

His full-bodied commitment was nothing new, as his successors in the chief's office of the Forest Service could attest. Since his removal in 1910, Pinchot had kept a close eye on the internal tensions and external pressures that the agency endured. Second chief Henry Graves, and his replacement William B. Greeley, well understood (and, not occasionally, were understandably troubled) that the founder of the Forest Service had a deep and abiding emotional bond with the agency he had created.

Pinchot's had not been an everyday presence as chief, to be sure, but that did not mean he could not be called back to help the Forest Service, even on the most seemingly minor of issues. During the second week of January 1914, while huddling with Pinchot about the Forest Service's proposed response to a grazing bill that was due for debate during the forthcoming session of Congress, then-chief Henry Graves, Pinchot's handpicked successor, asked for advice on a troubling personnel matter. Apparently a "Mrs. Pryor," a member of the Washington staff, had complained about her "working conditions." Pinchot immediately interviewed her, was persuaded that she had been "treated unjustly," and recognized that this situation contained some unspecified political fallout, as he noted in his diary: "The FS is in real danger because she has told Sen. [John Sharp] Williams [D-Mississippi] and will tell others." What bothered Pinchot most of all was that Graves did not appear to grasp the incident's significance. The next day he laid out his worries to Graves, conferred again with Mrs. Pryor, smoothed over her concerns, and then deflected what he called "a very determined" Senator Williams.8

There was little Pinchot would not do to stave off threats to the integrity of the Forest Service—even if that meant saving it from itself. Pinchot's response to Graves's hesitant handling of the Williams episode was tied to his growing fear in 1914 that the second chief was waffling on a larger issue—that of the appropriate relationship between the Forest Service and the lumber industry. Unlike Pinchot, who loved public dustups, Graves preferred to seek consensus with his potential opponents. Encouraged by his own proclivities and by his more accommodationist staff, especially William B. Greeley, who oversaw the agency's timber management programs, Graves had begun to map out a closer alliance between public foresters and private lumbering interests. This new direction was illustrated in the Graves-sponsored cooperative study of the lumber situation in the United States that the Forest Service, the Bureau of Corporations (later the Federal Trade Commission), and industry representatives conducted throughout the teens. These reports essentially concluded that private timber corporations were compelled to strip their forested lands even when timber prices were low, due to ongoing taxation and credit pressures. The Forest Service's response to this situation, Graves and Greeley believed, should be to manage its timber so as not to compete with private harvesting; the public good would best be served by sustaining private interests.[9]

Pinchot was shocked. Not only were these findings a "whitewash of destructive lumbering," but they managed at the same time to compromise the Forest Service's capacity to offer independent judgment and critical analysis, hardly the best means by which to serve the public interest. Although as chief he too had been interested in cooperative programs with the timber industry, and had sought ways by which to encourage the creation of a mutual agenda because of the power that lumbering lobbyists held in Congress, he was now convinced that accommodation meant capitulation.

That Pinchot reached this conviction in the mid-teens, that he then went on the offensive over the emergence of an alliance between the industry and the Forest Service, undercuts historian Mark Dowie's claim that Pinchot "could hardly have foreseen that the bureaucracy he thought would contain the greed and rapaciousness of timber men and miners would fall victim to the influence and, at times, corruption of the very people it was designed to contain." Pinchot did not suffer what Dowie labeled a "failure of foresight." From the outset, no one had seen this problem more clearly. In the early 1890s, he had corresponded with Dietrich Brandis about how to instill a sense of professional integrity into an agency that would operate in a political environment in which power and position often derived from partisan patronage. How to keep low-paid foresters free from temptation, safe from "peculation and corruption"? This problem required special handling, Brandis offered, due to the dispersed nature of a forest service, spread out and isolated over a vast terrain. It required the creation of "a Staff of Officers, animated by strong and delicate feelings of honor, [and] impelled and roused by enthusiastic zeal for the public good." That was the lesson he had learned in establishing the British forest system in India, a lesson that made good sense to Pinchot because of his experience as a Yale undergraduate. Like college classmates, agency employees would function most cohesively when bound together around a core set of shared values learned in the classroom, at work, and through play. Building such an esprit de corps, which the Pinchot-funded Yale forestry program pioneered in the United States through the camplike enthusiasm enveloping its summer school at Grey Towers, would embolden future forest rangers and officers to remain true to their school.[10]

The need to refresh these ties of fellowship and allegiance was not an occasional thing, Pinchot believed; their development and maintenance required a vigilant watchfulness. That had been easier to accomplish when he was chief than it would be after he left the service in 1910. But as the succeeding thirty-five years would demonstrate, whenever the moral standing of the Forest Service was in question, whether as a consequence of its own failings or as the result of outsider actors, Pinchot would go on the attack.[11]

That was why he had moved so fast to head off what he perceived were Graves's and Greeley's failures to uphold the public interest. That was why, too, he prodded the Society of American Foresters (SAF) and its several thousand members to join him in assessing the Forest Service's conduct in 1919. Few could have doubted but that SAF's Committee for the Application of Forestry, which Gifford Pinchot chaired and whose membership he helped select, would challenge the Forest Service's research and recommendations on the timber industry.

Any such doubts were dispelled when the report was published in the

December 1919 issue of the *Journal of Forestry,* the lead publication of the SAF: the title of the opening article, Pinchot's "The Lines Are Drawn," made it clear that a battle had been joined against the "continued misuse of forest lands privately owned." The widespread and "destructive lumbering on private timberlands is working a grave injury to the public interest and must be stopped," he proclaimed, but that could occur only if foresters joined together and fought against these depredations. "I use the word fight," the chairman trumpeted, "because I mean precisely that. Forest devastation will not be solved through persuasion, a method that has been thoroughly tried out for the past twenty years and has failed utterly." New tactics must be employed to ensure that "private owners of forest land," who are "so constituted and inspired that a change from within is not to be expected," are "compelled to manage their properties in harmony with the public good." That would come only from "[p]ressure from without, in the form of public sentiment, crystallized in compulsory public regulation." This alone "promises adequate results," he observed, an observation that carried with it a clarion call: with the "field cleared for action and the lines . . . plainly drawn," he who is "not for forestry is against it. The choice lies between the convenience of the lumbermen and the public good."[12]

It was Graves's turn to be shocked. Not because he fundamentally disagreed with Pinchot—by 1919, he too had begun to realize that lumber interests talked more about cooperation than they practiced it; he too thought that some regulation was necessary, though he stressed state rather than federal control. No, what bothered Graves was that the committee, by its emphasis on the need for federal controls over private enterprise, appeared to be pursuing what he labeled a "socialistic" agenda; worrisome too was that Pinchot, in undertaking "this scheme of his own," was attempting to supplant Graves and "become the hero in saving the forests of the country." Confirmation of the continuing regard with which the old chief was held emerged in a SAF straw vote on the Pinchot committee's findings—two-thirds affirmed their support of some form of national regulation of private lumber practices. Pinchot, it seemed, continued to do more to articulate and set the agenda of American forestry than did his successor.[13]

This was a difficult situation at best. These once-close friends now communicated, when they did, through third parties. Only indirectly would Pinchot learn in March 1920, in the midst of the contentious professional debate over the role of federal regulation in forestry, that Graves, worn down by illness and worn out by the politics of his job, had resigned as chief. Freed from Pinchot's shadow, he no longer had to fear, as apparently he had for several years, that his dominant friend (who in his most frustrated moments Graves called his "enemy") was poised to rebuke him for cozying up to the lumber industry. That shadow and the fear it could generate would be all too publicly realized during the eight-year term of Graves's assistant, William B. Greeley, who became the third chief of the Forest Service in April 1920.[14]

TRANSITION GAME

Years later, and with the prompting of an interviewer, Greeley's widow was pained to recall that her husband's accomplishments had gone unacknowledged in Gifford Pinchot's autobiography, Breaking New Ground: "Mr. Pinchot just had no use for Billy that was all," she remembered; to him, "Billy was a traitor." Although there was no reason for Pinchot to have included Greeley in his memoirs—they concluded with Pinchot's dismissal from the Forest Service in 1910, several years before Greeley became a central figure in agency matters—had Pinchot written the planned second volume, Greeley would have been the prime target of his scorn, pummelled as was the despised William Howard Taft in the first volume.[15]

Certainly Greeley and Pinchot were acutely aware of each other's perspectives throughout the 1920s, differing stances that consistently drew them into public confrontations of a kind and intensity that had not occurred between Pinchot and Graves, as strained as their relationship had been. This struggle, whether splashed across the pages of the Journal of Forestry or aired in congressional hearings, turned on different constructions of the Forest Service's mission, professional ideals, social significance, and political agenda. As Greeley put it, Pinchot "saw an industry so blindly wedded to fast and destructive exploitation that it would not change. I saw a forest economy overburdened by cheap raw material. Mr. Pinchot saw a willful industry. I saw a sick industry." And when they fought over these positions, they gave no quarter, making them more alike than they might have been willing to admit.[16]

The two had clashed even before Greeley replaced Graves, first over a 1916 report Greeley had authored on the economic troubles underlying the lumber industry. In that report Greeley had argued that fires, state tax codes, and glutted markets made it impossible for lumber companies to harvest responsibly. He and Graves advocated a more cooperative relationship with the timber companies and a greater sensitivity to the market forces that determined their actions, an argument that Pinchot denounced; with that denunciation, Greeley noted proudly, "I lost caste in the temple of conservation on Rhode Island Avenue."[17]

More sustained were Greeley and Pinchot's disagreements in 1919 over the need for federal oversight of private lumbering activities. When, in the *Journal of Forestry,* Pinchot had drawn a line in the sand, asserting that only strict national regulation would halt destructive lumbering, Greeley promptly drew his own. Not only were Pinchot's proposals of doubtful constitutionality, but they were in direct conflict with the powers and inclinations of the states, a situation that would "seriously confuse and hamper our national development of forestry." The states instead must be recognized, he wrote, as "the proper agency to deal with private lands within their borders"; any other approach was undemocratic, un-American.

That political principle, in Greeley's view, was reinforced by another concerning foresters' social concerns. They had no business involving themselves in what he called "purely industrial conditions"—that is, in the relations between employers and employees, and in questions of wages, benefits, and the workplace environment, subjects that were best left to the two contending parties themselves. "Let us stick to the subjects in which, as foresters, we can claim some degree of expert knowledge," he concluded, exhausting, for instance, "every opportunity for education, for showing the forest owners that the arrest of denudation is to their benefit." By this approach would the profession avoid what Pinchot had thought axiomatic, "a 'fight' between the public and the timber owners."[18]

Greeley knew he could not avoid a brawl with Pinchot. For his part, the former chief did not hesitate to rough up the new one. In a pair of rebuttals published in the *Journal of Forestry,* one just before Greeley assumed his new post and one just after, Pinchot dismissed Greeley's assertion that state control of the timber industry was preferable to national regulation, remarking that this would be counterproductive; state management would result in more litigation and conflict than would national. Moreover, federal control of public lands was the only effective way to counteract the power that special interests would exert in those states that witnessed the greatest devastation of timberlands. "It would be only necessary for the lumber interests . . . to prevent the passage of bills in three or four great lumber states in order to effectually cripple the whole plan of State control."[19]

Pinchot, who had long battled against such interests to secure and maintain the national forests, reminded his readers that what had kept the national forests inviolate (and the Forest Service independent) was "that both were free from State control," free from the meddling of the western states' timber industry. These public lands had been "saved in Congress by the support of the Central and Eastern states," he asserted, the very "forces" which the State control plan now proposes to eliminate from the critical points in the fight" to regulate private land exploitation. "The problem is National, and the Nation alone is strong and steady enough to handle it."[20]

Pinchot's political analysis had professional consequences, which he made certain to emphasize in his second rejoinder, "Where We Stand," published in the May 1920 issue of the *Journal of Forestry*. Its title, set in the first-person plural, assumed a direct correspondence between where Pinchot and foresters in general stood; as he asserted his claim to institutional memory, he positioned himself as the keeper of the flame, the definer of faith—*he* was "we." By this definition was Greeley an interloper, a flack for corporate interests who sought to undercut the Forest Service's integrity and its commitment to the public good.[21]

This point was more subtly made in an obituary of Eugene S. Bruce that Pinchot co-authored in the same issue of the *Journal of Forestry* in which "Where We Stand" appeared. Bruce, a lumberman in the Adirondacks when Pinchot met him in the late nineteenth century, "abandoned a career rich in promise," and at a "real sacrifice to his own financial future" threw his lot in with "a little band of foresters in Washington filled with enthusiasm but void of experience." Driven by a "clear vision of [the] better handling of the forests which he loved," he had a "grim determination to see this better handling realized" and, with "the zeal of a new convert to a great cause," fought unsparingly for his principles. Pinchot honored the memory of this lumberman who had become a forester as he would never do for a forester who acted like a lumberman, a dismissal that surely William Greeley, now in his first month as the new chief, recognized, and that his widow could still recall forty years later.[22]

The third chief was not dead on arrival, however. He proved an adept opponent, a skilled political player who challenged Pinchot's claims to define the profession's identity and ideological focus. In turn, he asserted his own with considerable success, in the process reshaping public foresters' sense of their duties, especially in the establishment of a cooperative relationship with the timber industry.

That Greeley would seek no reconciliation with Pinchot was evident in his deft handling of a series of legislative initiatives that surfaced in response to Pinchot-inspired legislation, specifically several versions of the so-called Capper bill. First introduced in May 1920, the bill was crafted to provide federal controls over timber cutting on private lands. To counter Pinchot's congressional supporters, and the legislation they proposed, Greeley encouraged industry executives to form the National Forestry Program Committee, then cooperated quietly with its efforts to promote more industry-friendly initiatives. This stealth campaign involved Greeley in drafting a bill that he gave to lumber lobbyists, who then dropped it into the legislative hopper. Pinchot was not the only one who knew how to manipulate the political process to his advantage.[23]

Greeley's legislative rebuttal, the Snell bill, named for its sponsor, Representative Bertrand Snell of New York, was introduced in December 1920; it advocated state control of lumbering practices and, due to its origins, quickly gained unanimous industry support along with a wide following among western foresters and forestry associations. Sparks flew at subsequent public hearings in Congress over the two competing bills, when Greeley and Pinchot predictably assailed each other's positions.

When the Capper bill failed to reach the Senate floor and the Snell bill, which did not have a Senate counterpart, languished in the House, Greeley quickly backed a successor, the Clarke-McNary Act of 1924, which secured bicameral sponsorship. Thus the issue of federal regulatory control over private lumbering flared anew, but with a startling difference. This time Greeley stacked the congressional hearings with witnesses friendly to his belief in state control and his contention that federal regulatory action mattered only in fire suppression. His opposition never mounted serious resistance. By June 1924, the act had swept through Congress, and Greeley stood in a cloakroom listening to the final vote in an exultant mood: "[I]t was a great thrill to be in on the kill—even if the victory was bloodless."[24]

That it was so, Greeley knew, was at least in part due to the fact that Pinchot, then governor of Pennsylvania, was distracted by his own legislative session in Harrisburg; he had dismissed the Clarke-McNary Act as a violation of the public trust, a gift to the lumber interests. Without his presence in the congressional discussion over the bill, there was, Greeley beamed, "no fight against the new and popular proposal from the West." His characterization of the Clarke-McNary Act's geographical source of support, however, neatly confirmed Pinchot's deep-seated fears that western lumbermen now dominated the Forest Service.[25]

This dominance would have ramifications for the agency's internal culture. Not only did Greeley's perspectives hold sway, but other voices were correspondingly muted. The most striking example of this was Raphael Zon. A Russian Jew and socialist, he had migrated to the United States in the late nineteenth century and studied forestry under Bernhard Fernow at Cornell. A brilliant and sharp-tongued scientist as well as an occasional and fiery editor of the *Journal of Forestry,* Zon was also a close associate of Pinchot's. His personality and politics—like Pinchot, he did not hesitate to advocate his belief in the necessity for federal regulation of private lumbering—led to his being eased out of the Washington office of the Forest Service to head up the Lakes States Forest Experiment Station in St. Paul, Minnesota. Zon had confronted Greeley once too often in staff meetings, and though he reported to a colleague in 1925 that his exile was "voluntary," it had been "suggested by Greeley."[26]

With the *Journal* in friendlier hands and the Society of American Foresters hewing to the nonregulatory line of the Greeley-led Forest Service, Pinchotites understandably felt isolated and of little consequence; the agency, one of them commented, was replete with Greeley "yes-men." Pin-

chot's disappointment was magnified by the fact that he had been instrumental in the creation of the agency, the profession's graduate programs,
the field's leading journal, and its professional organization. By the late
1920s, his continued pleas for a more socially responsible, politically engaged
forestry fell on deaf ears. No longer a member of the American Forestry
Association because of its capitulation to industrial interests, and rarely
asked to write for professional forestry publications, Pinchot felt excluded
from the world he had helped to create; he even stopped attending meetings of the Society of American Foresters. What Harry Graves had never
been able to accomplish, William B. Greeley had—the founder had been
uprooted.[27]

SHIFTING GROUNDS

Despite these professional setbacks, Pinchot sniped at Greeley's newly won
preeminence whenever he had a chance. In 1926, as Pennsylvania's chief
executive, he monitored a grazing bill that Greeley was sponsoring, and he
schemed with Harry Graves on how best to attack it when it came before
the House Committee on Agriculture. "Personally, I dislike the bill very
greatly in certain important respects," Pinchot wrote Graves, still at the
Yale School of Forestry, but "we can thrash that out when it gets before the
Committee"—before, that is, the two former chiefs would testify against
their successor's initiative in a public hearing. Pinchot gave Greeley fair
warning of his opposition and forthcoming testimony, informing him that
the grazing bill was "defective" in its specifics "but especially in this—that
it is obviously written from the point of view of protecting the special interests of a special group instead of protecting the interests of the general public." Such craven accommodation was galling. "I hope most earnestly that
you will not allow any bill of which this can properly be said, as it can of this
bill in question, to be introduced in Congress with the approval of the Forest Service. . . ." Not surprised that Greeley had once more failed to uphold
what Pinchot believed to be the agency's high ideals, his point was to
remind Greeley (and anyone who cared to listen) of this repeated failure.
He was trying to resuscitate a flagging opposition.[28]

He attempted to breathe more life into that opposition in the late 1920s, and did so from an increasingly leftist political platform. Emboldened by the insights he had gained during his first term as governor, and encouraged by his wife, Pinchot began to examine more radical responses to the problems confronting the forestry profession and the conservation movement, an examination that would lead him to support something he began to call "new conservationism."

Part of what was new was the emphasis he now placed on the protection and preservation of human life. While Pennsylvania's commissioner of forestry, and later as the state's governor, he had studied the social and environmental consequences of industrial forestry. He came to see that intensive logging not only stripped away forest cover but also left vulnerable the many communities that were located in, and once had depended on, the now-cutover lands. Pennsylvania was littered with ghost towns—places, such as Leetonia, Gardeau, and Cross Fork, that had boomed when the lumber companies arrived to liquidate the virgin forests of hemlock that few thought "would ever be cut out." The trees were quickly harvested, and just as rapidly the sawmills moved to the next dense stand, leaving behind a blighted landscape and a bewildered citizenry. "Discouragement and despair are written everywhere in the village" of Norwich, wrote Pinchot in 1923, noticeable "in the faces of the people as well as in the condition of the tumble-down houses and grass-covered streets." Only through an intense commitment to reforest the slash-littered environment would the land and the people recover.[29]

To combat these depredations, Pinchot had reenergized the state's forest commission and raised funds from the legislature to purchase and replant denuded landscapes. This restoration work was essential if the state forests were to assume the multiple functions assigned to them in the Governor Pinchot–inspired Administrative Code of 1923: "To provide a continuous supply of timber, lumber, wood and other forest products, to protect the watersheds, conserve the waters and regulate the flow of rivers and streams of the state, and to furnish healthful recreation to the public." He returned to these themes again and again when he stumped the state in 1928 in support of a $25 million "Forestry Bond" his successor, Governor John S. Fisher, had initiated. In hundreds of letters, and in articles and speeches, he praised the state forest system and expressed the belief that its expansion was critical to economic vitality, human health, and wildlife regeneration. "[R]eforesting the hills and valleys of Pennsylvania" was the only way "we can guarantee free hunting, fishing and camping grounds to our people," Pinchot asserted. A well-wooded state made dollars and sense.[30]

So would the purification of Pennsylvania's badly polluted streams and rivers. As with the timber industry, mining corporations and iron and steel operations had badly abused the landscape from which they wrenched their wealth, and used the state's waterways as sinks in which they poured sewage, sludge, and other effluent. Their collective despoliation found its counter, however poorly the legislature funded it, in a new agency that Pinchot established in his first term as governor.

Arguably the first state-level anti-pollution agency in the country, the Sanitary Water Board (SWB), a division of the State Department of Health, was charged with enforcing laws prohibiting pollution of the state's 4,400 streams, evaluating water quality, and proposing remedies to its decline. Its regulatory authority was upheld in 1924 on a ruling by Pinchot appointee and confidante Philip Wells, deputy state attorney general, which gave the SWB the power to stop industrial wastes from entering water supplies.

During the mid-twenties, the board generally sought voluntary agreements with industrial polluters, in the belief that legal threats would impel corporations to leave the state without repairing environmental damage. It thus successfully negotiated with the leather tanning industry and pulp and paper mills to evaluate and control the impact of their discharges into waterways; it struck similar agreements with coke producers and gas plants to halt the dumping of phenol wastes. Because the SWB staff recognized the interconnectedness of watersheds and the interstate implications of water flow, they joined with their counterparts along the Ohio River valley, and with the U.S. Public Health Service, for a series of meetings to determine a strategy for controlling industrial pollutants; out of these gatherings emerged the Ohio River Interstate Stream Conservation Agreement, signed in April 1924, in which "the signatories agreed upon uniform policy in regard to the protection of water supplies from phenol and other tarry acid wastes."[31]

Pinchot was not directly involved in these early steps in the abatement of water pollution, but he was their inspiration. Nor was he was fundamental to the one major lawsuit Pennsylvania brought against mining corporations, known as the Indian Creek pollution case, except in the not-insignificant sense that his attorney general, George Woodruff, had brought suit to stop the dumping of mine-acid drainage into the creek's watershed, which was befouling a local reservoir. After Pinchot left office, the state supreme court ruled that mine operators could be held liable for damaging potable water, a small but critical victory.[32]

Most of the credit for these successes goes to those to whom Governor Pinchot delegated this important work. It is true, too, as one historian has argued, that when "state political leaders, like Pinchot[,] attempted to find a delicate solution which might balance the economy and protect water users, few practical answers emerged." That more effective, national water-pollution legislation would not be enacted for another thirty years makes Pinchot's decision to push for the creation of the Sanitary Water Board and other oversight agencies particularly important. Without them, the state would not have had standing to investigate and regulate the complex links between industrial pollution, public health, and aquatic life. Surely it is also relevant that this connection was of direct, personal importance to Pinchot; his passion for fishing made him a staunch advocate for clean streams.[33]

Pinchot's commitment to a broader definition of conservation, his focus on the restoration of human communities and natural landscapes, and his vigorous defense of the political and economic rights of those who worked on farms and in factories, forests, and mills made his fellow foresters uncomfortable. Almost none thought that the pursuit of social and environmental justice was an essential plank in the conservationist agenda of the 1920s. Like William Greeley, they insisted that the economics of forest management was their only proper focus.

To shake that insistence, to challenge the Greeleyan faith in the beneficence of market forces, and to unmask industrial forestry's brutal and profligate ways, Pinchot financed the publication and distribution of George P. Ahern's 1928 tract, *Deforested America*. In his preface to this savage critique of the industry's depredations, Pinchot slammed those corporations that were "spending millions of dollars to forestall or delay the public control of

*One of Gifford Pinchot's
closest allies in the forestry
profession, Raphael Zon
edited the* Journal of
Forestry, *was an early
supporter of the New
Deal's shelterbelts, and
ushered Pinchot's auto-
biography,* Breaking
New Ground, *to its
posthumous publication.*

Forest History Society

lumbering, which is the only measure capable of putting an end to forest devastation in America." The lumber industry's diabolical public relations campaign was intended "to fool the American people into believing that the industry is regulating itself," he concluded. "That is not true, and Major Ahern has proved it beyond question."[34]

From distant St. Paul, Raphael Zon roared his approval of *Deforested America*—"Bravo! At least there are two militant voices raised against the camouflage spread about the practice of forestry by private timber land owners"—but he doubted that their angry words would become anything but a "a cry in the wilderness." The "forest profession," Zon continued, had "completely surrendered to the hegemony of the National Lumber Manufacturers' Association."[35]

Undaunted, Pinchot and Ahern hoped to encourage the spread of their message through the sponsorship of an essay contest for professional foresters (Pinchot was to foot the grand prize of $1,000). Its guidelines required submissions to explore "the actual forest situation in the U.S." and to offer practical remedies. The winners would be announced at the annual meeting of the Society of American Foresters, while the papers themselves would be read before the assembled professionals and later published in the *Journal of Forestry,* assuring maximum exposure. The contest's goal was to nurture and raise critical voices against the reigning discourse that proclaimed the unmitigated success of Greeley-promoted cooperation between private and public forestry. These counterclaims, Pinchot expected, would upstage, if not check, the self-congratulatory posture of the contemporary leadership of the American forestry movement.[36]

It was therefore fitting that Greeley selected this moment to submit his resignation as chief of the Forest Service, effective in late April 1928, clearing the way for him to become executive secretary of the West Coast Lumbermen's Association, headquartered in Seattle. Nothing could more perfectly symbolize his long-held allegiance to the needs of the lumbering interests, his chief critic concluded. By departing the Forest Service, Greeley was in effect going home. About Greeley's years as chief, Pinchot was emphatic: his administration had been "pitiful." With his departure, with his "malign influence" removed, "the foresters [are] returning to what they had known all along was the right point of view."[37]

This was a self-satisfied claim, but Pinchot had reason to hope that the profession would be more amenable to his expansive definition of conservation. A sign of this change in attitude, he reported to Zon, occurred in December 1928 when he and Ahern attended a meeting of the Washington chapter of SAF. Certain that *Deforested America* "would be the subject of a bitter attack," Pinchot had stayed in town to help defend Ahern's work. They were startled to find that such a defense was unnecessary. Instead, "[m]an after man got up and pointed out that [foresters] were not meeting the actual situation." Following these testimonies, the chapter then passed a resolution asking the Society of American Foresters to "appoint a committee to consider the facts and suggest a remedy" for forest devastation. This unqualified and unexpected endorsement of their arguments left Pinchot and Ahern "completely dazed."[38]

Another harbinger was that Robert Y. Stuart was named Greeley's successor. He had been Pinchot's deputy on the Pennsylvania Forest Commission from 1920 to 1922 and had replaced him when Pinchot resigned to run for governor. At the time, Stuart declared that his new work contained a "double honor—to be selected to lead the best state forest organization in the United States and to succeed Gifford Pinchot," an admiring note he maintained when tapped in 1923 to direct Pennsylvania's new Department of Forests and Waters. Stuart's ascension to the chief's office in Washington thus gave Pinchot and his coterie greater access to the agency's leadership and freedom to express their opinions about its policies.[39]

Illustrating his renewed faith that his ideas would be heard, Pinchot reactivated his membership in the Washington chapter of the Society of American Foresters; there and elsewhere, he regularly pressed the case for the inclusion of a social dimension to American forestry, and the implementation of national regulation of private forestry practices. Although Pinchot's perspectives did not emerge as explicit recommendations in Stuart's *A National Plan for American Forestry* (1933), a report that was the new chief's major accomplishment during his brief tenure, they were aired throughout the document, as were calls for significant increases in the amount of public ownership and management of forested lands. This recommitment to an expanded role for the Forest Service, this reassertion of what Pinchot believed was the agency's proper place in the making and execution of public policy, brought him considerable joy. In an open letter to his professional colleagues, Pinchot wrote: "[T]he time is ripe for a great advance in forestry in America"; now the Society of American Foresters must reject the "counsels of overcaution, inaction, and delay, and turn to the aggressive pursuit of clear cut objectives" that would put "an end to forest devastation." Our "central problem," he reaffirmed, was "public control of the axe."[40]

That problem received even closer scrutiny when Ferdinand Silcox was elevated to chief in 1933, following Stuart's tragic tumble out his seventh-floor office window at the Forest Service headquarters in Washington, D.C.; whether his fall was a suicide or the result of vertigo is unknown. Silcox, a former employee of the agency who most recently had worked in private forestry, seemed untainted by that industry's retrogressive politics, or so his keynote address to the 1935 annual meeting of the SAF signaled when it opened with a blunt refutation of Greeley's arguments. In identifying a "thrilling frontier where men battle for yet disputed principles," he called upon his peers to join in a struggle of ideas, a struggle that echoed Pinchot's conception of forestry's social obligations and its anti-industry perspective. Since "the primary objective of forestry is to keep forest land continuously productive," Silcox declared, supervision of private forestry practices could no longer be left in industry's hands. His assertion that public control and regulation must "take precedence over private profit" incensed lumber lobbyist William Greeley, but Pinchot greeted Silcox's crusading tone with evident relief. Under Silcox's direction, he wrote, the Forest Service would again become "the aggressive agent and advocate of the public good, and not the humble little brother of the lumbermen."[41]

Not since 1910, Pinchot asserted, had the agency assumed such a principled and combative posture; not in twenty years had it been in such good hands. A deeply satisfying consequence of his move back to Washington in 1927, this transition, Pinchot felt certain, would herald a renewed integration between himself and the agency he had brought to life. Characteristically, he cast this harmonic possibility in pugilistic terms, anxiously seeking a chance "to fight side by side with a leader like Silcox." That, the seventy-year-old Pinchot assured Zon, "is a grand prospect."[42]

The Widening View

FROM CHILDHOOD, Gifford Pinchot had yearned to sail through the South Pacific, an urge nurtured by reading stories of high-seas adventures filled with swashbuckling pirates and captains courageous. Playacting with friends in rowboats as they maneuvered off the shores of Nantucket and Long Island added ballast to his fantasy. In college, Pinchot's dream gained a partner: George Woodruff. "Once upon a time when all the world was young and all the trees were green, two sophomores at Yale (and sophomore means 'wise fool') decided that one day they would sail away to the South Seas in a schooner of their own," Pinchot would later write. "For the next three years they planned "their trip to the enchanted islands where all men and women would dearly love to go."[1]

In one sense, they were a mismatched pair of dreamers. Big, bulky, and powerful, captain of the Yale crew and starting right guard on the Yale offensive line, Woodruff "used to plow down the field, burdened but not stopped by the mass of opposing players that hid every vestige of him but his feet." Tall and lean, Pinchot had no such strength or heft; it was by dint of enthusiasm alone that he "just barely won his 'Y' as a substitute on the [football] team." Yet differences in outward appearance mattered little to these "pilgrims of hope," for whom a glimmering, evocative Pacific lay tantalizingly beyond the New Haven horizon.[2]

That vision persisted through the men's shared labors in the Forest Service and later in Harrisburg. But when in 1928 Pinchot proposed that they
actually act on their sophomoric fantasy, the gridiron hero, whom Pinchot
praised as "the foremost authority on the law of conservation" and who, in
his adult life as in football, had "kept carrying other people on his broad
back," was unable to leave. Pinchot set sail, but when he returned he dedicated the book of his travels to Woodruff, "friend and comrade in work and
play for forty years," a man whom he held "in lifelong affection, admiration, and respect."[3]

For Pinchot, the voyage was perfectly timed. Although he was sixty-
three when he and his family finally set sail in 1929, his health was excellent,
a vigor he attributed to his stint as governor. "I feel as if I had had a grand
time for the past four years," he told a reporter in early 1927, "the best four
years of my life. I cured my d[y]spepsia and gained twenty-five pounds."
His political strength in Pennsylvania was uncertain and yet could remain
untested, for there was neither a senatorial nor a gubernatorial race until
1930. As for the White House, as much as Pinchot would have liked to have
made a run for it, the Republican Party was not interested in him, selecting
Herbert Hoover as its standard bearer for the 1928 general election. Pinchot assumed that if Hoover won, the new president would not tap him for
the Cabinet, an assumption predicated on their sharp differences of opinion
over food relief programs during World War I and their current dispute
over the public control of electrical power.[4]

Pinchot's conjecture about his party's candidate proved accurate, if only
because when he announced his support for Hoover and was asked if he
would speak on the candidate's behalf, he agreed, but with a qualification.
Were he asked about his ideological differences with the Republican nominee, Pinchot wrote Representative Walter H. Newton, head of the party's
speaker's bureau, he would have to be honest. "If I am to advocate the election of Mr. Hoover on the stump, it must be . . . without evasion, misrepre-
sentation or campaign bunk." Not wanting a "campaigner to declare himself in such outspoken fashion," Newton declined Pinchot's services.[5]

Earlier that election season, the voters of the Fifteenth Congressional
District of Pennsylvania, which included Milford, had rejected the services
of the other politician in the family, Cornelia Pinchot. Her campaign in

the Republican primary in the spring of 1928 had been a long shot; she attempted to oust Louis T. McFadden, a seven-term Republican incumbent in a solidly Republican district. He had the added strength of running with the endorsements of *both* major parties (he had also won the Democratic primary) and against a woman whom Old Guard Republicans despised as much as they did her husband.

Given little chance of success, Cornelia campaigned with energy and verve, focusing on issues similar to those animating her husband's activism—she was pro-union, pro-farmers, and anti-Prohibition, but she also stressed the need for women in politics. Gifford agreed wholeheartedly and rallied to her cause, pressing the flesh throughout the district; her campaign manager, Peter Stahlnecker, had been Gifford's executive secretary in Harrisburg; and Henry Slattery even drafted speeches for her—all to no avail. Though by the narrowest margin in his career, McFadden won. Gifford offered this consolation: the money that poured into the incumbent's campaign from "the Pennsylvania Railroad, the Lehigh Valley Railroad, the big bankers, and the Pennsylvania State machine" had made the difference.[6]

Although disappointing, her loss helped clear the decks for the family's seven-month voyage to points south. Gifford and Cornelia spent the summer and fall scouring shipyards from the mid-Atlantic north to Maine, and telephoning yacht brokers in search of the perfect vessel. "I know little about ships and sailing," Gifford wrote, "for it takes years at sea to make a sailor," but the Pinchots knew enough to know that like "a Ford car, our ship must take us there and bring us back."[7]

Finally, in October 1928, they found the *Cutty Sark;* built in the Wilmington shipyard in 1902, it was a 148-foot, three-masted topsail schooner. Its cabins and staterooms were numerous enough to house a twelve-man crew, along with Gifford, Cornelia, and their son, "Giff," as well as one his friends, three scientists and their equipment, and a physician. After inspecting the schooner, the Pinchots "wanted her so badly that we couldn't wait for the mail but telephoned an offer to the agent from a hot dog stand on our way home."[8]

In the ensuing months, the couple poured thousands of dollars into refitting and repairing the *Cutty Sark,* purchasing new sails, an additional launch, and a set of lifeboats and skiffs. Other equipment was loaned by the National Museum of Natural History in Washington, D.C., and the Philadelphia Academy of Natural Sciences; for each institution, the researchers on what was grandly called the "Pinchot South Seas Expedition—1929" would collect specimens, known and unknown. About the need to contribute to scientific inquiry, the Pinchots were insistent, for theirs "was to be no mere yachting trip." They could not justify the expense on those grounds, and so modeled their voyage after Theodore Roosevelt's explorations of Africa and South America, as well as after the 1923 New York Zoological Society's foray to the Galapagos Islands, led by its director of tropical research, William Beebe. An "adventure seasoned with science," Gifford declared, "is the best kind."9

It was best, too, that the *Cutty Sark* bear a new name, one that exemplified the seaworthy schooner. "Once she was mine I named her after my mother," Pinchot wrote. "The best thing we could hope from any vessel was that she would turn out to be the kind of ship that Mary Pinchot was a woman." In the open seas, as her namesake had in life, the refurbished ship enfolded and protected its owner.10

PACIFIC IDYLL

With the full company on board, the *Mary Pinchot* set sail on March 31, 1929. The weather did not cooperate. "If glory can blaze in a cold wet rain on a sloppy dock and a sloppier deck, it blazed when we made our start." But they enjoyed an enthusiastic send-off, most of which was captured on film; Cornelia and Gifford had hired a naturalist-photographer to accompany them and a camera crew to record their launch. They were hoping to cash in on the publicity that the voyage might generate by building advance interest in the book that Pinchot projected he would write about their travels. (The book's sales would be accelerated when, after its publication, a documentary of their trip was screened publicly.) In addition, they were not unmindful of the potential political payoff that such a film might stimulate. "Two dozen movie cameras recorded our start," Pinchot wrote in his book about their travels, *To the South Seas* (1930), as if surprised by their abundant presence, "while a couple of talkie outfits required speech after speech

In 1929, the Pinchot family sailed aboard the Mary Pinchot, *a three-masted schooner, on a memorable cruise through the Caribbean and the South Pacific with an extended stay in the Galapagos.*

Grey Towers NHL

from Mrs. Pinchot, from me, and even from Giff." Though they were heading off to paradise, the senior Pinchots had their eye on the here and now.[11]

After a one-day delay to fix a malfunctioning ice machine, the *Mary Pinchot* slipped down the Delaware River, entered the Atlantic, and immediately plowed through "a multitude of tin cans, empty bottles, and burnt out electric light bulbs floating all over the sea," a portion of "New York's garbage that could swim." Testing their marksmanship, Giff and his close friend Steve Stahlnecker, the son of Pinchot's chief of staff in Harrisburg, opened fire on the flotsam and jetsam.[12]

On the cusp of adolescence, steady and inquisitive, intrigued by how things functioned and blessed with parents who had the wherewithal to give him every opportunity to explore his surroundings, thirteen-year-old Giff Pinchot would have the time of his life aboard the *Mary Pinchot*. The education the fair-haired boy had already received was apt preparation for what he would encounter afloat. Because of his parents' peripatetic lives, he had often been taught by tutors; in Harrisburg, he had been enrolled in an experimental primary school that his mother, deeply interested in the progressive educational theories of John Dewey, had founded. His formal schooling continued on board (as it would for his friend Steve, known as "Stiff"), with Cornelia, Gifford, and the resident scientists serving as instructors.

The boys thought the informal instruction they received was more valuable, and so convinced Cornelia. "Giff put over a deal on C.B. [Cornelia Bryce Pinchot] to the effect that every day we landed . . . he should be excused from lessons," his father laughed. When the *Mary Pinchot* sailed into the Galapagos, the islands "were just what Giff was looking for, and the bargain held. However, in the face of the prodigious history lesson written in rock and flora and fauna which soon lay open to us, we did not begrudge him his so-called holidays."[13]

Even the schooner named for the paternal grandmother he had never met had its educational possibilities. Giff came to an intimate knowledge of its inner workings, learning to rig its sails, man its helm, and race up into its crow's nest; from its deck and skiffs he absorbed his father's unending love of deep-sea fishing. As the *Mary Pinchot* made its way through the Caribbean, crossed the Isthmus of Panama via the canal that his father's hero, Teddy Roosevelt, had initiated, and then headed south and west to the Galapagos, the Marquesas, and the Tuamotu Archipelago before reaching its final destination of Tahiti, Giff's schooling unfolded. In seven months he became familiar, at least in passing, with some of the basic principles of geology, geography, marine biology, and cultural anthropology, a tutelage that indelibly influenced his future. Without a shred of interest in replicating his parents' volatile political careers, Giff would become a biological researcher of note, and a lifelong and passionate sailor. He would turn their avocations into his vocation.[14]

An ardent collector like his father, Giff was delighted with the scientific intent of the South Seas voyage; the collecting of objects and animals would begin in the Atlantic and continue until the *Mary Pinchot* finally dropped anchor in Papeete, Tahiti. After rounding Cape Hatteras, North Carolina, where they "crossed the line between the brilliant blue Gulf Stream full of gulf weed and the muddy looking grayish shore water as clearly defined as that between a sidewalk and the roadway in a street," the hunt commenced. When someone harpooned a seven-foot porpoise, Giff "shot it twice with his 38 revolver, and then we measured it and photographed it and cut it up, saving the skull and pieces of the skin for the National Museum, and the tenderloins and part of the liver for ourselves."

On Swan Island, Giff and Stiff watched with amazement as a marine lizard "they had frightened [on shore ran] on his two hind legs straight into the water, looking precisely like the great man-eating dinosaur in Conan Doyle's story of the 'Lost World.'" One of its kind found its way into the growing collection, where it was joined by a clutch of chameleons, frogs, and snails later captured on Old Providence Island. Henry A. Pilsbry, a conchologist on leave from the staff of the Philadelphia Academy, identified a pair of viviparous snails as belonging to a new genus, and thrilled his patrons when he named one *G. pinchotii* and the other *Giffordius corneliae* ("which being interpreted is 'Cornelia's Gifford,'" Pinchot noted, "a fact I gladly admit").[15]

As the *Mary Pinchot* entered the fecund Pacific, the region's marine and land biota yielded an even greater wealth of specimens. Off the Cocos, the sea "was simply jammed with fish," reminding the senior Pinchot of his angling twenty years earlier off the California coast. "Except in the great schools of Yellowtail at San Clemente in the old days, it seems to me I never saw fish bite so fast." As they struck, sharks sliced through the waves and "swallowed them whole," setting a scene of almost primeval power. With the seas crashing over a nearby point, and "the fiercely fighting fish, and the Sharks, Sharks, Sharks, it was a sort of daylight nightmare."[16]

More sharks, porpoises, wahoo, grouper, and tuna were hauled in; noddy and fern terns and men-of-war were gathered up, a collection of avian, marine, and terrene specimens that increased with each and every stop along the *Mary Pinchot*'s path through the southern Pacific. "Since we left Balboa no end of birds and snails have been collected by the scientists of the party," complained Morris Gregg, the Pinchots' secretary; "these specimen hunters have added so voluminously to their collections that . . . they have taken over the bath rooms as laboratories and exhibit rooms."

Worse than this appropriation of the limited space below decks was the "unbelievable and incredible stenches that emanate from those bath-roooms! The effluvium of decayed and decaying snails, and the sickening odor of dead birds, lizards, etc., are unspeakably awful. It has reached the point where one can hardly go into either of the two bathrooms even long enough to wash one's hands—and as for staying there longer, in order to do things intended to be done in all good bathrooms, that's rapidly becoming out of the question."

The one unexpected benefit of having tarried longer than planned in the Galapagos, Gregg noted, was that the *Mary Pinchot*'s fuel supplies had dwindled such that the party was forced to return to Panama; in Balboa, "all these damn specimens—bugs, lizards, tortoises, snails, etc.—will be crated up and started on their journeys to the National Museum and the Philadelphia Academy of Natural Sciences."[17]

The Pinchot party had lingered in the Galapagos for more than a month because Gifford Pinchot was fundamentally astounded by the unusual environment; Cornelia, too, according to Gregg, had "succumbed to [its] lethal spirit (or pretends she has—she's considerable of an actress, you know—and I suspect that a lot of her enthusiasm is feigned in order to please the Governor)." In either case, Gregg could not understand the spell the islands cast over his fellow voyagers. "William Beebe has called the damned things 'World's End'—and if anybody ever coined a more appro-priate name for them I would like to know his name—and also what he called them." For Gifford Pinchot, however, the Enchanted Islands were bliss. "I've never known the Governor to rhapsodize over any other thing since I've known him as much as he has over these damned Galapagos Islands," a puzzled Gregg wrote Slattery. "Certainly I would never have imagined that he was capable of such a fiery zeal over such miserable things as these islands are."[18]

Pinchot's "religious frenzies," as Gregg also tagged his boss's enthusi-asms, were fired by the rich, diverse, and ancient biota he everywhere encountered. Whether hiking along jagged cliffs, climbing up through lava fields, sloshing in and around tidal formations, or casting into the clear waters of Darwin Bay, he found himself immersed in what seemed the full range of biological time, an immersion that reminded him of the dangers of the human imprint and the immediate need for human stewardship.

That sensibility emerged in the aftermath of his successful pursuit of a sea bat (manta ray), which Pinchot described as "a creature from the ante-diluvian world that somehow survived into our time." Wanting one for the expedition's collection, he chased a number of them across Darwin Bay. When he finally struck his harpoon home and battled for more than two hours to land his victim, the ray was so vast that it took eight men to drag it to shore. Its sheer size and death struggle rattled Pinchot. "For years past," he admitted, "whenever I have killed a head of big game, remorse comes straightway to afflict me. So now the bitter tooth began to gnaw. . . . I was not a little oppressed by the bigness of my kill."[19]

Providing some sanction for the ray's death was the scientific collector's creed: "[W]e never killed unless there was a reason." That code, and the sense of regret that was embedded within it, led Pinchot to contemplate how to preserve the Galapagos. He recognized that the *Mary Pinchot*'s very presence in the islands was emblematic of the single greatest threat to the island's beguiling wildness. "As the Galapagos become better known, as what may be found there and felt there brings more and more visitors to the islands," Pinchot worried, "as methods of communication improve (and they surely will), as more and more boats touch at the islands, and more and more settlers come to live on them—one thing will surely happen if we let it happen, and that right quickly—the last natural stronghold of the fear-less wild will be destroyed." Staggered by how swiftly the Galapagos tor-toise, iguanas, penguins, and flightless cormorants had been exterminated, aware that he and his family and crew had entered "a region unmatched on earth in the ease and intimacy with which the strange and fascinating wild animals can be seen and studied," he concluded that such a region was very much worth saving. Its salvation lay in the "setting aside of several of the islands as wild life refuges, just as we have done so successfully in the Yel-lowstone National Park and elsewhere at home." Although he was uncer-tain whether the United States should encourage the Ecuadoran govern-ment to create the park, or "whether the League of Nations offers the proper channel," one thing was unmistakably obvious: "somehow it ought to be done."[20]

Pinchot's early call for a biological conservation zone in the Galapagos may have had no impact on Ecuador's subsequent actions. (In 1934 it set aside some of the islands he visited as a wildlife sanctuary, their uninhabited areas were declared a national park in 1959, and a more encompassing Marine Resources Reserve was established in 1986.) But Pinchot's argument for environmental protection of the islands and its flora and fauna is nonetheless significant on its merits. It is important, too, because its origin challenges historian Edward Larson's contention that the impulse to save the islands emerged from a different kind of ecological consciousness. He contends that among those pressing this cause were a host of mid-twentieth-century academic scientists associated with the International Union for the Conservation of Nature. They repudiated museum-specimen collecting expeditions such as Pinchot's, which hoped to save particular species by collecting them, "in favor of saving endangered species for study in the wild." Yet thirty years earlier, the amateur Pinchot had reached the same conclusion about the crying need for Galapagan preservation as a *consequence* of his experiences as a collector.[21]

Pinchot differed from the later advocates in another respect. They drew on the great African nature reserves as their model for what should occur on the islands. To convince his American readers of the necessity for the preservation of the Galapagos, Pinchot cited Yellowstone, one of the crown jewels of the U.S. national park system. His choice is remarkable in light of his tense relations with the Park Service. During his tenure as chief of the Forest Service, Pinchot had fully supported the construction of the O'Shaughnessy Dam in the Hetch Hetchy Valley of Yosemite National Park, a project that violated the park's sanctuary-like status. In subsequent years, he supported the agency's vigorous, if oft-unsuccessful, attempts to fend off congressional action that turned over some national forest acreage to the Park Service. Later, in the early 1930s, Secretary of the Interior Harold Ickes's attempt to absorb the Forest Service into a new department of conservation would bend before Pinchot's furious counterassault. It is telling that Pinchot, no friend of the rival service and often at odds with its preservationist mission, saw in Yellowstone the answer to the wounded Galapagos.[22]

Just as crucial as the conservation of the islands' flora and fauna, Pinchot believed, was the survival of the diverse human communities that he and his family encountered on their journey. He began to recognize this as an issue when he visited the San Blas Islands, located just off Panama's eastern coast. Its indigenous peoples, he commented, had "preserved the purity of its blood inviolate and still [permit] no white man to settle there." As fascinating was their adaptation to their environment. Pinchot noted that they lived "on little islands raised but a few feet above the water" and had constructed low-level seawalls from "pressed out sugar cane."[23]

The small, well-contained landmass forced the islanders to live compactly; "the most crowded districts of lower New York have little to brag of in comparison." Because of that density, Pinchot had difficulty maneuvering his tall frame through the community. He was at ease with the people, though, over whom he towered. After watching him interact with those whose language he could not speak, and exchange gifts with those whose culture he could not understand, Morris Gregg marveled that Pinchot "appeared to enjoy himself hugely among the San Blas Indians."[24]

He would mix just as easily with the Galapagans, Marquesans, and Tuamotuans he met along the *Mary Pinchot*'s route. He did so, it seems, because he bore little of the sense of cultural superiority that so often dominates contemporary American and European travelogues. Although he could be witheringly condescending to his political rivals, he exhibited no such condescension toward, and apparently felt no such rivalry with, those who called the Pacific home. He accepted that he and they came from different worlds, lived within different cultural strictures, and acted accordingly.

There were moments of mild imperial boast. When the *Mary Pinchot* made the transit through the Panama Canal, he assured his readers that they could "be proud of what Uncle Sam has done at the Canal," and should recall the reasons behind its high standards. "The Canal Zone is free from politics. What we have done there in honesty, efficiency, intelligence, and humanity of administration we can do anywhere else—on the same condition."

But such declarations of American prowess were rare, as rare as assertions of negative racial stereotypes. Indeed, Pinchot took pleasure in puncturing the racist assumptions that were built into the advice he regularly received to avoid certain islands and their presumably savage peoples. The descriptions, he wrote, "fairly sizzled," especially about the Galapagans: they "were said to vary from diseased and miserable wretches through petty thieves to wreckers, pirates, and murderers at large." The reality, he discovered, was quite the reverse, which led him to flip the discredited argument on its head. "The gap between civilized life in America, where we have grown to be the servants (or the masters) of each other's needs, and life in the Galapagos, where the civility of the uncivilized, the natural good manners of wild things, is the dominant note, is hard to bridge." The citizens of the United States had a good deal to learn from those who owned little but were masters of themselves.[25]

Pinchot's respect for the islanders' self-possession, and the organic communities that they lived within, would resonate with an industrial America then reeling from the first shocks of the Depression. These technologically more primitive cultures, living close to the land and in apparent social harmony, stood in sharp relief to the social dislocation already evident in the United States after the stock market crash, and to which the Pinchots would return in November 1929.

In the years following the publication of *To the South Seas* (1930), Pinchot's impressionistic evidence was replicated in the writings of a host of cultural critics who swept across the globe in search of more sustainable societies, places like the Mexico to which the *New Republic*'s Stuart Chase repaired, and reporting that it contained communities of "men without machines." Pinchot's close friend and fellow forester Bob Marshall went north to Alaska and returned after a year to publish *Arctic Village* (1933), a rough-hewn, earthy antidote to the malaise of industrialization. For another acquaintance, forester and wildlife biologist Aldo Leopold, the resolution lay in wilderness. His exquisite, late-1930s essays on hunting in Canada, Mexico, and other uninhabited terrain were opportunities to debunk the myth of progress. Those doubts of the modern were most brilliantly rendered from domestic sources in *Let Us Now Praise Famous Men* (1941), the collaborative work of photographer Walker Evans and writer James Agee, who took their inspiration from southern white tenant farm families. The plight and strength of poor southerners were later reimagined, with a slight shift in setting, in Aaron Copland's musical composition *Appalachian Spring* (1945). In a badly buffeted land, it was a gift to be simple.[26]

But unlike some of Pinchot's other contemporaries, who, in cultural historian Richard Pells's words, "felt more justified in offering a symbolic reproach to American materialism and greed than in outlining programmatic solutions to the depression," Pinchot was eager to develop a political response to the looming economic disaster. He was just sorry that he had to leave the Pacific to do so.[27]

It was thus with great regret that in October the *Mary Pinchot* party sailed from Toau, part of the Tuamotu Archipelago, to Tahiti, traveling south so that the Pinchots could return to the northern hemisphere. Their passage to the Tahitian port of Papeete, like their states of mind, was turbulent. "All night the sea was rough," Pinchot wrote, "but no rougher than having to leave Toau, where we wanted to stay, and ought to have stayed, at least a month." Fittingly, when they approached their new destination and "the sun cleared away the mists, Tahiti loomed up thirty miles away, a magnificent island full of mountain peaks," but its beauty could not compare to what had come before; "it left us cold."[28]

There was this hope—as the Pinchots and their companions left their schooner, which the crew would sail back to the States, and boarded a steamer to Hawaii, Gifford and Cornelia anticipated returning to the South Seas on the *Mary Pinchot* in the future. But a second voyage never transpired. The Great Depression had already begun to destroy the global economy by the time they reached Washington in November, and its impact on the family's finances was profound, as reflected in the need to dispose of the *Mary Pinchot* itself. After putting it up for sale at what Gifford and Cornelia thought was a "sacrifice" at $75,000, they finally settled for a rock-bottom $19,000.[29]

As sad as they may have been about having to forgo a return to the warm isles, on the level of remembrance the trip had been fully packed: "We caught some gorgeous fish, we had a glorious sail, we added, by however little, to the knowledge of [the] world in which we live," Pinchot affirmed in the last words of *To the South Seas*. "But best of all, I think, we brought new experience and new interest into our lives, and laid up for ourselves memories which will brighten many a summer day and bring cheer to many a winter fire."[30]

Cornelia and Gifford would give substance to those memories when they renovated portions of Grey Towers to open up its interior to the outdoor light, placed a large tiki from the Tuamotu Archipelago in its front hall, and scattered other mementos throughout the home. Outdoors, Cor-

At voyage's end, Gifford (second from left), *Cornelia* (wearing hat), *and Gifford Bryce Pinchot* (center) *pose with some of the members of the* Mary Pinchot's *crew.* Grey Towers NHL

nelia had inscribed into a courtyard surface a model of the *Mary Pinchot.* This carving directed guests to a newly constructed veranda complete with a "Finger Bowl," an outdoor dining table modeled after sixteenth-century Venetian water tables. Around it would sit the Pinchots and up to thirty guests on warm evenings, gently passing to one another across its placid waters "Polynesian bowls" laden with food.

As a teenager, Giff Pinchot disliked the interminable political "arguments between the more liberal Giffords and the more conservative Amoses" that were standard fare on "Finger Bowl" evenings, yet he also delighted in his parents' antics, which relieved the tension. At one lunch, noting that a guest on the opposite of the table needed butter, Cornelia slipped a pat onto her knife and flipped it across the pool. Although engrossed in a conversation with a "local politico," Gifford, without skipping a beat, "picked up the guest's butter plate, held it up like a baseball glove so that pat hit it and stuck to it. He handed it to the astounded guest who clearly didn't think that Emily Post would approve such odd table manners." In moments like these, the Pinchots were able to recreate for themselves the informal air and camaraderie that had prevailed aboard the *Mary Pinchot*.[31]

Not Down or Out

Though the Pinchots loved their Pacific sojourn and readily embraced the differences possible in the complex human ecologies they observed in the South Seas, they had every intention of returning to their own niche. "Conservation work to be done," Gifford observed toward the close of the voyage, "fixed November first as the last day for being back to Washington." That would give the couple an opportunity to lobby for pet legislation before Congress adjourned for its Christmas holiday, and it would put them in a better position to determine the prospects for a second term in Harrisburg.

They had never been too far removed from the political arena, in any event. By telegram and correspondence, Peter Stahlnecker and Harry Slattery had kept them abreast of breaking news. Most relevant was Stahlnecker's cable in the summer that Gifford Pinchot had a good chance of winning the 1930 Republican gubernatorial primary. "My interest in what you have written," Pinchot responded in August, "is so great that I have temporarily lost interest in the trip because of it."[32]

The Pinchots' political futures also influenced how they hoped to narrate and illustrate the story of their voyage. Morris Gregg suspected, for instance, that a "big upheaval" would occur "over the character of the pictures [Dr. Howard H.] Cleaves takes. Naturally enough he is anxious to get all the bird and 'wild life adventure' pictures he can, in order that they may be of maximum use to his WILD LIFE ADVENTURE lectures." The Pinchots had other ideas about the subjects—and thus the future use—of Cleaves's photographs. They wanted him "to concentrate a little bit more on the sort of pictures that will have publicity value for them," he confided to Slattery; "namely, pictures showing C.B.P. in her sailor habiliments doing a sailor's work—the Governor and Mrs. Pinchot staging an iguana hunt or cavorting around the beaches with sea lion pups—Mrs. Pinchot braving danger by leaping out of a skiff and wading through the surf to land."[33]

There is no question that the publication of *To the South Seas* was designed to promote the adventuresome Pinchots. In this respect the book did well, selling 8,000 copies in the first full year of the Depression. Its sales were aided by a documentary of the *Mary Pinchot*'s voyage (unambiguously entitled *Mr. and Mrs. Pinchot in Their Cruise of the South Seas*), which had a good run in New York City, and by other publicity. Just before the celebrated couple returned to the States, for example, a head shot of Gifford, with a full white beard, graced the pages of the Sunday *New York Times*. Out of sight for seven months, the Pinchots were making up for lost time.[34]

Yet being offstage had worked to their advantage in the tangle of Pennsylvania politics. While Gifford had been sailing, the fractious Republican Party was busily tearing itself apart in the run-up to the gubernatorial primary. Bill Vare, who had beaten Pinchot in the rough 1926 Senate primary only to have the U.S. Senate refuse to seat him, was backing Francis Shunk Brown; in political scientist Paul Beers's choice phrasing, Brown "was the type of Philadelphia patrician who pretends he stands above street politics even when there is mud on his spats." A second candidate then leaped into the fray, former congressman Thomas W. Phillips, Jr., whose campaign was financed through the Association Against the Prohibition Amendment. So intense was the jockeying for position that Pinchot, upon his return, hesitated to enter the campaign. "I don't want to make a fool of myself," he wrote old friend Clyde King. "On the other hand, I don't want to miss a chance of having a real pulpit again for four years."[35]

Only when assured the support of another of the state's kingmakers, Joe Grundy, would Pinchot formally announce his intention to seek another term. (As president of the state's Manufacturing Association, Grundy had backed Pinchot in 1922 and then had been appointed to fill the first two years of Vare's term in the U.S. Senate.) Running on his record ("One Good Term Deserves Another" was the slogan) and pounding away at the utility companies' power over the state's economy and politics, Pinchot set off on one of his patented whirlwind tours of the state. Knowing he would lose Philadelphia (which was Vare's turf) and hoping that the "wet" Phillips would drain votes from Brown (who advocated a referendum to reconsider

Prohibition), Pinchot hoped to slip through by appealing to his rural base of support and gaining once more the votes of miners and women. With their support, and by also carrying Pittsburgh, he won the primary.[36]

Unlike in 1922, however, winning the preliminary round did not assure him of a victory in the November general election. A furious Vare did the unthinkable: he threw his support to the Democratic nominee, John M. Hemphill. Vare brought with him considerable financial support from utility corporations hoping to silence Pinchot, along with a host of media endorsements. The Philadelphia boss would rather have seen the Republican Party lose than endure a Pinchot victory. Because Hemphill opposed Prohibition, however, "dry" Democrats crossed into Pinchot's camp, making them strange bedfellows with former distiller Andrew Mellon, long a target of Pinchot's scorn for his allegedly less than robust enforcement of federal Prohibition regulations. Reluctantly, the Mellon machine of Pittsburgh supported the man it loathed, preferring a Pinchot win to a party defeat.[37]

The final months of the campaign were brutal. Cornelia and Gifford Pinchot seemed to be in a constant state of motion, giving speeches, working county fairs, social clubs, and Grange meetings, and making extensive use of radio. Even fourteen-year-old Giff addressed the Milford faithful. In August, the elder Gifford evinced confidence about the outcome. "[U]nless something unexpected turns up the election seems reasonably safe," he informed his sister, "although the Philadelphia Gang is throwing its fortune with the wet Democrat nominee, who isn't personally very dangerous, and whom I am confident I can beat anyhow."

That fortune nearly purchased an upset. Despite the vast differences in party registration, on November 4, 1930, Pinchot beat Hemphill by less than 60,000 votes out of more than 2 million cast.[38]

Such a narrow margin of victory was not the only factor complicating the beginning of Gifford Pinchot's new term. The ever-worsening economy was taking its toll on the highly industrialized Keystone State, and would require an energetic response from the governor and legislature. Even before he took the oath of office, Pinchot was well aware that the only statistic increasing in Pennsylvania during the first years of the Depression was unemployment. In 1930, as he ran for office, more than 411,000 workers were out of a job (or 11.8 percent of the total workforce). "It isn't [going] to be a pleasant winter on either side of the big pond," he admitted to his sister in August. "Unemployment is getting to be very serious in the United States, and I am afraid [it] is likely to be more so."[39]

That was one prediction he would have preferred not to come true. One year later the number of jobless in Pennsylvania had doubled, and in 1932 it would soar to more than 1.3 million people, or approximately 37 percent. Worse, what those figures did not reflect was that many who held jobs were actually part-time laborers, a group that may have included upward of 800,000 workers. Their buying power was consequently reduced, as it was for those who were lucky to retain full-time employment. "[T]he average weekly industrial wage in Pennsylvania in May of 1929 was $27.53. By June 1931 it was $21.25."[40]

Believing that it "would be improper to spend any great amount of money" on his January 1931 inauguration due to "the widespread suffering and unemployment," Pinchot cut the ceremony's budget to $3,000. A symbolic act, this reduction presaged other deep cuts in the state's budget, which were necessary because of sharp revenue losses. Confronted with an entirely different scenario than in 1923, when he had to control unbudgeted and runaway spending, Pinchot felt ready for the challenge. "I dropped into a big fight even before I was inaugurated," he told Nettie in early February. "It is making pretty fair progress, I think, and it is going to be hot for months to come." But he had no intention of backing off. "This is lots more fun even than the last time, and I think we are going to get something done."[41]

CRISIS MANAGEMENT

Slashing expenditures was part of the Pinchot program, and in this the Republican-controlled legislature concurred. He reduced the number of state employees, saving more than $2 million in salaries; even though he rapidly increased funding for new programs, he paid for these with cuts in other projects and with new taxes. His first budget, in 1931, was set at $208.3 million, and the last, in 1933, had increased only to $217.8 million. Political historian Paul Beers has argued that Pinchot's drive to control

costs and balance expenses, a sign of his fiscal conservatism, was "extraordinary, perhaps the most remarkable of [its] kind, considering the circumstances, in Pennsylvania history."[42]

As the economy continued its downward spiral, Pinchot took additional
measures. One of these was to zero in on utility corporations that, he
argued, were gouging their customers. This claim generated enough publicity that he gained control of the Public Service Commission through
appointments of more friendly commissioners (including the omnipresent
George Woodruff), and as a consequence was able to have some impact on
rates. "What is going on here is getting wide publicity," he bragged to Nettie, "and we are having a real show-down in the matter of the way the utilities have been treating the people."[43]

Driving down the cost of utilities would not solve the larger problem of
increased misery. Securing direct relief and unemployment compensation,
Pinchot believed, at least would provide a short-term resolution. But to
secure either required convincing a reluctant legislature to increase taxes to
pay for these new expenses, and gaining the state supreme court's sanction.
In Pinchot's first term, the court had declared unconstitutional an Old-Age
Pension Act he had promoted, arguing that direct relief was illegal. Hoping to challenge that ruling, the governor called a special legislative session
in November 1931 to address the state's responsibility to the unemployed.
Within a month the assembly passed the Talbot Act, which provided $10
million for indigent care, a figure well below the $60 million Pinchot had
requested. To show his displeasure, he refused to sign the bill, but in April
the state supreme court, in a landmark decision, approved the expenditure,
opening the way for an expanded role for the government in social welfare.[44]

Even before the judiciary had acted, Pinchot sought ways around the
constitutional ban on direct aid to the poor. He created a loophole when, in
early November, he announced that "anyone who wants a job will be able
to get it at State Road Camps established in different parts of the Commonwealth." There, workers would "get a place to sleep and three square
meals a day, [and] will get a very small amount of money, far below regular
wages." To make more work, Pinchot had ordered that "road-making
machines not be employed." Although he realized that this might escalate
the per-mile costs of construction, that was a necessary evil; as the "Consti-

tution of Pennsylvania forbids direct relief, I have got to beat the devil around the bush somehow."[45]

For all his successful maneuvering on the state level, Pinchot was worried. He knew that Pennsylvania could not solve its economic woes by itself. He was certain that only federal intervention could prevail, and he had gone public with his concerns; he lobbied the Hoover administration to increase federal taxation of the rich to aid the poor, but was rebuffed. Speaking before the District of Columbia League of Women Voters in November 1931, he slammed the president's failure of nerve. "Is this nation, as a nation, to reach out a hand to help those of its people who through no fault of their own are in desperation and distress? Shall federal aid be granted in this great national crisis?" The answer, he asserted, was in the affirmative, and it was so because his experience governing had taught him that no other resolution was possible. "Gentle bed-side language can do nothing for us. We have tried it. We can afford no more of it." Pinchot called on the Hoover administration to embrace his guiding philosophy, that government "is the manager of society. It is the one agency which cannot shirk or pass on the blame for bad management." Only Washington could help Americans "determine, as a nation, where we want to go; how best we can get there; and then *go,*—with all the organized initiative, energy, and power of the nation behind us."[46]

Hoover did not accept Pinchot's assumptions, and never shared his conviction that "federal aid is our clear duty and our best hope of prompt and permanent recovery." The president's resistance to that argument, which Franklin Roosevelt one year later would exploit to such good effect on the 1932 campaign trail, helps explain Hoover's defeat in that election. In the interim, however, Hoover's inaction, Pinchot argued, was responsible for the nation's understandable unrest. "People are angry in this country— pretty much everywhere—and, in some places, bitter and anxious to make trouble," he observed in late October; "and I think we will have trouble before the winter is out."[47]

Troubling too was the need to send young Gifford, then fifteen, to California. He had not been eager to return to the governor's home in Harrisburg. "I think I am going to hate it because I hate all big cities. Country is a lot nicer, I say." A threat to kidnap him had led the family first to enroll him for the spring in school in Milford, the small town in which he felt most comfortable; the next fall they registered him at the Thatcher School, located in the rolling coastal mountains near Ojai, California. He did well there, academically and socially, and was "having a grand time in the Ojai Valley." An encouraging sign of Giff's maturation, his father noted, was his taking up of the pugilistic art. For the father, who once had had the distinction of knocking Theodore Roosevelt to the ground, fisticuffs was a mark of manhood, and he relished Giff's emerging skill. "[T]o my great delight, [he] is developing into a rather exceptional boxer for a boy his age."[48]

For all his physical development, Giff's departure, Gifford confessed to Nettie, had left "Leila and me with a sort of empty feeling. . . . " Antoinette commiserated: "How must both of you miss little Giffy terribly, but I expect you both have got your hands too full to have much time to have much free time for that." Hers was an accurate characterization of the obligations that pressed in on Pennsylvania's First Couple. "We do miss him a lot," Gifford concurred, "but, as you say, we do not have time to miss him very much. It is going to be as busy a winter as I have known."[49]

The governor might have said that about every season during his four-year term. The pace of the work was daunting, far more so than it had been during Pinchot's first term in Harrisburg. Because of the economic calamity, he called four special sessions of the legislature, which usually only met once every two years. The flood of correspondence across his desk, the number of delegations that came to lobby him, and the escalating level of distress were at times overwhelming.

The most difficult appeals were those that bespoke the special hardships that many children faced; their anguish, lack of food, and poor nutrition, as well as their loss of a stable family life, unsettled Pinchot. He used his office as a bully pulpit, lashing out at those who foreclosed on homes or ejected tenants. "I've just learned you're going to evict six families of miners from company houses," he wired the Huskin Coal Company in September 1933. "Their removal can't do the company any good. You may have a legal right but no moral right." Earlier that year he had pleaded more generally that Pennsylvanians not foreclose on properties, and then issued a proclamation to that effect. "Justice and mercy recommend this course. The welfare and safety of the State demand it."[50]

The bad news continued to roll in, however, and its most frequent bearer was Cornelia. She maintained a rigorous travel schedule, functioning as her husband's eyes and ears on matters social and political. "Leila continues to do a perfectly splendid work with her speeches throughout the state," he told his sister. "The job she has done is wonderful beyond all whooping. There is no one in Pennsylvania who begins to stand as well with the workers as she does."

Cornelia's insights gleaned while touring the state, and the public support she seemed to amass in the process, helped her husband keep pressure on the legislature to increase support for the unemployed. Its resistance to expanding the numbers of Pennsylvanians served, and the amount of relief distributed, infuriated Pinchot. "My greatest trouble is to get the regular Organization leaders of the legislature to understand that this relief question, with two million people being fed, is really worth their attention. So far they have only played with it." And although the amount of money on an individual level did not amount to much—in "not a few cases families are getting relief funds of only $1.50 or $2.00 a week. While they are not actually dying of hunger the situation isn't pretty. I am doing what I can to help but it isn't an easy job"—securing legislative approval for even that minimal outlay was difficult. The Republican-dominated assembly talked of doing "what the people need," Pinchot complained, and then would revert back to what he described as its "usual cheap and stupid politics."[51]

Hoping to elevate the political tone of the Fifteenth Congressional District, and making use of the many contacts and organizations with whom she had worked on her husband's behalf, Cornelia in 1932 mounted a second campaign against the incumbent, Louis McFadden. The issues she targeted for the May primary were consistent with her longtime work on social welfare and women's rights, and these gained added impetus from the Depression's assault on family economies and communal stability. As she had before, Cornelia set off on an exhaustive tour of the whole district, speaking indoors and out, all the while lambasting McFadden's record. Despite the large crowds she drew to her rallies, for a second time the district elected to stick with McFadden. "Leila was awfully tired at the end of her campaign and hasn't yet fully recovered," her husband observed. "She is up in Milford today gardening furiously, which is the best thing that could possibly happen to her."[52]

It was the best thing because that was Gifford's recipe for rejuvenation.

*Grey Towers provided
ample and much-needed
space for Pennsylvania's
First Couple to recover
from their arduous
political campaigning.*
Grey Towers NHL /
Forest History Society

In one of his many radio addresses during his term, he spoke of how he too would retreat to Grey Towers to sleep and eat, and go fly-fishing along his beloved Sawkill. (As land prices along its upper reaches fell during the Depression, he and Amos bought a number of farmsteads to expand their angling domain.) These respites kept him fit, or at least fit enough to fool his opponents. At the conclusion of an exceptionally difficult spring 1933 legislative session, the governor, then sixty-eight years old, was exhausted. "When I got through with it, I was pretty well all in," he wrote George Pardee, "but you can bet your boots and my boots too that the opposition didn't know it."[53]

That politics remained a combative sport was a reflection of Pinchot's long association with Theodore Roosevelt, a man whom he still credited as the formative force shaping his perspectives. But Pinchot was confronted with issues that his mentor never had to face, and consequently had to craft innovative responses to unique crises, the Depression foremost among them. As if to signal his realization of the distance that now separated him from TR and the "Square Deal" the president had advocated in the Progressive Era, Pinchot began to employ a different rhetoric. While delivering a campaign speech in Philadelphia in October 1930 in which he offered his assessment of the nation's economic collapse, he asked his audience: "Isn't it time for a new deal?"[54]

Rapid transformations in the body politic also pushed him beyond Progressive Era prescriptions. "I think you are right about the extraordinary change in the popular outlook in the country," he wrote Irish reformer Sir Horace Plunkett in June 1931. "So far as I am able to judge, the people generally are more aroused against the big corporations, and especially against the public utilities, than they were in TR's time." This ferment offered the first "real chance for a big step in the direction of real equality of opportunity in this country. Whether we take it, of course, nobody knows, but anyhow it is worth trying for." His experiments with state intervention in the development of economic and social policy, such as unemployment relief and workers' compensation, most resembled those of another Roosevelt, the then-governor of neighboring New York State. "Very few men found themselves, as did Roosevelt in Albany and Pinchot in Harrisburg," historian Otis Graham has argued, "under insistent pressures to move gradually leftward onto new tactical ground." Political activism had kept Pinchot ideologically fresh.[55]

And on the cutting edge. To relieve the crushing weight of unemployment, he set up emergency work relief camps throughout Pennsylvania. By February 1932, nearly 15,000 applicants had sought work under this program. During the day, the men were employed in the construction of state highways and country roads; at night, they lived in camps that were run with military-like regimen. The results seemed impressive. In his first term, Pinchot had spent approximately $260 million upgrading the state's roads; during the second he vastly extended the role of the state in building and maintaining the emerging highway system. Reasoning that cash-strapped townships could not upgrade or sustain the roadways under their jurisdiction, he urged the legislature in 1931 to transfer more than 20,000 miles of township roads to the state system. It did so by unanimous vote, and it was on these so-called "Pinchot roads" that the unemployed began their work; three years later, more than 70 percent of the expanded network of state roads was paved.[56]

Not only did this intensive labor to get "the farmers out of the mud" link long-isolated agricultural areas more directly with urban markets, and thereby directly aid one of Pinchot's most loyal constituencies, but the road workers themselves were reportedly transformed, nourished in body and soul. Such camps, a publicity release declared, "are a pleasing example of employment versus charity." They also served as an example to now-President Franklin Roosevelt; the national Civilian Conservation Corps was based in part on Pennsylvania's programs. That Pinchot seemed a step ahead of the New Deal led Bob Marshall to hope he might go even further. "What a splendid service he might do," he advised Raphael Zon in 1933, "if . . . he would step out completely and fearlessly as a thoroughgoing Socialist." Pinchot never came out of (or slipped into) that particular closet, but his solutions to the crises confronting rural and urban America revealed that his conservationism sported an evolving, human face.[57]

Its humanity was manifest most strikingly in the Pinchot administration's support for the state's industrial workers. When the bituminous miners staged a walkout in the summer of 1933, and coal companies refused to negotiate, Pinchot tried to jump-start negotiations by serving as a mediator. He released relief monies to sustain striking families, and toured the western Pennsylvania coal fields to urge strikers to refrain from violent conflict. The companies reacted by hiring private deputies, who fired on and beat up miners to provoke a reaction, but the result was not what they expected. Pinchot dispatched the National Guard and later the state police into the region to protect the strikers. "So far as I know," Pinchot observed, "that is the first time anything of that sort has been done in the whole history of labor troubles in the United States." As much as Pinchot relished the praise that came to him from liberal media such as *The New Republic,* and delighted in the defamatory editorials in the conservative press, he was especially pleased by the willingness of the miners to heed his call for peaceful protests. "The miners have been simply wonderful," he wrote Antoinette. "Their patience and good temper has been utterly beyond anything I believed possible." The same could not be said of what he called "the Steel Trust," which owned the most strike-ridden mines. Its actions, he raged, were "nothing so much as a vicious child—utterly unreasonable—utterly disregardful of its solemn pledges—cheating, lying, and doing its level best not to prevent trouble but to create trouble. And that it hasn't succeeded in spreading riot and bloodshed all over Western Pennsylvania is just nothing but the blessing of Providence."[58]

Strikers came to regard Cornelia Pinchot's presence in their midst as providential, too. During the 1933 strikes, she worked at her husband's side, a seemingly inexhaustible force. "Leila has been perfectly splendid in this, as in everything," a grateful governor noted. "One night she and I got through telephoning at 11:00 o'clock on strike matters, were called up again at 1:30, and went right through to breakfast. She has been a tower of strength to the labor people all the way through." So she proved when, in conjunction with Charlotte Carr, secretary of labor and industry, she joined picket lines, gave union-supportive speeches, and mediated labor disputes.

Significant on its own terms, Cornelia's activism had a larger importance, historian John Furlow has noted. Her words "gave the union movement official sanction" just as her status as Pennsylvania's First Lady legitimized her presence in hostile company towns. Because "[c]orporation officials did not dare intimidate or threaten a Governor's wife or . . . prevent her from making a public address, many workers were able to hear [a] pro-union message for the first time in their lives." Rebutting critics such as the *Philadelphia Record,* which complained that "Mrs. Pinchot and Miss Carr ought to stay home where they belong," Gifford proudly acknowledged that his wife had established herself as "this administration's best contribution to the cause of workers on farm or factory, mill or mine."[59]

The Pinchots also extended their sympathy for and support of another set of beleaguered Americans, the Jewish community. Their oppression was not local but international. In the early 1930s, Nazi-led persecution of German Jews accelerated; the party sanctioned boycotts against Jewish merchants, the dismissal of Jewish teachers, professors, and physicians from their posts, and the use of organized street harassment of Jews to constrict their public movements.

American Jews sought to raise the alarm, and at the center of these organizing efforts was one of Gifford Pinchot's friends, Rabbi Stephen S. Wise, the longtime spiritual leader of New York's Free Synagogue. He and Pinchot had met early in the twentieth century and had collaborated on forest-management measures in the Adirondack Mountains (where Wise had a summer home). Throughout the teens they appeared together in public forums devoted to the reformation of the political process and the amelioration of social ills, and over the years felt free to ask one another to support pet projects. Pinchot, for example, asked to list Wise's name on an appeal to President Hoover for the convening of an international conference on conservation; Wise congratulated Pinchot on his electoral victories and recommended candidates for positions in the Pinchot administrations. These enduring, reciprocal exchanges led Rabbi Wise to call once more on Pinchot to support a "monster rally" in New York's Madison Square Garden to protest the Nazis' openly oppressive actions, to be held on the night of March 27, 1933.[60]

Unable to attend himself, the governor delegated to his favorite spokeswoman the task of addressing the more than 30,000 Americans who jammed into the Garden. Joining an array of the celebrated and the powerful, including former New York governor Al Smith, Senator Robert F. Wagner, and an ecumenical host of religious leaders, Cornelia Pinchot blasted the actions of Hitler and his minions. The German leader "appeals for the advancement of German *kultur,*" she noted dryly, but how "can he reconcile that policy with the banishment of such men as [Albert] Einstein and [writer Lion] Feuchtwanger? Let him remember the lessons of history that the government that expelled the Jews always fell." Her criticism was also shaped, as it often was, by a focus on family. "As an American woman who has known Jewish mothers and wives in their homes I fiercely resent the outrages, the boycotts, and the injustices that have been perpetrated against Jewish homes in Germany." The message she read from her husband reiterated her arguments and voiced his solidarity with those who had rallied to the cause of the German Jews. "I am with you in demanding that

the German government's official disavowal of oppression must be translated immediately and actually into economic, political, and religious tolerance." If not, Governor Pinchot predicted, the German people will find
that "no government based on open or masked suppression of religious liberty can long endure."[61]

The response to the Pinchots' speeches was swift. "Am I right in my
opinion," asked George H. Payne, "that you are about the only distinguished gentile who has made a protest against the Hitler persecution of
Jews[?]" Although Pinchot was not in fact the only one to speak out, his
query reflected one of the reasons Wise had asked the governor to speak —
he had great name recognition. This was particularly true among the Jews
of Pennsylvania. "I cannot let this day pass without expressing to you the
appreciation of thousands of your fellow citizens for your ringing message
of denunciation," wrote Samuel Edelman, "and [for] the lofty, idealistic
and thrilling words of Mrs. Pinchot at the meeting held in protest of Nazi
atrocities against Jews." He then drew a parallel between the Pinchots'
willingness to speak up for the German Jews and their commitment to
social justice in the United States. "It is becoming more evident every day
that the masses of all creeds look to you for leadership [because] you never
fail them in the hour of trial."[62]

Gifford Pinchot had not always felt such an affinity for the Jewish people. As a young man he had given vent to the casual anti-Semitism of the
Anglo-American elite. Heading to Europe in 1890 to begin his forestry
studies, he had described a fellow passenger aboard the *Elbe* as a "self-satisfied, impertinent, ridiculous, good natured German Jew, Jew, Jew." Such
dismissive language occasionally cropped up in his diary and correspondence through the 1890s; those few Jews Pinchot encountered were identified *as* Jews, a testament to his inability and unwillingness then to distinguish between these particular individuals and their faith.[63]

The circumstance of mutual acquaintance and regard forced him to
rethink, and alter, his attitude. Among foresters, he developed quite close
relationships with Raphael Zon and Bob Marshall. Louis Brandeis had
become a critical advisor during the Ballinger controversy, and remained
such in subsequent years. Similarly extensive was his friendship with
another brilliant jurist, Felix Frankfurter. Pinchot also numbered Stephen

Wise and other Jewish progressives as allies in the shared cause of social reform, an alliance that would deepen during the 1920s and 1930s.

The timing and tightening of these friendships is important in another respect. Gifford's brother, Amos, whose leftist leanings in the Progressive Era had also brought him in contact with a coterie of Jewish intellectuals, including Wise, simultaneously began to repudiate his earlier relationships and the politics on which they were based. As Amos swung to the political right, he and his uncle Amos Eno joined the America First Committee in the mid-1930s to denounce the prospects of American entry into a brewing European war; "one of the more vocal members" of the isolationist organization, Amos served as president of its New York City chapter. From that position, he repeatedly denounced those, such as Rabbi Wise, who he believed were responsible for drumming up support for U.S. intervention overseas.[64]

Wise initially tried parrying Amos's criticisms of his anti-Nazi organizing in the United States: "[W]hat has come over you, one-time liberal," Wise wrote in 1937, "bless your heart and straighten out the kinks in your mind!" Amos never did, and instead became even more closely tied to right-wing isolationism, while Wise became more blunt in his rejection of Amos's growing rage against "Jewish interventionists." Writing to a mutual friend in 1941, Wise pointed out that "Jews as a group are not interventionists or isolationists or anything else, but as individuals they have the same right as Amos Pinchot to take a position." Moreover, he noted, that right was linked to this unalterable fact—"We are both American citizens."[65]

This claim of equal political status, Wise knew, was not something that Amos Pinchot and his ilk readily accepted; they trafficked instead in the perfidious allegation that Jews were "dual" citizens, which in the lexicon of the political right in Europe and the United States meant that they were more loyal to their "race" than to the nation in which they happened to reside. Another American who voiced this scurrilous charge was famed aviator and Hitler apologist Charles Lindbergh. "I am horrified by the Lindberghs," Wise told a friend, "and almost more horrified by those who, like [Amos] Pinchot, an old personal friend, are prepared to defend him on the specious ground that Jews must not object to be criticized or dealt with in a public way by those who disagree with them." All citizens in a democracy were free to debate public issues in the civic arena, access that Wise recognized was pivotal to American interests in the war itself. Amos Pinchot did not share this perspective, leading Wise to conclude: "[I]t may be that I am a better American than some Americans of older stock who are serenely complacent, not to say indifferent, to the fate of democracy throughout the world."[66]

About Gifford Pinchot, Wise never had to write such an indictment. Decades earlier, Pinchot had come to understand the distinctions between individual and group identity that Amos and others in their family refused to accept, and publicly doubted. In formally communicating his support for the plight of German Jews to the 1932 Madison Square Garden rally, Gifford was also sending a message to his kin. On this vital matter of conscience, belief was thicker than blood.

POLITICAL CONCLUSIONS

As the conscientious governor's term wound down, he revved up for the spring 1934 Republican primary for a seat in the U.S. Senate—or at least tried to do so. In December he was laid low by a debilitating case of shingles. Hospitalized in New York for three months, he then took an extended vacation until mid-April, putting him on hiatus for a total of four months, a period he likened to torture. "I felt as though I were wearing a straitjacket made of a red hot wire waste-basket." The already-thin governor lost twenty pounds and an incalculable amount of political ground. "I was only able to make as many speeches in the whole campaign," he confirmed to his sister, "as I made one day in my last campaign for the Governorship." For the first time, his age and health became campaign issues, but other deficits were familiar. Once more Pinchot had pitted himself against a tough incumbent, this time Senator David A. Reed; once more, he attacked his opponent as a creature of the Mellon machine; once more, he touted his progressive record as governor, anticipating that this would give him the decisive edge. And once more, he lost. But so would Reed in November, as would most Republicans on the state ticket, a sweep that Pinchot attributed to the reactionary forces still dominating the organization and to "the dis-

gust of the man in the street with the Old Deal." What was needed, the out-
going governor asserted, was "a New Deal for the Republican Party."[67]

It was not forthcoming, although a seventy-two-year-old Pinchot would
attempt to initiate the process in 1938 when he mounted yet another (and
final) bid for the governorship; he was crushed in the primary by almost
half a million votes. Even before that drubbing, the worst of his electoral
experience, Pinchot had acted as if his public career had (probably) run its
course. In his final speech to the Pennsylvania assembly in January 1935, he
adopted a far more conciliatory tone than he had employed in his 1927
address, during which he had excoriated the "gangster politicians" who ran
the Republican Party and the state. No such invective filled the air in 1935.
Rather, he praised the citizenry and civil servants for facing up to an
unimaginable set of difficulties. "No other administration, unless perhaps
during the Civil War, has had so hard a row to hoe," he noted, and "I most
earnestly hope and fervently pray that no other four years as difficult will
ever again face the people and the State Government of Pennsylvania." To
have been governor during these strenuous years was yet an honor. "[T]he
chance to be of use to the people of this Commonwealth was worth everything it cost and more."[68]

His bout with shingles had been one of those costs. Although he continued to do the state's work from his hospital bed, he would privately credit
Cornelia with "running the State of Pennsylvania when I was laid up."
Publicly, in his final message to the General Assembly, he applauded his
wife, "whose advice in this emergency was indispensable. Indeed, throughout both my terms Mrs. Pinchot's assistance in dealing with the human side
of government has been invaluable. In her the people of the Commonwealth have had an ally impossible to duplicate or replace."[69]

His shortcomings made him more expendable than she, but he turned
even these into a form of virtue. "Mistakes I have made in plenty, as any
man must, but I have honestly done my best and whatever may be said of
me, whatever you may think of me, this much you will admit. I have had
[no] master but the people of Pennsylvania and my own conscience."[70]

Capping these valedictory remarks was his final farewell. On a bitterly
cold day in January 15, 1935, he attended the inauguration of the new (and
Democratic) governor, George Earle. At its conclusion, with Cornelia by

his side, Pinchot, wearing his favorite battered, large-brim hat, walked toward the Capitol amid catcalls and jeers from Democratic loyalists. ("'So long, Giff,' someone shouted, and another chimed in, 'You ought to be ashamed of yourself.'") But when the couple reached and began to walk through the park that extends from the seat of government, cheers and shouts rang down from state employees gathered before the Capitol's windows. With the consummate timing of an actor sensing that the curtain was descending, Pinchot spun on his heel, swept off his hat, and bowed.[71]

Crosscut

I N T H E mid-1930s, at the height of the Great Depression that had battered the nation's economy for more than five years and had left millions of Americans unemployed, and at the close of his second term
as governor of Pennsylvania, Gifford Pinchot found himself in greatly
reduced financial circumstances and without a job. His income had been
slashed by more than two-thirds. To stay afloat, he and his brother Amos
had begun to sell off their families' past, disposing of properties that they
had inherited from their parents and grandparents. This partial liquida-
tion of assets staved off more desperate measures and situations but in turn
diminished future financial returns. "I have to scratch my gravel like everything to pay my debts and pay my taxes," he acknowledged to a friend. But
he knew that unlike the mass of his countrymen and women, he still had
money in the bank.[1]

What struck the now seventy-two-year-old former governor more
forcefully, what he could not abide, was not having steady work. To resolve
that untenable situation, he developed a plan—a Ten Year Plan. Shortly
after leaving office in 1934, he jotted down a list of ideas, goals, and questions that he expected to occupy the rest of his life. The list came in two
parts. The first group of items were of a practical nature—writing a will,
settling his estate and helping organize his family's financial and legal

affairs for the years after his death, and so forth. The second group focused on solidifying his legacy. He expected to finish his autobiographical tome on the history of forestry and conservation—what would become the posthumously published *Breaking New Ground;* write a volume about his two terms as governor of Pennsylvania; and publish another collection of "Fish Stories." In this ambitious catalogue of literary work, which would encapsulate and give meaning to his five decades of strenuous public service, lay an important admission. A full and active life was winding down.[2]

But he was also excited by the prospect of new ventures. Surely that is why he planned to have his "teeth fixed up," a mundane but significant act for a man who anticipated putting his best face forward for some time to come. That notion is reinforced by the very structure of the second half of his Ten Year Plan. It comprised a set of open-ended questions. Among the frankly political ones were queries about whether to mount a campaign to bolster the nation's security in the midst of Europe's rising troubles, and whether he should run for a third term as governor or take one more shot at a seat in the U.S. Senate.

Hunting for more to do, he also pondered how to incorporate within the concept of "new conservationism" a more ecological perspective on the American landscape. These concerns and the manner in which they were framed, themselves marks of a creative and restless mind, meant that nothing was certain, a state of being that both drove and worried Pinchot. In this sense the final question on his list was the most directly self-referential and critical: "Where's your program[?]"[3]

Where indeed. As the ensuing years revealed, he did not have one or, rather, never developed the programmatic certitude implied by a Ten Year Plan. During the final decade of his life, as he thought through his ideas and then tested them out in speeches, books, and forays into the political arena, he demonstrated yet again his remarkable ability to expose himself to, and change in the face of, fresh thinking. Yet his intellectual regeneration had its limits. Some were revealed in the tension that emerged between his growing conviction that conservationists must fight to preserve wilderness for its recreational value and spiritual qualities and their obligation to ensure the continued flow of material benefits to the greatest number of Americans. This was a healthy tension, to be sure, but his ability to maintain the balance between the two positions was tested during the second great national controversy of Pinchot's career. In the 1930s, he would square off with Roosevelt's interior secretary, Harold Ickes, over the transfer of the Forest Service from Agriculture; in his vigorous, reflexive defense of the agency, Pinchot would reveal just how brittle he could be.

OPENING CHAPTER

Clues as to how and why this tension came to be emerge in an unlikely source—Pinchot's revisions to *The Training of a Forester,* a popular manual he wrote to explain the defining characteristics of the profession he had done so much to introduce to American culture. The book contains very little direct autobiographical material from which to gain insight into the author's intellectual transformation. Its preface, moreover, aimed at young men who were considering their "life's work," adopts a tone that positively discourages notions of vocational uncertainty. "I urge no man to make forestry his profession," Pinchot warned, "but rather to keep away from it if he can. In forestry a man is either altogether at home or very much out of place." This language affirmed that there had been, and would always be, but one kind of "place," one form of experience, possible in the profession.[4]

Or so it would seem. But *The Training of a Forester* contains a surprise. The substantial revisions between 1914, when it was first published, and 1937, when the final (and fourth) edition appeared, indicate that Pinchot had grafted ecological insights onto utilitarian methodologies. This intellectual hybridization was itself largely inspired by his reaction to contemporary debates over the principles of conservation, a responsiveness that challenges one of Pinchot's own conceits. Although he liked to think of himself as someone who broke new ground, he was no less a reactive figure.

The first edition of *The Training of a Forester* appeared in the mid-teens and depended heavily upon the ethos of the Progressive Era. Built on the interlocking notions of efficiency, order, and rationality, and dedicated to the power of scientific analysis to resolve social problems, the ethos assumed that humanity has the capacity to remake, and thus to better, itself and the environment in which it lives.[5]

The Training of a Forester made similar claims about forestry, which its author defined as "the art of handling the forest so that it will render whatever service is required of it without being impoverished or destroyed." Those services are many, including the production of commodities such as "saw logs, telegraph poles, barrel hoops . . . or turpentine" or the maintenance of environments in which to "support cattle or sheep." Forests had other purposes, too, from the regulation of stream flow to the reduction of erosion to the advance of transportation. Nowhere in this edition did Pinchot acknowledge that a forest might have value unto itself, or at least hold a value different from those humanity then could conceive. Instead he trumpeted the ways in which the forest produced goods "for the service of man," and in the most efficient manner contributed to what he called the "housekeeping of the nation."[6]

This vantage point determined how foresters were taught to conceive of forests, too. In a lengthy section of *The Training of a Forester*, Pinchot dealt with curricular concerns, with the structure of forestry education, through which students would be introduced to the professional nomenclature. This knowledge was critical, for the "trained forester must know the forest as a doctor knows the human machine," and that meant being able to "distinguish the different trees of which the forest is composed, for that is like learning to read." A forester's grammar lessons involved a series of courses in dendrology (the science of trees), forest physiography (the physical geography of forests), and forest mensuration (qualitative data about forests and their understories). But the crux of a forester's education was silvics, "the knowledge of the relation of trees to light, heat, and moisture, to the soil, and to each other." These facts helped explain "the composition, character and form of the forest" and would enable foresters to determine "the success or failure of tree species in competition with one another," the development of individual trees in "height, diameter and volume," their "form and length of life," and their reproductive methodologies. Silvics unlocked a forest's life cycle.[7]

Silvics was also the key to forest management, which, as Pinchot observed, was "closely related to questions of forest finance." No forester's education would be complete without study of forest economics, which explored "the productive value of forests to their owners." In classifying the

"economic woods of the United States" and then determining the most efficient means by which to harvest them, foresters placed scientific analysis in
the service of resource exploitation.[8]

By tying forestry's legitimacy to its social utility, Pinchot acted as had
most of the other Progressive Era reformers who created the many new
academic professions, such as social work and sociology and political science, that blossomed throughout the late nineteenth and early twentieth
centuries. That is why he insisted that as forests were a "national necessity,"
so were foresters, for without them the United States would end up like
"Palestine, Greece, Northern Africa and Central India," now-stunted
regions that "offer in themselves the most impressive object lessons of the
effect upon national prosperity and national character of the neglect of the
forest. . . ." What would allow Americans, whose cultural identity was
derived from and dependent upon nature, to escape a similar fate? Scientific forestry. Its proponents were trained to break down a forest's con-
stituent elements and rebuild the wooded landscape, all with an eye for
increasing its economic contributions to the commonweal.[9]

That the forest could be studied and thus known, that its problems could
be analyzed and presumably fixed, was precisely analogous to the tack
urban reformers such as Jane Addams and Jacob Riis took when they wrote
about immigrant life in the burgeoning metropoli of Chicago or New
York. Pinchot was well aware of this link. When he opened an office as a
consulting forester in New York City in the mid-1890s, he leased space in
the United Charities Building, which historian Daniel Rodgers has identified as the epicenter of progressive social ferment. Other lessees included
the National Consumers' League, the National Housing Association, the
National Child Labor Committee, and a host of private social-service phi-
lanthropies. Pinchot readily mixed with these reformers, who shared his
faith in people's capacity to better the environment—both natural and
human. It was then that he came into contact with Jane Addams and joined
with her in her work on child welfare. Years later these connections
remained alive. In 1912 he was one of several civic, religious, and social
reformers invited to speak on "Social Justice" at Rabbi Stephen S. Wise's
Free Synagogue. The problems of the forest were at one with those of the
urban core.[10]

That made it easy for Pinchot to employ an urban metaphor to explain his profession's perspectives. "Just as in New York City, for example, the French, the Germans, the Italians, the Hungarians, and the Chinese each have quarters of their own, and in those quarters live in accordance with habits that distinguish each from all others," so too did trees take root in particular localities and "live in accordance with definite racial habits" every bit as precise as their human counterparts. To know those "peculiar characteristics" was the critical, first step in improving them.[11]

The Training of a Forester was itself a first step. Since the 1890s, Pinchot had been searching for a way to publish a primer on forestry that was at once a technical handbook and a missionary tract, one that informed as it proselytized. Mixed in with his insights about the nature of his craft were pointed admonitions about the dire political and social consequences if Americans did not thoroughly embrace the perspectives of professional forestry. Its concerns were integrated on the national level through the Forest Service, but that was not true for the millions of forested acres owned by individual states, most of which had passed precious little legislation regarding forestry. State foresters were thus urged to create "a right public sentiment" regarding their work, "prepare or endeavor to secure the passage of good State forest laws" that reclaimed cut-over lands and conservatively managed state forests, and battle "against the enactment of bad laws," particularly the pervasive forest taxation measures that forced "the destructive cutting of timber." State forestry, unlike its national counterpart, was in but a rudimentary stage of development.[12]

Private forestry was considerably less mature. "The concentration of timberland ownership in the United States," Pinchot asserted, "has put a few men in control of vast areas of forest," and for these monopolists, profits drove lumber production. That is why "the practice of forestry by private owners, except for fire protection, has made but little progress in the United States," frustrating the private forester, who "must usually be willing to accept a good many limitations on the technical side of his work." That frustration could be relieved, and privately owned lands better served, Pinchot proclaimed, only when "forest destruction will be legally recognized as hostile to the public welfare, and when lumbermen will be compelled by law to handle their forests so as to insure [their] reproduction. . . ."

Such tough legal remedies were "neither new nor tyrannical," and had been successful in "democratic Switzerland," but judging from conditions prevailing in the United States in the teens, Pinchot suspected it might take a generation before similar measures would catch hold in the American republic.[13]

It would take longer if foresters failed to remember that they were public servants. "Because he deals with a forest, he has his hand upon the future welfare of his country." No "[f]orester can safely allow himself to remain ignorant of the needs and purposes of his fellow citizens, or to be out of touch with the current questions of the day." For Pinchot, this established an important political equation—the "best citizen makes the best Forester, and no man can make a good Forester unless he is a good citizen also."[14]

This credo, reinforced by Pinchot's fervent declaration that foresters were "missionaries in a very real sense," shaped the marketing strategy Pinchot and J. W. Lippincott devised for *The Training of a Forester*. In January 1914, shortly before the book's publication, Pinchot wrote Lippincott that they needed "to talk over the matter of getting the book into the hands of the right people. A judicious campaign directed in the right quarters will, I feel confident, double the circulation the book might otherwise reach." By this he meant the spread of the book's arguments, not an increase in his royalties, and he thus put his mailing lists at the publisher's disposal, suggested particular reviewers for the book, and convinced Lippincott to reduce the volume's cost to $1 so that it would be easily within the reach of a wider reading public. In the Progressive war of ideas, price was no object; persuasion was all.[15]

VISIONS AND REVISIONS

Pinchot persuaded himself that with the publication of *The Training of a Forester* in 1914, professional forestry had reached a new point in its development. "In the United States," he declared, "forestry is passing out of the pioneer stage of agitation and education of public opinion, and into the permanent phase of the practice of the profession." He would not supply the leadership for this second stage, and the book's appearance provides a convenient demarcation in his career, which explains his cool reaction in 1916

when Lippincott proposed a second edition for the next year. Pinchot indicated he had neither the time nor the inclination to revise the original text.
Although the publisher brought out what it called a second edition in 1917,
it contained only minor revisions, and it remained unrevised for the next
fifteen years, giving it a long shelf life.[16]

By 1933 there were not many copies left on the shelves. That summer J.
Jefferson Jones, a Lippincott editor, wrote Pinchot that there were only fifty
copies of the book in stock, and the publisher wanted to bring out a third
edition. It did so in hopes of cashing in on the nation's revived interest in
forestry and conservation, which the Great Depression and the arrival of
Franklin Roosevelt's New Deal had brought to the fore. In "view of the
present wide interest in reforestation," Jones noted, "we believe it would be
advisable and helpful . . . to revise [The Training of a Forester] thoroughly
and [bring it] up-to-date before it is reprinted." Noting that the last edition
had appeared in 1917, he assumed that "much of interest and value could be
added." He wanted it added speedily, too, so as to coincide with the passage
of federal legislation concerning one of the president's pet projects, the Civilian Conservation Corps, or what Jones called the "reforestation camps."[17]

Pinchot was acutely aware of Roosevelt's growing interest in conservation, and the prospects this might hold for the nation's forests. In 1932, for
instance, the president-elect had asked the then-governor of Pennsylvania
to prepare a report on the status of America's woods. Aware of Pinchot's
pioneering efforts to purchase clear-cut lands and regenerate them by
hiring the state's unemployed workers, Roosevelt wished to determine
whether this experiment could be replicated nationally. Pinchot believed
that it could, and with the aid of foresters Raphael Zon and Bob Marshall,
he sent the president a tough and critical memorandum. Dominating their
response was an insistence that the only way to resolve the massive problems of environmental despoliation, which eroded the land and the quality
of people's lives, was to lease, buy, or take through eminent domain millions
of acres of private timberlands. In these forests, new jobs could be created—
such as replanting trees and building roads, bridges, dams, hiking trails,
and cabins—a public investment that would have important political and
social consequences. One of these was the demise of private forestry, or
what he and his colleagues sneeringly referred to as "industrial forestry";

current lumbering practices, they believed, were responsible for many of the current problems confronting rural, forested America. Nationalizing these lands, or a portion of them, and developing stiff regulations governing their use would finally establish public forestry's dominance over the American lumber industry. This approach would reduce the escalating unemployment rate, too, providing meaningful work and a steady income for the forgotten man and woman, who Pinchot expected would be hired to clean up, replant, and manage these new public lands. Best of all, the authors concluded, this was one federal investment that would pay for itself rapidly.[18]

This report stands as an important breakpoint in Pinchot's conception of the purposes and goals of American forestry, and it raised vital questions about who should control the nation's woods and to what ends. During the Progressive Era, he had hoped that in time private forests and forestry would be regulated by federal laws, but he had never called for outright public ownership. Now he believed that this was the only acceptable way to achieve woodland rehabilitation and social justice.[19]

Despite Pinchot's intellectual reorientation and political activism during the early 1930s, he was nonetheless caught off guard by Lippincott's renewed interest in *The Training of a Forester*. "To my great surprise," he wrote Herbert Smith in June 1933, "I have just had a request from the publishers to revise [the book] again." Pinchot, then governor of Pennsylvania, knew that he did not have the time for the extensive revisions necessary, and hoped that Smith would serve as ghostwriter. Smith hesitated, refusing to commit himself to the project before rereading an earlier edition. Once he had done so, he proposed instead that an entirely new edition be written. That, of course, was exactly what Pinchot was hoping to avoid in asking Smith to be his ghostwriter. But Smith said he was too old for the work, something he had realized while rereading the text. For him, the book was "a startling demonstration" not only of the transformation of forestry in the intervening years but of his own aging. "[W]ho but an old fellow would think of 20 years ago as though it were but yesterday and wonder that things are so far different than they were." Pinchot, who doubted that forestry had changed as much as it should have, and who by temperament and occupation was loath to succumb to nostalgic paeans to youthful accomplishments—at sixty-eight, he was happily governing one of the nation's largest states—nonetheless conceded that "the book was written for pioneer conditions, many of which no longer exist. . . . As you say, it certainly does mark the long road over which we have come."[20]

They would walk down that road one step farther. In early August Pinchot wrote Lippincott and indicated that he was unable to revise the text, a decision that the publisher regretted but understood. Editor Jones noted that they would again publish the unrevised text in expectation of receiving "most any day an order from the Reforestation camps—which may mean several hundred copies." Would it be harmful, the editor wondered, if the book was republished unrevised? Pinchot assured him that there would be no harm, although some minor revisions would be necessary. He then persuaded Smith to help update the facts and figures scattered throughout the text, and they even drafted "a new chapter containing some essential information about our forests." The volume reappeared on the publisher's list beginning in the early fall of 1933.

This third edition's reception was disappointing. It was not reviewed in either public or professional venues, and the expected sales to the Civilian Conservation Corps apparently never materialized, a disheartening response reflected in the royalty statement issued to Pinchot in January 1934: only fifty-six copies had been sold, netting the author $14.96. This was just as well, for as Pinchot understood, the edition did not reflect his altered thinking about the social and political context in which foresters operated, and did not contain his prescriptions for a profession he believed was badly in need of reform. A fourth and final edition would resolve some, though not all, of these concerns.[21]

TOWARD ECOLOGY

It was far easier to appreciate that *The Training of a Forester* needed updating than it was to find the time or energy to accomplish the necessary revisions. Still, by the summer of 1936, Pinchot had begun to contemplate how to revise the book and to cast about for a suitable, and younger, ghostwriter. With the help of Smith and Henry Graves, Pinchot recruited Robert P. Holdsworth, a member of the forestry faculty at Massachusetts State Col-

lege in Amherst. Fortunately, Holdsworth was close at hand, spending that
summer at Grey Towers, organizing the former chief forester's archives
and preparing synopses of some of its holdings. In short order, the two men
developed a warm relationship, based as much on Holdsworth's evident
research abilities as on the men's shared love of fishing and tennis. "Words
fail me," Holdsworth would write Pinchot later that fall, "when it comes to
expressing thanks for the great kindness which enveloped me at Grey
Towers from the very moment of my arrival. Never in my life have I spent
so interesting and satisfactory a summer." Pinchot, in turn, was no less gra-
cious. "We can certainly reciprocate everything that you say for we keenly
enjoyed you being here, and are looking forward with equivalent anticipation to your work here next summer."[22]

Work they did. Beginning in early July 1937, Holdsworth and Pinchot
began to rewrite *The Training of a Forester.* To be more precise, Holdsworth, who had read the book over the winter and had come to believe in
its "destiny," reworked portions of each chapter and then passed them to
Pinchot. He heavily edited Holdsworth's first draft, both for style and content, a month-long procedure that followed the text through a second and
third draft. The book, which was published in December, was thus a collaborative effort, a relationship Pinchot acknowledged by splitting the
book's royalties with Holdsworth and, in the preface to this edition, calling
it "our joint project."[23]

But Pinchot's name was on the book's spine, and he thereby assumed
responsibility for its ideas, some of which differed significantly from those
advanced in previous editions. In particular, there were important changes
in his discussions of the character of forestry education and in the conception of a forest itself. The earlier emphasis, for instance, on silvics, forest
economics, and lumbering, three crucial elements in defining forestry's
utilitarian orientation, was tempered by the insertion of new material that
fell under the rubric of "forest ecology." He advised his readers that while
one must study and be able to identify "the various kinds of trees" and their
"individual habits of growth and life," they must also "understand them as
members of plant communities" and be able to discuss these communities'
"relationships to each other and to climate and physiography," to soils and
humus. Trees were rooted in diversity.[24]

In the new edition, forestry was branching out in other ways, too. Under the heading of "forest protection," a subject ignored in earlier editions, Pinchot spoke of students' need to study entomology. That was in good measure due to the damage various insects could inflict on "forest vegetation," of course, but in studying "how their attacks are made, how they may be discovered, and the best ways by which such attacks can be mitigated or controlled," the forester was compelled to adopt new methods of "cutting the forest during its various stages of development . . . to control or minimize the evil effects of attacks by insects, fungi, and other enemies." Not all insects were injurious; the well-trained forester must have a sophisticated understanding of the dynamic interactions within the forest community, and respond accordingly.[25]

Pine beetles and spruce bud worms were not the only nonhuman organisms to complicate, even alter, the forester's perspective. "The conservation of our native forest wildlife is of growing importance," Pinchot affirmed, and as a result he claimed that a "general study of forest animals, fish and birds should be included in the Forester's training," as should classes in wildlife management. Such coursework was essential because what "birds and animals do to and in the forest is not yet fully known." Caution in handling this "very real and highly interesting and essential part of a forest" was essential, he concluded, so that its "animal citizens" would not be destroyed.[26]

Human needs never could dominate forests, Pinchot conceded when he defined them as "a complex community with a life of its own." What mattered instead was that nature "governs the mutual lives and works of [this community] under a strict code of natural laws, so that despite the warfare, the pulling and hauling, and the helping, the forest tends in the long run to be kept pretty well in balance." This insight had important implications for the forester's art. "The Forester, therefore, must know about these elements of the forest and their behavior," for "he, too, must work toward maintaining the balance of nature." The woodsman must work within nature's economy; utilitarian forestry had been undercut.[27]

Pinchot accepted that the harvesting of wood products must be balanced by legitimate and competing human claims on forested environments. He was not opposed to logging per se, and always promoted forestry's economic contributions, as he did on the very first page of the 1937 edition of *The Training of a Forester* when he declared that "the forest is a great renewable resource, which . . . need never be exhausted of its riches." But now he argued that one of these riches was that "woodlands are beautiful." Happily, this "'good' which the forest offers so freely to all men cannot be measured in board feet and cords, in dollars and cents," Pinchot observed. "It is immeasurable because it reaches and uplifts our inner selves," a spiritual and aesthetic appreciation that confounds long-held assumptions about his unbending, lifelong commitment to the preeminence of efficiency and productivity. His change of heart led a reviewer for *American Forests* to conclude that "those now established in the profession will find [the book] a means of re-orienting themselves in their chosen profession."[28]

Pinchot's reorientation depended, ironically enough, on the very utilitarian credo that is so closely associated with him (by way of Jeremy Bentham): "the greatest good, for the greatest number, for the longest run." What would happen, for instance, if the definition of the greatest good changed over time, a shift in part dictated by what the greatest number construed as good? That question is decidedly political, and it is no surprise that Pinchot, who throughout his long career had been alert to new currents in scientific scholarship and public activism, responded once more.

In the late teens and early 1920s, some foresters started to incorporate into their work new forms of scientific analysis of the environment that stressed the interconnectedness of flora, fauna, and habitat; a few even adopted the language and precepts of ecology, a term invented in the mid-nineteenth century in Germany. One of ecology's first American exponents had been C. Hart Merriam, who as chief of the Bureau of the Biological Survey had pioneered in the field of habitat studies, and who had been a mentor and friend of Pinchot's during the younger man's first years in Washington.

Another critical figure was botanist Frederic E. Clements, often considered one of the founders of modern ecology. He concluded from his research that plant communities on a site acted as if they were a single organism, and that this organism passed through an identifiable cycle of development, stages of succession that culminated in what he called "climax communities." Because he believed that all plants and all habitats evolved similarly,

Clements criticized foresters, among others, for failing to adopt this ecological insight; he attributed their failure to the fact that they gave close attention to tree reproduction "and little or [none] at all [to] the shrubs and herbs of the forest floor." These smaller plants, he argued, were the "indicators" of forest habitat and of its evolutionary processes, an approach Pinchot inserted in the final version of *The Training of a Forester* when he acknowledged that the "herbs and woody shrubs beneath the trees, play great parts in forest life."[29]

Foresters such as Raphael Zon and Aldo Leopold had already incorporated ecology into their work in forest management by the time Pinchot adopted the term "forest ecology" in *The Training of a Forester*. He had it right, therefore, when in his preface to the book's final edition he indicated that it had been reworked to "keep in tune with times," which was another way of acknowledging that once it (and he) had been behind the curve. But only slightly so. It would would take another twenty years before ecological insights would become a regular feature in forestry education.[30]

Political influences also impelled Pinchot to articulate a more holistic vision of forests and their place in American culture. While serving as Pennsylvania's commissioner of forestry in the early 1920s, and later as the state's governor, Pinchot was aggressively lobbied by a number of conservation organizations. They were persistent in their demands that the state purchase private woodlands to expand or create new state forests, develop recreational areas, and preserve the rapidly disappearing remnants of Pennsylvania's old-growth forests. Part of their strategy, naturally dovetailing with Pinchot's political aspirations, was to offer him a chance to speak to their constituencies. In these luncheon addresses or evening talks, he sought to locate a happy medium between the economic or utilitarian perspective he had advocated as chief of the Forest Service, and a more preservationist posture that apparently fit better with his audiences' vision. The fit was uncomfortable at times. The "destruction of our forests is a question of the health and pleasure of the public," he admitted in a speech in 1919, "but it is far more a question of business and economy."[31]

Yet even that tilt toward practicality came into question when Pinchot signed his Arbor Day proclamation of 1923: "Trees, apart from their practical side, make for better manhood and womanhood by inspiring higher thoughts and cleaner ideas about life." That assertion created a catch. What seemed useful economically could undermine human development. The governor's resolution was to expend state monies to purchase and rehabilitate terrain that lumber companies had logged excessively. "And what we plant let us protect so that Pennsylvania . . . may become Penn's Woods again in very truth."[32]

He took his rhetoric seriously, and used tax dollars to expand the state forest system. He intervened, as well, to halt the sale of one of the state's last large tracts of hardwoods. He did so, he informed the Fairmount Park Art Association, for he believed that government should "protect and not destroy" such "precious possessions," made all the more so because of their antiquity. "The old stumps and fallen logs are covered with moss, and the whole effect is that of a dense, rich and most beautiful primeval forest. If [the sale] had not been stopped [it] would have ruined this uniquely valuable forest." The demands of electoral politics had compelled a redefinition of what Pinchot considered the "greatest good," of what constituted "value," a professional consequence of which emerged in his reconceptualization of *The Training of a Forester*.[33]

Taking Stock

Breathing new life into the text helped resuscitate the book. Its brisk sales were facilitated, too, when Lippincott shrewdly brought it out in time for a rush of Christmas orders. Months later it would receive another boost, securing what Holdsworth called "two very kindly reviews" in the major forestry journals. The royalties for the first year were impressive, totalling $474.30, a figure substantially larger than the third edition had accumulated in its four years on the market. True to his word, Pinchot sent Holdsworth a check for half the amount. "You certainly deserve it," he wrote, knowing how much he had depended on the younger man's energy to produce this new edition. "I have a sort of feeling that you ought to have the whole."[34]

Holdsworth demurred, for it was reward enough that professional colleagues and the public were reading their joint production. "The little book must be doing something," he observed, "and I rather think that it will travel quite a distance."[35]

So had Pinchot. His articulation of some of the central precepts and guiding principles of American forestry changed over the lifetime of *The Training of a Forester.* These alterations were at once semantic, the shifting of nomenclature or vocabulary, and reflective of a richly layered and principled response to shifts in the political landscape and social environment. Responding to changing circumstances, Pinchot also willingly rewrote his own history when he reimagined the book's focus, a conscious revisionism that suggests that this old forester, like the trees he so lovingly studied, was generative to the end.

Turf Wars

He could also be unswervingly loyal, almost to the point of inelasticity, a trait that would complicate his allegiance to new perspectives. What brought this to the fore was a perceived threat to the Forest Service, whose fate Pinchot could not ignore even if it meant setting aside newfound allegiances, losing old friends, and challenging a president whose values he shared.

When Franklin D. Roosevelt swept to victory in the fall of 1932, signaling the return of the Democrats to the White House after an absence of twelve years, the good citizens of Washington, D.C., were ecstatic, especially those with property to rent. Among these were Cornelia and Gifford Pinchot, who, although lifelong Republicans, showed no reluctance in exploiting the change in administrations. Just days after Roosevelt's triumph, Cornelia Pinchot queried Harry Slattery, the family's legal representative in the capital: "Don't you think it might be advisable to jack up all the real estate agents again about 1615 [Rhode Island]?," the site of the palatial Pinchot home in the District. "I would awfully like to rent it to some of the rich Democrats that come in."[36]

One of the well-heeled new Cabinet officers to whom the Pinchots spoke was not a Democrat at all—Harold Ickes, incoming secretary of the interior and one of Gifford Pinchot's old political allies from the progressive wing of the Republican Party. Because of their longstanding friendship, the Pinchots thought they might entice Ickes into becoming their lessee. Despite their best efforts, Ickes selected another domicile, but the extensive sales job was not a complete failure, for it revived a dormant relationship between the two men. Both hoped its revival would be mutually beneficial. As Ickes commented in his diary shortly after a postinaugural visit with Pinchot, "[H]e really acts delighted at my being here in this job and constantly refers to it when I see him." The interior secretary, in turn, "was glad to have the opportunity" to consult with Pinchot on "several office policies."[37]

Their shared delight would not endure, because Ickes, as part of the administration's reorganization efforts, would push for the creation of a new department of conservation, with the Forest Service at its core. Pinchot, who viewed this bureaucratic reshuffling in apocalyptic terms, did everything he could to sabotage Ickes's plans. He was successful, and the Forest Service remained within Agriculture, but to understand why the intense debate occurred at all requires a backward glance at the historical context in which the language, mechanisms, and goals of administrative reform previously had been worked out in the executive branch. This earlier context helps explain Pinchot's impulse for and resistance to bureaucratic change.[38]

It was the first Roosevelt who set the stage for what would occur during his cousin's later presidency. Theodore Roosevelt issued what is considered the first call for a substantial reorganization of the executive branch after a May 1905 meeting with Gifford Pinchot and James Garfield, then commissioner on corporations. The Keep Commission (named for its chairman, Charles H. Keep, assistant secretary of the treasury), on which Pinchot and Garfield would sit, was mandated "to investigate ... what changes are needed to place the conduct of the executive business of the Government in all its branches on the most economical and effective basis in the light of the best modern business practice." What the Keep Commission discovered during its four years of investigations was what it expected to find—a bloated bureaucracy that lacked clear lines of authority, was wary of interdepartmental cooperation, and was fraught with waste and inefficiency. To combat these problems, the commission recommended the creation of a centralized procurement office and a streamlined form of management and decision-making. These recommendations, a grateful president acknowledged later in his autobiography, "resulted in the promulgation of a set of working principles for the transaction of public business which are as sound today as they were when the Committee finished its work."[39]

Its most substantial contribution was the establishment of a precedent empowering the president to reorganize the executive branch. This meant that particular agencies could be transferred from one department to another, all in pursuit of what Theodore Roosevelt had called "good team work." Had this notion been established earlier, the nation's forest reserves, located within Interior, might have been transferred more easily to Agriculture, there to be united with Pinchot's foresters. In working on the commission, then, Pinchot helped develop a post hoc justification for this bureaucratic shift, without which there could have been no Forest Service. How ironic that succeeding secretaries of the interior would seize upon this very justification to legitimize their attempts to recapture the national forests and their guardians. Pinchot, who would be intimately involved in fending off each of these "attacks" upon the Forest Service, was repeatedly hoist on his own petard.[40]

FOREST FIRES

How was it possible for Pinchot to continue to have such influence over the agency's status? Why did those who had replaced him as chief of the agency tolerate his looming presence? The answer lies in an odd link between Pinchot's psychological needs and the ominous political context in which the Forest Service operated, a link that left its mark on the agency's bureaucratic culture.

For his part, Pinchot could not, would not let go of his intense allegiance to the Forest Service. He gave voice to how integral it was to his identity at a celebration commemorating the Forest Service's fortieth anniversary in 1945: "I have been . . . a governor now and then, but I am a forester all the time—have been, and shall be, all my working life." He meant what he said about forestry, too, though in his implied disdain for politics he was just being politic; no one was more sensitive to or fixated on the nuances of national forestry legislation.[41]

And no one knew this better than his successors at the Forest Service, over whose shoulder a scolding Pinchot forever peered, much like a domineering father. Yet his "sons" helped create the very paternal monster some of them came to loathe, enabling Pinchot forever to star, Harold Ickes would shrewdly note, in his "own little personal drama." The stage would be set whenever Interior threatened to reclaim the Forest Service, as happened in almost every administration. When the threat materialized, the then-current chief of the beleaguered agency (and, just as frequently, the secretary of agriculture) would urge Pinchot to bring his many talents to its defense. If confrontational public testimony during congressional hearings would do the trick, he complied. If a sharply worded radio address or a hyperbolic press release would turn the tide, he headed for the recording studio or typewriter. Money was no object, either; he would spend thousands of dollars on postage for mass mailings. Working a crowd of representatives and senators behind the scenes remained a special pleasure; that was why, in 1935, Chief Ferdinand Silcox, confronted with a bill that targeted the agency, pleaded with Pinchot to point "out to some of your personal contacts in the Senate and House the dangers of this bill and why it should not pass."[42]

A meddlesome parent was useful, and Pinchot would prove most helpful in the late 1930s when the President's Committee on Administrative Management issued its report on reorganization of the federal government; its proposals would send tremors through an already-defensive Forest Service and strip it of some of its protective cover, leading it to rely upon Pinchot even more than it had in the past.

The committee, chaired by Louis Brownlow, had been charged with evaluating the functioning of the White House staff, probing the executive branch's personnel and fiscal management, and assessing the executive's accountability to Congress. "There is but one grand purpose" to this extended evaluation, the Brownlow Report noted, "namely, to make democracy work." At that moment it was not functioning as it ought, a discovery that justified the sweeping and integrated changes the committee proposed. The most sensitive of those proposals was the call for a fundamental realignment of the Cabinet; the most controversial was the creation of a new department of conservation.[43]

Absorbing the functions of the Department of the Interior, the new agency would have an expanded mandate—to "advise the President with regard to the protection and use of the natural resources of the nation and the public domain" and to "administer the public lands, parks, territories and reservations, and enforce the conservation laws with regard to public lands, and mineral and water resources. . . ." With this, Interior's Harold Ickes, who had been seeking just such a resolution for the past several years, was overjoyed. He threw his full weight behind the so-called Reorganization Bill, which incorporated the Brownlow Committee's ideas and which was submitted to Congress in 1937, hoping that transferring "all conservation activities" to the new department would "prevent overlapping and clashing and jealousies in the future."[44]

No such luck. Then-contemporary jealousies provoked such a firestorm of protest that the department of conservation died before it was born. Pinchot was not alone in immediately sensing the challenge the proposal contained for the Forest Service. The moment the Brownlow Report appeared, he avidly read it through. "It is not a bad document," he observed, but it was "written from the point of view of men with little experience in actual administration. This is curious, because Brownlow as Commissioner for the District ought to know something about Government work." That failure was the least of the report's problems. Its declared financial savings did not amount to much, Pinchot believed. "It is ridiculous that it proposes economies amounting to only one-half to one and one-half per cent over the present emergency set-up." More absurd, to his mind, was the recommendation that the Forest Service be transferred out of Agriculture, which the president fully supported in his message submitting the Reorganization Bill to Congress. Deeply disappointed, the former chief noted in his diary that this "seems to make it certain that the Forest Service will go to Interior Department. Tough luck, after stopping it so many times."[45]

There would be one last, pitched battle. In fervent opposition was the Department of Agriculture, for it would lose a significant portion of its responsibilities were the Reorganization Bill to be enacted. At least that is how its secretary, Henry Wallace, and Wallace's subordinate, Ferdinand Silcox, chief of the Forest Service, interpreted its import. The Brownlow Report had narrowed Agriculture's work to agricultural research and education, granting it oversight of "the conservation and development of private lands and other resources affecting the agricultural supplies of the Nation." Lost, too, would have been the department's traditional responsibility for the public domain—forests, grazing, and mining. Not happy about this sharply diminished set of activities, and distrustful of the realignment of the two departments such that the Forest Service and related agencies would have been transferred to Interior, Wallace and Silcox battled long and hard to scuttle the Reorganization Bill.[46]

The president finally ordered Agriculture's leadership to stop sabotaging his legislative agenda, a gag order that silenced the public character of their rear-guard actions. To pick an open fight with Ickes, they enlisted the agency's white knight, Gifford Pinchot. He took up the lance with delight and tilted with the interior secretary over the radio, in speeches, and in an intense lobbying campaign that carried him throughout the country and up and down the corridors of power in Washington. Each man occasionally managed to read the other's speeches even as they were being written, and thus was well prepared to counterattack; each found allies in the media and used them freely. Without shame, each abused the other, heaping invective and calumny upon his opponent, defaming one another's character and past achievements.

Take the verbal fisticuffs that broke out over a 1937 speech Pinchot gave to the Izaak Walton League, a conservationist organization to which both men belonged. In it, Pinchot denounced Ickes's conception of a department of conservation that would leave Agriculture caring for private woodlots, charging that this would increase rather than decrease governmental waste and inefficiency. Given that there were "more than 30 million acres of private lands inside the boundaries of the National Forests," he observed, this would mean that "forestry on one side of the fence would be handled by one Department, and on the other side of the same fence by another Department." Such "dual control" was confusing and unnecessary.[47]

It was also dangerous. If successful in taking "the publicly owned National Forests out of the Department of Agriculture, where they have been admirably handled for a generation, and return[ing] them to the renamed Interior Department, whose treatment of them was a national scandal," Ickes would open the way for a pillaging of the public domain. "The fact is the Interior Department is Uncle Sam's real estate agent," and it was not a good idea to "let your real estate agent keep house for you." Here, Pinchot linked the Reorganization Bill to an earlier, discredited transfer scheme that Interior Secretary Albert Fall, infamous for the Teapot Dome scandal, had promoted in the 1920s; Harry Slattery and Pinchot had derailed that effort through their investigations into, and the publicity they generated about, the transfer of U.S. Navy oil reserves to private corporations. Pinchot vowed similarly to deflect this latest assault on the Forest Service. In any event, he was happy to draw attention to the parallels he believed existed between the two transfer controversies. What "Honest Harold" was doing in 1937 was "no more worthy of respect . . . than it was when [Fall,] that distinguished enemy of the whole conservation policy[,] was pushing it."[48]

The proposed new department was neither a New Deal nor the real deal, Pinchot charged; it was actually a "smokescreen" for Ickes's egregious political ambitions. Grabbing the Forest Service was part of the interior secretary's strategy "to take possession of a large section of the rest of government at the same time," a grab that boded ill for democratic government in an age of Hitler, Mussolini, and Stalin. "Too much power is bad for some people," Pinchot blared, "and this case is no exception." In his view, Ickes was an old evil masquerading in "new clothes."[49]

The irascible secretary, meanwhile, could not wait to undress his assailant, and to do so before the very same audience assembled at the Isaak Walton League convention. Ickes was rebuffed, however, when he sought access to the podium, and became incensed when the league's officers, citing a prohibition in the organization's by-laws, refused to provide him with a copy of its membership list, preventing him from rebutting Pinchot via mail. So Ickes took to the air instead, delivering stinging replies over the radio that garnered considerable press coverage. In one of these attacks, in which he declaimed against those who opposed the idea of a department of conservation, Ickes observed that the new department's opponents, "who have been given special privileges in the past with respect to our lands, forests and mines," were clever enough not to confront the president openly. "They find it better to work by indirection; to make use of a sincere but misguided zealot," Gifford Pinchot. By "jittering his way about the country," this "senate-reject of Pennsylvania" had become "the Lot's wife of the conservation movement," backward-looking, a crusader who sits "astride his hobbyhorse . . . facing the tail instead of the head."[50]

Pinchot's retrogressive posture was matched by the company he now kept. In his attacks upon what he called "Pinchot's Folly," Ickes rebuked the forester for his bizarre desire to "keep the conservation activities of the Government separate, disunited and antagonistic"; this forced him to be in cahoots with those he once despised, among them William Greeley, one of the lead lobbyists for the timber industry. "Do you wonder that some question the sincerity of this man," Ickes purred, "who yesterday fought the great lumber interests, charging them with ruthless exploitation, and today walks down Pennsylvania Avenue arm and arm with them?" Or that the man who so roundly abused the secretary of the interior had but the year before so highly praised him when he inscribed a copy of his book *Just Fishing Talk* to "Harold Ickes, whose courage, conscience and common sense have made him one of the most outstanding public servants of his time, with the affection and admiration of his friend, Gifford Pinchot."[51]

That hurt. Pinchot snapped back in a press release that he had been so little interested in what his "former friend, Irritable Interior Ickes" had had to say that he had gone "off to bed instead of listening in." Feigning indifference was never Pinchot's style, so he concluded on a rougher, more petulant note. "Hard-boiled Harold may think he knows more about Conservation and what is best for Conservation than I do. But just because I happened to be the first man to formulate the Conservation policy, and have spent my life in that work, is no real reason why I need to take lessons in it from a Chicago lawyer," a studied response that both deftly dodged Ickes's charges of collusion and partisan politics and provided Pinchot with a powerful emotional appeal. His storied past gave him a moral claim on the present.[52]

HOME FRONT

For all the pleasure Pinchot derived from this anti-transfer brawl, and the frequent opportunities it gave him for "ripping Ickes up the back," the momentous struggle was only one element in an intensely busy life. While dueling with Ickes in 1937, Pinchot was that summer, with Holdsworth, rewriting *The Training of a Forester,* and grinding away on his autobiography. In conjunction with the latter, his daily rounds included gathering documents, dictating portions of his and his mother's diaries, and traveling to Asheville to revisit the scene of his first professional labors.

As the year wore on, he overcame his initial reluctance to launch a third campaign for governor of Pennsylvania. Throughout the fall he met with potential supporters, spoke before public forums, and reenergized dormant alliances with labor unions and women's organizations; in retrospect, his disastrous showing in the spring 1938 primary underscored the power of political ambition to fool even a seasoned campaigner into thinking his support was more substantial than it was.[53]

Cornelia Pinchot felt too the seductive allure of office, so much so that in 1936 she did something quite unusual. After her two defeats at the hand of Representative Louis McFadden, she ran for a congressional seat in a Philadelphia district in which she did not live; the end result was the same, however. This loss would be her final one, but it did not halt her public activism. From the 1930s until her death in 1960, she remained an ardent champion of the poor, women, and the working class.

In the Great Depression especially, she defended the rights of labor to unionize, to work within safe environments, and to earn decent wages. She was a much-sought-after speaker at union halls and industrial plants. In 1933 she had to wire the Hosiery Workers her regret at not being able to meet with them, for she was "tied up . . . with the Sweatshop Committee and then [am] going to Pittsburgh to help the steel workers organize." Four years later, she was stretched just as thin, meeting with hosiery workers, addressing automobile strikers in Detroit and Flint, Michigan, and walking Congress of Industrial Organizations (CIO) picket lines.

She used her presence to publicize workers' aspirations. When management charged that strikers occupying automobile factories were destroying property, she rebutted the allegations by publishing an eyewitness account praising union members' housekeeping skills, noting that they kept work spaces "in the utmost good order—the place neat as a pin, and everything peaceful." Owners who pleaded poverty were roundly criticized if they did not raise wages and reduce stress on assembly lines. A "most important discovery" of her tours of Michigan industrial plants, her husband reported, "was that a great majority of the automobile workers get less than one thousand dollars a year—and that the speed-up is driving the older workers out of the business." These and other inequities drove her to greater efforts as the Depression continued to undercut the nation's economic prospects.[54]

The Pinchots' political engagements shaped the interior life of 1615

Rhode Island Avenue. It was there that the couple read and rewrote one another's speeches, set up interviews with friendly reporters, and held luncheons and dinners in which labor organizers sat down with political representatives, lobbyists, and diplomats. Radicals and reactionaries broke bread together and then listened to post-prandial talks on the global economy, Europe's grim political future, or the shifting status of the nation's two major parties. In the 1920s, a journalist had commented that the Pinchots' homes functioned like political boardinghouses. Cornelia "spends her apparently inexhaustible vitality in a continuous effort to tie up politics more closely to life" and did so, the reporter for the *Saturday Evening Post* concluded, "to make the two come together, meet, touch, fuse, get fresh points of contact, and so release big, revitalizing forces in both." This was just as true of the Pinchot home in the 1930s. Whether at large dinner parties or small soirees, political discourse set the table. "We always talk at meals," she said in a 1931 radio address. "I cannot imagine people who have feelings for each other and have interests in common not doing it, about books, funny things, people, politics." Throughout their thirty-two-year marriage, Cornelia and Gifford believed that political debate was "the best of all indoor sports."[55]

Their son never shared their enthusiasm and had no intention of following in the family business. When in the mid-1930s Gifford Bryce entered the family college—Yale, as a member of the class of 1938—it was not as a stepping stone to a career in public service. Instead, his emphasis would be on the sciences, with the expectation of becoming a doctor.

His parents were shrewd enough to let their son chart his own course, but they were not so hands-off that they took little interest in his affairs. His father's diary is replete with notations of Giff's movements between New Haven, Milford, Washington, and points beyond. Woven in were frequent comments about their shared enthusiasm for rod and reel and for flying airplanes, an activity Giff pioneered and then convinced his parents to take up (they both earned their licenses). In a late June 1934 letter to his dying sister Nettie, which she would not live to read, Gifford bragged about his son's prowess. "Leila and Giff and I have been taking to aviation furiously of late. . . . [But] Gifford has already made such progress that he flies alone, and I understand he flies very well. I wasn't so keen about his learning, but you can't stop them nowadays."[56]

His life took off in other ways. In June 1936, at the conclusion of his sophomore year, he married Sally Richards. Like her husband, Sally came from a wealthy family; her father was a prominent New York attorney, and the family lived on New York's Park Avenue and had a country retreat in Wilton, Connecticut. She attended the exclusive Brearley School, graduated from Vassar in 1935, and was an avid sailor, having grown up sailing on Long Island Sound and nearby waters. The couple was a good and close match. The senior Pinchots readily embraced their daughter-in-law, were grateful that she helped their son stay focused on his career ambitions, and took pleasure in her company. "Giff and Sally arrived with [their dogs] Nietzsche and George Rat the first thing in the morning," Gifford wrote of one of their many visits. "Fooled around with them a lot during the day and had a fine time." Sally, in turn, came to respect the particular magnetism of her parents-in-law that drew so many into their homes in Washington and Milford. "Gifford was very proper, moral, conventional—for *good*," she once observed. "Leila was a natural rebel—loved to upset people by doing outrageous things. They complemented each other. It was a delight to be with them." Giff seconded his wife's appreciation. After watching his father pull strings to facilitate last-second changes in the young couple's 1937 voyage to Europe, for example, Giff's parting words warmed his father's soul: "I'm certainly glad to be a Pinchot."[57]

ICKES REDUX

The Forest Service was similarly delighted to have Gifford Pinchot maneuvering on its behalf. On the same day in 1937 that Giff and Sally sailed for Europe on the *Aquitania,* the former agency chief was already back in Washington, meeting with Harry Graves and Herbert Smith to develop a strategy to further foil Harold Ickes's plans to fold the Forest Service into the proposed department of conservation. The next day he met with the ailing current chief, Frederick Silcox, and warned him that "the Service must use the powers it has to prevent the Park Service and the Interior Department [from] generally running away with it." Silcox "agreed thoroughly with my point of view," he recorded. The intense bureaucratic infighting would continue, with Pinchot very much at the center of the ever-swelling controversy.[58]

His poor health forced a truce, however temporary. In 1938, as he recuperated at home from an illness, Ickes sent him a bunch of roses and a conciliatory note. Their reconciliation appeared to deepen the next January, when Pinchot was involved in an automobile accident on the streets of Washington. He had left a function at the Cosmos Club in a taxi when the "driver got the idea that his cab and a streetcar could occupy the same space," Pinchot later joked with his nephew Harcourt Johnstone, "an idea that was immediately disproved." He made light of the crash, but the emotional trauma stressed an already diseased heart. He had had a heart attack some years earlier, and as a consequence of this later shock, Pinchot suffered a string of four new attacks and was confined to his bed until the summer. One of his many visitors was Harold Ickes, whose concern touched the invalid. "I am truly glad," Pinchot wrote in thanks, that "in spite of our disagreements on certain policies, our old friendship of thirty years is to be renewed."[59]

The amity did not last. In 1940, with the bill to reorganize the executive branch stalled in Congress, Ickes let loose a new series of allegations designed to sully Pinchot's reputation and revive the legislative process to create a full-fledged conservation agency. Turning historian, the secretary revisited the most hallowed of controversies surrounding the Forest Service and Interior, the Ballinger-Pinchot affair of 1910. At its height, Ickes had been a young Progressive enamored with the call to public service. One of those he had admired had been Gifford Pinchot, and he had firmly supported him throughout his conflict with Taft's secretary of the interior. Ickes had believed in the justness of the chief forester's attacks upon a corrupt and grasping department and in his bold challenge to its muddled secretary. He remained convinced of Pinchot's "heroic stature" and that "Richard Ballinger had been guilty of maladministration" until he, too, went toe-to-toe with the forester. When in 1940, with some affectation, Ickes suggested he "was made aware . . . that there was at least some question as to whether Ballinger had been the evil man that Gifford Pinchot and others had sought to represent him," he determined "that it was my duty to search out the truth, and, if I should find that he had been unjustly dealt with . . . to clear Ballinger's name publicly. . . ."[60]

Justice must be served, and so must Ickes's ends, for there was little doubt about the conclusions he would reach. He quickly published two blistering reevaluations of Pinchot's confrontation with Ballinger, one as a *Saturday Evening Post* article and the other as an official Department of the Interior report. Both fully exonerated Ballinger, whom Ickes dubbed an "American Dreyfus," and both draped him in a cloak of martyrdom, portraying him as yet another hapless victim of a Pinchot-inspired witch hunt. That Ickes saw parallels between this historical case of an innocent man driven to a premature grave and Ickes's contemporary death struggle with a relentless, wicked foe was laid out in the scathing conclusion of the departmental finding. "There are many subsequent events that sustain the charge that . . . the unremitting and vindictive efforts of Pinchot have been devoted to smearing and tearing down the Department of Interior." What Ickes called "this long outpouring of hate" had served "the Pinchot clique as a symbol of a deed accomplished and as an encouragement to keep up the fight." This feisty interior secretary would not be intimidated. The current department "[is] stronger than when Pinchot first selfishly began to wage war against it," and this time, Ickes vowed, the "Great Forester" would fall on his own sword, becoming the battle's "chief casualty."[61]

Pinchot studiously ignored Ickes's revision of the historical record, a silence he expected would infuriate the loquacious interior secretary. "One of the meanest things I have done . . . was to refuse to answer Ickes at all," Pinchot wrote to a friend; "I think my refusal to do so has cut him to the bone."[62]

By these two men's puerile and contentious behavior, one might conclude that a significant piece of public policy was to be decided on the basis of ad hominem attacks. So it partly was. Through these vituperative personal assaults, both men attempted to rally support throughout the country. But Pinchot, who had had much experience fronting for the first Roosevelt, understood that this later confrontation had less to do with Ickes personally than with him as an agent of the second Roosevelt. By repeatedly attacking his former friend, Pinchot hoped to raise the costs of reorganization so high that Roosevelt would be forced to back off his pledge to transfer the Forest Service to Interior. This strategy accounted for the number and ferocity of Pinchot's speeches and his repeated calls for like-minded conservationists to flood Washington with letters and telegrams to bolster congressional opposition to the proposed department of conservation. This, too, is why he worked hand-in-glove with the "Forest Lobby," a powerful set of western senators and representatives whose states and districts they believed would benefit from the retention of the Forest Service in Agriculture. The battle over the agency was also a convenient weapon in their struggle to shape the president's agenda, so they frequently warned Roosevelt that if he transferred the Forest Service they would sabotage other cherished elements of his New Deal program. Making good on that threat required an enraged public that would destabilize the electoral campaigns of 1940. By that spring, the Ickes-Pinchot dispute had created just such an uproar.[63]

It is striking that Ickes chose precisely this moment to publish his scathing revision of the Ballinger-Pinchot affair. Dredging up that past could only have reminded voters of how another sitting president, struggling (and failing) to contain a damaging controversy enveloping his administration's conservation policy, had been battered at the polls. Franklin Roosevelt had no interest in replicating William Howard Taft's fate, as he demonstrated some months before the 1940 presidential election. During a tense showdown with the "Forest Lobby," he dramatically tore up the executive order authorizing the transfer of the Forest Service to Interior. Stunned, Ickes believed this signaled that his own position was "bankrupt intellectually and emotionally," and quickly tendered his resignation; the president just as swiftly refused his theatrical capitulation. But in trying to bow out, Ickes acknowledged that he, not Pinchot, had become the battle's "chief casualty."[64]

As entertaining as the Ickes-Pinchot brawl was to some, it diverted attention from a critical question implicit in the Brownlow Report—what was the best way to administer, conserve, and use the nation's natural resources? This was a question that had long preoccupied Pinchot. Indeed, it had been the basis of his musings some thirty years earlier when, while riding through Washington's Rock Creek Park, he had what he described as a flash of inspiration about the integrative power of the idea of conservation. It seemed to offer a way to unify the disparate efforts of individual government bureaus charged with overseeing discrete elements of the nation's public lands and the resources they contained. He would later draw a parallel between his notion of conservation and the motto of the United

States: "*E Pluribus Unum* is the fundamental fact of our political affairs," he argued in *Breaking New Ground,* and "*E Pluribus Unum* is and always must be the basis in dealing with natural resources. Many problems fuse into one great policy, just as many states fuse into one great Union."[65]

The compelling need to unify the federal conservation response had not changed for Pinchot when Harold Ickes raised the issue in the 1930s. What had changed was that it was Ickes, as secretary of the interior, who used this idea to advance what Pinchot believed were his political ambitions. To foil the secretary's goals to transfer the Forest Service into a department of conservation, Pinchot now argued on particularistic grounds. Because trees in the national forests were a crop, they and the agency that oversaw them necessarily fell under the purview of Agriculture.[66]

Unfortunately, neither Pinchot nor Ickes addressed this larger issue to any great degree. Instead, knowing that American political culture thrived on sensationalism and titillation, they attacked and counterattacked accordingly. Scoring points mattered more than offering a substantive debate on the merits of the report's conclusions about the federal government's responsibility for and approach to conservation. This failure on their part had important consequences. As historian Richard Polenberg has pointed out, few contemporary observers "managed to view the transfer issue in proper perspective." A broad spectrum of conservation societies, for instance, "devoted so much effort to denouncing the Reorganization bill" that in their "zeal to protect one administrative agency," they "blocked the creation of an executive department which, in the long run, could have provided leadership and coherence for the conservation movement." Whether "coherence" was then lacking, whether it could emanate from the federal government in the first place, is almost beside the point. Such a unified bureaucracy has never been developed and tested.[67]

Left unexamined too were the Forest Service's assumptions about its proper place within the federal bureaucracy. It waged a desperate and ultimately successful campaign to remain where it had always been, a remarkable achievement given that it had to fight off a powerful president. But the struggle to survive overwhelmed the possibility of detached reflection upon the role federal foresters had already begun to play in the maintenance of the American landscape. During the 1920s, the agency had started developing recreational activities in national forests. Among these were hunting and fishing, boating, and skiing, and these new uses represented a break from the agency's traditional, almost exclusive emphasis on timber production. This new aspect of the agency's land-use policy would expand rapidly with the aid of New Deal largesse; the Civilian Conservation Corps was especially active in constructing recreational infrastructure on the public lands under the Forest Service's control. Robert Marshall and Aldo Leopold added additional impetus to these alterations. Beginning in the 1920s, these two men, who a decade later would found the Wilderness Society, articulated the need for wilderness preservation and proposed that the first preserves be carved out of the national forests.

None of these developments within the Forest Service were without powerful internal detractors who considered the new activities to be more consistent with Interior's mission than with Agriculture's, thus blurring the distinction between the Park and Forest Services. Had these men not been in leadership positions, the agency might have had more impetus to accept the proposed transfer.[68]

There might have been a greater receptivity had a different Gifford Pinchot shown up when Silcox and Wallace recruited him to defend the Forest Service in the late 1930s. His advocacy of the ecological implications of "new conservationism" might have eased a transfer to a department of conservation, but in the face of what Pinchot and the Forest Service's leadership viewed as a hostile takeover, that possibility went unrealized. The intense debate, then, generated little interest in the kind of critical self-reflection, intellectual creativity, and keen insight that had driven the evolution of Pinchot's *The Training of a Forester.*

Climax

THE RAVAGED landscape staggered him. Standing on a slope overlooking Montana's Bitterroot Valley in the summer of 1972, gazing down at the marks of a vast clear-cut that fell away from his feet—severe erosion, deep skid trails, and piles of slash—Gifford Bryce Pinchot gave vent to what he thought was a familial frustration. "[I]f my father had seen this," averred the only child of the famed forester, "he would have cried." Those words were recorded by one of those on the hill that day with Pinchot. A second, later, and more blunt report, published without attribution, had him assuring his listeners that such devastation "would have killed the Old Man."[1]

It was not incidental that the son, a founding member of the board of directors of the Natural Resources Defense Council (NRDC), evoked this image of a keening Gifford Pinchot at the height of a raging controversy over clear-cutting in national forests. Founded in 1970, the NRDC followed in the tradition of the National Conservation Association (which Pinchot's father had started in 1909) by combining political analysis, scientific research, and legal criticism to lobby Congress, shape environmental legislation, and, if necessary, seek redress in the courts. In search of the best grounds from which to initiate a lawsuit against the Forest Service for its mismanagement of federal lands, members of the NRDC board, including a then-fifty-six-year-old Gifford Bryce Pinchot, toured the Bitterroot National Forest and the other prime candidate for the test case, the Monongahela National Forest in West Virginia; the Monongahela ultimately was selected. Pinchot's reaction to the Bitterroot's torn-up terrain was thus as heartfelt as it was calculated.[2]

Among those who immediately picked up on its calculation, and sought to counter its effect on public opinion, were those who worked within the profession the senior Pinchot had done so much to promote. *American Forests,* the organ of the American Forestry Association, pumped out a series of pieces critical of the scion of forestry's first family. In a May 1973 editorial, it linked Gifford Bryce's critical commentary to the "increasing tendency in America to indict, try and condemn forestry practices in drumhead courts without due process." The father, it asserted, "would not have approved of this. He was basically a fair man." In a memoir published in the same number, Paul Oehser, a longtime editor at the Smithsonian and a conservationist, anointed the senior Pinchot as forestry's "patron saint." With sainthood came staunch defenders of the faith, one of whom, in a follow-up article in *American Forests,* rushed to insulate the revered icon from his flesh and blood. Al Wiener, a timber appraisal specialist with the Forest Service, was convinced that Gifford Bryce's words were tantamount to heresy. Offended that the son and his fellow travelers in the environmental movement were attempting to appropriate Gifford Pinchot to *their* cause, Wiener claimed that the dead forester would have had no truck with such "amateur dilettantes." He cited chapter and verse from *Breaking New Ground* to reveal Pinchot's commitment to clear-cutting, sustained yield, and multiple use, principles of forestry that many environmentalists abhorred and that, through the lawsuit the NRDC had filed against the Monongahela National Forest, they were seeking to regulate, if not eliminate.[3]

In so arguing, Wiener deliberately narrowed the range of Pinchot's ideas on forest management. More, in unearthing early-twentieth-century clear-cutting practices that Pinchot had proposed for various national forests, Wiener was assuming that the former chief's commitment to these proposals endured across time. They had not. After an extended evaluation of western public lands in September 1937, for instance, Pinchot was per-

*While touring the national
forests in 1937, Gifford
Pinchot became convinced
that clear-cutting of some
western forests was neither
scientifically justified nor
politically acceptable.*
Grey Towers NHL

suaded that clear cutting was not always the most appropriate harvesting
strategy. "One of the things which struck me most," he wrote Regional
Forester C. S. Buck about their inspection tour through the national forests
in Oregon, "was your wisdom in preferring the high forest selection system
as against clear cutting." This approach, with its emphasis on the cutting of
individual trees, Pinchot continued, "convinced me completely that what
you are doing is not only the right thing for the forest but also very much
the right thing in its effect on public sentiment." The former chief promised Buck—whose anti-clearcutting position was controversial within the
agency and profession—that he would back him up; that "is one of the
things I want to talk about when I see the head men in Washington." He
kept his word in this case, and later went public with his opposition to wartime clear-cuts, denouncing them as "tree butchery." How appropriate that
when Wiener threw the book at Gifford Bryce Pinchot—"[t]he elder Pinchot's writings might cause one to speculate as to whether the son's com-

ment might have generated as much anger as laughter"—the joke was on him.[4]

Wiener's mistaken impression had larger implications. He and the Forest Service of the 1970s seemed not to understand, as Pinchot had in the 1930s, that public opinion was a fundamental part of good forest management. Compounding their mistake was their failure to remember that Pinchot had declared the public interest an inviolable principle from the very outset. In *The Use of the National Forests,* a 1907 Forest Service publication, the then-chief had asserted that the public forests "exist to-day because the people want them. To make them accomplish the most good the people themselves must make clear how they want them run." And when the public spoke, the Forest Service must listen. "The officers are paid by the people to act as their agents and to see that all the resources of the Forests are used in the best interest of everyone concerned. What the people as a whole want will be done." Had late-twentieth-century federal foresters accepted this democratic dictum and responded with greater openness to the concerns that Gifford Bryce Pinchot, the NRDC, and other environmentalists publicly raised about the agency's management style and harvesting strategies, it might not have been sued in federal court. Because it did not so respond, the Monongahela lawsuit was only the first of a flurry of legal actions that damaged the agency's internal morale and blackened its public reputation. That fallout, too, would have "killed the Old Man."[5]

Yet Gifford Pinchot probably would have drawn some comfort from the fact that more than a quarter of a century after his demise, he continued to provoke arguments. Friends and foes, defenders and detractors still argued over his significance, still debated the meaning of his utterances, still invoked his memory to justify their commitments. In life, he once had been likened to a religious enthusiast—"he preaches and excites," the *Washington Post* observed in 1905, "as devotedly as Peter the Hermit heralding a crusade." In death, he remained a sacred, galvanizing force.[6]

That Pinchot could be made to sanction the disparate public policy positions of some late-twentieth-century foresters and environmentalists suggests how malleable these representations of him and his ideas had become; a mark of one's posthumous relevance is to be continually revised, and thus reborn. Gifford Pinchot anticipated, even as he contributed to, this revisionist impulse: throughout his last years he revisited his past arguments and accomplishments and reworked and tried to extend his legacy, all with an eye for how he would be read and interpreted over time.[7]

BOOK ENDS

There could be no interpretation of his life more profound than his own, he sternly advised future readers of his autobiography, *Breaking New Ground*. Its opening words set the narrator's perspective—"This is my personal history of how Forestry and Conservation came to America"—and established his omniscience. "[T]he story of an eyewitness," *Breaking New Ground* was "written to tell not only what happened but also why and how it happened." Seeing events though his eyes, and accepting thereby his version of the creation and evolution of the forestry and conservation movements, was, Pinchot claimed, the best way for his audience to obtain "a true picture of what it took to bring [them] to America."[8]

This authorial vision was not really constructed for the casual reader. Uppermost in Pinchot's mind were later generations of scholars who of necessity would come to his memoir without having firsthand knowledge of the people, times, or places that were described in it. It was to these engaged professionals that he insisted on autobiography's precedence over all other forms of historical writing. An eyewitness account, he wrote, beat "documentary history all hollow" and did so because the latter relied exclusively on primary evidence. A "document may represent a fact, or it may represent the concealment of a fact," he noted, and it therefore may be "honest or it may be false." To distinguish between the two required the kind of "personal recollection" that Pinchot proffered. After all, there "are many portions of the American story of Forestry and Conservation which will never be rightly understood unless the men who had a part in them supply the background of facts actually experienced," experience that "alone can explain what the documents really mean."[9]

This left Pinchot in an enviable position. As the "only living witness" to much of the history he was to recount, as the writer of a memoir that would not be "decorated and delayed by references to authorities"—he *was* the authority—he compelled his audience to embrace his insights. As to the veracity "of nearly every statement" on *Breaking New Ground*'s more than five hundred pages, he concluded, "you will have to take it or leave it on my say-so."[10]

Pinchot's sense of his own omniscience was everywhere apparent in his memoir, including early on when he addressed the intellectual origins of forestry in America. There were precious few, in his telling. While conceding that George Perkins Marsh's *Man and Nature* (1864) had been an "epoch-making" tome, Pinchot disputed its impact by asserting that only a handful of Americans had ever read it. The pioneering, late-nineteenth-century forestry efforts of Bernhard E. Fernow were also damned with faint praise. As Pinchot observed in a book that amply recounted his own long and successful career as a forester, Fernow, who had been "head of the Government's forest work and of the forest movement in America," once had advised a young Pinchot to take up the profession "but only as second fiddle to something else." But at least Fernow, Charles Sargent, and John Muir, each of whom contributed to the late-nineteenth-century national dialogue about the pressing need for conservation and scientific forestry, made it into the text. George Bird Grinnell, who was Theodore Roosevelt's earliest and closest advisor on conservation, who founded the Boone and Crockett Club (which Pinchot later would join), and who as editor of *Forest and Stream* gladly published the up-and-coming forester, received the silent treatment; *Breaking New Ground* never records his considerable activism and substantial influence.[11]

Being ignored had its advantages in a narrative that Pinchot framed in terms of an epic struggle between those who agreed with him and those who did not. It was written as if his public career had been a Manichean brawl pitting conservationists, who battled on behalf of the public good, against their dread enemies, the plutocrats and their underlings. Surely William Howard Taft, if he had had the choice, would have preferred not to have been mauled, for more than a hundred pages, in a blistering attack that lampooned his physique, mocked his "so-called judicial temperament," and poured scorn on his character. "[L]ike many another failure in high places, [he] was an admirable lieutenant but a poor captain." Because he lacked the ability to lead, Pinchot asserted, Taft quickly became "the accomplice and the refuge of . . . all the swarm of big and little thieves and near-thieves, who, inside and outside of the law, were doing everything they knew to get possession of natural resources which belonged to the people and should have been conserved in the public interest." In the interest of fairness, Pinchot agreed that Taft "may really have believed his position to be right," but his heart was not in the concession. After all, *Breaking New Ground* was crafted to bury, not to praise, the former president. Besides, as Pinchot pointed out in his preface, Taft had already received inflated credit at the hands of kept biographer Henry F. Pringle, who "attributes the Conservation policy, which was Theodore Roosevelt's greatest contribution to the world, mainly to Taft, the man who betrayed it. . . ."[12]

As fun as settling old scores could be, and as necessary as this was to the literary ends to which his autobiography was being put, Pinchot felt burdened by a project he pungently denounced as this "wretched autobiographical screed of mine." He tried to shuck that burden whenever he could. Typical was his reaction in the late spring of 1941. Faced with a long summer's residence at Grey Towers, where he planned to tackle the pivotal chapters involving Taft and the Ballinger-Pinchot controversy, Pinchot instead sent feelers through Supreme Court Justice Felix Frankfurter to the White House about the possibility of securing work in Roosevelt's third administration. That he preferred to swelter in Washington's heat and humidity rather than to relax in Milford's cool was a measure of his desperation. This bit of proffered self-sacrifice was rebuffed, however. In early June, Frankfurter "advised me strongly to go on and finish my book. I take it that means no Government job," Pinchot noted reluctantly.[13]

It is not that he lacked for help. By the late 1930s, to speed the production of what he called his "thrice accursed" book, Pinchot had assembled a team of researchers to organize and pore through a rambling archive of his correspondence, diaries, and journals, as well as to search through his extensive library of books and public documents, to provide evidence and context for his book's arguments. He also had convinced Herbert Smith, who by this time had retired from his editorial work for the Forest Service, to take up his accustomed position as Pinchot's amanuensis. Smith's sudden death in July 1944 was a deep personal blow. They had known one another for more than fifty years, and without Smith at his side, Pinchot was almost at a loss. But into the void slid forester Raphael Zon, another, albeit younger,

*When his health began to fail in the early 1940s, Gifford
Pinchot engaged Raphael Zon and others to help him
complete the writing of his autobiography.*
Forest History Society

associate who had ghostwritten for Pinchot in the past. A vigorous editor
and a polemicist in his own right, Zon would prod Pinchot when prodding
was needed, and by 1945, as its author's health began to fade, *Breaking New
Ground* took on its final shape. On August 10, 1945, a day before he turned
eighty, a frail Pinchot could exult: "FINISHED BOOK!"[14]

Not quite: What he had completed was more of a rough draft than the
polished manuscript that would unfold in tandem with Pinchot's last days.
As Pinchot's legendary energy flagged, as he shuttled between hospital and
home in a losing battle with what would be diagnosed belatedly as leuke-
mia, Zon completed the book's writing and editing and ushered it through
publication. His dedication to the project raised eyebrows. Some in the Forest Service who watched the then-retired Zon toil over his editorial work—
he had been loaned an office in the agency's Washington headquarters—
wondered just whose perspectives the completed manuscript reflected.

"Nobody knows how much [Zon] cut out of what Pinchot put in, or what Smith cut out," Leon Kneipp mused, leading him to suggest that this substantial copy-editing, and the former chief's many bouts with debilitating illness, produced a book that "really doesn't represent Pinchot at his best. Probably if he'd undertaken more systematically to finish it while he still maintained all of his supreme mentality, it would have been a much better book."[15]

It was good enough, at any rate, to elicit precisely the kind of mixed reception such a contentious volume predictably would receive; having largely defined the world in black-and-white terms, *Breaking New Ground* generated reviews that conformed to and confirmed the embattled political landscape its author had reinvoked. Old allies rose up in approbation, and Harold Ickes took one last whack at his by-then-deceased rival. The autobiography was "somewhat less than a half-told tale," Ickes opined, marred by its author's subjectivity and his conceit that he was a "zealot who had discovered a great new empire which he was to claim by right of discovery."[16]

His zealousness, Pinchot had discovered when he had read the book's last chapter to a May 1945 gathering at his home of the Washington section of the Society of American Foresters (SAF), also irritated some of his forestry colleagues. His talk that day began quietly enough, opening with a query about the meaning of his life as a conservationist; it soon exploded with a rhetorical heat that would leave not a few of his listeners fuming.[17] Initially, they would find little to object to when he laid down what he considered to be the first of "three great purposes" of conservation, that is, "wisely to use, protect, preserve, and renew the natural resources of the earth." After he moved beyond this boilerplate, some in the audience began to squirm. His second principle, that natural resources should be used only in "the common interest" and distributed at a "fair and reasonable charge," implied a delivery mechanism entailing governmental regulatory control in some form of public and private production.

To a good portion of the SAF members, this was akin to waving a red flag. Pinchot obligingly (and fully) unfurled that offensive banner with his third principle—conservationists must "see to it that the rights of the people to govern themselves shall not be controlled by great monopolies through their power over natural resources." Foresters must be vigilant, ever ready to hurl themselves into a political struggle to defend what he called "the public interest."[18]

The time to erect the defensive perimeters was at hand, Pinchot went on. "Concentrated Wealth" had manipulated the levers of power in the past, he proclaimed, and would continue to do so; it would maintain its "strangle hold over the general welfare" by lulling the citizenry into accepting "its exactions, especially the methods by which it gets power, as normal and natural." These "Economic Royalists" accustomed "people to their tyranny by a constant stream of praise . . . of free enterprise," he charged, and subsequently silenced their opposition by thoroughly discrediting "liberal movements and leaders" through their "ever increasing control of the press, the radio, and other news outlets." The fight now must be joined, for despite this overwhelming control, the monopolistic sway could be broken, and America could "move on from a social order in which unregulated profit is the driving force" to one "in which equality of opportunity will cease to be a dream."[19]

Pinchot sensed that this "new order" was in the offing, a progressive outcome that depended on foresters championing federal control of natural resources, resurrecting a responsive and representative government, and fostering the vital "drive and stimulus of mixed races adventuring in a new land." This was the "public good" they were sworn to protect, he declaimed. Learning to come to its defense had been the single most important lesson he had learned since that summer day fifty-five years earlier when his father had first asked a young Gifford if he would like to become a forester.[20]

Many of his listeners in May 1945 wished he had answered no. Conceding in his diary that "some were very much against" his bold speech, he guessed that the majority had felt as he did. Yet the sum of his opposition was greater than he was willing to admit. Since the late teens, members of the SAF and the American Forestry Association had rebelled against Pinchot's intensifying commitment to federal ownership of forested lands and his expanding sense of forestry's social responsibilities, one reason why he had forsworn his membership in these organizations.

With the selection of Robert Stuart and Frederick Silcox as chiefs of the Forest Service in the late 1920s and early 1930s, respectively, and of Earl Clapp to serve as its acting chief when Silcox died in 1939, Pinchot's views seemed to regain their primacy. That did not last, one signal of which was the publication of a series of editorial attacks in *American Forests* on Clapp's support of federal control of public lands and strong regulation of timber production. Pinchot was enraged by the attacks. He replied in an open letter in 1943. "I protest both against this utterly unjustified attempt to discredit a man whose record of leadership in the Forest Service does him high honor, and against the equally unjustified attack on the Service, which has done more for forestry in America than all other organizations put together." He recognized that the AFA journal had gone after Clapp "because [he] stands, as Silcox stood, as Graves stands, and as I stand, for government control of cutting on private lands, the only measure that has ever anywhere in the world permanently guaranteed the safety of forests." Pinchot understood, too, that when he denounced the journal's capitulation to "the lumber interests" and bemoaned that it was "no longer a useful influence," he had only one option. "Nearly ten years ago I was elected an honorary member of the American Forestry Association . . . [but] because I have lost confidence in the Association, I can no longer continue my membership, and I hereby resign."[21]

Within a decade of his resignation, those who disputed his political vision—members of the AFA, the Forest Service, and those in the SAF audience before whom he had spoken in 1945—had thoroughly triumphed. Their victory depended on two alterations in American politics and economy. With the advent of the Cold War and the rising fear of the Soviet Union, policies that even appeared to smack of socialism were in jeopardy; taking advantage of this new rhetoric were those within the profession who opposed federal regulation of production, a keystone of Pinchot's agenda. Jeopardized as well was Pinchot's more conservative approach to land management. The postwar housing boom allowed the Forest Service to pursue an accelerated harvesting strategy, the rising quotas of which were met by the adoption of massive clear-cuts in the national forests. In now pushing timber sales, argued Arnold W. Bolle, dean of the Forest School of the University of Montana, the Forest Service "changed from a custodial agency to one aimed at commodity production." As it continuously upped production rates, the Forest Service "appeared to be advocating the 'cut out and get out' policy it had been established to oppose." With that, its mission, and the institutional culture in which Pinchot (and Pinchotism) once had thrived, had been wiped clean.[22]

Evidence of this expunging emerges in a series of oral histories given by retired foresters of that era. Many of these men fondly remembered Pinchot and the camaraderie he inspired—one went so far as to call him "our *beau ideal*"—but they were also quick to distinguish his warm personality from what they perceived to be his inflammatory language and relentless attempts to politicize the profession. At times led on by interviewers hostile to the Pinchotian approach, but mostly driven by their own desire to distance themselves from his radicalism, they shook their heads over his antagonism of the lumber industry, blamed that conflict for the difficulties the Forest Service had encountered, and were thankful the hostilities had lessened since his death in 1946. They would never reemerge, either, predicted Royal Kellogg, who had retired from the agency in 1910 for a career in the lumber business. "Mrs. Pinchot is trying to revive some of that," he noted of her 1950 article in the *Journal of Forestry* that recycled her husband's key arguments against a close association with the lumber interests. "[S]he's for some very radical ideas. As radical as Pinchot's most radical ones . . . but she isn't going to get anywhere."[23]

A placid present and a tranquil future even allowed others to reconsider past indiscretions, notably their youthful, visceral reaction to the Ballinger-Pinchot crisis. "You understand, of course, that we were greatly prejudiced in favor of Pinchot and terribly antagonistic towards President Taft," confessed one. "I'm rather ashamed of that attitude now." This retrospective sense of shame was a bad sign for Pinchot's faith that *Breaking New Ground* would cement his reputation and posthumously extend his influence. He had become dispensable.[24]

PAST OVER

Even before Pinchot died, he had become something of a laughingstock. Contemporaries detected a desperate quality to his quest for continued usefulness. While the White House may have gently turned aside his plea for a post in 1941, others were more disdainful of the aged man's desires to serve and be seen. One of those, H. Gleason Mattoon, who in 1942 was the secretary of the Pennsylvania Forestry Association, may have gone further than simple disdain, helping to set up Pinchot for an embarrassing fall.

Pinchot, then seventy-six, played no small role in his own tumble. That spring, hearing what he described as "very disturbing rumors" of government lease contracts that would allow devastating clear-cuts in the state forests of the Keystone State, and that contained no provision for these lands' reforestation, he moved with characteristic haste. He fired off a letter to Albert Stewart, the state's secretary of forests and waters, that began to turn rumor into fact: "I cannot imagine that such complete disregard of the interests of the State and the State Forests can have been sanctioned by the Department of Forests and Water." He reminded Stewart that the arboreal treasures under his care "deserve to be treated with utmost care for their protection, reproduction, and perpetuation, for the service of our citizens, and the beauty and prosperity of the Commonwealth." To ensure that the head of Forests and Water, who was a journalist by trade, was keeping faith with the people and the land, Pinchot pulled rank—he requested a copy of the offending contract, as was his right "as a citizen, as a former Secretary of Forests and Water, and as a former Governor."[25]

Rankled, the political appointee shot back that "this being an election year I expected to hear from you regarding Pennsylvania forestry," and then hooted that Pinchot would give such credence to rumors that defamed the department's personnel, as the timber harvest was being conducted "with the advice and consent of [those] men in whom you had confidence when you were Governor." Stewart, at least, was confident that they were "doing a job of practical forestry rather than a job of purely theoretical or political forestry."[26]

This distinction, and the implied denigration it contained, curiously re-emerged in a later exchange of letters between Pinchot and Gleason Mattoon. Seeking a way to counter Stewart's attacks on him, and simultaneously to raise public consciousness about what he charged was "the false and specious excuse" that wartime emergencies required forest devastation, Pinchot arranged for Mattoon to join him in an examination of the cutting operations. He had also invited Henry Graves, whose professional insight would be crucial in identifying Pennsylvania's problems and establishing that "it is of genuine importance for the whole progress of forestry

Gifford Pinchot and Henry Graves gather in New Haven in 1940 to celebrate the fortieth anniversary of the Yale School of Forestry. The Pinchot family's financial support had made it possible to open the school, and Graves had served as its first dean.
Forest History Society

in the U.S. to get [its failures] straightened out." Pinchot wanted Graves on the tour for protection as well. "[I]f I go alone, it will be easy to charge (because [Governor Arthur] James beat me [in 1938]) . . . that I am doing it for political motives. If you are along, that charge would die aborning." Graves was unable to leave New Haven, however, and the allegations Pinchot suspected might be unleashed against him would appear shortly after he and Mattoon completed their travels.[27]

In late June Pinchot and Mattoon spent two days touring the field. Pinchot then drafted a series of letters they would sign, send to Governor James and Secretary Stewart, and then release to the state's media. By all accounts the trip went smoothly, and Pinchot came away thinking that

Mattoon shared his belief that they had witnessed some instances of egregious forest management. Mattoon refused to sign on, however, alleging that Pinchot's ideological bias had blinded him. "Our disagreement is fundamental, stemming from opposing political philosophies. . . ." Pinchot's advocacy of governmental ownership of forested lands clashed with Mattoon's faith in "private enterprise," leading them to read the logging sites in polar opposite ways. Where "you saw a 'destructive attack' on the State forests; I saw needed timber for barracks and crates and other war uses."[28]

Each man had a party line, but what Pinchot did not know was that others were listening in on the conversation. Mattoon had shared their correspondence with Stewart, so that when Pinchot released his letter enumerating the problems he had identified, Governor James immediately published a rebuttal that quoted at length from Mattoon's denunciation of Pinchot's interpretive prejudices. The *Journal of Forestry* further embarrassed the former chief of the Forest Service when it republished the exchange, adding to Pinchot's pique. This humiliation was only just, Mattoon believed. "Gifford Pinchot, in his day, was a great forester, but the insidious virus of political ambition has warped his judgment and impelled him into foolish moves"—one of which had been to trust the secretary of the Pennsylvania Forestry Association.[29]

However humiliated, Pinchot would not back down. Trusting his political instincts, he continued to lambaste the celerity with which American forests were being harvested during World War II. He was all for patriotism. "If the war needed every last tree in Pennsylvania, we should give it of course." But he was unconvinced that such wholesale sacrifice was necessary. Even granting that "we must have huge quantities of wood—huge even for the prodigal United States," this was no justification "for killing the goose that laid the golden egg," for "cutting as if we were going to need no wood after the war is over. This is pure foolishness." Those who argued otherwise were being deceived by the lumber companies and their political servants. The timber industry, like other American corporations, wrapped its hunger for substantial earnings in the flag; their new motto, he told Graves, ought to be *"Profita omnia excusat"* (profit excuses all). Their hunger for hegemonic power worried him more. "Personally, I have never seen as dangerous [an] amount of the big special interests trying to get control of

the government as the effort now going on," he confided to a friend in
March 1945. "I have long been tired of the Big Boys—men to whom the
only thing in the world worth considering is profits. There are, it seems to
me, a considerable number of things that are better worthwhile."[30]

PACIFIC DESIGNS

World peace was one of them. The correct path to it, he determined as hostilities flared throughout Europe and Asia during the late 1930s, was not to
embrace America First isolationism, as did other old Progressives, including his brother, Amos Pinchot. To avoid world conflagration required
instead the creation of broad international controls to rein in nationalistic
ambitions, controls that must be fashioned around the principles of conservation.[31]

He was certain that ignorance of conservationism lay at the root of all
global conflict. As he argued in an address to the Eighth American Scientific Conference in 1940, civilized life was not possible without natural
resources, the most basic of which was land. The "demand for new territory, made by one nation against another," he declared, "is a demand for
additional natural resources." The quest for economic dominance and
imperial control had been, and remained, "among the greatest causes of
war."[32]

To wage peace required a recognition of the interdependence of peoples
and nations. No nation was self-sufficient, and the "welfare of every nation
depends on access to natural resources which it lacks." It was, he thought,
quite possible to determine "fair access," but only if an overarching political
organization was established, the first task of which would be to gather
data on individual countries' resource bases and needs, as well as current
(and projected) levels of consumption and conservation. Data must also be
collected on the status of "wildlife" (not "game"), he argued—an indication
that Pinchot recognized this project entailed tabulating more than just
human needs. The final stage was for a United Nations–like body to be
empowered to design general policies and specific regulations to control
resource exploitation, protect and preserve threatened species, and secure
enduring prosperity—all of which would promote a just and permanent

peace. Only in this way could humanity ensure that war would not continue to determine the fate of the earth.[33]

Amos, by contrast, was weighed down by more gloomy perceptions of that fate. Viscerally opposed to World War II and just as adamant in his dissent from the Rooseveltian urge to centralize power, he found himself increasingly isolated. Boxed in politically, despondent over the 1938 suicide of his daughter Rosamond, and depressed in part because he could not shake his dependency on alcohol, Amos turned his hand against himself. While visiting his uncle William Eno in Westport, Connecticut, in August 1942, he slipped into a bathroom and used a safety-razor blade to slit veins in the upper part of one of his arms. Discovered and revived, he never really recovered from his wounds, both physical and psychological; they contributed to his death two years later, in February 1944. With his sister Antoinette also deceased, Gifford, as he had been for the first years of his life, was for his last an only child.[34]

He would greatly miss his brother and sister, with whom he had maintained vital, politically charged, and intricate relations over the course of their shared lives. But Gifford did not allow his newly singular status, and the impending mortality it promised, to unnerve him (at least not publicly). Symptomatic of this was his abiding faith in conservation and his creative interpretation of its manifold possibilities. To build wider support for his assertion that peace and conservation were ineluctably hooked together, for instance, he assiduously lobbied members of the Roosevelt administration. W. C. Lowdermilk, an assistant chief of the Soil Conservation Service, agreed with Pinchot's assessment that conservation was "a way out of this hellish frenzy of destruction," and was bucked up by one of the older man's displays of charm. "This is a real thing that you and I are working on, and it ought to be *kept after*." Pursued too was Secretary of State Cordell Hull, whom Pinchot urged to expand his hitherto narrow conception of conservation, as something limited to agriculture, and to recognize its broader implications. "[W]ithout conservation," the secretary learned, "the people on the earth can neither live happily, nor permanently endure." Even President Roosevelt—especially the president—was courted. Following his third-term budgetary report, Roosevelt received Pinchot's applause—it "was grand, hit just the right notes"—and this sycophantic nudge. "[T]he omission of any reference to *'conservation'* among the many other programs specified as needing post-war planning was not I am sure in the part which you yourself wrote."[35]

Pinchot's persistence paid off; his political acumen had not dimmed. But it did not hurt that his ideas converged with those of a president who was devoting some attention to postwar political and economic reconstruction, one essential element of which was the establishment of the United Nations. As a small part of the planning for the new organization's mission, and at Roosevelt's behest, Pinchot in the summer of 1944 drafted a letter "to Allied Governments proposing a Conference on the conservation of natural resources as a necessary requirement for permanent peace." Delighted that the president "spoke so highly of the plan," certain that it "would add a useful element of practical idealism to the international picture," Pinchot refined the proposal throughout the fall and made a final pitch to Roosevelt just before the latter left Washington for what would be his final rounds of talks with the allied powers at Yalta, held in February 1945. The ailing chief executive first assured Pinchot that he would brief Churchill and Stalin on the proposed international conference. Later, he also apparently concurred with the forester that a first step toward demonstrating the commitment of the United States to this vision of the pacific purpose of conservation was the enactment of legislation to halt "destructive cutting" in the national forests. Pinchot was elated.[36]

Then he was deflated by "the dreadful news of the President's death" on April 12. Yet within a month, Pinchot was angling for the new president's ear. By November he had made such a racket that Truman, who accepted that a conference "was a good thing" on its merits, apparently assented to "keep *G.P.* out of his hair," Harold Ickes reported. But when the global conference to champion the role of conservation in the maintenance of world peace finally convened in 1949 at Lake Success, New York—its formal title was the UN Scientific Conference on the Conservation and Utilization of Resources—it had been gutted of much of its original visionary quality and practical idealism. Highly technical in its orientation, it also lacked political punch. UN Secretary-General Trgve Lie opened the session with the solemn promise that the conference would have "no policy-making responsibilities, for it will neither bind governments nor formulate recommendations to be submitted to them." Without legislative authority and regulatory power, Pinchot would have told the secretary-general, the conference had little point.[37]

That is exactly what Cornelia Pinchot, an official delegate to the conference, declared when she addressed the six hundred attendees. "To sidestep the human and political implications of conservation," she charged, "to deal with it exclusively in terms of materials, matter, and technical processes, is to take a long step backward from where we stood a generation ago." She bluntly challenged Secretary Lie's decision to "hobble with restrictions" the creative minds and "creative mechanisms of democracy" that should have been unleashed at Lake Success. "What upside-down, Humpty Dumpty nonsense is this? I should like to ask Mr. Lie since when did scientists become so dangerous that they are not to be trusted even with [a] little power"? Deeply disappointed, she regarded the UN conference "less as a dream come to fruition than as a noble opportunity sidestepped."[38]

That Gifford Pinchot's dream had been deferred, that the august international body would not catch up to his conceptions until a UN-sponsored environmental conference in 1972, suggests how prescient his work had been in this respect. Over time, he had developed a creed that served as a harbinger of some of the ideas and tactics characteristic of modern environmentalism. His assertion that international agreements are essential to restrain resource exploitation and the despoliation of fragile landscapes such as the Galapagos Islands are central elements in the political agenda that underlies, for example, the Kyoto Accords (1997), which have been developed to control the effects of ozone depletion. They are also crucial to the motivations of such contemporary organizations as the Natural Resources Defense Council, which has used the legal system to foster tighter regulation of the environment, and Greenpeace (established in 1971), which has been at the forefront of those actively exposing the failures of various nations and economic actors to abide by international environmental laws. As Greenpeace's very name suggests, it is an heir to Pinchot's fundamental conviction that world peace and conservation are inextricably bound together. The human community, he came to believe, must think globally and act globally.[39]

The particular needs of local communities—their stressed ecosystems and battered human populations—also required action. Pinchot's "new conservationism," which had emerged during his two terms as governor of Pennsylvania, reflected his keen awareness of and rapid political responses to a degrading and exploitative economic system; with Cornelia, he had battled to ensure the right of all children, men, and women to live within sustainable communities and to inhabit a clean landscape. Deep ecologists and ecofeminists were not the first to recognize the intersection of politics and economics, social justice, and the environment.

Nor did post–World War II environmental activists invent the contentious choreography that has so long framed the drama of environmental politics. For that, credit goes to Pinchot and John Muir and their paired struggle in the early twentieth century to assert leadership over and control of the agenda of the conservation movement. The dynamic they developed, a kind of dance between moderate and radical forces, helped define their activism and that of their detractors. This complicated legacy was invoked—however unwittingly—when Dave Foreman jokingly described Earth First!, the radical environmental organization he founded in 1980, as a "secretly controlled" offshoot of mainstream environmental groups that could be "trotted out at hearings to make the Sierra Club or the Wilderness Society look moderate."[40]

That there are important intellectual links between Pinchot and the character and content of postwar environmentalism is not to say that Pinchot was a "green," that he had fleshed out a biocentric vision and lived according to Gaia. Rather, his legacy lies in his green*ing,* in his deliberate effort to reach an ever more complete understanding of the tangled interactions between the civilized and the wild. In this, he represents nothing less than the ever-widening range of strategies available to Americans, from the nineteenth century to the present, who were and are concerned with the maintenance of a healthy and peaceful world, and who have sought and continue to seek ways to bring that more benign state to life. The lessons Pinchot drew from his experiences evolved into an intellectual openness and moral engagement that his son, while standing on a hillside overlooking the Bitterroot Valley in 1972, invoked as he chastised the Forest Service in the name of the father.[41]

Grounded

There is a certain symmetry to that moment in Montana. In acting as he had, Gifford Bryce revealed the degree to which he had internalized a principle his father had taught him—to keep the land was to keep the people. The interdependent character of stewardship had been central to the senior Pinchot's private musings and public activism, and it also lay at the core of one of his most compelling short essays, "Time Is Like an Ever Rolling Stream." He had written it in the mid-1920s in response to a question his ten-year-old son had posed while they were fishing side by side along the Sawkill: "Dad, how long has this brook been here?"[42]

The father had no idea, at least not in terms of geological time, but the narrative he spun for his child integrated their forebears with the landscape in which they lived for many generations, a storyline that was as elegiac as it was prospective. "Men may come and men may go, but the Sawkill brook flows on—feeding its trout, protecting its insect, molluscan, and crustacean life—a home and a hiding place for myriads of living creatures—a thing of beauty and a joy forever," he began. As he developed this ode to the cyclical character of life, he infused it with a palpable sense of place. Along the Sawkill's banks "giant Pines and Hemlocks have germinated and grown, flourished and died, decayed and vanished"; under this verdant canopy "deer and bear drank and listened as they drank"; its fertile soil was crisscrossed by the tracks of moose, wolves, and panthers, and overhead kingfishers "clattered up and down the gorge." The rushing waters, meanwhile, sculpted a shifting streambed, "and floods ground out great potholes with their in-arching rims."[43]

In the beginning all was good, but such would not last. In the by-now-classic trope of environmental narration, Pinchot's Edenic vista would cloud with the advent of human civilization. "When the redmen came," he commented, "the life of the brook changed, but only a little. For they were no slaughterers, but conservationists, blood and bone, and took no more than the natural increase." Europeans took a good deal more. Hefting "new weapons of destruction" and evincing a "new zeal for slaughter," they made "new demands on nature for the means to live a new kind of life." Before these demands fell the "primeval forests," most of the indigenous

The Sawkill, which flows through the Pinchot estate
in Milford, has been the family's favorite fishing site for
generations. Like his father and his mother, Gifford
Bryce Pinchot was a lifelong, avid angler.
Grey Towers NHL

animals, and the Native American people; giving way too was "the old order, grown out of thousands of generations of adjustment, and the old balance, painfully won through the . . . internecine struggles of myriad forms of life." The cost for this "better living"? A culture that had reaped where it had not sown.[44]

Early generations of the Pinchot family had been among the profligate European pioneers, young Gifford Bryce was told. His émigré great-grandfather, Cyrille, who "threw himself into the life of this new country with a vigor which distinguished him," was an especially vigorous sawyer — "[t]he tribes of Pine and Hemlock along many streams paid him tribute." The income from lumbering enabled him to snap up a goodly share of Milford real estate, including the very riparian environment that was the essay's focus. At this point the emphasis of "Time Is Like an Ever Rolling Stream" shifted, along with the family's fortunes. The narrator thereafter

spoke not of raw commercial enterprise, but of each succeeding generation's fascination with an activity distinguishing the leisured life the Pinchots' material success had bought—the time to fish.[45]

On James Pinchot, his father, the author lavished praise for his skill as an
angler and for the sharpness of his eye; through his tutelage, a young Gifford "became a lover of the Sawkill and its sister little rivers." He learned to
be sensitive to their every riffle and pool and to the meanings written into
the charred remains of a lightning-sparked fire that had altered the "lives
of land and water dwellers for a few or many generations." From his father
came the desire to attend to every detail of the fisherman's craft (not the
least of which was to ensure that all hooks had been debarred, "broken off
with a pair of sharpnosed pliers"). Standing by his father's side in mid-
stream was where a young Gifford came to recognize that a fisherman's
pursuit of mastery was chimerical.[46] Certainly these were the very sensibilities Gifford Pinchot hoped to pass on to his son, through deed and word.
"Time Is Like an Ever Rolling Stream" testified to his desire to write himself into the land and the heart of a curious child.

In the 1970s, as commercial development in Milford and surrounding
Pike County threatened to despoil the region's rural character and
adversely affect the water quality of the Sawkill and other streams, Gifford
Bryce pulled together a coalition of local activists, including his son Peter
Pinchot, to stave off destruction. Using state water pollution codes that had
been updated since, but drew their legal precedence from the first such leg-
islation enacted during Gifford Pinchot's initial term as governor, the Pike
County activists secured stronger environmental protections for the region's
watersheds. Such actions were consistent with, and even demanded by,
Gifford Bryce's earlier acknowledgment of his patrimony. At his father's
open-air funeral service at Grey Towers on October 7, 1946, he had slipped
Gifford's favorite fishing rod into his casket.[47]

CODA

Gifford Pinchot would have been pleased with the nature of the posthumous honors bestowed upon him. Conservation societies and governments
alike marked individual trees and denoted full forests in his memory. A less

A perennial politician, Gifford Pinchot made good use of this broad-brimmed, floppy brown hat. Along with his full mustache, it became part of his public persona.
Grey Towers NHL

monumental, but maybe even more inspired, botanical recognition had come his way while he had been very much alive. In 1905, George B. Sudworth, a dendrologist in the newly created Forest Service, had linked his chief to a subspecies of juniper, *Juniperus pinchotii*. Its range encompasses some of the most arid terrain of far west Texas and Arizona, and its presence flags an abused and overgrazed landscape. It flourishes "on dry hillsides and in deep cuts and slashes in rocky soil," a tough, durable small tree that ranchers in the region forever seek to eradicate. Their efforts go for naught. As Sudworth noted, *Juniperus pinchotii* has an unusual regenerative capacity, a "marvelous power of sprouting from charred or cut stumps."[48]

Notes

PROLOGUE

1. Gifford Pinchot, Diary, May 7, 1891, Gifford Pinchot Papers, Library of Congress. (Unless otherwise noted, all referenced letters, diaries, and journals are located in this archive.)
2. Pinchot, Diary, May 8, 1891, May 4, 1891.
3. Pinchot, Diary, May 7–8, 1891; Stanford E. Demars, *The Tourist in Yosemite, 1855–1985* (Salt Lake City: University of Utah Press, 1991), 30–31.
4. Pinchot, Diary, May 8–9, 1891; his inability to see Yosemite as it was may have had something to do with his having previously seen photographs of it—a diminishing of its power through a prior, if secondhand, encounter.
5. Pinchot, Diary, May 9–10, 1891.
6. Pinchot, Diary, May 10, 1891; Gifford Pinchot, *Breaking New Ground* (New York: Harcourt Brace Jovanovich, 1947), 44–45.
7. Pinchot, *Breaking New Ground*, 45; John Muir, *The Mountains of California* (New York: Penguin Books, 1985), 191.
8. Roderick Nash, *Wilderness and the American Mind* (New Haven: Yale University Press, 1967), 181; John Muir, *The Yosemite* (New York: The Century Co., 1912), 255–62.
9. Address by Governor Pinchot at Lewisburg, Pa., March 20, 1924.
10. Gifford Pinchot, *Fishing Talk* (Harrisburg: Stackpole Books, 1993), 163–65; originally published as *Just Fishing Talk* (Harrisburg: The Telegraph Press, 1936).
11. Ibid., 44. William B. Cronon, "The Trouble with Wilderness: Or Getting Back to the Wrong Nature," in Char Miller and Hal Rothman, eds., *Out of the Woods: Essays in Environmental History* (Pittsburgh: University of Pittsburgh Press, 1997), 28–50. John Brinckerhoff Jackson, "Beyond Wilderness," in his *A Sense of Place, A Sense of Time* (New Haven: Yale University Press, 1994); and Michael Pollan, *Second Nature: A Gardener's Education* (New York: Atlantic Monthly Press, 1991), debunk the romanticism of those who segregate humanity and nature. See also Char Miller, "An Open Field," *Pacific Historical Review,* February 2001, 69–76. For counterarguments to Cronon's argument in particular, see the following comments in *Environmental History,* January 1996: Samuel Hays, "The Trouble with Bill Cronon's Wilderness," 29–32; Michael Cohen, "Resistance to Wilderness," 33–42; Thomas R. Dunlap, "But What Did You Go Out to the Wilderness to See?," 43–46, and Cronon's reply, 47–55. For a more general critique, see Eric Katz, *Nature as Subject: Human Obligation and Natural Community* (London: Rowan & Littlefield Publishers, Inc., 1997), 3–12, passim. Samuel Hays, "From Conservation to Environment: Environmental Politics in the United States Since World War II," in Miller and Rothman, eds., *Out of the Woods,* 101–26, indi-

rectly lays out some of the shifts in American intellectual and cultural history that account for the decline in Pinchot's popularity.

12. Mark Dowie, *Losing Ground: American Environmentalism at the Close of the Twentieth Century* (Cambridge: MIT Press, 1995), 17, notes that Muir "remains at the heart of the American environmental imagination." Stephen Fox, *The American Conservation Movement: John Muir and His Legacy* (Madison: University of Wisconsin Press, 1985), and Nash, *Wilderness and the American Mind,* also track Muir's centrality to the evolution of the environmental movement. Gabriel Kolko, *The Triumph of Conservatism* (New York: Quadrangle Books, 1963), 111, challenges Pinchot's reform image and integrity. In contrast, Richard Cartwright Austin, *Baptized to Wilderness: A Christian Perspective on John Muir* (Atlanta: The John Knox Press, 1987), which appears as the first number of a series on environmental theology, testifies to the religious light in which Muir is currently bathed: "In America," Austin writes, "we have had an advocate for nature whose spiritual insights rival those of Francis of Assisi for the Middle Ages" (2). No one will ever draw such parallels for Pinchot—not for him the glow of transcendent Christianity, argues Mark Stoll in *Protestantism, Capitalism, and Nature in America* (Albuquerque: University of New Mexico Press, 1997). "Pinchot rigidly divided his private and public lives: spirituality and mysticism had no part in his gospel of conservation." Stoll then proceeds to demonstrate the moral underpinnings of Pinchot's conservation philosophy, 151–59.

13. Michael Cohen, *The Pathless Way: John Muir and American Wilderness* (Madison: University of Wisconsin Press, 1984), 326; Stoll, *Protestantism, Capitalism, and Nature,* 159–69, plays off Cohen's observation by probing the Hetch Hetchy controversy through a useful comparison of Pinchot's rhetoric of "Evangelical Science" with Muir's of "Paradise Lost."

14. Frederick Turner, *Rediscovering America: John Muir in His Time and Ours* (New York: Viking, 1985), 322–23; Fox, *American Conservation Movement,* 289–90. Thurman Wilkins, *John Muir: Apostle of Nature* (Norman: University of Oklahoma Press, 1995), makes the same argument about Muir's ultimate victory over Pinchot, 253; Paul Cutright, *Theodore Roosevelt: The Making of a Conservationist* (Urbana: University of Illinois Press, 1986), 234–35, also makes much of Pinchot's later nomination to the Conservation Hall of Fame, suggesting that Pinchot had much less influence on Roosevelt's conservation principles than is usually believed.

15. Stephen Fox, "Gifford Pinchot and His Place in the American Conservation Movement," *Theodore Roosevelt Association Journal,* Summer 1987, 7–10; Roderick Nash, "Gifford Pinchot," in Nash, *In These Beginnings: A Biographical Approach to American History* (New York: Harper & Row, 1984), 99–147. T. H. Watkins, "Father of the Forests," *American Heritage,* February–March 1991, 86–98, is a partial exception; see also Bob Pepperman Taylor, *Our Limits Transgressed: Environmental Political Thought in America* (Lawrence: University of Kansas Press, 1992), for a compelling comparative analysis of

Henry David Thoreau and Pinchot; Aldo Leopold, *A Sand County Almanac* (New York: Oxford University Press, 1968).

16. Fox, "Pinchot," 7–10; Nash, "Pinchot," 99–147.

17. Although Robert Gottlieb does not include Pinchot among the sources of the environmental justice movement that emerged in the late 1990s, he deserves to be: Robert Gottlieb, "Reconstructing Environmentalism: Complex Movements, Diverse Roots," in Miller and Rothman, eds., *Out of the Woods,* 144–60.

18. Aldo Leopold, *Sand County Almanac,* 129–32; Fox, "Pinchot," 8.

19. Gifford Pinchot, *To the South Seas* (Philadelphia: The John C. Winston Co., 1930), 344.

20. Lawrence Buell, *The Environmental Imagination: Thoreau, Nature Writing, and the Formation of American Culture* (Cambridge: The Belknap Press of Harvard University Press, 1995), and Nash, *Wilderness and the American Mind,* address this literary tradition.

21. Pinchot, *Fishing Talk,* 185, 189. He felt no such restraint about sharks, however; 188–89.

22. Cornelia Pinchot, "Gifford Pinchot and the Conservation Ideal," *Journal of Forestry,* February 1950, 85–86.

23. His 1924 warning to the Pan American Union that tropical forests would soon be obliterated if not brought under careful regulation, for instance, was confirmed in the United Nations–sponsored Santiago Declaration (1995) that established internationally accepted criteria for and indicators of sustainable forest management. Gifford Pinchot, "A Forest Devastation Warning," *Pan American Cooperation in Forestry Conservation* (Washington, D.C.: Government Printing Office, 1925), 5–9; the Santiago Declaration is located at http://www.fs.fed.us/global/pub/links/santiago.htm.

CHAPTER 1. THE WORLD OF HIS FATHER

1. "Gifford Pinchot Who Fathered Conservation," *Washington Herald,* March 1912, Pinchot Scrapbooks, reel 1, GP-LC. All quotations in the next two paragraphs come from this article.

2. Gifford Pinchot, *Breaking New Ground* (New York: Harcourt Brace, 1947), 2. John Reiger, *American Sportsmen and the Origins of Conservation,* third edition (Corvallis: Oregon State University Press, 2000), explores the range and development of the idea of conservation in America, as does Donald J. Pisani, "Forests and Conservation, 1865–1890," in Char Miller, ed., *American Forests: Nature, Culture, and Politics* (Lawrence: University Press of Kansas, 1997), 15–34.

3. Gifford Pinchot, *Fishing Talk* (Harrisburg: Stackpole Books, 1993), 71–75. The book that introduced Americans to the sylvan Adirondacks was William H. H. Murray, *Adventures in the Wilderness; or Camp Life in the Adirondacks,* ed. William K. Verner (Syracuse: Syracuse University Press, 1970), 9–15. Warder H. Cadbury, "Introduction," in ibid., 11–75, sets Murray's book in its intellectual and cultural context; see also Philip G. Terrie, "Imperishable

Freshness: Culture, Conservation and the Adirondack Park," *Forest & Conservation History*, July 1993, 133–37. Karl Jacoby, "Class and Environmental History: Lessons from 'The War in the Adirondacks,'" *Environmental History*, July 1997, 324–42, discusses the social transformation of the region following its "discovery" by the urban elite.

4. One of those they encountered was President Noah Porter of Yale College. Mary Pinchot, "Biographical Sketch"; Pinchot, *Fishing Talk*, 71–73; Murray, *Adventures in the Wilderness*, 10.

5. Pinchot, *Fishing Talk*, 71–73; Warder H. Cadbury, "Introduction," in Murray, *Adventures in the Wilderness*, 11–12, 32–75.

6. Pinchot, *Fishing Talk*, 74.

7. Pinchot, *Fishing Talk*, 73–74; E. R. Wallace, *Descriptive Guide to the Adirondacks* (New York: Forest and Stream Publishing Co., 1876), 140–41.

8. Pinchot, *Fishing Talk*, 73.

9. Ibid., 73–74; Reiger, *American Sportsmen*, passim, offers insights into male bonding on such trips as this one, and into the sportsman's code. Annette Kolodny, *The Lay of the Land: Metaphor as Experience and History in American Life and Letters* (Chapel Hill: University of North Carolina Press, 1975), explores the evolving character of a "female" landscape against which men test themselves.

10. Pinchot, *Fishing Talk*, 74; Reiger, *American Sportsmen*; Kolodny, *Lay of the Land*.

11. Pinchot, *Fishing Talk*, 74–75.

12. All of which he in turn passed on to his own readers through his *Fishing Talk*.

13. William Fortescue, *Revolution & Counter-Revolution in France, 1815–1852* (New York: Basil Blackwell, 1988), 1–16; Guillaume de Bertier de Sauvigny, *The Bourbon Restoration* (Philadelphia: University of Pennsylvania Press, 1966), 93–111.

14. Cyrille Pinchot's actions in France are discussed in "Edgar Pinchot," in *Commemorative Biographical Record of Northeastern Pennsylvania* (Chicago: T. H. Beers, 1900), 277; and in Alfred Mathews, *A History of Wayne, Pike and Monroe Counties, Pennsylvania* (Philadelphia: R. T. Peek, 1886), 862–63. Napoleon's collapse is detailed in Daniel Resnick, *The White Terror and the Political Reaction after Waterloo* (Cambridge: Harvard University Press, 1966); Sauvigny, *Bourbon Restoration*, 102–7, 117–19, 134–35. Pinchot, *Breaking New Ground*, 10, offers a third version of his grandfather's exploits, noting that he was forced to leave France for participating in a plan to free Napoleon from St. Helena.

15. Mathews, *History of Wayne, Pike and Monroe Counties*, 860–61.

16. Not for them the prescriptions for the harmonic tranquillity and meditative agrarian life that another Frenchman had proclaimed from his farm, Pine Hill, in nearby Chester, New York, in the late eighteenth century: see J. Hector St. John de Crevecoeur, *Letters from an American Farmer* (New York: Pen-

guin Books, 1981), 71; Gay Wilson Allen and Roger Asselineau, *St. John de Crevecoeur: The Life of an American Farmer* (New York: Viking Penguin, 1987), 32–45; Mathews, *History of Wayne, Pike and Monroe Counties,* 860–61.

17. The early history of Milford is detailed in Mathews, *History of Wayne, Pike and Monroe Counties,* 860–64; William Bross quoted in ibid., 883–86.

18. John Brodhead to Pinchot, August 9, 1839, August 30, 1839; John Wallace to C. C. D. Pinchot, April 15, 1834, May 6, 1834; Wallace to Pinchot, May 5, 1835; Seth Couch to Pinchot, February 9, 1836; John Brodhead to Pinchot, May 19, 1837; R. R. Boughton to Pinchot, September 18, 1837. For a historical analysis of this preindustrial pattern of lumbering, see Thomas R. Cox, "Transition in the Woods: Log Drivers, Raftsmen, and the Emergence of Modern Lumbering in Pennsylvania," *Pennsylvania Magazine of Biography and History,* July 1980, 345–64; Robert K. McGregor, "Changing Technologies and Forest Consumption in the Upper Delaware Valley, 1780–1880," *Journal of Forest History,* April 1988, 69–81.

19. Gordon S. Whitney, *From Coastal Wilderness to Fruited Plain: A History of Environmental Change in Temperate North America from 1500 to the Present* (Cambridge: Cambridge University Press, 1995), details the impact of railroads on the consumption of wood. See Michael Williams, *Americans and Their Forests: A Historical Geography* (New York: Cambridge University Press, 1989), 146–89, for information on the "quickening pace" of industrial production in antebellum America. See also Thomas Cox et al., *This Well Wooded Land: Americans and Their Forests from the Colonial Times to the Present* (Lincoln: University of Nebraska Press, 1985), 110–90; McGregor, "Changing Technologies," 69–81; James Elliot Defenbaugh, *A History of the Lumber Industry of America,* 2 vols. (Chicago: The American Lumberman, 1907), 563–64.

20. Mathews, *History of Wayne, Pike and Monroe Counties,* 863. On tax matters, see Cyrille Pinchot file, Grey Towers National Historic Landmark (NHL), Milford, Pa.; the profitability of his work was such that he reportedly plunked down $30,000 to buy a horse farm, one of his passions; Carol Severance, "The American Art Collection of James Pinchot" (seminar paper, Cooperstown Graduate Programs, Fall 1993), 1–2, copy on file at Grey Towers NHL, Milford, Pa.

21. On turnpike development, see correspondence between Fred Bailey and C. C. D. Pinchot, February 18, 1840; June 11, 1842; March 7, 1843; April 13, 1843; June 17, 1843; November 20, 1847; April 15, 1851; "The Milford and Owego Turnpike," in Emily C. Blackman, *History of Susquehanna County, Pennsylvania* (1873), 511; Rhamanthius M. Stoker, *Centennial History of Susquehanna County, Pennsylvania,* revised edition (Baltimore: Regional Publishing Co., 1974), 47–49; Bross recollections in Mathews, *History of Wayne, Pike and Monroe Counties,* 883.

22. Edward H. Mott, *Between the Ocean and the Lakes: The Story of the Erie* (New

York: John S. Collier, 1901), 89–90, 345. The legislative and legal maneuverings are tracked in George H. Minor, *The Erie System,* second edition (Cleveland: The Gates Legal Publishing Co., 1936), 165–66.

23. Mott, *Between the Ocean and the Lakes,* 345–46; H. S. Mott to C. C. D. Pinchot, April 14, 1854, April 23, 1854, April 28, 1854; Minor, *Erie System,* 173; Frederick Bailey to C. C. D. Pinchot, April 15, 1851.

24. Bailey to Pinchot, April 15, 1851; Stocker, *Centennial History of Susquehanna County,* 47–48, 655; Mott, *Between the Ocean and the Lakes,* 345–46.

25. Biographical data is drawn from Mathews, *History of Wayne, Pike and Monroe Counties,* 863–65, 868, 892–93; *A Commemorative Biographical Record of Northeastern Pennsylvania,* 270, 277, 369, 580; Mott, *Between the Ocean and the Lakes,* 344–45; Edward Mott, *Pike County Folks,* a popular and patronizing compendium of back country tales, is a reflection of the distance—literary and physical—that this one former resident had traveled from his birthplace. Edgar's experience in New York is chronicled in Char Miller, "All in the Family: The Pinchots of Milford," *Pennsylvania History,* Spring 1999, 140–41.

26. John Weir to James Pinchot, May 17, 1870; James Pinchot to C. C. D. Pinchot, September 24, 1871.

27. James Pinchot to his mother, August 21, 1871; James Pinchot to C. C. D. Pinchot, June 16, 1864; James Pinchot to C. C. D. Pinchot, December 30, 1869; Richard L. Bushman, *The Refinement of America: Persons, Houses, Cities* (New York: Knopf, 1992), 238–79, 313–401.

28. Mathews, *History of Warren, Pike and Monroe Counties,* 863–64; David Chase, "Superb Privacies: The Later Domestic Commissions of Richard Morris Hunt, 1878–1895," in Susan R. Stern, ed., *The Architecture of Richard Morris Hunt* (Chicago: The University of Chicago Press, 1986), 164–65; Paul R. Baker, *Richard Morris Hunt* (Cambridge: MIT Press, 1980), 337–40; Bushman, *Refinement of America,* 353–401.

29. James W. Pinchot to C. C. D. Pinchot, March 5, 1845; Henry Fitch to James Pinchot, November 1, 1846; Henry Fitch to James Pinchot, November 9, 1849. On Fitch's work for the Erie, see Mott, *Between the Ocean and the Lakes,* 379–80; Edward Hungerford, *Men of Erie: A Story of Human Effort* (New York: Random House, 1946), 95.

30. James Pinchot to C. C. D. Pinchot, August 16, 1852. Albert Fishlow, *American Railroads and the Transformation of the Ante-Bellum Economy* (Cambridge: Harvard University Press, 1965), 201n, indicates that railroads "captured a very large share of the traffic" in internal migration in the 1850s. The Erie Railroad was one of the most successful in this regard, hauling, for instance, more than 50,000 migrants in 1855. This speaks well to Fitch's abilities and James Pinchot's intuition that his former schoolmaster was well positioned to help sell the Pinchots' lands.

31. Partridge, Pinchot & Warren advertisement, July 12, 1858; New York City population figures and residential patterns appear in Edward K. Spann, *The New Metropolis: New York City, 1840–1857* (New York: Columbia University

Press, 1981), 432–33; Ivan D. Steen, "Palaces for Travelers: New York City's Hotels in the 1850s as Viewed by British Visitors," *New York History,* April 1970, 269–86; James Pinchot quoted in Gifford Pinchot, "Biographical Sketch of James W. Pinchot," July 7, 1936; M. Nelson McGeary, *Gifford Pinchot: Forester-Politician* (Princeton: Princeton University Press, 1960), 3. William Seale, *The Tasteful Interlude: American Interiors through the Camera's Eye, 1860–1917,* second edition (Nashville: American Association for State and Local History, 1981), 10–27, details the shifting tastes in decoration that fed Pinchot's business, as does Florence Montgomery, *Textiles in America, 1650–1870* (New York: Norton, 1984), passim.

32. James Pinchot to C. C. D. Pinchot, November 5, 1854; Henry Ward Beecher quoted in Clifford E. Clark, Jr., *Henry Ward Beecher: Spokesman for a Middle-Class America* (Champaign: University of Illinois Press, 1978), 77–78; William G. McLaughlin, *The Meaning of Henry Ward Beecher: An Essay on the Shifting Values of Mid-Victorian America, 1840–1870* (New York: Knopf, 1970), 98–118.

33. James Pinchot to C. C. D. Pinchot, March 13, 1855, March 16, 1855; McGeary, *Gifford Pinchot: Forester-Politician,* 3. James Pinchot's collapse may be attributable as well to the death of his youngest brother, Cyril, in 1858 or 1859. James had been like a father to Cyril: at the same time that James heard from his father on health matters, so he had counselled Cyril to remedy *his* sickly demeanor, intensify his work habits, straighten out his waywardness, and reform his soul. In an unrelenting stream of letters, James alternately challenged, provoked, and scolded Cyril, displaying an overbearing concern stemming from the fact that James helped underwrite Cyril's education, first at boarding school and later at Union College. Hypervigilance about the state of one's health was a kind of family neurosis, and it clearly carried over into the lives of James's children, who often complained about their father's over-solicitousness. James's intense concern about his children may well have been caused by Cyril's demise just before he graduated from college; James may have become determined not to fail his children as he perhaps felt he had his brother: James Pinchot to Cyril H. Pinchot, April 10, 1855, May 16, 1855, June 7, 1855, January 24, 1856, October 25, 1856, July 21, 1857, November 24, 1858.

34. Thomas Couture, Charcoal Sketch of James W. Pinchot, April 5, 1873, Grey Towers NHL Collection, Milford, Pa.; Launt Thompson to James Pinchot, July 23, 1863.

35. The wedding was announced in the *New York Times,* May 27, 1864; Jervis McEntee to James Pinchot, May 23, 1864; Eastman Johnson wrote a hilarious description of how he overslept in a May 25, 1864, letter to James Pinchot; Mary Pinchot to James Pinchot, May 21, 1865; James Pinchot to Mary Pinchot, 1865.

36. Mary Pinchot to James Pinchot, August 21, 1888.

CHAPTER 2. RELATIVE POWER

1. Gifford Pinchot, Diary, June 13, 1913; M. Nelson McGeary, *Gifford Pinchot: Forester-Politician* (Princeton: Princeton University Press, 1960), 240–41.

2. Pinchot, Diary, April 15, 1913; Char Miller, "Keeper of His Conscience? Roosevelt, Pinchot and the Politics of Conservation," in Natalie A. Naylor et al., eds., *Theodore Roosevelt: Many Sided American* (Interlaken, N.Y.: Hofstra University and Heart of the Lakes Publishing Co., 1992), 231–44; McGeary, *Pinchot,* 94–100; Theodore Roosevelt, *An Autobiography* (New York: The MacMillan Co., 1913), 428–61.

3. Pinchot, Diary, July 2, 1913.

4. Mary Pinchot to Theodore Roosevelt, June 13, 1913, Series 1, Reel 176, Theodore Roosevelt Papers, Library of Congress.

5. Ibid.

6. Roosevelt, *Autobiography,* 429; Mary Pinchot to Theodore Roosevelt, June 13, 1913, June 20, 1913.

7. Mary Pinchot, "Recollections."

8. Ibid.

9. James Hammond Trumbull, *The Memorial History of Hartford County, Connecticut, 1633–1884* (Boston: Edward L. Osgood, 1886), 357, 361.

10. Charles Cunningham, *Timothy Dwight, 1752–1817* (New York: The MacMillan Co., 1942), 293–334; Ralph Henry Gabriel, *Religion and Learning at Yale* (New Haven: Yale University Press, 1958), 54–71; Brooks Mather Kelley, *Yale: A History* (New Haven: Yale University Press, 1974), 115–19; on Timothy Dwight's Federalist politics, see David Hackett Fischer, *The Revolution of American Conservatism: The Federalist Party in the Era of Jeffersonian Democracy* (New York: Harper & Row, 1965), 134–35, 286–87, 296–97.

11. On Anson Phelps's unorthodoxy, see Richard J. Purcell, *Connecticut in Transition: 1778–1818,* new edition (Middletown: Wesleyan University Press, 1963), 197; on Reeve, Gould, and the Litchfield Law School, see James Willard Hurst, *The Growth of American Law: The Law Makers* (Boston: Little, Brown & Co., 1950), 258–60.

12. Morton J. Horwitz, *The Transformation of American Law, 1780–1860* (Cambridge: Harvard University Press, 1977), 1–30.

13. Robert Stevens, *Law School: Legal Education in America from the 1850s to the 1980s* (Chapel Hill: University of North Carolina Press, 1983), 3–4, 11; Albert J. Harno, *Legal Education in the United States* (reprint, Westport, Conn.: Greenwood Press, 1980), 26–34; Herbert Parker, *Courts and Lawyers of New England,* vol. 3 (New York: The American Historical Society, Inc., 1931), 666–71; Francis R. Aumann, *The Changing American Legal System: Some Selected Phases* (Columbus: Ohio State University Press, 1940), 96–97.

14. "Elisha Phelps," in *Biographical Directory of the United States Congress, 1774–1989* (Washington, D.C.: Government Printing Office, 1988), 1,641, and in *The National Cyclopaedia of American Biography,* vol. 11 (Ann Arbor: Uni-

versity Microfilms, 1967), 323; Purcell, *Connecticut in Transition,* xii–xvii, 146–89, 237–64. Politics was a family affair: although Jeffrey O. Phelps did not have his brother Elisha's educational attainments—neither the Yale degree nor the Litchfield pedigree—he nonetheless served as a state representative and a county judge from Hartford County; another brother, Noah Amherst Phelps, was a judge and served as secretary of state of Connecticut; Trumbull, *Memorial History of Hartford County,* 361.

15. Trumbull, *Memorial History of Hartford County,* 360; Mary Pinchot, "Recollections"; "Elisha Phelps," *Biographical Dictionary of the United States Congress,* 1,641.

16. Mary Pinchot, "Recollections"; Mary Mason, Simsbury Historical Society, provided an inventory of the Phelpses' home.

17. "John Smith Phelps," in Allen Johnson and Dumas Malone, eds., *The Dictionary of American Biography,* vol. 14 (New York: Charles Scribner's Sons, 1935), 530; *Cyclopaedia of American Biography,* vol. 12, 307; Mary Pinchot, "Recollections."

18. *Dictionary of American Biography,* vol. 14, 530; Phelps supported, for example, California and Oregon's admission to the Union, and passed legislation for inter- and intrastate railroad development.

19. Mary Pinchot, "Recollections."

20. Ibid.; Samuel Flagg Bemis, *John Quincy Adams and the Union* (New York: Knopf, 1956), 539–44; Albert J. Kirwen, *John J. Crittenden: The Struggle for the Union* (reprint, Westport, Conn.: Greenwood Press, 1962), 282–84. While star-gazing, Mary missed a good speech at Pierce's inaugural: Lara Gara, *The Presidency of Franklin Pierce* (Lawrence: University Press of Kansas, 1991), 47–48; Roy Franklin Nichols, *Franklin Pierce: Young Hickory of the Granite Hills* (Philadelphia: University of Pennsylvania Press, 1958), 232–36. John Phelps's political career, like that of so many of his generation, was interrupted by the Civil War: he raised his own regiment from southwestern Missouri to fight for the Union, he was one of the heroes of the battle of Pea Ridge, Arkansas, and Lincoln appointed him military governor of Arkansas. His steadfast Unionism did not work to his political advantage once the hostilities ceased, however; he was too northern for Missouri's unreconstructed southern vote, too much the Democrat for the then-triumphant Republicans. After several tries, he finally became the governor of Missouri, serving one term, 1876 to 1880. See Christopher Phillips, *Damned Yankee: The Life of General Nathaniel Lyon* (Columbus: University of Missouri Press, 1990); Hans Christian Adamson, *Rebellion in Missouri: 1861* (Philadelphia: Chilton Co., 1961); John McElroy, *The Struggle for Missouri* (Washington, D.C.: The National Tribune Co., 1909); Edwin C. McReynolds, *Missouri: A History of the Crossroads State* (Norman: University of Oklahoma Press, 1962); William E. Parrish, *A History of Missouri,* 3 vols. (Columbia: University of Missouri Press, 1971).

21. *New York Times,* January 22, 1898; April 13, 1899, 14; April 16, 1899, 11; May 7, 1899, 9; Richard L. Bushman, *The Refinement of America: Persons, Houses, Cities* (New York: Knopf, 1992), 370–82.

22. Henry Lane Eno, "The Eno Family: The New York Branch," *New England Historic and Genealogical Society,* 1920, 1–26.

23. Amos Eno to Lucy Phelps, February 16, 1834.

24. J. Eugene Smith, *One Hundred Years of Hartford's Courant: From Colonial Times through the Civil War* (New Haven: Yale University Press, 1949), 158–76; Trumbull, *Memorial History of Hartford County.* Eno and Phelps's decision to leave Hartford apparently coincided with the departure of a number of its other young, ambitious clerks, who also found success in New York City, including John Collins, Morris Earle, and Edwin Morgan, who later became a U.S. senator and governor of New York: see Walter H. Barrett, *The Old Merchants of New York City* (reprint, Westport, Conn.: Greenwood Press, 1968), 136, 138–39. Barrett was a pseudonym for Joseph Alfred Scoville; James A. Rawley, *Edwin Morgan, 1811–1883: Merchant in Politics* (New York: Columbia University Press, 1955), 3–7.

25. Barrett, *Old Merchants of New York City,* 138–39; Edward Pessen, *Riches, Class and Power Before the Civil War* (Lexington: D. C. Heath, 1973), debunks Barrett's and similar claims.

26. Alexis de Tocqueville, *Democracy in America,* vol. 1 (New York: Vintage Books, 1945), 54; Edward Pessen, "The Wealthiest New Yorkers of the Jacksonian Era: A New List," *New York Historical Society Quarterly,* April 1970, 145–72.

27. Pessen, *Riches, Class and Power Before the Civil War*; Edward K. Spann, *The New Metropolis: New York City, 1840–1857* (New York: Columbia University Press, 1981), 205–41.

28. *New York Herald,* July 26, 1855, quoted in Spann, *New Metropolis,* 112; *New York Times,* February 22, 1898, 1.

29. *New York Times,* February 22, 1898; James D. McCabe, Jr., *Lights and Shadows of New York Life* (Philadelphia: National Publishing Co., 1872), 308–13; Bushman, *Refinement of America,* 359.

30. "The Fifth Avenue Hotel; New York," *Harper's Weekly,* October 1, 1859, 634; McCabe, *Lights and Shadows of New York Life,* 308–13; Theodore James, Jr., *Fifth Avenue* (New York: Walker and Co., 1971), 87–89, 125; Bushman, *Refinement of America,* 359; Ivan D. Steen, "Palaces for Travelers: New York City's Hotels in the 1850s as Viewed by British Visitors," *New York History,* April 1970, 269–84.

31. Bushman, *Refinement of America,* 370–82; Trumbull, *Memorial History of Hartford County,* 354–56; "Amos R. Eno," in Rossiter Johnson, ed., *The Twentieth Century Biographical Dictionary of Notable Americans* (Boston: The Biographical Society, 1904); on James Pinchot's patron activities, see Carol Severance, "The American Art Collection of James W. Pinchot," unpublished

manuscript, Grey Towers National Historic Landmark, Milford, Pa.; John E. Ellsworth, *Simsbury: Being a Brief Historical Sketch of Ancient and Modern Simsbury, 1642–1935* (Simsbury: The Simsbury Committee for the Tercentenary, 1935), 159–61. The next generation of Enos continued to improve and gentrify the town's appearance, most notably Antoinette Eno Woods, who donated more than $300,000 to build a massive "colonial" town hall in her parents' honor. At its dedication in May 1932, Gifford Pinchot, then governor of Pennsylvania, gave the keynote address, in which he extolled his aunt's beneficence to "this beautiful town," a beauty that depended in good part on the Eno family's multigenerational contributions to the prevailing construct of what constituted beauty.

32. Mary Pinchot, "Recollections"; Barrett, *Old Merchants of New York City*, 48–50; Pessen, *Riches, Class and Power Before the Civil War*, 172–79; Peter G. Buckley, "Culture, Class, and Place in Antebellum New York," in John Hull Mollenkopf, ed., *Power, Culture and Place: Essays on New York City* (New York: Russell Sage Foundation, 1988), 25–27, 34–38.

33. Mary Pinchot, "Recollections."

34. Mary Pinchot, "Recollections." There is a nice echo of Kirkland's literary concerns in Mary's observation of the advance of the great unwashed upon once-civilized lower Manhattan. Kirkland's most famous work, *A New Home—Who Will Follow* (1839; reprint, New York: Garrett Press, 1969), chronicled her family's move into Michigan Territory and depicts the struggle to maintain genteel respectability amid the rough western culture. It was a struggle that the Kirklands ultimately quit, moving to New York City in the early 1840s to pursue careers in writing and teaching; the frontier, urban and rural, was contested ground. William S. Osborne, *Caroline M. Kirkland* (New York: Twayne Publishers, Inc., 1972), 26–28, 156–57. On Kossuth's visit to the United States, see John M. Komlos, *Kossuth in America: 1851–1852* (Buffalo: East European Institute, 1973), 75–96.

35. Mary Pinchot, "Recollections," 14–15. That her experience of courtship was without clear adult supervision or control was typical of middle-class women, too; see Ellen Rothman, *Hearts and Hands: A History of Courtship in America* (New York: Basic Books, 1984).

36. *New York Times,* May 14, 1884, 1; May 15, 1884, 5; May 16, 1884, 1; January 1, 1888, 12; Hugh M. Herrick, compiler, *William Walter Phelps* (New York: The Knickerbocker Press, 1904), 141–46.

37. *New York Times,* January 1, 1888, 12; Herrick, *Phelps,* 141–46.

38. See the extensive coverage of John C. Eno's flight to Canada in *New York Times,* May 14–June 30, 1884, passim; Mary Pinchot to William T. Sherman, January 4, 1891; Sherman to Chester Arthur, June 16, 1884, Chester Arthur Papers, Library of Congress; *New York Times,* March 20, 1894, 9; June 23, 1899, 14.

39. James Pinchot to Mary Pinchot, January 15, 1886; *New York Times,* March 20,

1894, 9; June 23, 1899, 14; William T. Sherman to Benjamin Harrison, February 1889, Benjamin Harrison Papers, Library of Congress; Sherman to Mary Pinchot, January 4, 1891.

40. William T. Sherman to Mary Pinchot, June 16, 1884; Pinchot to Mary Pinchot, November 16, 1893.

CHAPTER 3. RISING SON

1. Mary Pinchot, Diary, August 11, 1886.
2. Gifford Pinchot, *Breaking New Ground* (New York: Harcourt Brace Jovanovich, 1947), 2.
3. George Perkins Marsh, *The Earth as Modified by Human Action, A New Edition of Man and Nature* (New York: Charles Scribner's Sons, 1882), 280; David Lowenthal, *George Perkins Marsh: Prophet of Conservation* (Seattle: University of Washington Press, 2000), 290–312. Gifford first discussed Marsh's book in a March 21, 1886, letter to his mother; Amos's gift is currently located in the library of Grey Towers National Historic Landmark, Milford, Pa., with an inscription that reads: "Gifford Pinchot, Aug. 11th, 1886, from AREP"; I am grateful to Carol Severance, curator of Grey Towers, for information about the book and its provenance. See also Gifford Pinchot, *Breaking New Ground* (New York: Harcourt Brace Jovanovich, 1947), xxiii, 1–3; Pinchot to Mary Pinchot, April 27, 1886, describes the planting of trees and roses around the house.
4. Gifford's extended family's response to his conversations was to give him books on forestry; he was reportedly overjoyed to receive numerous such presents for Christmas 1885; Pinchot to James Pinchot, December 26, 1885; M. Nelson McGeary, *Gifford Pinchot: Forester-Politician* (Princeton: Princeton University Press, 1960), 15–16; Pinchot to James Pinchot, December 11, 1885; Pinchot to Mary Pinchot, December 26, 1885.
5. McGeary, *Gifford Pinchot: Forester-Politician,* 9.
6. Mary Pinchot, Memo Book of 1880; James Pinchot, Journal of a Tour of England and the Continent, undated; Gifford Pinchot, Diary, 1878–1880; Pinchot to Mary Pinchot, October 29, 1880; James Pinchot to Mary Pinchot, August 25, 1880.
7. James Pinchot to Pinchot, October 6, 1880, October 14, 1880, November 3, 1880. The father did not yank the son's chain, however, but decided to control from afar, insisting that henceforth Gifford write his parents once a day: James Pinchot to Pinchot, October 14, 1880.
8. Mary Pinchot to Pinchot, October 10, 1880, November 13, 1880, November 26, 1880; Pinchot to Mary Pinchot, September 2, 1880, September 30, 1880.
9. The quote comes from McGeary, *Gifford Pinchot: Forester-Politician,* 9.
10. William G. Saltonstall, *John Phillips: Merchant, Shipowner, Landed Proprietor, and Founder of Phillips Exeter Academy* (New York: The Newcomen Society in North America, 1951), 18; James McLachlan, *American Boarding Schools: A Historical Study* (New York: Charles Scribner's Sons, 1970), 219–41.

11. A. H. Gesner to Pinchot, October 17, 1883.

12. Ibid.

13. Gesner to Pinchot, October 17, 1883; Charles Rosenberg, *No Other Gods: On Science and American Social Thought* (Baltimore: Johns Hopkins University Press, 1976), 2–3; see also Nathan Reingold, *Science, American Style* (New Brunswick: Rutgers University Press, 1991), 1–49. Gesner's compromise was also perfectly in line with that ascribed to the New Haven scholars, several of whom would become Gifford Pinchot's teachers at Yale; see Louise L. Stevenson, *Scholarly Means to Evangelical Ends: The New Haven Scholars and the Transformation of Higher Learning in America, 1830–1890* (Baltimore: Johns Hopkins University Press, 1986), 67–86.

14. Pinchot to Mary Pinchot, February 21, 1882; F. W. Farrar, *The Life and Work of St. Paul* (New York: E. Dutton, 1879); Pinchot to James Pinchot, January 1, 1882; the Reverend Niles to Pinchot, March 21, 1882; Pinchot to James Pinchot, May 18, 1882; J. W. Davis to James Pinchot, September 12, 1883.

15. James Pinchot to Pinchot, February 17, 1882; Pinchot to Mary Pinchot, October 2, 1882.

16. Pinchot to Mary Pinchot, March 1, 1882; James Pinchot to Pinchot, April 24, 1882; James Pinchot to Pinchot, November 3, 1882, Pinchot to James Pinchot, December 3, 1882.

17. James Pinchot to Pinchot, December 12, 1882, January 10, 1883, April 20, 1883, May 17, 1883. For discussions of the Progressive Era's rhetorical emphases, see Gifford Pinchot, *The Fight for Conservation* (New York: Doubleday, Page, 1910); Robert Wiebe, *The Search for Order* (New York: Hill and Wang, 1967); Clayton Koppes, "Efficiency, Equity, Esthetics: Shifting Themes in American Conservation," in Donald Worster, ed., *The Ends of the Earth: Perspectives on Modern Environmental History* (Oxford: Oxford University Press, 1988); and Samuel Hays, *Conservation and the Gospel of Efficiency: The Progressive Conservation Movement, 1890–1920* (New York: Atheneum, 1969).

18. For a discussion of the cultural and medical foundations for Trudeau's theories, see Robert Taylor, *Saranac: America's Magic Mountain* (Boston: Houghton Mifflin, 1986), 1–65; David L. Ellison, *Healing Tuberculosis in the Woods: Medicine and Science at the End of the Nineteenth Century* (Westport, Conn.: Greenwood Press, 1994), 8–18; Georgina D. Feldberg, *Disease and Class: Tuberculosis and the Shaping of Modern North American Society* (New Brunswick: Rutgers University Press, 1995); Edward David Livingston Trudeau, M.D., *An Autobiography* (Garden City, N.Y.: Doubleday, Page & Co., 1916).

19. Pinchot to James Pinchot, January 8, 1884, January 13, 1884, January 18, 1884.

20. Pinchot to James Pinchot, February 24, 1884; Gifford Pinchot would spend the next year studying for the Yale examinations, including a summer session in New Haven, before officially entering the school in the fall of 1885.

21. Pinchot to James Pinchot, January 18, 1884; Pinchot to Mary Pinchot, Febru-

ary 12, 1884; Pinchot to James Pinchot, February 18, 1884; Pinchot to Mary Pinchot, February 12, 1884; see Jerry Hantover, "The Boy Scouts and the Validation of Masculinity," in Elizabeth H. Pleck and Joseph H. Pleck, *The American Man* (Englewood Cliffs, N.J.: Prentice-Hall, Inc., 1980), 285–301; Joe L. Dubbert, "Progressivism and the Masculinity Crisis," in Pleck and Pleck, *American Man,* 303–20; Pinchot to Mary Pinchot, February 24, 1884.

22. James Pinchot to Amos Pinchot, November 15, 1885; Mary Pinchot to James Pinchot, January 9, 1886.

23. George Wilson Pierson, *Yale College: An Educational History, 1871–1921* (New Haven: Yale University Press, 1952), 66–80; Brooks Mather Kelley, *Yale: A History* (New Haven: Yale University Press, 1974), 235–72; Noah Porter quoted in Stevenson, *Scholarly Means to Evangelical Ends,* 55.

24. Kelley, *Yale,* 270–74; Pierson, *Yale College,* 80–86.

25. Kelley, *Yale,* 273–97.

26. Pinchot, *Breaking New Ground,* 3; McGeary, *Gifford Pinchot: Forester-Politician,* 13.

27. Pinchot to James Pinchot, September 27, 1885; Pinchot to James Pinchot, June 10, 1885; James Pinchot to Pinchot, September 30, 1885; Dr. C. R. Agnew to Pinchot, October 19, 1885; Pinchot to Mary Pinchot, November 3, 1885; Pinchot to James Pinchot, December 11, 1885; Pinchot to Mary Pinchot, December 26, 1885.

28. Pinchot to Antoinette Pinchot Johnstone, June 22, 1934.

29. Pinchot to Theodore Roosevelt, November 22, 1904; *New York Times,* October 6, 1946, 56, corrected on October 10, 1946, 27.

30. Pinchot, *Breaking New Ground,* 1.

31. Pinchot to Mary Pinchot, February 22, 1886, September 26, 1886; James B. Reynolds to Pinchot, November 23, 1888; on the Northfield Conferences, see James B. Reynolds et al., eds., *Two Centuries of Christian Activity at Yale* (New York: G. Putnam's Sons, 1901), 241–51. Pinchot, *Breaking New Ground,* 71; Pinchot to Mary Pinchot, November 5, 1887; J. E. Donnelly to Pinchot, July 20, 1888; Pinchot to Mary Pinchot, October 9, 1888.

32. Pinchot to Mary Pinchot, October 9, 1889; Pinchot to James Pinchot, October 14, 1889; Pinchot, Diary, January 1889.

33. Pinchot, Diary, January 5, 1889; Bernhard Fernow to Pinchot, March 10, 1889; Pinchot, *Breaking New Ground,* 5.

34. Pinchot to James Pinchot, undated, 1889; internal evidence suggests the letter was written in the late spring; see also February 16, 1889.

35. On the Townsend Prize, see Amos Eno to Pinchot, May 29, 1889; the content of Pinchot's commencement speech is noted in Pinchot, *Breaking New Ground,* 6. Pinchot's prospects as a missionary or a forester may have been different, even dramatically so, but that the two occupations for him were on a par reinforces Charles Rosenberg's insight into the intersection of scientific and religious careers in the late nineteenth century: Rosenberg, *No Other Gods,* 3.

36. Mary Pinchot to James Pinchot, August 21, 1888; Pinchot, *Breaking New Ground,* 1–5. On Pinchot's childhood, see Char Miller, "The Greening of Gifford Pinchot," *Environmental History Review,* Fall 1992, 4–6; McGeary, *Gifford Pinchot: Forester-Politician,* 8–16; Gifford Pinchot, "An Address of Gifford Pinchot, Esq., Delivered at the Celebration on Center Square, August 28, 1889, to Commemorate the Second Centennial of the Republic," in *Milford Dispatch,* August 29, 1889; William Bross to Pinchot, September 9, 1889.

CHAPTER 4. AN AMERICAN IN NANCY

1. The Pinchot Scrapbooks are located in the Gifford Pinchot Papers, Library of Congress; see Gifford Pinchot, *Breaking New Ground* (New York: Harcourt Brace Jovanovich, 1947), passim; "Sketch of Gifford Pinchot," 2nd National Conservation Congress, September 1910, Box 19, File 1908–1910, Harry A. Slattery Papers, Special Collections Library, Duke University. The relationship between Pinchot's youthful enthusiasm and professional accomplishments also determines the narrative thrust of Dale White's juvenile biography, *Gifford Pinchot: The Man Who Saved the Forests* (New York: Julian Messner, 1957); on the role of scientific expertise during the late nineteenth and early twentieth century, see Samuel P. Hays, *Conservation and the Gospel of Efficiency: The Progressive Conservation Movement, 1890–1920* (New York: Atheneum, 1969), passim.

2. Gifford Pinchot, Diary, 1889–1890, 1–2.

3. Pinchot, Diary, 1889–1890, 3–10.

4. Pinchot, Diary, October 18, 1889; Pinchot to James Pinchot, October 18, 1889.

5. Pinchot, Diary, October 22, 1889.

6. Ibid.

7. Pinchot, Diary, October 22, 1889; Pinchot to Mary Pinchot, November 9, 1889.

8. Pinchot, Diary, October 25, 1889; John E. Findling and Kimberley D. Pelle, eds., *Historical Dictionary of World's Fairs and Expositions, 1851–1988* (Westport, Conn.: Greenwood Press, 1990), 108–16; Char Miller, "The Pivotal Decade: American Forestry in the 1870s," *Journal of Forestry,* November 2000, 6–10.

9. Pinchot, Diary, October 24, 1889.

10. Pinchot, Diary, October 24, 1889; inexplicably, M. Nelson McGeary wrote that Pinchot's diary was silent on his reactions to his visit to the Folies, when in fact it is quite explicit. McGeary, *Gifford Pinchot: Forester-Politician* (Princeton: Princeton University Press, 1960), 22; on the Brandis visit, see Pinchot to James Pinchot, October 30, 1889; Pinchot to parents, November 14, 1889.

11. Stephanie Pincetl, "Some Origins of French Environmentalism: An Exploration," *Forest & Conservation History,* April 1993, 80–85; Bernard Kalaora and Antoine Savoye, *La Forêt Pacifiée: Sylviculture et Sociologie au XIXe Siècle* (Paris: Editions L'Harmattan, 1986), 15–34.

12. Pinchot to Mary Pinchot, May 9, 1890; Pinchot, *Breaking New Ground,* 11.

13. Pinchot, Diary, May 14, 1890.

14. Pinchot, *Breaking New Ground,* 13.

15. James C. Scott, *Seeing like a State: How Certain Schemes to Improve the Human Condition Have Failed* (New Haven: Yale University Press, 1998), 11–22.

16. Ibid., 22. See also Gifford Pinchot, "Government Forestry Abroad," *Publications of the American Economic Association,* VI (May 1891), 191–238; Hays, *Conservation and the Gospel of Efficiency*; Pinchot to Mary Pinchot, February 12, 1890; Mary Pinchot to Pinchot, November, 1889; Pinchot to Mary Pinchot, February 12, 1890; James B. Reynolds to Pinchot, August 5, 1890.

17. Pinchot to parents, January 26, 1890.

18. Pinchot to parents, January 5, 1890; Pinchot to James Pinchot, March 2, 1890; Pinchot, "Sihlwald," *Garden and Forest,* July 30, 1890, 374; August 6, 1890, 386; August 13, 1890, 397; Pinchot, *Breaking New Ground,* 11, 15–19; Char Miller, "A High-Grade Paper: *Garden and Forest* and Nineteenth-Century American Forestry," *Arnoldia,* vol. 60, no. 2, 19–22.

19. Pinchot to Mary Pinchot, July 20, 1890; Pinchot to James Pinchot, March 2, 1890, July 20, 1890; James B. Reynolds to Pinchot, August 5, 1890; Pinchot, *Breaking New Ground,* 16–22.

20. Dietrich Brandis to Pinchot, November 19, 1889; Pinchot to Mary Pinchot, December 30, 1889, April 18, 1890; Pinchot, *Breaking New Ground,* 19–22.

21. Pinchot to Mary Pinchot, December 30, 1889, April 18, 1890.

22. Pinchot to Mary Pinchot, February 12, 1890; Pinchot to James Pinchot, February 18, 1890, April 28, 1890, May 6, 1890; Pinchot, *Breaking New Ground,* 19–22; Pinchot to Mary Pinchot, November 6, 1890; Pinchot, Diary, September 14, 1890; Pinchot to Mary Pinchot, November 23, 1890; Pinchot, "Government Forestry Abroad," 32–33, 37–38, 41.

23. Brandis to Pinchot, October 14, 1890; some weeks he received no less than nine letters from his family; Pinchot to Mary Pinchot, November 23, 1890.

24. Pinchot to Mary Pinchot, April 30, 1890; Pinchot to James Pinchot, August 3, 1890, in which he quotes extensively from Bernhard Fernow's letter; McGeary, *Gifford Pinchot: Forester-Politician,* 24–25.

25. Pinchot, Diary, August 1, 1890, notes that Charles S. Sargent indicated that the "general standing" of the Agriculture Department, Forestry Division, and Fernow "were not satisfactory"; Pinchot to James Pinchot, August 3, 1890; Pinchot to Mary Pinchot, August 4, 1890; James Pinchot to Pinchot, August 19, 1890, August 30, 1890; McGeary, *Gifford Pinchot: Forester-Politician,* 23–24.

26. Andrew Denny Rodgers, *Bernhard Eduard Fernow: A Story of North American Forestry* (Princeton: Princeton University Press, 1951), 14–18; Pinchot to James Pinchot, August 4, 1890; Pinchot to James Pinchot, November 9, 1890.

27. Charles S. Sargent to Pinchot, April 25, 1890, June 6, 1890; Pinchot to James Pinchot, May 11, 1890, May 18, 1890; James Pinchot to Mary Pinchot, June 5, 1890; Miller, "High-Grade Paper," 19–22; S. B. Sutton, *Charles S. Sargent and the Arnold Arboretum* (Cambridge: Harvard University Press, 1970), 131–33,

178, 224. Pinchot would build his career in forestry and politics on just such an insight into the press's role in shaping opinion: see Stephen Ponder, "Gifford Pinchot: Press Agent for Forestry," *Journal of Forest History,* January 1987, 26–35.

28. Pinchot, "Sihlwald," *Garden and Forest.* His articles in *G & F* generated enthusiastic responses, according to its publishers and editors: see W. A. Stiles to Pinchot, July 11, 1890, September 4, 1890; Charles S. Sargent to Pinchot, July 28, 1890; James B. Reynolds to Pinchot, August 5, 1890; James Pinchot to Mary Pinchot, June 5, 1890; Pinchot to James Pinchot, June 9, 1890. Pinchot earlier had proposed drawing upon another close family connection, Whitelaw Reed, whose *New York Tribune,* he thought, might also be interested in a set of articles on forestry's significance; Pinchot to Mary Pinchot, December 12, 1889; Pinchot to Mary Pinchot, April 30, 1890; Brandis to James Pinchot, March 20, 1890; Pinchot to James Pinchot, October 17, 1890.

29. Bernhard Fernow to Pinchot, October 30, 1890, December 5, 1890, May 18, 1890.

30. Pinchot to Mary Pinchot, November 23, 1890; Pinchot, "Government Forestry Abroad," 7–9.

31. Pinchot, "Government Forestry Abroad," 22–23.

32. Ibid., 32–33, 41.

33. Pinchot to James Pinchot, August 31, 1890; on the Adirondacks, see Sutton, *Charles S. Sargent,* 97–104; Philip Terrie, *Forever Wild: A Cultural History of Wilderness in the Adirondacks* (Philadelphia: Temple University Press, 1985); Frank Graham, Jr., *The Adirondack Park: A Political History* (New York: Knopf, 1978); Hays, *Conservation and the Gospel of Efficiency,* 191–92; Roderick Nash, *Wilderness and the American Mind* (New Haven: Yale University Press, 1967), 116–21; Charles Dudley Warner, *In the Wilderness* (Syracuse: Syracuse University Press, 1990).

34. Pinchot to Mary Pinchot, November 23, 1890.

35. Pinchot, Diary, December 20–23, 1890.

36. Pinchot, Diary, December 18–20, 1890; Bernhard E. Fernow, "Practicability of an American Forest Administration" (Baltimore: American Economic Association, 1891), 77–78, 90–92; Fernow to Pinchot, December 18, 1890.

37. Pinchot, Diary, December 30–31, 1890.

CHAPTER 5. THE DAMAGED FABRIC

1. Gifford Pinchot, *Breaking New Ground* (New York: Harcourt Brace Jovanovich, 1947), 40.

2. Gifford Pinchot, Diary, April 1891.

3. Pinchot, Diary, April 1891; Pinchot, *Breaking New Ground,* 40–42.

4. Pinchot, Diary, April 16–19, 1891.

5. Pinchot nowhere indicates that family ties were the source of his work for Phelps, Dodge in Arizona and earlier in Pennsylvania, but the link seems indisputable. The Phelps-Eno families had been in business and in bed

together for several generations. See chapter 1 for a discussion of these family ties. Pinchot, *Breaking New Ground,* 36–37, 40.

6. Pinchot, *Breaking New Ground,* 40–41, 43.

7. Pinchot, Diary, March 1891.

8. Pinchot, Diary, November 12, 1891; Pinchot, *Breaking New Ground,* 38–39.

9. Witold Rybczynski, *A Clearing in the Distance: Frederick Law Olmsted and America in the Nineteenth Century* (New York: Scribner, 1999); Laura Wood Roper, *FLO: A Biography of Frederick Law Olmsted* (Baltimore: Johns Hopkins University Press, 1973); and Norman T. Newton, *Design on the Land: The Development of Landscape Architecture* (Cambridge: Harvard University Press, 1971), detail Olmsted's storied career; Frederick Law Olmsted, "Park," in Charles E. Beveridge and David Schuyler, eds., *Creating Central Park, 1857–1861,* vol. 7 of *The Papers of Frederick Law Olmsted* (Baltimore: Johns Hopkins University Press, 1983), 354–55. For a fine discussion of Olmsted's aesthetic, see Anne Whiston Spirn, "Constructing Nature: The Legacy of Frederick Law Olmsted," in William B. Cronon, ed., *Uncommon Ground* (New York: Norton, 1995), 91–113. Her chapter concludes with an insight that is relevant to Pinchot's work at Biltmore and beyond: "There is always a tension in landscape between the reality and autonomy of the nonhuman and its cultural construction, between the human impulse to wonder at the wild and the compulsion to use, manage, and control," 113.

10. Rybcynski, *Clearing in the Distance,* 380–84, 400–405; Roper, *FLO,* 410; Spirn, "Constructing Nature," 91–113. For a thick description of the rapid deforestation of sections of the American landscape, see Gordon G. Whitney, *From Coastal Wilderness to Fruited Plain: A History of Environmental Change in Temperate North America from 1500 to the Present* (New York: Cambridge University Press, 1996), 131–226.

11. Roper, *FLO,* 416–17; Newton, *Design on the Land,* 346–51; Frederick Gutheim, "Olmsted at Biltmore," in Dana F. White and Victor A. Kramer, *Olmsted South: Old South Critic/New South Planner* (Westport, Conn.: Greenwood Press, 1979), 239–46.

12. Roper, *FLO*; Gutheim, "Olmsted at Biltmore," 242.

13. Gifford Pinchot, *Biltmore Forest* (Chicago: R. R. Donnelley & Sons, 1893); Pinchot, *Breaking New Ground,* 47–69; Harold T. Pinkett, *Gifford Pinchot: Private and Public Forester* (Urbana: University of Illinois Press, 1970), 23.

14. Pinchot to Dietrich Brandis, March 5, 1892.

15. William B. Cronon, *Changes in the Land: Indians, Colonists, and the Ecology of New England* (New York: Hill & Wang, 1983), 108–26.

16. John Reiger, *American Sportsmen and the Origins of Conservation,* third edition (Corvallis: Oregon State University Press, 2000), 88–91.

17. Henry S. Graves, "Background of a New Profession," quoted in Henry Clepper, *Professional Forestry in the United States* (Baltimore: Johns Hopkins University Press, 1971), 16.

18. Bernhard E. Fernow to Pinchot, January 20, 1892; Pinchot to Fernow, January 31, 1892; Fernow to Pinchot, February 2, 1892.

19. Pinchot to Fernow, July 17, 1893; Fernow to Pinchot, July 20, 1893; Andrew Denny Rodgers III, *Bernhard Eduard Fernow: A Story of North American Forestry* (Princeton: Princeton University Press, 1951), 166–69; Reiger, *American Sportsmen,* 90.

20. James Pinchot's close relationship with various artists emerges in his correspondence in the Gifford Pinchot collection at the Library of Congress and in Anthony F. Janson, *Worthington Whittredge* (Cambridge: Cambridge University Press, 1989), 132–33, 154–56, passim; Ila Weiss, *Poetic Landscape: The Art and Experience of Sanford R. Gifford* (Newark: University of Delaware Press, 1987), 105, 147–48, 153.

21. Weiss, *Poetic Landscape,* 259–60; Janson, *Whittredge,* 81–90; Barbara Novack, "The Double-Edged Axe," *Art in America,* January–February, 1976, 44–50; Nicolai Cikovsky, Jr., "'The Ravages of the Axe': The Meaning of the Stump in Nineteenth-Century American Art," *Art Bulletin,* December 1979, 610–26.

22. Samuel Avery to James Pinchot, December 25 [n.d.], quoted in Carol Severance, "The American Art Collection of James W. Pinchot, 1831–1908" (M.A. thesis, Cooperstown Graduate Program, 1993), 117

23. "Terrible beauty" quote in *American Paradise* (New York: Metropolitan Museum of Art, 1987), 231; Donald Worster, *Nature's Economy: The Roots of Ecology* (San Francisco: Sierra Books, 1977), 266–69.

24. More than forty years before Aldo and Estella Leopold (and their children) began to restore their Sand County farm in Wisconsin, the Pinchots were engaged in a massive restoration project on their cutover estate. Leopold would have been familiar with their efforts because he attended the Yale School of Forestry's summer camp at Grey Towers; one aspect of whose teaching was to apply land management techniques to continue the restorative process that James and Mary Pinchot had initiated in the late 1880s. Aldo Leopold, *A Sand County Almanac* (New York: Oxford University Press, 1968), 3–92; Curt Meine, *Aldo Leopold: His Life and Work* (Madison: University of Wisconsin Press, 1988), 71–83.

25. I am grateful to Carol Severance of Grey Towers National Historic Landmark, Milford, Pa., for her insights into the relationship between the river and the homestead. Succeeding generations of the Pinchot family have been in the forefront of efforts in Milford to fight off development schemes along the Sawkill's watershed and thus to preserve it as a wild river.

26. Spirn, "Constructing Nature," 100–102.

27. Pinchot to Brandis, August 21, 1893; Pinchot, *Breaking New Ground,* 53.

28. Pinchot, *Biltmore Forest*; Fernow to Pinchot, July 9, 1894.

29. Gifford Pinchot, "Forestry and the Woodlot," *Garden and Forest,* March 2, 1892, 104–5; Pinchot, *Biltmore Forest.*

30. Robert Wolf, "National Forest Timber Sales and the Legacy of Gifford Pin-

chot: Managing a Forest and Making It Pay," in Char Miller, ed., *American Forests: Nature, Culture, and Politics* (Lawrence: University Press of Kansas, 1997), 87–108, argues that Pinchot and his successors at the Forest Service have never managed to make the national forests pay; see, too, William E. Shands and Thomas E. Waddell, *Below-Cost Timber Sales in the Broad Context of National Forest Management* (Washington, D.C.: The Conservation Foundation, 1988). For a fuller discussion of this complex issue, see Paul Hirt, *A Conspiracy of Optimism: The Management of the National Forests Since World War Two* (Lincoln: University of Nebraska Press); making similar arguments is Brian Balough, "Scientific Forestry and the Roots of the Modern American State: Gifford Pinchot's Path to Progressive Reform," presented to the American Society for Environmental History Meeting, April 2001.

31. Carl Schenck, *Birth of Forestry in America: Biltmore Forest School, 1898–1913* (Santa Cruz, Calif.: Forest History Society, 1955), 19–21; Pinchot, *Breaking New Ground,* 65.

32. Pinchot to parents, August 26, 1892; Pinchot to James Pinchot, September 8, 1892, September 18, 1892; Pinchot, *Breaking New Ground,* 66–67; Pinchot to Beatrix Jones, September 12, 1892.

33. Schenck, *Birth of Forestry in America,* 8–26; Pinchot, *Breaking New Ground,* 65–66.

34. Schenck, *Birth of Forestry in America,* 27–30.

35. Ibid., 40–41.

36. Ibid., 51–52.

37. Ibid., 53–54.

38. Pinchot, *Breaking New Ground,* 68.

39. Ibid., 65–67.

40. Schenck, *Birth of Forestry in America,* 167–200; Char Miller and James G. Lewis, "A Contested Past: Forestry Education in the United States, 1898–1998," *Journal of Forestry,* September 1999, 38–41.

41. Pinchot to Mr. Wetmore, March 21, 1893.

42. Pinchot, Diary, April 1–5, 1937; *Breaking New Ground,* 69, 28.

CHAPTER 6. A POLITICAL TWO-STEP

1. Although Linnie Marsh Wolfe does not date the episode, a remarkable lacuna that has led subsequent historians to select various dates for when it might have occurred, it is clear from Pinchot's diary that he met John Muir in the lobby on September 6, 1897. But that is all the diary confirms. Gifford Pinchot, *Breaking New Ground* (New York: Harcourt Brace Jovanovich, 1947), 122–32; Gifford Pinchot, Diary, 1897, reel 1; on Pinchot's public relations campaign, see Stephen Ponder, "Gifford Pinchot: Press Agent for Forestry," *Journal of Forest History,* January 1987, 26–35.

2. Pinchot, Diary, September 5, 1897; Pinchot, *Breaking New Ground,* 122–32; Stephen Ponder, "Conservation, Community Economics, and Newspaper-

ing: The Seattle Press and the Forest Reserves Controversy of 1897," *American Journalism,* 1986, 50–60, analyzes the decided impact Pinchot's visit had on public opinion in Seattle.

3. Pinchot, Diary, September 5, 1897; Pinchot, *Breaking New Ground,* 103. On the National Forest Commission, see Michael Cohen, *The Pathless Way: John Muir and American Wilderness* (Madison: University of Wisconsin Press, 1984); Linnie Marsh Wolfe, *Son of the Wilderness: The Life of John Muir* (New York: Knopf, 1945); Roderick Nash, *Wilderness and the American Mind* (New Haven: Yale University Press, 1982).

4. Pinchot, *Breaking New Ground,* 103; Wolfe, *Son of the Wilderness,* 275–76, recounts the hotel lobby denunciation.

5. Wolfe, *Son of the Wilderness,* 275–76. Elements of this story are replicated in Thurman Wilkins, *John Muir: Apostle of Nature* (Norman: University of Oklahoma Press, 1995), 201–2; Michael L. Smith, *Pacific Visions: California Scientists and the Environment, 1850–1915* (New Haven· Yale University Press, 1987), 163; Frederick Turner, *Rediscovering America: John Muir in His Time and Ours* (New York. Viking Press, 1985), 312; Jim Dale Vickery, *Wilderness Visionaries* (Merrillville, Ind.: ICS Books, 1986), 88–91; Lawrence Rakestraw, "Sheep Grazing in the Cascade Range: John Minto vs. John Muir," *Pacific Historical Review* (November 1958), 371–82, employs the story, too, but dates it three years later. See Char Miller, "What Happened in the Rainier Grand's Lobby? A Question of Sources," *Journal of American History,* March 2000, 1,709–1,916.

6. Pinchot, Diary, 5 September 1897.

7. The entries to Pinchot's diaries for September 6, when the incident was supposed to have taken place, do not corroborate Marsh's account but are instead positively banal. Pinchot ran errands in the morning, which included getting a medical checkup and having his outfit repaired, all in preparation for his departure from Seattle on a four o'clock train heading east. Surely he would have penciled in such a momentous confrontation as Marsh describes, especially given the fact that he had been so careful to record his extensive and happy interactions with Muir on the previous day. He was, moreover, a man who regularly used his diary as a way of venting his grievances and settling scores. That he did not do so in this case suggests that there may not have been a score to settle; a close reading of the Seattle newspapers for the days in and around the supposed event uncover no discussion of a conflict in the hotel's lobby.

8. Cornelius Bliss was the secretary of the interior. In none of the three oral histories compiled with William E. Colby and located in the Bancroft Library, University of California, Berkeley, is the Seattle hotel incident recalled. This does not mean that it did not happen, of course, but is suggestive of the tale's apocryphal character; John Muir to Pinchot, December 16, 1897. Muir to Robert Underwood Johnson, August 3, 1898, John Muir Papers, Bancroft Library, University of California, Berkeley, supports the notion that Muir

knew Pinchot's support of grazing was qualified in important ways and was not in the same category as Binger Hermann's.

9. Pinchot, *Breaking New Ground,* 177–80. Turner, *Rediscovering America,* 312, also notes the complexity of Pinchot's position on the question of grazing in the forest reserves. Muir and Pinchot spent five days together in August 1899, among other things studying sheep devastation in northern California; see Pinchot, Diary, August 8–12, 1899. John Muir, "The Wild Parks and Forest Reservations of the West," in Muir, *Our National Parks* (Boston: Houghton Mifflin, 1909), 33, provides a concise view of his reaction to sheep and shepherds in the Sierra Reserve: "sheep in uncountable hordes . . . trample it and devour every green leaf within reach; while the shepherds, like destroying angels, set innumerable fires, which burn not only the undergrowth of seedlings on which the permanence of the forest depends, but countless thousands of the venerable giants." Like Muir, Pinchot "never did love a sheepherder." Pinchot, *Breaking New Ground,* 178.

10. M. Nelson McGeary, *Gifford Pinchot: Forester-Politician* (Princeton: Princeton University Press, 1960); Harold T. Pinkett, *Gifford Pinchot: Private and Public Forester* (Urbana: University of Illinois Press, 1970); Barry Walsh, "Gifford Pinchot, Conservationist," *Theodore Roosevelt Association Journal,* Summer 1987, 3–7; Henry Clepper, *Professional Forestry in the United States* (Baltimore: Johns Hopkins University Press, 1971).

11. Cohen, *Pathless Way,* xiii. Stephen Fox reveals that he chose to write about Muir because he "noticed that of the early pioneers of the conservation movement, only one—John Muir of the Sierra Club—still seemed an active force in the movement today"; Fox, *American Conservation Movement: John Muir and His Legacy* (Madison: University of Wisconsin Press, 1985), ix.

12. McGeary, *Gifford Pinchot: Forester-Politician*; Pinkett, *Gifford Pinchot: Private and Public Forester*; Walsh, "Gifford Pinchot," *Theodore Roosevelt Association Journal,* 3–7; Clepper, *Professional Forestry.* Two articles that explore the evolution of the relationship between the Forest Service and the Park Service are Susan Schrepfer, "Establishing Administrative 'Standing': The Sierra Club and the Forest Service, 1897–1956," in Char Miller, ed., *American Forests: Nature, Culture and Politics* (Lawrence: University Press of Kansas, 1997), 125–42; Hal K. Rothman, "'A Regular Ding-Dong Fight': The Dynamics of Park Service–Forest Service Controversy During the 1920s and 1930s," in Miller, ed., *American Forests,* 109–24.

13. On Pinchot's public relations campaigns, see Steven Ponder: "Federal News Management in the Progressive Era: Gifford Pinchot and the Conservation Campaign," *Journalism History,* Summer 1986, 42–48; "Conservation, Community Economics, and Newspapering, *American Journalism,* 1986, 50–60; "Gifford Pinchot," *Journal of Forest History,* 26–35. Discussions of Muir's public relations campaigns are found in Cohen, *Pathless Way,* and Fox, *American Conservation Movement.* The biographer's craft depends on empathy, on trying to get inside one's subject so as to bring her or him to life. That this

might lead to the taking of sides, to adopting the world view of one's subject, is not a shock, as this book itself testifies.

14. Cohen, *Pathless Way,* 320.

15. Pinchot to Fritz-Greene Halleck, October 26, 1892; Pinchot, *Breaking New Ground,* 74.

16. Cohen, *Pathless Way,* 320; William Badé, *Life and Letters of John Muir,* vol. 2, 265.

17. John Muir to Louise Muir, June 13, 1893, in Badé, *Life and Letters of John Muir,* vol. 2, 265–66, recounts Muir's whirlwind social life in New York that June.

18. Ibid.; Ronald H. Limbaugh, *John Muir's 'Stickeen' and the Lessons of Nature* (Fairbanks: University of Alaska Press, 1996).

19. Muir to Pinchot, April 16, 1894; Pinchot to Muir, June 19, 1893, September 17, 1893.

20. Muir to Pinchot, April 16, 1894; Pinchot to Muir, September 13, 1893; *Boston Herald,* March 20, 1891, Pinchot Scrapbooks, reel 1, 5. The *New York World* weighed in similarly: "It is a good sign," it wrote of Pinchot's budding career, "when men of means and position throw themselves so completely into a profession that is more likely to bring them fame than ducats": February 10, 1895, Pinchot Scrapbooks, reel 1, 12.

21. Pinchot to Muir, September 13, 1893; Pinchot to Muir, April 8, 1894; Pinchot to Muir, May 23, 1894.

22. Muir to Pinchot, April 16, 1894.

23. Pinchot to parents, July 20, 1896; Pinchot, *Breaking New Ground,* 101–2.

24. Cohen, *Pathless Way,* 317–20; Smith, *Pacific Visions,* 159–61.

25. Pinchot to Dietrich Brandis, May 20, 1896.

26. Brandis to Pinchot, June 12, 1896.

27. Pinchot to parents, July 20, 1896; Wilkins, *John Muir,* 190–96; Smith, *Pacific Visions,* 160–61; Pinchot, Diary, August 26, 1896.

28. Muir to Pinchot, July 26, 1896; James Pinchot to Pinchot, August 9, 1896; Pinchot to Muir, July 23, 1896.

29. Linnie Marsh Wolfe, *John of the Mountains: The Unpublished Journals of John Muir* (Madison: University of Wisconsin Press, 1979), 357.

30. Ibid., 363; Pinchot to Muir, October 21, 1896; Muir to Pinchot, October 28, 1896; Pinchot, *Breaking New Ground,* 100–103.

31. Pinchot, *Breaking New Ground,* 100–103; Muir to Pinchot, October 28, 1896, December 17, 1897.

32. Pinchot to Muir, July 2, 1897; Muir to Pinchot, July 8, 1897. Several months later, Muir apparently changed his mind about the value of Pinchot's new job; Muir to Charles S. Sargent, October 28, 1897.

33. Pinchot to James Pinchot, July 6, 1897; Muir to Pinchot, December 16, 1897.

34. Muir to Pinchot, July 8, 1897; Pinchot to Muir, December 9, 1896, July 2, 1897; Pinchot, Diary, March 21–22, 1897; Pinchot was the only member to vote against Sargent's proposal; Arnold Hague, who supported Pinchot's position, "did not vote."

35. Pinchot, Diary, August 8–12, 1899; Pinchot to Muir, August 20, 1899; Pinchot to Muir, February 2, 1900; Muir to R. U. Johnson, August 16, 1899; Pinchot, *Breaking New Ground*, 170–71. The essays in Muir's *Our National Parks* (1909) particularly speak to his belief in the health-giving qualities of forests, a perspective with which Pinchot also had grown up.

36. Pinchot, *Breaking New Ground*, 119–22; Cohen, *Pathless Way*, 292–94; Fox, *American Conservation Movement*, 112–15; Pinchot to Muir, October 21, 1896.

37. Pinchot, Diary, October–December 1896; Pinchot, *Breaking New Ground*, 105–6; Sargent to Muir, May 3, 1897.

38. John Muir, "A Plan to Save the Forests," *Century*, February 1895; John Muir, "The American Forests," 336–42, and "The Wild Parks and Forest Reservations of the West," 1–36, in *Our National Parks*, also speak to the productive use of forests, use that was in line with Pinchot's understanding of that term; Cohen, *Pathless Way*, 297–301.

39. Ibid.

40. Roderick Nash, *Wilderness and the American Mind*, chapter 10; Smith, *Pacific Visions*, 159–66; Muir to R. U. Johnson, March 23, 1905.

41. Pinchot to William E. Colby, February 17, 1905, Robert Underwood Johnson Papers, Bancroft Library, University of California, Berkeley. Pinchot sent a copy of this letter to Muir as a concise statement of his views; Muir to Pinchot, May 27, 1905. It is, at least, the last letter in Pinchot's files; for ongoing discussions of this issue and Pinchot's attempts to secure better information about the valley, and to reexamine his arguments, see Pinchot to Norman Hapgood, April 30, 1908; Pinchot to Frederick Bade, May 11, 1908; Bade to Pinchot, October 1908; Pinchot to Marsden Manson, May 15, 1909; Marsden Manson to Pinchot, May 22, 1909; J. Horace McFarland to Pinchot, May 19, 1909; Pinchot to McFarland, May 21, 1909; Pinchot to McFarland, December 16, 1909; McFarland to Pinchot, December 18, 1909; all in Records Group 95, Entry 22, Box 4, National Archives.

42. Nash, *Wilderness and the American Mind*, chapter 10; Smith, *Pacific Visions*, 159–66; copies of Pinchot to Marsden Manson, May 28, 1906, and November 15, 1906, are located in Robert Underwood Johnson Papers, Bancroft Library, University of California, Berkeley; they are also cited in *The Independent*, August 8, 1910, 375–76; see also Terry Gifford, ed., *John Muir: His Life and Letters and Other Writings* (Seattle: The Mountaineers, 1997), 377–80.

43. Muir to James Garfield, September 6, 1907, John Muir Papers, Bancroft Library, University of California, Berkeley; Pinchot, who visited Muir during a break in the 1907 Irrigation Conference in Sacramento, hoped to return to discuss Hetch Hetchy in detail with Muir, but was unable to do so due to the "press of work": Pinchot to Muir, September 6, 1907; Pinchot to Roosevelt, October 11, 1907, quoted in Nash, *Wilderness and the American Mind*, 164.

44. Pinchot to Frederick Perry Noble, September 18, 1913, Robert Underwood Johnson Papers, Bancroft Library, University of California, Berkeley; Nash, *Wilderness and the American Mind*, 170–71.

45. Muir to Robert Underwood Johnson, September 11, 1913, September 3, 1910, Robert Underwood Johnson Papers, Bancroft Library, University of California, Berkeley.

46. Bernhard Fernow to Pinchot, July 15, 1890, September 19, 1890; Pinchot, Diary, February–March 1891; McGeary, *Gifford Pinchot: Forester-Politician,* 21–26.

47. Fernow to Pinchot, February 2, 1892; Pinchot to Maurice Hutton, February 23, 1907; Muir to Pinchot, October 28, 1896; Pinchot to Muir, October 21, 1896, December 9, 1896; McGeary, *Gifford Pinchot: Forester-Politician,* 25–27.

48. Pinchot, *Breaking New Ground,* 130–31; McGeary, *Gifford Pinchot: Forester-Politician,* 37–43.

49. Sargent to Muir, June 27, 1898, John Muir Papers, Bancroft Library, University of California, Berkeley; Sargent to Muir, quoted in Turner, *Rediscovering America,* 325.

50. Robert Underwood Johnson, *Remembered Yesterdays* (Boston: Little, Brown, & Co., 1923), 304–5.

CHAPTER 7. KEEPER OF HIS CONSCIENCE?

1. Gifford Pinchot, Diary, December 26, 1898, February 4–10, 1899; Gifford Pinchot, *Breaking New Ground* (New York: Harcourt Brace Jovanovich, 1947), 144–46.

2. Ibid.

3. Ibid.; nineteen months later, while hiking on Mount Marcy in September 1901, Roosevelt learned that President McKinley was dying; Stephen Fox, *The American Conservation Movement: John Muir and His Legacy* (Madison: University of Wisconsin Press, 1985), 124.

4. Kathleen Dalton, "Why America Loved Teddy Roosevelt: Or, Charisma Is in the Eyes of the Beholders," in Robert J. Brugger, ed., *Our Selves/Our Past: Psychological Approaches to American History* (Baltimore: Johns Hopkins University Press, 1981), 269–91; Roosevelt to Pinchot, March 2, 1909, in Etling Morison, ed., *The Letters of Theodore Roosevelt* (Cambridge: Harvard University Press, 1954), vol. 6, 1,541 (hereafter cited as *Letters*); Roosevelt to Kermit Roosevelt, February 10, 1904, in *Letters,* vol. 4, 724; M. Nelson McGeary, *Gifford Pinchot: Forester-Politician* (Princeton: Princeton University Press, 1960), 65–67.

5. McGeary, *Gifford Pinchot: Forester-Politician*; Pinchot, *Breaking New Ground*; Robert Underwood Johnson, *Remembered Yesterdays* (Boston: Little, Brown, & Co., 1923), 310; Samuel Hays, *Conservation and the Gospel of Efficiency: The Progressive Conservation Movement, 1890–1920* (Cambridge: Harvard University Press, 1959), and Clayton R. Koppes, "Efficiency, Equity, Esthetics: Shifting Themes in American Conservation," in Donald Worster, ed., *The Ends of the Earth: Perspectives on Modern Environmental History* (Oxford: Oxford University Press, 1988), 230–51.

6. Henry F. Pringle, *Theodore Roosevelt: A Biography* (New York: Harcourt

Brace Jovanovich, 1984), 303; Theodore Roosevelt, *An Autobiography* (New York: The MacMillan Co., 1913), 313, 428–30, addresses the question of Pinchot's influence on the president's policies, as does Robert Underwood Johnson, *Remembered Yesterdays*; Lewis L. Gould, *The Presidency of Theodore Roosevelt* (Lawrence: University Press of Kansas), 40–41, 199–201. More-negative reflections of that influence appear in Fox, *American Conservation Movement*, 130; Michael Cohen, *The Pathless Way: John Muir and American Wilderness* (Madison: University of Wisconsin Press, 1984), 296–97, 323–29; Linnie Marsh Wolfe, *Son of the Wilderness: The Life of John Muir* (New York: Knopf, 1945), 275–76, 311–14. Pinchot biographers, for their part, stress the close ties between the president and the forester to burnish the latter's luster: McGeary, *Gifford Pinchot: Forester-Politician,* 56–57, 65–67, 109; Harold T. Pinkett, *Gifford Pinchot: Private and Public Forester* (Urbana: University of Illinois Press, 1970), 53–55; Harold K. Steen, *The U.S. Forest Service* (Seattle: University of Washington Press, 1970), 69–100.

7. Joseph Nimmo, *Report in Regard to the Range and Ranch Cattle Business of the United States* (New York: Arno Press, 1972), 46–55.

8. Nimmo, *Report,* 46–55. He noted, however, that long-term leases were not in the public interest: it would be better if these "lands now held by the Government shall be dedicated to the rearing of men rather than the rearing of cattle," 48.

9. William D. Rowley, *U.S. Forest Service Grazing and Rangelands: A History* (College Station: Texas A&M University Press, 1985), 3–21; National Academy of Sciences 1896 report quoted in Henry Clepper, *Professional Forestry in the United States* (Baltimore: Johns Hopkins University Press, 1971), 74.

10. Gifford Pinchot, *A Primer of Forestry, Part 1 — The Forest* (Washington, D.C.: Government Printing Office, 1899), 69–73; Gifford Pinchot, "Grazing in the Forest Reserves," *The Forester,* November 1901, 276–80; "Alarming Forest Conditions in Colorado," *The Forester,* November 1901, 280; Gifford Pinchot, *The Use of the National Forests* (Washington, D.C.: U.S. Department of Agriculture, 1907), 12–13, 21–23.

11. Christopher McGrory Klyza, *Who Controls the Public Lands? Mining, Forestry, and Grazing, 1870–1990* (Chapel Hill: University of North Carolina Press, 1996), analyzes the development of conservation and land management policies in the federal context; see also Bob Pepperman Taylor, *Our Limits Transgressed: Environmental Political Thought in America* (Lawrence: University of Kansas Press, 1992); Mark Stoll, *Protestantism, Capitalism, and Nature in America* (Albuquerque: University of New Mexico Press, 1997), 141–69; Clepper, *Professional Forestry,* 69–81; Elmo Richardson, *The Politics of Conservation* (Millwood, N.Y.: Kraus Reprint, 1980), 17–46. Pinchot's take on this development is articulated in his *The Fight for Conservation* (New York: Doubleday, Page & Co., 1910), 79.

12. Pinchot, *Breaking New Ground,* 319–26.

13. Ibid.; the "greatest good" concept is imbedded in the 1905 letter to Pinchot

from James Wilson, secretary of agriculture, in which the mission of the new Forest Service is outlined, a letter that Pinchot ghostwrote; *Breaking New Ground,* 261–62; Hays, *Conservation and the Gospel of Efficiency,* 122–46; Taylor, *Our Limits Transgressed,* 14–27.

14. Pinchot, *Breaking New Ground,* 319–26. As Taylor observes, "Pinchot's optimistic views about the abundance of natural resources provided him with a link between scientific management and democratic politics. Not only would public management produce the necessary material basis for a democratic society, but it would actually promote democratic values by setting an example of patriotic public service": *Our Limits Transgressed,* 27.

15. Pinchot, *Breaking New Ground,* 133–76.

16. E. T. Allen to Henry Graves, July 13, 1900, quoted in Steen, *U.S. Forest Service,* 61–62.

17. Pinchot, *Use of the National Forests,* 33–34; Pinchot, *Breaking New Ground,* 147–53; Steen, *U.S. Forest Service,* 63–64.

18. Pinchot, *Use of the National Forests,* 26; Hal K. Rothman, "'A Regular Ding-Dong Fight': The Dynamics of Park Service–Forest Service Controversy During the 1920s and 1930s," in Char Miller, ed., *American Forests: Nature, Culture, and Politics* (Lawrence: University Press of Kansas, 1997), 109–12; Steen, *U.S. Forest Service,* 77–78, 122–29. On the Weeks Law, see William E. Shands and Robert G. Healy, *The Lands Nobody Wanted: Policy for National Forests in the Eastern United States* (Washington, D.C.: The Conservation Foundation, 1977).

19. Lawrence Rakestraw, ed., "Gifford Pinchot, Agnes V. Scannell, and the Early Days of the U.S. Forest Service," *Oregon Historical Quarterly,* Spring 1991, 60–75; Harold T. Pinkett, "The Forest Service: Trail Blazer in Record-Keeping Methods," *American Archivist,* October 1959, 419–26.

20. Steen, *U.S. Forest Service,* 77.

21. Pinkett, *Gifford Pinchot: Private and Public Forester,* 81–86; Stephen Ponder, "Gifford Pinchot: Press Agent for Forestry," *Journal of Forest History,* January 1987, 26–35. Under its first director, Stephen Mather, the Park Service was just as relentless in its pursuit of publicity and popular support through the use of new media; see Rothman, "'A Regular Ding-Dong Fight,'" 112–15.

22. Stewart Udall, *The Quiet Crisis* (New York: Holt, Rinehart and Winston, 1963), 103–4. Udall was also sharply critical of what he believed were Pinchot's philosophical shortcomings: "He always had a blind spot to wildlife and wilderness values," 108.

23. "Philip Wells in the Forest Service Law Office," *Forest History,* April 1972, 23.

24. The Supreme Court rulings are quoted in Clepper, *Professional Forestry,* 80–81, 70–71; and in Harold K. Steen, *U.S. Forest Service,* 86–89.

25. Rowley, *U.S. Forest Service Grazing and Rangelands,* 3–54; Thomas Alexander, "From Rule of Thumb to Scientific Range Management," in Char Miller, ed., *American Forests: Nature, Culture, and Politics* (Lawrence: University Press of Kansas, 1997), 179–94; Clepper, *Professional Forestry,* 69–81.

26. Hamlin Garland, *Cavanagh: Forest Ranger* (New York: Harper & Brothers Publishers, 1910), 201; Garland, "My Aim in Cavanagh," *World's Work*, October 1910, 135–69.

27. G. Michael McCarthy, *Hour of Trial: The Conservation Conflict in Colorado and the West, 1891–1907* (Norman: University of Oklahoma Press, 1977), 200–210, passim, offers the fullest account of the ensuing battle between regional interests and federal power; also persuasive is Richardson, *Politics of Conservation*, 17–46.

28. Pinchot, *Breaking New Ground*, 299–300.

29. In two letters of the same date—Theodore Roosevelt to Pinchot, February 9, 1907, Theodore Roosevelt Papers, Library of Congress—Roosevelt indicates that he and Pinchot, whatever their later bravado, were acutely aware of the political risks of their actions. Responding to telegrams sent from and speeches delivered in the West, Roosevelt noted, "[W]e must be careful that we do not invite a reaction by going too far in the creation of the new reserves." In the other letter, he similarly expressed their shared concern: "We have gone ahead very fast indeed, and I think it extremely important that we should not do more than we can stand." Pinchot, *Breaking New Ground*, 299–302; McCarthy, *Hour of Trial*, 200–210.

30. *Glenwood Avalanche-Echo*, June 12, 1907, quoted in McCarthy, *Hour of Trial*, 177; "Czar Pinchot" cartoon, *Rocky Mountain News*, September 20, 1908; Richardson, *Politics of Conservation*, 35–40.

31. Pinchot, Diary, March–July 1907, tracks his interviews with various western leaders and his evaluation of the relative seriousness of their protests; McCarthy, *Hour of Trial*, 221–26.

32. Pinchot's speech in Denver was reprinted in the *Idaho Daily Statesman*, June 21, 1907.

33. Quoted in Richardson, *Politics of Conservation*, 39.

34. *Idaho Daily Statesman*, June 21, 1907; Pinchot, "Grazing in the Forest Reserves," 276.

35. Pinchot, *Use of the National Forests*, 25.

36. *Idaho Daily Statesman*, June 21, 1907. In an earlier article, "Grazing in the Forest Reserves," 276–80, Pinchot argued further that the deep-seated antagonisms between interest groups vying for limited grazing land on public lands forced the Forest Service, in the guise of its local forest rangers, to adjudicate between these competing forces. To facilitate the rangers' task of resolving these vexing disputes, Pinchot advocated a ranger-mediated policy of consensus building in which all groups and interests recognized at the outset that they would not—because the conditions of the land would not allow them to—obtain all that they might hope to secure; see also Pinchot, *Fight for Conservation*, passim, and Rowley, *Grazing and Rangelands*, 44–47.

37. Hays, *Conservation and the Gospel of Efficiency*, 192–96; Roderick Nash, *Wilderness and the American Mind* (New Haven: Yale University Press, 1967), 161–81; Fox, *American Conservation Movement*, 139–47; Mark Stoll, *Protes-*

tantism, Capitalism, and Nature in America (Albuquerque: University of New Mexico Press, 1997), 159–69; Kendrick A. Clemens, "Politics and the Park: San Francisco's Fight for Hetch Hetchy, 1908–1913," *Pacific Historical Review,* May 1979, 185–215; Taylor, *Our Limits Transgressed,* 82–88; *The Wilderness Idea,* Florentine Films, 1989. James G. Lewis, "History, Lies, and Videotape: Historical Documentaries in the Classroom," *OAH Council of Chairs Newsletter,* April and June 1997, 1–5, offers critical commentary on the film and its presentation of the debate over Hetch Hetchy.

38. The sheer size of Roosevelt's conservation-oriented achievements remains profound—so much so that President Bill Clinton's secretary of the interior, Bruce Babbitt, apparently used Roosevelt's impressive achievements to shame his boss into developing a more robust environmental record; Paul Larmer, "Mr. Babbitt's Wild Ride," *High Country News,* February 12, 2001, 1; see also "Interior View: Bruce Babbitt Took the Real West to Washington," *High Country News,* February 12, 2001, 8–11, and Char Miller, "It's the Environment, Stupid," *Trinitonian,* March 1, 2000, 11; Nash, *Wilderness and the American Mind,* 162–64; Paul R. Cutright, *Theodore Roosevelt: The Making of a Conservationist* (Urbana: University of Illinois Press, 1985), 210–27; Gould, *Presidency of Theodore Roosevelt,* 200–202.

39. Roosevelt to John Muir, and Roosevelt to John Burroughs, quoted in Cutright, *Roosevelt: The Making of a Conservationist,* 249; Fox, *American Conservation Movement,* 124–27.

40. Muir quoted in Fox, *American Conservation Movement,* 126.

41. Roosevelt to Robert Underwood Johnson, January 17, 1905, *Letters,* vol. 4, 1,104.

42. Pinchot to Roosevelt, October 11, 1907, quoted in Nash, *Wilderness and the American Mind,* 164.

43. Roosevelt to John Muir, September 16, 1907, *Letters,* vol. 5, 793; the indefiniteness to which the president referred carried on after he left office. See Pinchot to Norman Hapgood, April 30, 1908; Pinchot to Marsden Manson, May 15, 1909; Pinchot to Horace McFarland, May 21, 1909; Pinchot to Manson, December 16, 1909; all in Records Group 95, Entry 22, Box 4, National Archives.

44. Roosevelt to Muir, September 16, 1907, *Letters,* vol. 5, 793.

45. Nash, *Wilderness and the American Mind,* 164–70; Richardson, *Politics of Conservation,* 43–45.

46. Theodore Roosevelt, *Works,* vol. 17 (New York, 1926), 618–19; Nash, *Wilderness and the American Mind,* 168.

47. Roosevelt, *Autobiography,* 429.

48. Roosevelt to R. U. Johnson, December 17, 1908, in *Letters,* vol. 6, 1,428.

49. Muir to Johnson, September 11, 1913, Robert Underwood Johnson Papers, Bancroft Library, University of California, Berkeley; Pinchot to William Colby, February 17, 1905. As Pinchot told Horace McFarland, president of the American Civic Association and, with Muir, a lead critic of the adminis-

tration's policy on Hetch Hetchy, "One thing I thoroughly agree with you in, that the Lake Eleanor site should be developed to its fullest capacity, and its insufficiency should be demonstrated before the city is allowed to touch Hetch-Hetchy," Pinchot to McFarland, May 21, 1909, Records Group 95, Entry 22, Box 4, National Archives. Pinchot continues to shield Roosevelt in the historiographical accounts of conservation in the Progressive Era. Every commentary that depicts Pinchot as a pernicious influence on the president, as his dark side—and there are many—unconsciously reinforces the symbiotic relationship the two men fashioned in the first years of this century. See in particular Cutright, *Roosevelt: The Making of a Conservationist,* 234–35, and Fox, *American Conservation Movement,* passim. Cohen, *Pathless Way,* 325, inflates Pinchot's reputation by titling him the secretary of agriculture, a job Pinchot may have wanted but never obtained.

50. James Pinchot to Pinchot, April 9, 1907.

51. Ibid.

52. Roosevelt to Henry Cabot Lodge, March 1, 1910, in *Selections from the Correspondence of Theodore Roosevelt and Henry Cabot Lodge, 1884–1918,* vol. 2 (New York: Charles Scribner's Sons, 1925), 361; James Penick, Jr., *Progressive Politics and Conservation* (Chicago, 1968), passim.

53. Roosevelt to Lodge, March 1, 1910, in *Correspondence of Theodore Roosevelt and Henry Cabot Lodge,* 361; *McGeary,* Gifford Pinchot: Forester-Politician, 56; F. J. Dyer, "Gifford Pinchot," *Alaska-Yukon Magazine,* May 1910, 371.

CHAPTER 8. FAMILY AFFAIRS

1. Gifford Pinchot, Diary, June 22, 1913.

2. On Peter Cooper's political beliefs, see Edward C. Mack, *Peter Cooper: Citizen of New York* (New York: Duell, Sloan and Pearce, 1949), 357–84; on Edward Cooper's rocky mayoral term, 177–78, 294–95; and Allan Nevins, *Abram Hewitt; with some account of Peter Cooper* (New York: Harper & Brothers, 1935), 432–34, 267–319. See also "Peter Cooper," "Edward Cooper," and "Lloyd Stephens Bryce," in Allen Johnson and Dumas Malone, eds., *Dictionary of American Biography* (New York: Charles Scribner's Sons, 1935), 409–10, vol. 4, 397, vol. 3, 205–6; Cornelia Bryce Pinchot, "In Search of Adventure," in Elaine Showalter, *These Modern Women: Autobiographical Essays from the Twenties* (New York: The Feminist Press, 1989), 125.

3. On Cornelia Bryce Pinchot's political aspirations, see John W. Furlow, Jr., "Cornelia Bryce Pinchot: Feminism in the Post-Suffrage Era," *Pennsylvania History,* October 1976, 330–31; Lisa K. Hill, "'All in the Day's Work': Cornelia Bryce Pinchot and the Decade of the 1920s" (unpublished honors thesis, History Department, University of Texas, 1989), 4–6; Cornelia Bryce Pinchot, "In Search of Adventure," 125.

4. Pinchot to Frances A. Kellor, April 15, 1913, quoted in M. Nelson McGeary, *Gifford Pinchot: Forester-Politician* (Princeton: Princeton University Press, 1960), 250.

5. Pinchot, Diary, June 23, 1913.

6. Pinchot, Diary, July 31–August 1, 1914, August 5, 1914; *New York Times,* August 15, 1914, 7; August 16, 1914, Section 15, 1.

7. Cornelia Bryce Pinchot quoted in Hill, "'All in the Day's Work,'" 6; Cornelia Pinchot, "In Search of Adventure," 124–26. The *New York Times* account of the Bryce-Pinchot wedding indicates that Cornelia had in fact been a debutante: August 15, 1914, 7.

8. Horace Walker to Pinchot, January 21, 1891.

9. Walker to Pinchot, October 11, 1891. "C.B." was a bit of Skull and Bones slang that Pinchot and his fellow members continued to use after graduation in their letters about girlfriends.

10. Florence Adele Stone, with commentary by Louis Auchincloss, *Maverick in Mauve: The Diary of a Romantic Age* (Garden City, N.Y.: Doubleday & Co., 1983), 15–29. I am grateful to Timothy Smith for guiding me to this source.

11. Ibid., 74.

12. Ibid., 74, 82.

13. Ibid., 79; Pinchot enjoyed the speculative turn of the press enough to clip and save their musings about his bachelorhood; see Pinchot Scrapbooks, reel 1, "Pinchot: A Millionaire with a Mission," *Current Literature,* October 1909, 391.

14. Stone to Pinchot, March 28, 1892, quoted in Stone, *Maverick in Mauve,* 16–17.

15. James G. Bradley, "The Mystery of Gifford Pinchot and Laura Houghteling," *Pennsylvania History,* Spring 1999, 199–214. I am indebted to the late Jim Bradley for his pioneering exploration of the relationship between Gifford Pinchot and Laura Houghteling, particularly his insights into its spiritual and spiritualist dimensions. Although his work makes no use of the historiographical context in which their love flowered and ignores some correspondence that challenges his interpretive framework, his effort remains a substantial contribution. I am indebted as well to Doris Stillman of Columbia University for sharing the results of her careful reading of the Pinchots' collection of books on spiritualism; see her "Spirit: Notes on references to spiritualism in books in Grey Towers Library," Grey Towers National Historic Landmark, Milford, Pa. The couple's first meeting at "Strawberry Hill" may have occurred on February 7, 1892, or so Pinchot would state when reconstructing the early stages of their brief relationship in a set of notes he scribbled down after Laura's death in 1894. The incident at the bridge apparently occurred on April 25, 1892: see Gifford Pinchot, Notes, Letterbox, Grey Towers National Historic Landmark, Milford, Pa.

16. Julia Sullivan to Pinchot, quoted in Bradley, "Mystery of Gifford Pinchot and Laura Houghteling," 202.

17. Pat Corbin to Pinchot, September 7, 1893; Walker to Pinchot, March 14, 1893; Sam [?] to Pinchot, July 17, 1893; James B. Reynolds to Pinchot, September 11, 1893.

18. Walker to Pinchot, July 19, 1893.

19. Walker to Pinchot, July 19, 1893; Pinchot to Mary Pinchot, March 30, 1893.
20. James and Mary Pinchot's visceral reactions are laid out in their son's responses: Pinchot to parents, October 1893 (this letter is misdated as 1894, but internal evidence makes it clear it was written a year earlier); Pinchot to Mary Pinchot, October 20, 1893; Pinchot to parents, October 25, 1893.
21. Antoinette, who lived at home, was unable to create the maneuvering room her brother secured by virtue of his residence in Asheville. Pinchot to Mary Pinchot, October 20, 1893; Pinchot to parents, October 1893. Pinchot, Diary, July 1891, recounts some of his family's reactions to Alan Johnstone and his suit; see James Pinchot's blunt rebuttal to Johnstone's father's assumption that an engagement between their children had been agreed upon: Lord Dewent to James Pinchot, March 26, 1891; James Pinchot to Lord Dewent, April 14, 1891. That two years later Alan Johnstone would fully support Gifford's surreptitious courtship of Laura underscores the connection between Antoinette's and Gifford's courtships: "I do hope your matrimonial affairs are going as you could wish. You may rely on my doing my best to smooth matters and to stick by you," Alan Johnstone to Pinchot, December 6, 1893; Johnstone to Pinchot, December 18, 1893.
22. Pinchot to Mary Pinchot, October 20, 1893; Pinchot to parents, October 1893.
23. Pinchot to parents, October 1893. Gifford's concession about William Houghteling may have been shared by others: in a biography of his evidently much more talented son, industrialist James L. Houghteling, there is but one sentence about the father, "a man most noted for his sterling honesty and public spirit."
24. Antoinette Pinchot to Mary Pinchot, quoted in Bradley, "Mystery of Gifford Pinchot and Laura Houghteling," 203; Pinchot to parents, October 1893.
25. Pinchot to parents, October 25, 1893.
26. Pinchot to James Pinchot, January 5, 1894; Julia Sullivan quoted in Bradley, "Mystery of Gifford Pinchot and Laura Houghteling," 205. Senator Stockbridge himself would suddenly die several months after his niece's demise: "Francis Brown Stockbridge," in *The National Cyclopaedia of American Biography,* vol. 1 (New York: James T. White, 1898), 460.
27. Alan Johnstone to James W. Pinchot, February 9, 1893; Mary Pinchot to Amos Pinchot, February 8, 1893; Bradley, "Mystery of Gifford Pinchot and Laura Houghteling," 206–7.
28. Pinchot to James Pinchot, January 5, 1894.
29. Pinchot, Diary, March 17, 1894, April 15, 1894.
30. Carl Schenck, *Birth of Forestry in America: Biltmore Forest School, 1898–1913* (Santa Cruz, Calif.: Forest History Society, 1955), 21–22; Pinchot, Diary, May 16, 1895, June 13–14, 1894. See also Bradley, "Mystery of Gifford Pinchot and Laura Houghteling," 26–27. He often used the first-person plural to describe such moments, such as this notation on August 8, 1894: "Today we finished reading John Halifax together."

31. Bradley, "Mystery of Gifford Pinchot and Laura Houghteling," 32–33, pulls together some of the titles the couple read. Twain's scathing critique of this fiction is developed in Howard Kerr, *Mediums, and Spirit–Rappers, and Roaring Radicals: Spiritualism in American Literature, 1850–1900* (Urbana: University of Illinois Press, 1972), 169–80, and R. Laurence Moore, *In Search of White Crows: Spiritualism, Parapsychology, and American Culture* (New York: Oxford University Press, 1977), 7, 8–39, 133–68. See also Ann Braude, *Radical Spirits: Spiritualism and Women's Rights in Nineteenth-Century America* (Boston: Beacon Press, 1989), and Russell M. Goldfarb and Clare R. Goldfarb, *Spiritualism and Nineteenth-Century Letters* (Rutherford, N.J.: Fairleigh Dickinson University Press, 1978).

32. Pinchot, Diary, August 2, 1894, April 22, 1896, May 4, 1896; Bradley, "Mystery of Gifford Pinchot and Laura Houghteling," 30–32.

33. Pinchot, Diary, January 18, 1896, March 24, 1906; Gifford Pinchot, *The Fight for Conservation* (New York: Doubleday, Page, 1910), frontispiece. For a different interpretation of Pinchot's behavior, one that misses the familial dynamics in his decision not to marry, see McGeary, *Gifford Pinchot: Forester-Politician*: "There is no question that the loss [Laura's death] had a profound effect on Pinchot. . . . His slow recovery from the shock helped to explain his continued bachelorhood until the age of forty-nine"; 33.

34. Mary Pinchot, Diary, December 22, 1907–February 9, 1908, tracks the family's responses to James Pinchot's declining health.

35. Pinchot to Calvin Cobb, March 3, 1908.

36. James Pinchot to Pinchot, February 11, 1891.

37. James Pinchot to Pinchot, October 8, 1892.

38. Gifford Pinchot, *Breaking New Ground* (New York: Harcourt Brace Jovanovich, 1947), 152; Char Miller and James G. Lewis, "A Contested Past: Forestry Education in the United States, 1898–1998," *Journal of Forestry*, September 2000, 38–43.

39. Pinchot to Theodore Roosevelt, January 3, 1904.

40. Ibid.; Pinchot, Diary, January–February 1905; Pinchot, *Breaking New Ground*, 235–62.

41. Pinchot, *Breaking New Ground*, 235–62; Harold K. Steen, *The U.S. Forest Service* (Seattle: University of Washington Press, 1970), 71–76.

42. *Detroit News,* January 30, 1910. Commenting on the delight she took in the maturation of her progeny, and noting that they had "grown more than I," Mary Pinchot singled out Gifford for praise: he had developed "more than one could have imagined." Mary Pinchot, Diary, December 31, 1909; Mary Pinchot to Pinchot, August 27, 1890; McGeary, *Gifford Pinchot: Forester-Politician,* 8–9.

43. Nancy Pittman Pinchot, "Amos Pinchot: Rebel Prince," *Pennsylvania History,* Fall 1999, 170.

44. Mary Pinchot to James Pinchot, 1901 (undated).

45. Amos Pinchot to Pinchot, June 23, 1901.
46. Stephen McKenna, "The Hon. Lady Johnstone," *London Times,* July 5, 1934; Harcourt Johnstone to Pinchot, July 1934.
47. Ibid.; on Johnstone's career, see Jaime Reynolds and Ian Hunter, "'Crinks': An Outline of the Career of the Right Honourable Harcourt Johnstone (1895–1945)," manuscript in author's possession; Nancy Pittman Pinchot, "Amos Pinchot," 170.
48. Nancy Pittman Pinchot, "Amos Pinchot," 168–69.
49. Amos Pinchot to Pinchot, April 11, 1893, August 1896.
50. Pinchot, Diary, April 29–July 29, 1989; Pinchot to James Pinchot, July 5, 1898, July 17, 1898; Nancy Pittman Pinchot, "Amos Pinchot," 170–71.
51. Ibid.
52. Amos Pinchot to Woodrow Wilson, November 11, 1916, quoted in Amos R. E. Pinchot, *History of the Progressive Party, 1912–1916,* ed. Helene Maxwell Hooker (New York: New York University Press, 1958), 69–70.
53. Nancy Pittman Pinchot, "Amos Pinchot," 174–76.
54. Amos Pinchot to Mary Pinchot, August 14, 1914; Pinchot, Diary, April 26, 1914, confirms the family's discussion about the potential conflict with the two brothers campaigning simultaneously. Amos R. E. Pinchot, *History of the Progressive Party,* 53, indicates that there was debate among Progressive Party operatives about the brothers' chances if both ran.
55. By his first wife, Amos would have two children, Gifford (who, because of his height, and to distinguish him from his shorter cousin, was dubbed "Long Giff") and Rosamond; by his second wife, Ruth Pickering, he would have two more: Mary and Antoinette.
56. Pinchot, Diary, July 30, 1914. Bradley suggests that Mary Pinchot and Edith Bryce arranged their children's marriage, but offers no evidence to support this argument that robs Gifford and Cornelia of a role in their own courtship—an argument, moreover, that hardly squares with Cornelia's and Gifford's commanding personalities. Once their engagement was announced and a wedding date set for the autumn, Mary Pinchot asked them to accelerate the timing of the nuptials to help make sure they would occur while she was still living: *New York Times,* August 16, 1914, 15.

CHAPTER 9. A POLITICAL NATURAL

1. Jeannette Paddock Nichols, *Alaska* (New York: Russell & Russell, 1963), 369–70; Herman Slotnick, "The Ballinger-Pinchot Affair in Alaska," *Journal of the West,* April 1971, 342–43; Herbert N. Casson, "Alaska Catechism," *Alaska-Yukon Magazine,* May 1910, 353. The whole May 1910 issue of this magazine was devoted to Alaskans' reactions to the Ballinger-Pinchot affair.
2. Ibid.
3. Pinchot to J. E. Engstad, May 25, 1909.
4. Pinchot to James Garfield, April 29, 1909, May 26, 1909; Pinchot to Horace

Plunkett, March 8, 1909, July 13, 1909; Pinchot to Calvin Cobb, July 13, 1909; Gifford Pinchot, *Breaking New Ground* (New York: Harcourt Brace Jovanovich, 1947), 408–10.

5. Pinchot Scrapbooks, reel 2, November 1909; Oscar Lawler to Richard Ballinger, July 21, 1909, quoted in James Penick, Jr., *Progressive Politics and Conservation: The Ballinger-Pinchot Affair* (Chicago: The University of Chicago Press, 1968), 75–76.

6. Penick, *Progressive Politics and Conservation,* 178–80.

7. Pinchot, *Breaking New Ground,* 398; M. Nelson McGeary, *Gifford Pinchot: Forester-Politician* (Princeton: Princeton University Press, 1960), 132; Penick, *Progressive Politics and Conservation,* 79–84.

8. The literature on the Ballinger-Pinchot controversy is vast. The best secondary analysis is Penick, *Progressive Politics and Conservation*; I've also drawn from the insights of Harold T. Pinkett, *Gifford Pinchot: Private and Public Forester* (Urbana: University of Illinois Press, 1970), 114–29, and Harold K. Steen, *The U.S. Forest Service* (Seattle: University of Washington Press, 1970), 101–2. Pinchot's lengthy recapitulation is located in *Breaking New Ground,* 391–451. Indispensable too is *Investigations of the Department of the Interior and the Bureau of Forestry,* Senate Document 719, Sixty-first Congress, Third Session, which comprises thirteen volumes.

9. Penick, *Progressive Politics and Conservation,* 100–104.

10. *Seattle Post-Intelligencer,* July 13, 1909, quoted in Pinchot, *Breaking New Ground,* 416–17.

11. Pinchot to William Howard Taft, August 10, 1909, in *Investigations,* vol. 2, 62–63.

12. Pinchot to John Bigelow, October 4, 1909; Pinchot to Frank Flint, October 15, 1909.

13. Taft to Richard Ballinger, quoted in *Investigations,* vol. 4, 1,187–89; Taft to Pinchot, September 13, 1909.

14. Gifford Pinchot, *Fishing Talk* (Harrisburg: Stackpole Books, 1993), 202–6; Pinchot, *Breaking New Ground,* 430.

15. Pinchot, *Fishing Talk,* 206–8.

16. "Pinchot's Battle in Dark with Dangerous Swordfish," publisher uncited, September 21, 1909, Pinchot Scrapbooks, reel 2, 206; "'Resign? Never!' Declares Pinchot," *Los Angeles Examiner,* September 21, 1909, Pinchot Scrapbooks, reel 2, 206; "Diplomatic Press Invades Camp Sanctity," publisher uncited, Pinchot Scrapbooks, reel 2, 207.

17. Pinchot to Mary Pinchot, September 6, 1909.

18. "Pinchot Fears 'Dollar Reign,'" publisher uncited, September 23, 1909, Pinchot Scrapbooks, vol. 2, 208.

19. "Ballinger and Pinchot Strangers to Each Other," publisher uncited, Pinchot Scrapbooks, vol. 2, 210.

20. Pinchot, *Breaking New Ground,* 432–39; Pinchot to Taft, November 4, 1909,

1908–1915 file, Harry A. Slattery Papers, Special Collections Library, Duke University, recapitulates the concerns he raised in Salt Lake and embellishes them.

21. Pinchot, *Breaking New Ground,* 447–51, excerpts the Dolliver letter; see also Pinchot to Dolliver, January 5, 1910, in *Congressional Record,* January 6, 1910, 378; Penick, *Progressive Politics and Conservation,* 140–42.

22. Archie Butt, *Taft and Roosevelt: The Intimate Letters of Archie Butt,* vol. 1 (New York: Doubleday, Doran, 1930), 245, 253–56.

23. Gifford Pinchot to Senator Dolliver, January 5, 1910, in *Investigations,* vol. 3, 178–79; Pinchot, *Breaking New Ground,* 447–51; Thornton T. Munger, "Recollections of My Thirty-Eight Years in the Forest Service, 1908–1946," *Timberlines,* supplement to vol. 16, December 1962, 12–14. Munger, who had dinner with Pinchot that night, amply confirms the forester's exultation at his firing; Penick, *Progressive Politics and Conservation,* 137–42.

24. *Washington Star,* January 10, 1910; *Washington Post,* January 10, 1910; "Statement of Gifford Pinchot on leaving the Forest Service," January 13, 1910, Harry A. Slattery Papers, Special Collections Library, Duke University; Pinchot, *Breaking New Ground,* 454–55; Steen, *U.S. Forest Service,* 102–3.

25. *Washington Star,* January 10, 1910, 1, 10.

26. Pinchot, *Breaking New Ground,* 459. Pinchot had encouraged Henry Graves to choose forestry as his career, helped finance his education in Europe, secured his first job, and collaborated with him in writing *The White Pine* (1896); and when, in 1898, Pinchot became chief of the Division of Forestry, forerunner of the Forest Service, Graves became his assistant chief before becoming dean of the Yale School of Forestry. Given these close professional ties, it is hardly surprising that Pinchot would select his "first disciple" to replace him; see Herbert A. Smith, "The Old Order Changes," *Journal of Forestry,* March 1920, 203–10.

27. Herbert A. Smith, "Memorandum Re Graves' Appointment as Forester," September 11, 1941, Box 576, Gifford Pinchot Papers, Library of Congress. Pinchot could not support A. P. Davis for another reason—employed as he was in the Interior Department, the agency that Richard Ballinger headed and with which Pinchot had been fighting until his firing; Pinchot, *Breaking New Ground,* 459–60; Steen, *U.S. Forest Service,* 104. Graves remembers that he put himself forward as Pinchot's replacement; Henry Clepper, *Professional Forestry in the United States* (Baltimore: Johns Hopkins University Press, 1971), 56. Several months earlier, a similar, Yale-connected set of correspondents had tried to prevent Taft from imploding. In October 1909, Congressman William Kent had written Yale Secretary Anson Stokes and President Hadley hoping they would intercede with the president, who "seems to be blundering in an almost criminal way. . . . I cannot contemplate with anything but horror the likelihood of Pinchot being forced out of his position, which is inevitable unless Taft changes his attitude." Intercession would be a

long shot, Kent knew, because "Taft has been sojourning with corporation people, with Ballingers, Hammonds and reactionaries of all kinds, and I have no doubt is beginning to see the necessity of ridding himself of Pinchot." But the Eli network was obliged to act: "Yale College has claimed Taft with great *eclat.* It is about time that an effort should be made from New Haven to save him from his friends and from his lack of vision." William Kent to Anson Stokes, October 21, 1909, Gifford Pinchot Papers.

28. James G. Lewis, "'Trained by Americans in American Ways': The Establishment of Forestry Education in the United States, 1885–1911 (Ph.D. dissertation, Florida State University, 2001), chapter 5; McGeary, *Gifford Pinchot: Forester-Politician,* 35–36.

29. Pinchot to Roosevelt, December 31, 1909.

30. Penick, *Progressive Politics and Conservation,* 137–64, offers a deft recounting of this strategy; Pinchot, *Breaking New Ground,* 468–95, confirms it, as does Amos R. E. Pinchot, *History of the Progressive Party,* ed. Helene Maxwell Hooker (New York: New York University Press, 1958), 14–16; Pinchot's testimony in *Investigations,* vol. 4, 1,143.

31. Brandeis to Norman Hapgood, February 27, 1910, in Melvin I. Urofsky and David W. Levy, eds., *Letters of Louis D. Brandeis,* vol. 2, 321–24. See also the broader run of his correspondence on the hearings, 306–65, 370–80; Pinchot, *Breaking New Ground,* 475–78.

32. George Wharton Pepper, *Philadelphia Lawyer* (Philadelphia: Lippincott, 1944), 82–84, recounts his grave disappointment with some of Pinchot's actions, which Pinchot rebuts in *Breaking New Ground,* 470–73. The two men's later accounts of their antagonism were surely shaped by the fact that in 1926 they ran against one another for the U.S. Senate from Pennsylvania, a rough three-way contest in which Pepper defeated Pinchot, who was then in his first term as governor of the Keystone State.

33. Amos Pinchot to George W. Pepper, May 3, 1910, quoted in Penick, *Progressive Politics and Conservation,* 150.

34. Ibid.

35. Pinchot, *Breaking New Ground,* 470–71; Pinchot to Roosevelt, May 9, 1910. Louis Brandeis was just as effective in getting the word out to journalists, believing they were "his irreplaceable ally." To *American Magazine*'s Finley Peter Dunne, he wrote: "You said that you found difficulty in getting at the facts. I am therefore taking the liberty of sending you a copy of our brief, and have also asked the Clerk of the Committee to send you a copy of the oral arguments," materials he readily distributed to a number of other reporters; Phillipa Strum, *Louis D. Brandeis: Justice for the People* (Cambridge: Harvard University Press, 1984), 132–37. Taft, by contrast, failed to make use of publicity to support his actions, and Ballinger, who did, bungled the job. According to Stephen Ponder, a historian of journalism, Taft was the last president not to have an effective press officer in the White House; Stephen Ponder,

"'Nonpublicity' and the Unmaking of a President: William Howard Taft and the Ballinger-Pinchot Controversy of 1909–1910," unpublished manuscript in author's possession.

36. Pinchot, *Breaking New Ground,* 490–92.

37. Gifford Pinchot, Press Release, December 12, 1910; Pinchot, *Breaking New Ground,* 490–92.

38. Ibid.

39. Wes Hildreth, compiler, *Historical Chronology of Muir Woods and Vicinity* (Muir Woods National Monument, 1966); February 13, 1938, memorandum; December 7, 1945, memorandum between the custodian of Muir Woods and the director of the National Park Service, Muir Woods National Monument archives. I owe a great debt to Mia Monroe of the Muir Woods National Monument for sharing these documents with me; Mia Monroe to Char Miller, May 7, 2001, e-mail correspondence.

40. Forerunners of the NCA included the nineteenth-century organizations the Sierra Club (1893) and the Audubon Club (1905). The NCA differed from these groups in its exclusive goal of political advocacy on the federal level. John Reiger, *American Sportsmen and the Origins of Conservation* (Corvallis: Oregon State University Press, 2000), offers a careful assessment of the effectiveness of these and other early volunteer organizations; Susan R. Screpfer, "Establishing Administrative Standing: The Sierra Club and the Forest Service, 1897–1956," in Char Miller, ed., *American Forests: Nature, Culture, and Politics* (Lawrence: University Press of Kansas, 1997), 125–42. John Opie, *Nature's Nation: An Environmental History of the United States* (New York: Harcourt Brace Jovanovich, 1998), 417–29, details the rise of nongovernmental environmental organizations.

41. McGeary, *Gifford Pinchot: Forester-Politician,* 205; "Statement by Mr. Pinchot," June 7, 1910, in Harry A. Slattery Papers, Special Collections Library, Duke University.

42. "Statement of Mr. Pinchot on Agricultural Appropriations Amendment," March 2, 1911, in Harry A. Slattery Papers, Special Collections Library, Duke University; Gifford Pinchot, Diary, March 3, 1911; McGeary, *Gifford Pinchot: Forester-Politician,* 206.

43. Gifford Pinchot, *The Fight for Conservation* (New York: Doubleday, Page & Co., 1910), 3–4.

44. David Lowenthal, *George Perkins Marsh: Prophet of Conservation* (Seattle: University of Washington Press, 2000), 290–312.

45. Ibid., 29–30, 146–47; Bob Pepperman Taylor, *Our Limits Transgressed: Environmental Political Thought in America* (Lawrence: University of Kansas Press, 1992), 15–21, insists on a democratic reading of Pinchot's conservationism and rescues him from scholars, such as Samuel P. Hays, who have long pigeonholed Pinchot as simply a technocratic manager; see Samuel Hays, *Conservation and the Gospel of Efficiency: The Progressive Conservation Movement, 1890–1920* (New York: Atheneum, 1969), passim.

46. Pinchot, *Fight for Conservation,* 146.

47. Capturing some of this yearning for TR was an exchange in contemporary humorist Wallace Irwin's syndicated feature, "Interviews of a Japanese Schoolboy" (which Pinchot clipped):

> "Unless Public Conscience [Roosevelt] return to America pretty soonly there will be no property for poor folks to camp on." This from Hon. Gifford.
> "When are Public Conscience expected back?" This from me.
> "Before 1912, I hopes," says he, looking coaxingly in direction of Africa.

Washington Star, October 17, 1909, in Pinchot Scrapbooks, vol. 2.

48. Kenneth W. Hechler, *Insurgency: Personalities and Politics of the Taft Era* (New York: Russell & Russell, 1964), 15–59; Theodore Roosevelt to Pinchot, January 17, 1910.

49. Roosevelt to Pinchot, March 1, 1910, in Etling Morison, ed., *The Letters of Theodore Roosevelt* (Cambridge: Harvard University Press, 1954), 50–51.

50. Henry Cabot Lodge to Roosevelt, January 8, 1910, January 15, 1910, in *Selections from the Correspondence of Theodore Roosevelt and Henry Cabot Lodge, 1884–1918,* vol. 2 (New York: Charles Scribner's Sons, 1925), 356–59.

51. Ibid.

52. Roosevelt to Lodge, April 6, 1910, in ibid., 363–67.

53. Pinchot, *Breaking New Ground,* 502.

54. Ibid.; Pinchot to James Garfield, April 27, 1910; McGeary, *Gifford Pinchot: Forester-Politician,* 176–78.

55. Roosevelt to Lodge, April 11, 1910, in Morison, *Letters of Theodore Roosevelt,* 367–74.

56. Amos R. E. Pinchot, *History of the Progressive Party,* 112–17; Roosevelt to Pinchot, August 17, 1910, in Morison, *Letters of Theodore Roosevelt,* vol. 7, 113–14; Martin L. Fausold, *Gifford Pinchot: Bull Moose Progressive* (Syracuse: Syracuse University Press, 1961) 43–45.

57. Theodore Roosevelt, *The New Nationalism* (Gloucester, Mass.: Peter Smith, 1971), 3–33.

58. Pinchot to Roosevelt, August 18, 1910.

59. Roosevelt to Pinchot, June 29, 1910; Pinchot to Roosevelt, July 6, 1910, August 18, 1910; Roosevelt to Pinchot, August 17, 1910; Roosevelt to Theodore Roosevelt, Jr., October 19, 1910, November 11, 1910; Roosevelt to Henry L. Stimson, November 16, 1910; all in Morison, *Letters of Theodore Roosevelt,* 113–17, 144–45, 159–61, 165.

60. Pinchot to Henry Wallace, quoted in Fausold, *Gifford Pinchot: Bull Moose Progressive,* 92.

61. Ibid., 128–93; McGeary, *Gifford Pinchot: Forester-Politician,* 242–60.

62. Fausold, *Gifford Pinchot: Bull Moose Progressive,* 32; McGeary, *Gifford Pinchot: Forester-Politician,* 196–97; Pinkett, *Gifford Pinchot: Private and Public Forester.*

CHAPTER 10. GOVERNING AMBITIONS

1. Gifford Pinchot, *Fishing Talk* (Harrisburg: Stackpole Books, 1993), 123–25; I am indebted to John Reiger for his insights into the significance of this episode in Pinchot's life; see John F. Reiger, *Two Essays in Conservation History* (Milford, Pa.: Grey Towers Press, 1994), 19–21.

2. Pinchot, *Fishing Talk,* 126–27; Gifford Pinchot, Diary, May 10–13, 1913; Kerry W. Buckley, *Mechanical Man: John Broadus Watson and the Beginnings of Behavioralism* (New York: Guilford Press, 1989), 54–55. Watson began his work in the Tortugas in 1907 and continued it for several summers.

3. Pinchot, *Fishing Talk,* 131–32.

4. Ibid., 131–33.

5. Ibid.

6. Ibid., 133–34.

7. Ibid., 136.

8. Pinchot, Diary, November 9–18, 1912.

9. Theodore Roosevelt to Kermit Roosevelt, December 3, 1912, in Etling Morison, ed., *The Letters of Theodore Roosevelt* (Cambridge: Harvard University Press, 1954), vol. 7, 660; the issue of Perkins is tracked from 661 to 684.

10. Pinchot to Roosevelt, December 17, 1912.

11. Martin L. Fausold, *Gifford Pinchot: Bull Moose Progressive* (Syracuse: Syracuse University Press, 1973), 228–33.

12. Gifford Pinchot to Henry Cabot Lodge, April 2, 1917; M. Nelson McGeary, *Gifford Pinchot: Forester-Politician* (Princeton: Princeton University Press, 1960), 260–63.

13. Fausold, *Gifford Pinchot: Bull Moose Progressive,* 238; Nancy Pittman Pinchot, "Amos Pinchot: Rebel Prince," *Pennsylvania History,* Fall 1999, 184–93.

14. Cornelia Pinchot to Harry Slattery, November 29, 1922. Slattery was intrigued by her request and asked to speak with her: "When I see you I can tell you of a slant on the Mr. Amos end that I think has good in it," Slattery to Cornelia Pinchot, December 10, 1922, Harry A. Slattery Papers, Special Collections Library, Duke University; Pinchot to Amos Pinchot, November 28, 1922.

15. Pinchot to Amos Pinchot, January 18, 1919; Gifford Pinchot, *Breaking New Ground* (New York: Harcourt Brace Jovanovich, 1947), 390; McGeary, *Gifford Pinchot: Forester-Politician,* 268–69.

16. "Statement of Gifford Pinchot, President, National Conservation Association, on radium legislation," June 17, 1914, February 4, 1914.

17. Pinchot to John Grace, November 15, 1916, November 22, 1916; National Conservation Association, Press Release, June 30, 1916, December 16, 1916.

18. Pinchot to George Pardee, October 8, 1919; Paul B. Beers, *Pennsylvania Politics Today and Yesterday: The Tolerable Accommodation* (University Park: Pennsylvania State University Press, 1980), 71–72; Joseph Albert Falco, "Political Background and First Gubernatorial Administration of Gifford

Pinchot, 1923–1927" (Ph.D. dissertation, University of Pittsburgh, 1956), 50–63; McGeary, *Gifford Pinchot: Forester-Politician,* 267–68.

19. Falco, "Gifford Pinchot, 1923–1927," 9–44; Beers, *Pennsylvania Politics,* 84–85.

20. Ibid.

21. J. Horace McFarland to Charles S. Sargent, May 2, 1922, Charles Sargent Papers, Arnold Arboretum Archives; Ernest Morrison, *J. Horace McFarland: A Thorn of Beauty* (Harrisburg: Pennsylvania Historical and Museum Commission, 1995), 153–72.

22. *Philadelphia Bulletin,* quoted in Beers, *Pennsylvania Politics,* 87.

23. Cornelia Pinchot, "Address at Grange Picnic, Lookout, Penna.," *Milford Dispatch,* September 3, 192? [date unclear], Grey Towers National Historic Landmark Archives.

24. Pinchot to James Pinchot, November 9, 1890; McGeary, *Gifford Pinchot: Forester-Politician,* 244–45.

25. Albert Shaw, "Pennsylvania's Reform Governor," *Review of Reviews,* February 1923, 169; "Inaugural Address by Gifford Pinchot," *Review of Reviews,* February 1923, 171–73; Falco, "Gifford Pinchot, 1923–1927," 125.

26. Cornelia Pinchot to Amos Pinchot, undated, Amos Pinchot Papers, Library of Congress; by internal evidence, this letter was probably written in January or February 1920.

27. Amos Pinchot to Cornelia Pinchot, January 3, 1920, Amos Pinchot Papers.

28. Nina Burleigh, *A Very Private Woman: The Life and Unsolved Murder of Presidential Mistress Mary Meyer* (New York: Bantam Press, 1998), 30.

29. Fausold, *Gifford Pinchot: Bull Moose Progressive,* 177–78.

30. William Hard, "Pinchot for President," *The Nation,* October 31, 1923, 482–83.

31. "Women Are After Him: Chief of Forestry Bureau Has Got into Hot Water," *Milford Dispatch,* April 15, 1906.

32. Fausold, *Gifford Pinchot: Bull Moose Progressive,* 95.

33. Pinchot to Amos Pinchot, September 13, 1914.

34. Falco, "Gifford Pinchot, 1923–1927," 84–87.

35. *Philadelphia Record,* March 25, 1922; *Philadelphia North American,* May 1, 1922; Beers, *Pennsylvania Politics,* 84–86; Falco, "Gifford Pinchot, 1923–1927," 85–87.

36. *Harrisburg Telegram,* May 18, 1922.

37. *New York Times,* August 27, 1922; McGeary, *Gifford Pinchot: Forester-Politician,* 281.

38. Pinchot to Antoinette Pinchot Johnstone, April 5, 1922; Pinchot to Horace Plunkett, July 1, 1922.

39. *Philadelphia Public Ledger,* January 5, 1927; Beers, *Pennsylvania Politics,* 87–90.

40. Pinchot to Harcourt Johnstone, May 25, 1926.

41. Pinchot quoted in Beers, *Pennsylvania Politics,* 87–88; Pinchot to Charles G. Dawes, quoted in Falco, "Gifford Pinchot, 1923–1927," 318–19.
42. "Inaugural Address by Gifford Pinchot," *Review of Reviews,* February 1923, 172.
43. Beers, *Pennsylvania Politics,* 74–75.
44. Pinchot to Ralph Pulitzer, May 19, 1924, quoted in Falco, "Gifford Pinchot, 1923–1927," 222.
45. Falco, "Gifford Pinchot, 1923–1927," 223–25.
46. Pinchot quoted in Beers, *Pennsylvania Politics,* 75.
47. Pinchot to Calvin Coolidge, August 14, 1923, Harry A. Slattery Papers, Special Collections Library, Duke University.
48. Falco, "Gifford Pinchot, 1923–1927," 233–39.
49. Ibid.; Beers, *Pennsylvania Politics,* 80.
50. *New York Times,* February 17, 1926, March 20, 1926; Falco, "Gifford Pinchot, 1923–1927," 248–56; Beers, *Pennsylvania Politics,* 88–89.
51. Jean Christie, *Morris Llewelyn Cooke: Progressive Engineer* (New York: Garland Publishing, Inc., 1983), 68–74.
52. Morris Cooke to Pinchot, October 25, 1923, December 12, 1923, December 18, 1923, Cooke Papers, Franklin Delano Roosevelt Papers, Hyde Park, N.Y. I am most grateful to Sarah Phillips for sharing her research into the Giant Power Survey.
53. Thomas K. McCraw, *TVA and the Power Fight, 1933–1939* (Philadelphia: J. B. Lippincott Co., 1971), 21–23.
54. Cooke to Pinchot, October 25, 1923, December 12, 1923, December 18, 1923, Cooke Papers, Franklin Delano Roosevelt Papers, Hyde Park, N.Y.; *Philadelphia Inquirer,* July 5, 1925.
55. Cooke to Pinchot, March 10, 1924, Cooke Papers, Franklin Delano Roosevelt Papers, Hyde Park, N.Y.
56. Ibid.; Christie, *Morris Llewelyn Cooke,* 76–77.
57. Christie, *Morris Llewelyn Cooke,* 79–84.
58. Pinchot to Antoinette Pinchot Johnstone, September 28, 1926.
59. Message to the General Assembly, January 5, 1927, reported in *Philadelphia Public Ledger,* January 5, 1927; all subsequent quotations from the speech come from this version.
60. Ibid.
61. Pinchot to Antoinette Pinchot Johnstone, February 5, 1927.

CHAPTER 11. CHIEFLY POLITICS

1. "Pinchot Plans Battle Here to Save Nation's Resources," *Washington Star,* January 9, 1927.
2. "Pinchot, in Washington, Planning to Rekindle Old Roosevelt Fire," *Philadelphia Public Ledger,* January 29, 1927; all subsequent references to this interview come from this source.
3. Ibid.; *Washington Star,* January 9, 1927.

4. Brian Balogh, "'A Better Informed Amateur Than the Others': Gifford Pinchot and the Professional Foundation of State Building," delivered to the Southern California Colloquium in the History of Science, Medicine and Technology, April 29, 2000, 10–17. I am grateful to Professor Balogh for sharing his insights into the significance of this element of Pinchot's career.

5. Richard Lowitt, *George W. Norris: The Persistence of a Progressive, 1913–1933* (Champaign: University of Illinois Press, 1971), 197–216, tracks the battles over Muscle Shoals; Lowitt credits Pinchot with being the first to recognize the threat to public control that Henry Ford's proposal entailed; Pinchot to Harry Slattery, June 13, 1928; Slattery to Pinchot, June 16, 1928; both in Harry A. Slattery Papers, Special Collections Library, Duke University.

6. Slattery to Walter Lippmann, January 9, 1922, Harry A. Slattery Papers, Special Collections Library, Duke University.

7. *Washington Star,* January 9, 1927.

8. Gifford Pinchot, Diary, January 8–9, 1914.

9. William B. Greeley, *Some Public and Economic Aspects of the Lumber Industry,* USDA Report no. 14, 1917; William B. Greeley, *Forests and Men* (Garden City, N.Y.: Doubleday, 1951), 101–14; Henry S. Graves, "A Policy of Forestry for the Nation," *Journal of Forestry,* December 1919, 901–10; Harold K. Steen, *The U.S. Forest Service* (Seattle: University of Washington Press, 1970), 104–13.

10. Dietrich Brandis to Pinchot, January 7, 1895, July 7, 1895, February 17, 1898; James G. Lewis, "'Trained by Americans in American Ways': The Establishment of Forestry Education in the United States, 1885–1911" (Ph.D. dissertation, Florida State University, 2001); Char Miller, "The Prussians Are Coming! The Prussians Are Coming! Bernhard Fernow and the Origins of the USDA Forest Service," *Journal of Forestry,* March 1991, 23–27, 42.

11. Mark Dowie, *Losing Ground: American Environmentalism at the Close of the Twentieth Century* (Cambridge: MIT Press, 1995), 18; Greeley, *Forests and Men,* 101–44. On Pinchot's earlier willingness to acknowledge and work within timber companies' needs, see Gifford Pinchot, "Forestry on Private Lands," *Annals of the American Academy of Political and Social Science,* May 1909, 8–11; Richard Clow, "Timber Users, Timber Savers: The Homestake Mining Co. and the First Regulated Timber Harvest," in Char Miller, ed., *American Forests: Nature, Culture, and Politics* (Lawrence: University Press of Kansas, 1997), 71–86; Robert Ficken, "Gifford Pinchot Men," *Western Historical Quarterly,* April 1982, 165–78.

12. On the composition of the committee, see F. E. Olmsted to Raphael Zon, May 5, 1919, Raphael Zon Papers, Minnesota Historical Society; Gifford Pinchot, "The Lines Are Drawn," *Journal of Forestry,* December 1919, 901–2.

13. Henry S. Graves diary, quoted in Steen, *U.S. Forest Service,* 178.

14. Harry Slattery, Pinchot's personal secretary, was the usual conduit between the two wary men; Graves diary, quoted in Steen, *U.S. Forest Service,* 143. See also Herbert A. Smith, "The Old Order Changes," *Journal of Forestry,* March

1920, 203–10, which argues that Graves's chief claim to fame was as "the man who consolidated what his predecessor had won, and prevented the undoing of the work so well under way." But then that is usually the labor that disciples undertake, which is why they *are* disciples.

15. Mrs. William B. Greeley, Oral History Interview, June 28, 1960, Forest History Society, Durham, N.C.

16. Greeley, *Forests and Men,* 118.

17. Ibid.

18. Ibid.; William B. Greeley, "Self Government in Forestry," *Journal of Forestry,* February 1920, 103–5.

19. Gifford Pinchot, "National or State Control of Forest Devastation," *Journal of Forestry,* February 1920, 106–9; Gifford Pinchot, "Where We Stand," *Journal of Forestry,* May 1920, 441–47.

20. Ibid.

21. Pinchot, "Where We Stand," 441–47.

22. Henry S. Graves, Gifford Pinchot, and Raphael Zon, "Eugene Sewell Bruce," *Journal of Forestry,* May 1920, 439–40.

23. Steen, *U.S. Forest Service,* 179–81.

24. There was one direct interchange between them that would later trouble Greeley's widow. After the two men had offered contrary testimony, she recalled, a member of the congressional committee asked Pinchot: "[H]ow does it happen that this young successor of yours believes this way?," to which Pinchot reportedly replied, "'Oh well, he's young,' or something to the effect that the lumbermen had 'pulled the wool over his eyes.'" Mrs. William Greeley, Oral History Interview, June 28, 1960, Forest History Society, Durham, N.C.; Greeley, *Forests and Men,* 104–5, 109–10. Pinchot managed one public, if indirect blast at the assumptions that underlay the Clarke-McNary Act: see his "The Blazed Trail of Forest Depletion," *American Forests,* June 1923, 323–28, 374. Running commentary on the various legislative proposals and their fates appears in Henry Clepper, *Professional Forestry in the United States* (Baltimore: Johns Hopkins University Press, 1971), 139–42; Steen, *U.S. Forest Service,* 173–95.

25. Greeley, *Forests and Men,* 109–10.

26. On Zon, see Norman J. Schmaltz, "Raphael Zon: Forest Researcher," part 1, *Journal of Forest History,* January 1980, 25–39; Samuel Dana to Ward Shepard, March 8, 1925.

27. Dana to William Greeley, June 18, 1925; Greeley to Dana, April 3, 1926; both in Raphael Zon Papers, Minnesota Historical Society; Char Miller, "Sawdust Memories," *Journal of Forestry,* February 1994, 8–12; Clepper, *Professional Forestry,* 145.

28. Pinchot to Graves, March 24, 1926; Pinchot to Greeley, March 16, 1926.

29. Pinchot, "Blazed Trail of Forest Depletion," 328–29; Gifford Pinchot, "How the National Forests Were Won," *American Forests,* October 1930, 615–20.

30. "Pinchot Out for Forestry Bonds," *Butler Eagle,* October 19, 1928; "Pinchot

Tells Need of Forests Owned by State," *Norristown Register,* October 18, 1928; "Walton League Backs Forest Bond Issue; Ex-Gov. Pinchot to Address Meeting," *Greenville Record-Argus,* October 27, 1928; "How Shall We Vote on the Forestry Bond Issue? Vote 'Yes'—Says Mr. Pinchot," *Pennsylvania Farmer,* September 29, 1928, 6, 17.

31. Pinchot also established the Department of Forests and Water, which among other things was also focused on water quality issues; Joel A. Tarr, "Searching for a 'Sink' for an Industrial Waste," in Char Miller and Hal K. Rothman, eds., *Out of the Woods: Essays in Environmental History* (Pittsburgh: University of Pittsburgh Press, 1997), 163–80. Pinchot's personal interest in unpolluted waters was of a piece with similar desires of the state's huge number of anglers. Under the aegis of the Isaak Walton League, a national sportsmen's association that had considerable clout in Pennsylvania, recreationists helped pressure government and industry to protect water quality. Nicholas Casner, "Angler Activist: Kenneth Reid, the Isaak Walton League, and the Crusade for Federal Water Pollution Control," *Pennsylvania History,* Autumn 1999, 535–53.

32. Beers, *Pennsylvania Politics,* 89.

33. Beers, *Pennsylvania Politics,* 89; William B. McCaleb, "Progress in Controlling Stream Pollution in Pennsylvania," *Outdoor America,* May 1928, 22–24; John H. Fertig, "Pollution and Law," *Outdoor America,* June 1926, 20–22, 51–53, 68.

34. Pinchot, preface to George Ahern, *Deforested America* (Washington, D.C.: privately published, 1928), 7.

35. Zon to Pinchot, December 22, 1928, November 26, 1929, Raphael Zon Papers, Minnesota Historical Society.

36. Pinchot to Graves, November 30, 1928; Zon to Pinchot, December 22, 1928; Zon to Pinchot, November 26, 1929; Pinchot to Zon, November 15, 1929, Raphael Zon Papers, Minnesota Historical Society.

37. Pinchot to Zon, December 26, 1928.

38. Ibid.

39. *Philadelphia North American,* August 19, 1922; Slattery to Robert Y. Stuart, April 19, 1922; Stuart to Slattery, April 20, 1922; both in Harry A. Slattery Papers, Special Collections Library, Duke University.

40. On the Pinchot-Stuart relationship, see Michael Williams, *Americans and Their Forests: A Historical Geography* (Cambridge: Cambridge University Press, 1989), 460–61; Pinchot to Society of American Foresters (SAF), *Journal of Forestry,* April 1931, 628–29; Pinchot to SAF, January 20, 1935, quoted in M. Nelson McGeary, *Gifford Pinchot: Forester-Politician* (Princeton: Princeton University Press, 1960), 405–6.

41. Ferdinand Silcox, "Foresters Must Choose," *Journal of Forestry,* March 1935, 198–204; Pinchot to Zon, June 26, 1934.

42. Pinchot to Zon, June 26, 1934, October 3, 1934.

CHAPTER 12. THE WIDENING VIEW

1. Gifford Pinchot, *To the South Seas* (New York: John C. Winston and Co., 1930), 1.
2. Ibid.
3. Ibid.
4. *Philadelphia Public Ledger,* January 29, 1927.
5. Pinchot to Walter H. Newton, reprinted in *New York Times,* October 17, 1928; Pinchot knew his offer would be rebuffed, pointing out to Newton that "[u]nder the circumstances you will probably not want me to speak."
6. Pinchot to Antoinette Pinchot Johnstone (hereafter APJ), May 2, 1928; Lisa K. Hill, "'All in the Day's Work': Cornelia Bryce Pinchot and the Decade of the 1920s" (senior thesis, University of Texas at Austin, April 1989), 26–36.
7. Pinchot, *To the South Seas,* 5–7.
8. Ibid.
9. Ibid.; William Beebe, *Galapagos: World's End* (New York: G. Putnam's Sons, 1924), was required reading on board the *Mary Pinchot*; see below for some of the responses to the islands. See also Edward J. Larson, *Evolution's Workshop: God and Science on the Galapagos Islands* (New York: Basic Books, 2001).
10. Pinchot, *To the South Seas,* 7.
11. Ibid., 16.
12. Ibid., 16–17.
13. Ibid., 99–100; Hill, "All in the Day's Work," 37–48.
14. Gifford Bryce Pinchot, *Giff and Stiff in the South Seas* (Philadelphia: The John C. Winston Co., 1933). See also Gifford Bryce Pinchot, "Marine Farming," *Scientific American,* December 1970, 14–21.
15. Pinchot, *To the South Seas,* 18–37.
16. Ibid., 59–63.
17. Morris Gregg to Harry Slattery, July 14, 1929, Harry A. Slattery Papers, Special Collections Library, Duke University.
18. Ibid.
19. Pinchot, *To the South Seas,* 144–58.
20. Ibid., 193–95.
21. Larson, *Evolution's Workshop,* 184–88.
22. Hal K. Rothman, "'A Regular Ding-Dong Fight': The Dynamics of Park Service–Forest Service Controversy During the 1920s and 1930s," in Char Miller, ed., *American Forests: Nature, Culture, and Politics* (Lawrence: University Press of Kansas, 1997), 109–24. See chapter 13 of this book for a discussion of the explosive debate between Pinchot and Ickes in the 1930s.
23. Pinchot, *To the South Seas,* 40–53.
24. Ibid.; Gregg to Slattery, July 14, 1929, Harry A. Slattery Papers, Special Collections Library, Duke University.
25. Pinchot, *To the South Seas,* 99, 109–11.
26. Richard H. Pells, *Radical Visions and American Dreams: Cultural and Social*

Thought in the Depression (New York: Harper & Row, 1974), 97–150; Robert Marshall, *Arctic Village* (New York: H. Smith and R. Haas, 1933); Aldo Leopold, *A Sand County Almanac* (New York: Oxford University Press, 1970), 137–62; James Agee and Walker Evans, *Let Us Now Praise Famous Men* (Boston: Houghton Mifflin, 1960).

27. Pells, *Radical Visions and American Dreams,* 101.

28. Pinchot, *To the South Seas,* 476–79.

29. M. Nelson McGeary, *Gifford Pinchot: Forester-Politician* (Princeton: Princeton University Press, 1960), 344–45.

30. Pinchot, *To the South Seas,* 492.

31. Gifford B. Pinchot, "Politics and Baked Alaska in the Fingerbowl," *Milford Dispatch,* August 17, 1989, 3; Carol Severance to author, April 16, 2001.

32. Pinchot to Peter Stahlnecker, August 13, 1929.

33. Gregg to Slattery, July 14, 1929.

34. Ibid.; McGeary, *Gifford Pinchot: Forester-Politician,* 344.

35. Pinchot to Clyde King, February 17, 1930.

36. Beers, *Pennsylvania Politics,* 92–93; McGeary, *Gifford Pinchot: Forester-Politician,* 346–50; John W. Furlow, Jr., "An Urban State under Siege: Pennsylvania and the Second Gubernatorial Administration of Gifford Pinchot, 1931–1935" (unpublished Ph.D. dissertation, University of North Carolina, 1973), 51–54.

37. Furlow, "Urban State under Siege," 57–60; Beers, *Pennsylvania Politics,* 93–94.

38. *Milford Dispatch,* August 17, 1989, 3; Pinchot to APJ, August 7, 1930; McGeary, *Gifford Pinchot: Forester-Politician,* 356–57.

39. Pinchot to APJ, August 7, 1930.

40. Ibid.; Beers, *Pennsylvania Politics,* 96.

41. Pinchot to Charles R. Davis, January 10, 1931; Pinchot to APJ, February 10, 1931.

42. Beers, *Pennsylvania Politics,* 98–99.

43. Pinchot to APJ, March 30, 1931.

44. Beers, *Pennsylvania Politics,* 96–97; Pinchot to APJ, September 28, 1931, October 24, 1931.

45. Pinchot to APJ, October 24, 1931.

46. Gifford Pinchot, "Release for the Rich or Relief for the Poor," an address to the District of Columbia League of Women Voters, November 30, 1931.

47. Ibid.; Martin L. Fausold, *The Presidency of Herbert C. Hoover* (Lawrence: University Press of Kansas, 1985).

48. Pinchot to APJ, June 6, 1931.

49. Furlow, "Urban State under Siege," 61; Pinchot to APJ, September 28, 1931.

50. Pinchot to Huskin Coal Co. (telegram), September 18, 1933; Pinchot, Proclamation, March 23, 1933; Furlow, "Urban State under Siege," 237–43.

51. Pinchot to APJ, March 30, 1933, November 14, 1933, June 6, 1932.

52. Pinchot to APJ, June 6, 1932.
53. Pinchot to George Pardee, May 29, 1933; Furlow, "Urban State under Siege," 93–94; McGeary, *Gifford Pinchot: Forester-Politician,* 373.
54. *Philadelphia Inquirer,* October 29, 1930, 1, 2; Furlow, "Urban State under Siege," 236.
55. Furlow, "Urban State under Siege," 314–69; Pinchot to Horace Plunkett, June 6, 1931; Otis Graham, *An Encore for Reform: The Old Progressives and the New Deal* (New York: Oxford University Press, 1967), 63. Ronald L. Feinman, *Twilight of Progressivism: The Western Republican Senators and the New Deal* (Baltimore: Johns Hopkins University Press, 1981), examines a group of former progressives who, unlike Pinchot, were unable to evolve politically. Pinchot went even further in his political migration. In June 1944, he called on Franklin Roosevelt after meeting with Republican Wendell Willkie, who had run against Roosevelt in 1940. Willkie had proposed, and Pinchot had agreed, that progressive Republicans had nowhere to turn, and that the same was probably true of liberal Democrats. Pinchot served as an envoy to the president, carrying a germ of an idea that Willkie first advanced—that, with Roosevelt, he and Pinchot and like-minded Republicans work to create a new party, a fusion of progressives. Samuel I. Rosenman, one of Roosevelt's close political advisors, was dispatched to secretly discuss the prospects with Willkie and found the Republican as enthusiastic about the plan as Pinchot had reported. Nothing came of the idea for party realignment, for Willkie would be dead by that November and Roosevelt would die six months later, but the episode is one more sign of Pinchot's political adaptability. Samuel I. Rosenman, *Working with Roosevelt* (New York: DaCapo Press, 1972), 463–70.
56. "Emergency Labor Camps in Pennsylvania," *Monthly Labor Review,* June 1932, 1,289–91.
57. Ibid.; Graham, *Encore for Reform,* passim, argues that in the end Pinchot opposed the New Deal, though he acknowledges that Pinchot was difficult to characterize. Pinchot was a Republican, after all, and challenged some New Deal programs. But it is also clear where his sympathies (and political agenda) lay in the years immediately preceding (and following) Roosevelt's election in 1932—even if these clashed with his own political aspirations. See Pinchot to Horace Plunkett, April 27, 1931. In 1940, and again in 1944, he publicly supported Roosevelt in his successful bids for reelection; this was one old Progressive who became a New Dealer.
58. Pinchot to APJ, October 5, 1933. *The New Republic,* August 9, 1933, 1, praised Pinchot's sending of troops to support strikers, noting that previously Gifford and Cornelia Pinchot "almost single-handedly helped textile strikers in several cities to win a series of strikes." Pinchot also worked closely with labor unions in the timber industry. McGeary, *Pinchot,* 302–11, 316–17, 376–81.
59. Pinchot to APJ, October 5, 1933; Furlow, "Urban State Under Siege," 341–44; McGeary, *Gifford Pinchot: Forester-Politician,* 302–11, 316–17,

376–81; John W. Furlow, "Gifford Pinchot: Public Service and the Meaning of Conservation," *Theodore Roosevelt Association Newsletter,* Summer 1987, 13–14; Gifford Pinchot, "Address to the Amalgamated Clothing Workers of America," September 14, 1933; Pinchot, "Address to the Pennsylvania National Guard Association," October 28, 1933; *Philadelphia Record,* May 19, 1934, 2; *The New Republic,* August 9, 1933, 1.

60. Pinchot to Stephen S. Wise, September 1, 1911; Wise to Pinchot, September 12, 1911; Pinchot to Wise, June 13, 1922; Pinchot to Wise (telegram), January 25, 1926; Pinchot to Wise, February 16, 1929; Pinchot to Wise, November 21, 1930; Wise to Pinchot, November 6, 1931, all in Stephen S. Wise Papers, American Jewish Historical Society. Wise to Pinchot (telegram), March 24, 1933, Gifford Pinchot Papers, Library of Congress.

61. *New York Times,* March 28, 1933, 1, 6, 12–13; Address by Mrs. Cornelia Bryce Pinchot, March 27, 1933; Pinchot to Wise, March 27, 1933; Pinchot to Wise (telegram), March 27, 1933; Statement by Gifford Pinchot, March 29, 1933; Pinchot to Rabbi Davidson, March 27, 1933.

62. George H. Payne to Pinchot, April 20, 1933; Samuel Edelman to Pinchot, March 30, 1933.

63. Gifford Pinchot, Diary, 1888–89, 3–10.

64. *New York Times,* August 7, 1942, 9.

65. Wise to Amos Pinchot, February 24, 1937; Wise to Warren Marks, October 24, 1941; both in Wise Papers, American Jewish Historical Society, Brandeis University, Waltham, Mass.

66. Wise to Marks, October 24, 1941.

67. Pinchot to APJ, May 29, 1934; APJ to Pinchot, May 18, 1934; Furlow, "Urban State under Siege," 481–96.

68. Furlow, "Urban State under Siege," 481–96; *New York Times,* January 2, 1935.

69. Furlow, "Urban State under Siege," 469; *New York Times,* January 2, 1935; McGeary, *Gifford Pinchot: Forester-Politician,* 385–86.

70. *New York Times,* January 2, 1935; Furlow, "Urban State under Siege," 495–98.

71. *New York Times,* January 16, 1935, 4; Beers, *Pennsylvania Politics,* 81.

CHAPTER 13. CROSSCUT

1. Amos Pinchot to Pinchot, April 5, 1933; Pinchot to A. K. Fisher, June 10, 1933.

2. Gifford Pinchot, "A Ten Year Plan," Box 644, Gifford Pinchot Papers, Library of Congress.

3. Ibid.

4. Gifford Pinchot, *The Training of a Forester* (Philadelphia: Lippincott, 1917), 6–7 (hereafter cited as *Training,* 1917); American Library Association *Booklist,* June 1914, 404, picked up on and endorsed Pinchot's sense that he alone could provide "expert" advice on this question.

5. Clayton Koppes, "Efficiency, Ethics and Esthetics," in Donald Worster, ed., *The Ends of the Earth: Perspectives on Modern Environmental History* (Oxford: Oxford University Press, 1988). These ideas were not indigenous to the United States, but were products of a decades-long and fertile transatlantic interchange between Europe—especially Germany and Great Britain—and North America. In his own small way, Gifford Pinchot contributed to this intellectual transfusion when he studied in Europe in the 1890s, later transferring some of the principles of European forestry into the Forest Service. On the intellectual origins of progressivism, see Peter Coleman, *Progressivism and the World of Reform* (Lawrence: University Press of Kansas, 1987); the impact of German ideas on American forestry is explored in Char Miller, "The Prussians Are Coming! The Prussians Are Coming! Bernhard Fernow and the Origins of the USDA Forest Service," *Journal of Forestry,* March 1991, 23–27, 42; and in Char Miller, "Wooden Politics: Bernhard Fernow and the Quest for a National Forest Policy," in Harold K. Steen, *The Origins of the National Forests* (Durham, N.C.: Forest History Society, 1992), 287–300.

6. *Training,* 1917: 113–19, 23–25.

7. *Training,* 1917: 18–19, 131–34. His delineation of Progressive Era forestry curricula is confirmed in Henry S. Graves and Cedric H. Guise, *Forest Education* (New Haven: Yale University Press, 1932); Andrew Denny Rodgers, *Bernhard E. Fernow: A Story of North American Forestry* (Princeton: Princeton University Press, 1951); George A. Garrett, "Gifford Pinchot and Forestry Education," *Journal of Forestry,* August 1965, 597–660; Henry Schmitz, *The Long Road Travelled: An Account of Forestry at the University of Washington* (Seattle: Arboretum Foundation, 1973); Paul Cassamajor, ed., *Forestry Education at the University of California: The First Fifty Years* (Berkeley: California Alumni Foresters, 1965).

8. *Training,* 1917: 123–40. Pinchot was not in favor of unrestrained corporate forestry; over the years, and with increasing intensity, he called for tighter government regulation. Some of the costs of the Progressive Era's marriage of science and capitalism emerge in Clayton Koppes, "Efficiency, Equity, Esthetics," in Worster, *Ends of the Earth.*

9. *Training,* 1917: 22–23; Robert Wiebe, *The Search for Order* (New York: Hill & Wang, 1968).

10. Daniel T. Rodgers, *Atlantic Crossings* (Cambridge: Harvard University Press, 1998), 27–28.

11. *Training,* 1917: 22–23. The intellectual link between Pinchot's and Addams's approaches was not accidental; they met one another through political and social gatherings and corresponded over time, sharing ideas and methods of reform. Jane Addams, *Spirit of Youth and the City Streets* (New York: The MacMillan Co., 1909).

12. *Training,* 1917: 84–88.

13. *Training,* 1917: 106–8.

14. *Training,* 1917: 84, 64–67.

15. Pinchot to J. W. Lippincott, January 1, 1914; Lippincott to Pinchot, January 24, 1914.

16. *Training,* 1917: 27–28; J. W. Lippincott to Pinchot, January 26, 1917, February 26, 1917. Pinchot felt so little proprietary concern for *The Training of a Forester* that in 1933, when he again decided that he did not have the time to revise it significantly, he proposed to the Lippincott firm that it publish the work of another forester in his book's stead. "It is a very generous act on your part to call attention to another work that would seem to be directly competitive with your book," Jefferson Jones of Lippincott responded, "and, were it not for this, we would be very interested." Pinchot to Jefferson Jones, August 30, 1933; Jones to Pinchot, August 31, 1933.

17. Jones to Pinchot, June 8, 1933.

18. Edgar R. Nixon, ed., *Franklin D. Roosevelt and Conservation, 1911–1945* (New York: Arno Press, 1972), 129–32.

19. Ibid.

20. Herbert A. Smith to Pinchot, July 4, 1933; Pinchot to Jones, July 11, 1933; Pinchot to Smith, July 18, 1933; Smith to Pinchot, July 20, 1933; Pinchot to Smith, July 22, 1933.

21. Royalty statements are incomplete, but it appears the second edition sold better than its successor: during the six months preceding January 1932, for example, 118 copies of the book were sold. Sales of the third edition were slower: by January 1934, 56 copies had been sold; by April 1936, 50; and by June 1937, just months before the appearance of the final edition, sales were but 34 copies; receipts located in Box 326, Gifford Pinchot Papers, Library of Congress.

22. Gifford Pinchot, Diary, June–August 1936; Morris Gregg to Pinchot, July 31, 1936. Holdsworth's monthly salary while at Grey Towers was $330; Robert Holdsworth to Pinchot, September 10, 1936; Pinchot to Holdsworth, September 16, 1936. Graves reported to Smith that Pinchot "seemed much pleased with Holdsworth. Your suggestion about enlisting Holdsworth's interests was inspirational"; Graves to Smith, September 22, 1936; Pinchot, Diary, March 22, 1937.

23. Pinchot had always used ghostwriters for his books and speeches, but as the original drafts reveal, he clearly labored over the words and ideas to make them his own, to make them sound like him. A quick example, drawn from one of the drafts of the 1937 version of *The Training of a Forester* (hereafter cited as *Training,* 1937), demonstrates Pinchot's editorial activity and acuity. Holdsworth's version: "After the Technical Forester has made a thorough estimate of the timber on one of these natural logging units, he can tabulate from his data a large amount of practical information. He will have at hand, for example, figures which give the total volume of timber on the unit. These figures will be broken down to show the amount of volume represented by each species and the volume of each species contained in the trees, both above and below the specified diameter limits." Pinchot's revisions: "After the

trained Forester has made a thorough estimate of the timber on any natural logging unit, he will have at hand much practical information, such as the total volume of each species, and the volume of each species above and below the specified diameter limits." His attention to grammar and language was evident throughout, see "Training of a Forester," July 13, 1937, draft; Pinchot to Holdsworth, November 11, 1937; *Training*, 1937: v; Holdsworth to Pinchot, November 29, 1937.

24. *Training*, 1937: 81–83. Pinchot's discussion of curriculum surely leaned heavily on Holdsworth's close association with forestry education, though as a member of the board of directors of the Yale School of Forestry, and having been at the forefront of forestry educational reform initiatives throughout his career, Pinchot no doubt was familiar with these curricular changes firsthand; see Graves and Guise, *Forest Education*, 15–20.

25. *Training*, 1937: 86–87, 1–2, 8–9; Graves and Guise, *Forest Education*, 151–52.

26. *Training*, 1937: 93, 7–9; Aldo Leopold, *Game Management* (New York: Scribner, 1933). Graves and Guise, *Forest Education*, 161–62, takes a more utilitarian view of wildlife management.

27. *Training*, 1937: 9.

28. *Training*, 1937: 1, 10, 14; Donald Worster, *Nature's Economy: The Roots of Ecology* (San Francisco: Sierra Books, 1977), 226–69; Max Oealschlaeger, *The Idea of Wilderness: From Prehistory to the Age of Ecology* (New Haven: Yale University Press, 1991), 201, 209; *American Forests*, July 1938, 333.

29. Worster, *Nature's Economy*, 189–225; Anna Bramwell, *Ecology in the 20th Century: A History* (New Haven: Yale University Press, 1989), 22–31; Frederick E. Clements, *Plant Succession and Indicators*, revised edition (New York: H. W. Wilson Co., 1928), 220–24, 420–37. Clements's ideas about "climax communities" and "succession" anticipated some late-twentieth-century ecological thought, but they have fallen out of favor: Andrew Brennan, *Thinking About Nature* (Athens: University of Georgia Press, 1988), 46–48, 53–54, 101–2; *Training*, 1937: 7; Aldo Leopold, *Sand County Almanac* (New York: Oxford University Press, 1968); Curt Meine, *Aldo Leopold: His Life and Work* (Madison: University of Wisconsin Press, 1988), 340–505; Harold K. Steen, *The U.S. Forest Service* (Seattle: University of Washington Press, 1970), 317–18.

30. *Training*, 1937: iv. But he was not too far behind that curve: the term ecology appears but once in Graves and Guise, *Forest Education*, a four-hundred-page evaluation of contemporary forest curricula, and does not appear in any of the following: Cassamajor, ed., *Forestry Education at the University of California*; Schmitz, *The Long Road Travelled*; Henry Clepper, "Forestry Education in America," *Journal of Forestry*, July 1956, 455–57; and Henry Clepper and Arthur B. Meyer, eds., *American Forestry: Six Decades of Growth* (Washington, D.C.: Society of American Foresters, 1960).

31. John W. Furlow, Jr., "An Urban State under Siege: Pennsylvania and the Second Gubernatorial Administration of Gifford Pinchot, 1931–1935" (unpub-

lished dissertation, University of North Carolina, 1973); Gifford Pinchot, "Forestry and Conservation," speech dated 1919 but not more fully cited.

32. Gifford Pinchot, "Proclamation: Arbor Day and Bird Day," February 27, 1923; Gifford Pinchot, "Address before the Carlisle Civic Club," May 3, 1920.

33. Gifford Pinchot, "Address to the Fairmount Park Art Association," January 15, 1920; Pinchot, "Address before the Carlisle Civic Club," May 3, 1920.

34. Pinchot to Holdsworth, November 13, 1937, November 11, 1938.

35. Holdsworth to Pinchot, November 29, 1937, July 31, 1938, November 10, 1938.

36. Cornelia Pinchot to Harry A. Slattery, November 11, 1932, Harry A. Slattery Papers, Special Collections Library, Duke University.

37. Gifford Pinchot to Harold Ickes, March 23, 1933; M. Nelson McGeary, *Gifford Pinchot: Forester-Politician* (Princeton: Princeton University Press, 1960), 409; Harold Ickes, *The Secret Diary of Harold Ickes: The First Thousand Days, 1933–1936* (New York: Simon & Schuster, 1953), 17.

38. Rothman, "'A Regular Ding-Dong Fight': The Dynamics of Park Service–Forest Service Controversy During the 1920s and 1930s," in Char Miller, ed., *American Forests: Nature, Culture and Politics* (Lawrence: University Press of Kansas, 1997), 109–24.

39. For all its work, the Keep Commission was not entirely successful. The usually optimistic Pinchot noted that it was impossible to do "away with all the going stupidities and wastes of time and money. That was too much to expect"; Pinchot, *Breaking New Ground* (New York: Harcourt Brace Jovanovich, 1947), 296–99; Theodore Roosevelt, *An Autobiography* (New York: The MacMillan Co., 1913), 399–400; Harold Pinkett, "The Keep Commission, 1905–1909: A Rooseveltian Effort for Administrative Reform," *Journal of American History,* 297–312.

40. Roosevelt, *Autobiography,* 400; Pinkett, "Keep Commission," 303, 312; Louis Brownlow et al., *Report of the President's Committee on Administrative Management* (Washington, D.C.: Government Printing Office, 1937), 1–3; Pinchot, *Breaking New Ground,* 297–98. Pinchot recognized the connection between the Keep Commission findings and the transfer battles with Harold Ickes; Pinchot to Smith, June 11, 1935. Subsequent presidents have followed Franklin Roosevelt's precedence, most recently Jimmy Carter, Ronald Reagan, and Bill Clinton; see Char Miller, "A Cautionary Tale," *Journal of Forestry,* 6–10.

41. Pinchot quoted in Harold T. Pinkett, *Gifford Pinchot: Private and Public Forester* (Urbana: University of Illinois Press, 1970), 149.

42. Harold Ickes to Pinchot, May 18, 1940; Pinchot regularly corresponded with President Roosevelt on the question of the transfer, a correspondence that was part of a larger strategy to derail such threats. See Pinchot to Franklin D. Roosevelt, April 18, 1933, a copy of which he sent to Henry A. Wallace, secretary of agriculture, with the comment that he, Pinchot, "was ready to follow it up any time you will let me know that it ought not to wait any longer";

Roosevelt to Pinchot, April 21, 1933; Gifford Pinchot, Press Release, July 9, 1935; Ferdinand Silcox to Pinchot, August 1, 1935.

43. *President's Committee on Administrative Management,* 3, 32–33.

44. Richard Polenberg, *Reorganizing Roosevelt's Government: The Controversy over Executive Reorganization, 1936–1939* (Cambridge: Harvard University Press, 1966), contains the best analysis of the Brownlow Report and the battles it spawned; Harold Ickes, *The Secret Diary of Harold Ickes: The Inside Struggle, 1936–1939* (New York: Simon & Schuster, 1954), 20–21; see also Ickes, *First Thousand Days,* 417–19, 534–39, 604–5.

45. Pinchot, Diary, January 12–27, 1937.

46. *President's Committee on Administrative Management,* 32; Ickes, *Inside Struggle,* 23.

47. Gifford Pinchot, "Old Evils in New Clothes," *Journal of Forestry,* May 1937, 435–36; Pinchot had distributed advance copies of this speech to potential supporters in Congress, including old ally Senator George Norris of Nebraska; the senator "heartily agreed in opposing the transfer of the Forest Service, and said he expected to make a speech about it when it came up"; Pinchot, Diary, April 26–30, 1937.

48. Pinchot, "Old Evils in New Clothes," 435–36; Gifford Pinchot, "Notes of talk with Secretary Fall, on Friday afternoon, July 29, 1921; Gifford Pinchot, open letter, December 21, 1921, January 3, 1922; Burt Noggle, *Teapot Dome: Oil and Politics in the 1920s* (Westport, Conn.: Greenwood Press, Publishers, 1980), 22–31; Margaret L. Davis, *Dark Side of Fortune: Triumph and Scandal in the Life of Oil Tycoon Edward L. Doheny* (Berkeley: University of California Press, 1998), 137–39; David H. Stratton, *Tempest over Teapot Dome: The Story of Albert B. Fall* (Norman: University of Oklahoma Press, 1998), 211–18.

49. By curious fate, Ickes had hired Harry Slattery, on Pinchot's strong recommendation, to join his staff in 1932; when the reorganization fight erupted, Ickes suspected that Slattery had remained loyal to his old employer, and fretted that he was funneling internal, confidential documents to the dreaded foe. Pinchot delivered a somewhat different form of his speech to the February 1937 meeting of the Allegheny Branch of the Society of American Foresters, and revised it further for talks given to the American Forestry Association (May 1937) and the California State Chamber of Commerce (October 1937). One version was published as "Old Evils in New Clothes," *Journal of Forestry,* May 1937, 435–38. The Izaak Walton League's magazine, *Outdoor America,* May–June 1937, 8, also offered a recap of the speech in which it praised his "clear and dramatic" analysis of the dangers inherent in the Brownlow Report, noting particularly that the new department of conservation would "divide up the natural resources, not on the basis of use and protection, but on the artificial and constantly changing basis of ownership." The editors also applauded Pinchot's rejection of the report's bifurcation of federal forestry's functions, in which issues related to private lands would stay in Agriculture, and management of public forested lands would be

moved to Interior. About Pinchot's politicking, *Outdoor America* was less happy. "Unfortunately, the Governor brought out other considerations having political implications in which the League has no interest. . . . "

50. Harold Ickes, "We Must Husband Our Resources," an address on Star Radio Forum, November 1, 1937, File 21, Society of American Foresters Collection, Forest History Society, Durham, N.C.

51. Ickes, "We Must Husband Our Resources"; Harold Ickes, "Not Guilty: Richard Ballinger—An American Dreyfus," *Saturday Evening Post,* May 25, 1940; Ickes, *Inside Struggle,* 131–32, 238–39, 293–95; Polenberg, *Reorganizing Roosevelt's Government,* 100–22; Miller, "Sawdust Memories," 10–11; Gifford Pinchot, *Fishing Talk* (Harrisburg: Stackpole Books, 1993); T. H. Watkins, *Righteous Pilgrim: The Life and Times of Harold Ickes, 1874–1952* (New York: Henry Holt, 1990), 560–62. Ickes never forgot an insult, real or perceived. When, in 1940, he finally addressed the Izaak Walton League, he promptly castigated his hosts for allowing Pinchot to attack him in such partisan ways in 1937, then turned around and did the same thing, lashing out in a twenty-three-page diatribe against his chief antagonist; Harold Ickes, "Babes in the Woods," *Outdoor America,* April 1940, 8–10.

52. Pinchot, "Reply to Harold Ickes Radio Attack of November 1, 1937." Jeanne N. Clarke has proposed that Ickes's investment in the transfer fight was quite personal and "had very much to do with his relationship with the president." Were he to win the transfer war, his stature within the administration would be elevated, but there was also an element of "sibling rivalry" to his ambition. "The lives of three men—Theodore Roosevelt, Gifford Pinchot, and Franklin Roosevelt—were all linked to forests and the Forest Service. They were all men whom Ickes admired and emulated in his own public career. . . . His acceptance by this vital group would be assured if the president, who[m] he practically worshipped, gave him stewardship over the nation's forests. Harold Ickes needed that prize in order to feel secure about his relationship with Roosevelt and about his place in history," Jeanne N. Clarke, *Roosevelt's Warrior: Harold Ickes and the New Deal* (Baltimore: Johns Hopkins University Press, 1996), 241–43. Ickes had the bad luck to tangle with Pinchot, who had his own psychological investments in the preservation of the Forest Service's historic ties to Agriculture, which only heightened the tension of this remarkable pyschodrama.

53. Pinchot, Diary, January–December 1937.

54. Pinchot, Diary, January–February 1937.

55. Elizabeth Frazer, "Mrs. Gifford Pinchot, Housewife and Politician," *Saturday Evening Post,* August 26, 1922, 15–16, 85; John W. Furlow, "Cornelia Bryce Pinchot: Feminism in the Post-Suffrage Era," *Pennsylvania History,* October 1976, 334–38.

56. Pinchot to Antoinette Perry Johnstone, June 22, 1934. Antoinette died on July 1, 1934; Harcourt Johnstone to Pinchot (telegram), July 1, 1934.

57. Sally Pinchot quoted in Carol Severance, "Cornelia Bryce Pinchot, 1881–

1960," a talk presented to the USDA Forest Service Management Policy Seminar, February 22, 1993, 3; Pinchot, Diary, September 15, 1937.

58. Pinchot, Diary, September 15–17, 1937.

59. Pinchot to Harcourt Johnstone, June 21, 1939; Ickes, *Inside Struggle,* 565; Pinchot to Harold Ickes, April 13, 1939. McGeary, *Gifford Pinchot: Forester-Politician,* 411–18, makes a small error; he indicates in the text—though the dates cited in the letters cited in the endnotes show otherwise—that Pinchot and Ickes patched things up only once, in 1938; there were in fact two brief moments of peace.

60. Harold Ickes, "Not Guilty: An Official Inquiry into the Charges Made by Glavis and Pinchot against Richard A. Ballinger, Secretary of the Interior, 1909–1911" (Washington, D.C.: Government Printing Office, 1940), 1.

61. Ickes, "Not Guilty," passim. Before he began the research into the Ballinger-Pinchot files, Ickes was already convinced of Pinchot's guilt "because I myself know what a zealot Pinchot is": Harold Ickes, *The Lowering Clouds* (New York: Simon & Schuster, 1953–54), 111.

62. Pinchot to R. Wright, July 6, 1940; Pinchot to Ruth Pinchot, June 1, 1940; Amos Pinchot to Pinchot, May 24, 1940; Pinchot to Charles Beard, June 4, 1940. Ickes resented Pinchot's linking him with Interior's tainted past; see Harold Ickes to Pinchot, May 18, 1940, passim; "Pinchot's Reply to Harold Ickes," November 4, 1937.

63. Some of Pinchot's almost daily contacts with the "Forest Lobby" are recounted in "Transfer Fight of 1940—2nd Attempt," a thirteen-page memorandum detailing their discussions and the coordination of their political activities during the critical fight; Polenberg, *Reorganizing Roosevelt's Government,* chapter 5; Ickes, *Lowering Clouds,* 125–31, 135–36, 279–81.

64. Roosevelt refused Ickes's resignation, as he had in the past and would other such letters the secretary occasionally offered. Ickes, *Lowering Clouds,* 114–17, 125–31, 133, 135–36, 162–63, 279–81, 412–13; Polenberg, *Reorganizing Roosevelt's Government,* 191–95, 122.

65. Pinchot, *Breaking New Ground,* 322–35.

66. Ickes, *First Thousand Days,* 418; Pinchot, "Old Evils in New Clothes," 435–38; Watkins, *Righteous Pilgrim,* 560–62.

67. Polenberg, *Reorganizing Roosevelt's Government,* 121–22.

68. Steen, *U.S. Forest Service,* 152–62; Rothman, "'A Regular Ding-Dong Fight,'" 109–24.

CHAPTER 14. CLIMAX

1. The first quote comes from Arnold W. Bolle, "The Bitterroot Revisited: A University Re-View of the Forest Service," in Char Miller, ed., *American Forests: Nature, Culture, and Politics* (Lawrence: University Press of Kansas, 1997), 170. Bolle, then dean of the School of Forestry at the University of Montana, had organized the trip to the Bitterroot Valley. Included in the

group was Dale Burk, a reporter for the *Missoula Missoulian,* whose articles brought Gifford Bryce Pinchot's words to the attention of the national press. The second quote attributed to Pinchot comes from *American Forests,* September 1973, 2. Gifford Pinchot was well aware that clear-cutting raised scientific and political issues; see Pinchot to C. J. Buck, September 9, 1937.

2. The test case of the Natural Resources Defense Council (NRDC) was successful; Bolle, "Bitterroot Revisited," 14–15, briefly chronicles the lawsuit, one consequence of which was the passage of the National Forest Management Act of 1976. For a more complete discussion of the Bitterroot and Monongahela controversies, see Paul Hirt, *A Conspiracy of Optimism: Management of the National Forests Since World War Two* (Lincoln: University of Nebraska Press, 1994), 245–51. On the development of the NRDC and similar organizations in the late 1960s and early 1970s, see John Opie, *Nature's Nation: An Environmental History of the United States* (New York: Harcourt Brace Jovanovich, 1998), 417–29.

3. "The Blow That Probably Wouldn't Have Killed Father" (unsigned editorial), *American Forests,* May 1973, 9; Paul Oehser, "Gifford Pinchot's Peace Concepts," *American Forests,* May 1973, 43–44; Paul Henry Oehser, *Who's Who,* 41st edition, 1980–81; Al Wiener, "Gifford Pinchot Would Have Laughed," *American Forests,* November 1973, 12–13, 34–37; Pinchot to C. J. Buck, September 9, 1937. The *American Forests* campaign to blunt Gifford Bryce Pinchot's words generated its own mini-controversy of protest and counterprotest: see *American Forests,* August 1973, 4, 48–49; September 1973, 2; November 1973, 2; December 1973, 3, 64; January 1974, 2–3.

4. Wiener, "Gifford Pinchot Would Have Laughed," 12–13.

5. Hirt, *Conspiracy of Optimism*; Bolle, "Bitterroot Revisited," 163–76; Char Miller, "On Rewriting Forest History," in Miller, ed., *American Forests,* 9–10; Gifford Pinchot, *The Use of the National Forests* (Washington, D.C.: U.S. Department of Agriculture, 1907), 25–26.

6. *Washington Post,* June 25, 1905, Pinchot Scrapbooks, reel 1, 124.

7. There were, and are, a goodly number of environmentalists who have little interest in claiming Pinchot as one of their own, but even as they invariably use him as a marker for what they do not believe, they testify to his continuing power to shape contemporary discourse; see Char Miller, "The Greening of Gifford Pinchot," in Miller, *Gifford Pinchot: The Evolution of an American Conservationist,* Pinchot Lecture Series (Milford, Pa.: Grey Towers Press, 1992), 43–48.

8. Gifford Pinchot, *Breaking New Ground* (New York: Harcourt Brace, 1947), xxii; some of these ideas were earlier developed in Char Miller, "On Rewriting Forest History," in Miller, ed., *American Forests,* 1–2.

9. Pinchot, *Breaking New Ground,* xxii–xxiii; the irony is that the *Kirkus* review of the book complains that it was too thoroughly documented: November 1, 1947, 620.

10. Pinchot, "On Writing History," in *Breaking New Ground,* xxii–xxiv.

11. Pinchot, *Breaking New Ground,* 5; on the broad range of George Bird Grinnell's accomplishments, see John Reiger, *American Sportsmen and the Origins of Conservation* (Corvallis: Oregon State University Press, 2000) and *The Passing of the Great West: Selected Papers of George Bird Grinnell* (Norman: University of Oklahoma Press, 1982).

12. Pinchot, *Breaking New Ground,* xxii; Henry F. Pringle, *The Life and Times of William Howard Taft: A Biography* (New York: Farrar & Rinehart, 1939).

13. Gifford Pinchot, Diary, June 1, 1941. The journal entries for that summer detail the mood swings he felt while writing this particular set of chapters. Some days in June and July recorded great progress; others, such as this July 16 comment—"still Ballinger"—were a grim reminder of a writer's difficulties in composing his thoughts. On August 1, there was relief: "Anna May found my letter of December 31, 1909 to TR in Africa—a great help." This was followed by several more months in which he was convinced he was nearly finished, only to be disappointed anew when the work dragged on through August and September. Any author can sympathize with this emotional roller coaster.

14. Pinchot quoted in M. Nelson McGeary, *Gifford Pinchot: Forester-Politician* (Princeton: Princeton University Press, 1960), 245; Pinchot, Acknowledgments, in *Breaking New Ground*; "Conservation's Communicator: An Interview with Henry E. Clepper" (1976), Forest History Society, Durham, N.C., 12–13. On Zon's personality and politics, see Norman J. Schmaltz, "Raphael Zon: Forest Researcher," part 1, *Journal of Forest History,* January 1980, 25–39; part 2, April 1980, 87–97.

15. Leon Kneipp, "Land Planning and Acquisition, U.S. Forest Service," Oral History Interview, Forest History Society, Durham, N.C., 36; Schmaltz, "Raphael Zon," part 2, 96.

16. Among the favorable reviews were *The Nation,* February 2, 1948, 162; *The Christian Science Monitor,* January 28, 1948, 14; *Christian Century,* February 11, 1948, 65; and *Journal of Forestry,* February 1948, 135–42; Harold Ickes, *New York Times,* November 23, 1947, 6.

17. Henry Clepper, "Gifford Pinchot and the SAF," *Journal of Forestry,* August 1965, 590–92.

18. Pinchot, *Breaking New Ground,* 504–6.

19. Pinchot, *Breaking New Ground,* 508.

20. Pinchot, *Breaking New Ground,* 508–10.

21. Pinchot to W. S. Rosencrans, April 8, 1943, in Henry S. Graves Papers, Manuscripts and Archives, Yale University.

22. Bolle, "Bitterroot Revisited," in Miller, ed., *American Forests,* 163–65.

23. Unless otherwise noted, the following oral histories are located in the Forest History Society archives, Durham, N.C.: Emanuel Fritz, "Teacher, Editor, and Forestry Consultant," 27–29, 77; J. P. Kinney, "The Office of Indian Affairs: A Career in Forestry," 16–19, 92; William D. Hagenstein, 27–28;

Royal Kellogg, Interview I, 13–14, unpaged section; A. B. Recknagel, 14; Royal Kellogg, Interview II, 2–3; "R. S. Kellogg Retires," *The Paper Industry,* March 1950, 1,408; Dr. and Mrs. Wilson Compton, 55–57; Charles Connaughton, 51, 72; Walter J. Damtoft, 4–5; Inman F. Eldredge, passim; there were those, like Scott Leavitt, who did not join the swelling chorus of critics who accentuated Pinchot's negative qualities and denigrated his contributions; 30–31. See also John W. Keller, "Recollections of Gifford Pinchot," Bancroft Library, University of California, Berkeley; Cornelia Bryce Pinchot, "Gifford Pinchot and the Conservation Ideal," *Journal of Forestry,* February 1950, 83–86.

24. Fearing that Pinchot had become dispensable, Henry S. Graves concluded his lengthy review of *Breaking New Ground* by apologizing for his extensive paraphrasing of the text. He had done so, he wrote, because "[y]ounger men may find some of the book rather difficult reading. I have called attention to events which seem to me most significant. It is my hope that my narrative may tempt foresters and others really to read the book"; *Journal of Forestry,* February 1948, 142, 29, 77; Kinney, "Office of Indian Affairs," 16–19, 92.

25. Pinchot to G. Albert Stewart, April 18, 1942. This letter and the correspondence that follows are located at the Pennsylvania Forestry Association, Harrisburg. Many of these letters were reprinted in Robert H. Rumpf, "The Pinchot-Mattoon Controversy," *Pennsylvania Forests,* Winter 1977, 16–22.

26. Stewart to Pinchot, April 23, 1942.

27. Pinchot to Henry Graves, June 17, 1942; Pinchot to Graves, June 25, 1942, Graves Papers, Manuscripts and Archives, Yale University.

28. Gleason Mattoon to Pinchot, July 2, 1942. Pinchot was stunned to learn of Mattoon's volte-face: "The only subject on which we did not disagree," he responded, "was an incidental reference to the matter of State as against National control of forests, which could have nothing whatever to do with whether or not the cuttings we were examining had been well or badly done, whether they amounted to permanent forestry, or destructive lumbering"; Pinchot to Mattoon, July 8, 1942.

29. Pinchot released a second statement, following the governor's rebuttal, which sharply critiqued the prevailing argument among politicians and the timber industry that the war justified a rapid harvest: Pinchot, "Release," August 24, 1942; Pinchot, Diary, June 26–August 26, 1942; Mattoon to George Wharton Pepper, January 18, 1945, in Rumph, "Pinchot-Mattoon Controversy," 22–23. In this letter to Pepper, Mattoon revealed that he thought Pinchot a pathetic figure, as illuminated in an anecdote he shared with Pepper, a former U.S. senator who had been Pinchot's counsel during the Ballinger-Pinchot controversy, and against whom Pinchot had run for the Senate in 1926. Noting that on their tour of the state forests they had traveled in Pinchot's chauffeur-driven car, a convertible Crossley, Mattoon said the drive "developed into a political fence mending trip by G. In many towns he would direct the chauffeur to pull to the curb in the busiest section, where upon he would stand up

and gaze up and down the street until a crowd collected. The [o]pen Crossley attracted the first ones. Then someone would recognize the governor and he would greet them with a certain paternalistic enthusiasm which they seemed to relish." Mattoon, by contrast, relished this signifier of Pinchot's last hurrah. On the relationship of Pinchot and Pepper, see Amos R. E. Pinchot, *History of the Progressive Party,* ed. Helene Maxwell Hooker (New York: New York University Press, 1958), 239, and George Wharton Pepper, *Philadelphia Lawyer: An Autobiography* (Philadelphia: J. B. Lippincott Co., 1944), passim.

30. Pinchot, "Release," August 24, 1942; Gifford Pinchot, "Regulation of Private Forests," *Journal of Forestry,* September 1942, 732–733. Pinchot made additional inspection trips to state forests and encouraged sportsmen's clubs and the CIO to support his call to an end to clear-cutting: Pinchot, Diary, July 28–29, 1942; August 8, 10, 20, 26, 1942; Pinchot to R. H. Wagoner, March 27, 1945.

31. Otis Graham, *An Encore for Reform: The Old Progressives and the New Deal* (New York: Oxford University Press, 1967), 32–34; Ronald L. Feinman, *Twilight of Progressivism: The Western Republican Senators and the New Deal* (Baltimore: Johns Hopkins University Press, 1981), 176–202; Richard Pells, *Radical Visions and American Dreams: Cultural and Social Thought in the Depression* (New York: Harpers, 1973). Amos Pinchot was one of the founders of America First: see Helene Maxwell Hooker, "Biographical Introduction," in Amos R. E. Pinchot, *History of the Progressive Party,* 82–84.

32. Gifford Pinchot, "Conservation as a Foundation for Permanent Peace," *Nature,* August 10, 1940, 183–85.

33. Ibid., 185.

34. *New York Times,* August 7, 1942, 1, 9; August 8, 1942, 13; August 9, 1942, 45; Nancy Pittman Pinchot, "Amos Pinchot: Rebel Prince," *Pennsylvania History,* Fall 1999, 194–96; Nina Burleigh, *A Very Private Woman: The Life and Unsolved Murder of Presidential Mistress Mary Meyer* (New York: Bantam Press, 1998), 70–71.

35. Gifford Pinchot, "Conservation as a Foundation of Permanent Peace," *Nature,* August 10, 1940, 184–85; W. C. Lawdermilk to Pinchot, May 16, 1940; Pinchot to Lawdermilk, May 24, 1940; Cordell Hull to Pinchot, March 27, 1940; Pinchot to Hull, April 5, 1940; Pinchot to Franklin Roosevelt, undated. Pinchot's other lobbying efforts included convincing Congress to publish his speech (H. H. Bennett to Pinchot, May 17, 1940); generating the passage of a Society of American Foresters resolution in favor of his ideas (*Journal of Forestry,* August 1940, 656–57); and securing the approval of another resolution by the Committee on Agriculture of the Governing Board of the Pan American Union to establish a Resources Committee, (Pinchot, Diary, June 3, 1940). A year later, Pinchot reported that Cordell Hull "approves vigorously" of his plan for an international conservation congress: Pinchot, Diary, February 25–26, 1941.

36. Townsend Hoopes and Douglas Brinkley, *Franklin Roosevelt and the Creation of the United Nations* (New Haven: Yale University Press, 1997); Pinchot to Franklin Roosevelt, July 29, 1944, August 26, 1944, September 8, 1944, January 21, 1945; Pinchot to Mrs. John Boettiger, January 21, 1945, January 22, 1945. Pinchot, ever the politician, linked his work on this plan with his support for Roosevelt's 1944 campaign: among the reasons this Republican was voting for the Democratic candidate, "Statement of Gifford Pinchot," August 29, 1944, was Roosevelt's desire to lead us "to permanent peace" and his proven ability to free "the world from the dread and danger of future wars," language Pinchot often employed in his speeches about the value of an international set of accords concerning conservation. Embedded in his September 8, 1944, letter to the president pressing the case for a conservation conference was this political plea: "Leila [Cornelia] and I are organizing a Committee of Independent Voters for Roosevelt in Pennsylvania, which we hope will do you no harm." On Roosevelt's concern for "forest butchery," see Roosevelt to Women's Conservation League, April 2, 1945, cited in an unattributed newspaper dated May 17, 1945, in Gifford Pinchot Papers, Library of Congress.

37. Gifford Pinchot, Diary, January–December 1945, offers a running commentary on his lobbying campaign; additional letters between Pinchot and Roosevelt are reproduced in Edgar R. Nixon, ed., *Franklin D. Roosevelt and Conservation, 1911–1945* (New York: Arno Press, 1972), 591–94, 644–48, and in Frank Smith, ed., *Conservation in the United States: Land and Water, 1900–1970* (New York: Chelsea House, 1971), 376–82. Pinchot, Diary, April 12, 1945; Harold Ickes, Diary, November 14, 1945, Harold Ickes Papers, Library of Congress; Cornelia Bryce Pinchot, "Gifford Pinchot and the Conservation Ideal," *Journal of Forestry,* February 1950, 83–86; and John W. Furlow, Jr., "Gifford Pinchot: Public Service and the Meaning of Conservation," *Theodore Roosevelt Association Newsletter,* Summer 1987, 15–16, charge that the conference was a failure because it did not keep faith with Pinchot's idealism; "Mobilizing Science for Peace," *UN Bulletin,* September 1, 1949, 230; "Man and His Resources," *UN Bulletin,* September 15, 1949, 338–45. That the conference proved a pale version of Pinchot's original conception makes it a perfect reflection of the general dilution of the idealism that had brought the UN into being; see Hoopes and Brinkley, *FDR and the Creation of the UN,* 208–9.

38. Cornelia Pinchot, "Conservation," 1949, Cornelia Pinchot Papers, Library of Congress.

39. Donald Worster, *Nature's Economy: The Roots of Ecology* (San Francisco: Sierra Club Books, 1977); Robert Gottlieb, *Forcing the Spring: The Transformation of American Environmental Movement* (Washington, D.C.: Island Press, 1993); and Opie, *Nature's Nation,* 404–33, track the emergence of modern environmental thought.

40. Dave Foreman quoted in Michael Parfit, "Earth First!ers wield a mean mon-

key wrench," *Smithsonian,* April 1990, 184–204; Foreman expands on this theme in his *Confessions of an Eco-Warrior* (New York: Harmony Books, 1991), 17–21.

41. See "The UN Conference on the Human Environment," in Roderick Nash, ed., *The American Environment: Readings in the History of Conservation* (New York: Knopf, 1975), 307–15. This paragraph draws on arguments in Char Miller, "The Greening of Gifford Pinchot," *Environmental History Review,* Fall 1992, 16.

42. Gifford Pinchot, *Fishing Talk* (Harrisburg: Stackpole Books, 1993), 238.

43. Ibid., 233–34.

44. Ibid., 234–35; Pinchot's belief that Native Americans are inherently conservationists, a faith the larger culture has come to accept uncritically, is debunked in Shepard Krech III, *The Ecological Indian: Myth and History* (New York: Norton, 1999).

45. Ibid.

46. Ibid., 234, 236–38. In "The Road to Better Fishing," Maryland Sportsmen's Luncheon Club, March 30, 1937, Pinchot argued that barbless fishing would help restore "wild fish" to America's rivers: "The way to better fishing is to kill less fish." Those rivers and streams also needed restoration: once "full of old logs and brush," which provided "vastly more places for trout . . . to hide and breed and grow," these natural "obstacles" have been cleared away in a misguided effort to improve their flow. For a shrewd and compelling commentary on Pinchot's angling aesthetic, see John Reiger, "Gifford Pinchot with Rod and Reel," in Reiger, *Two Essays in Conservation History* (Milford, Pa.: Grey Tower Press, 1994), 1–36.

47. *Milford Dispatch,* August 17, 1989, 3; *New York Times,* October 6, 1946, 56; October 7, 1946, 30; October 8, 1946, 23. For someone who was so devoted to his alma mater of Yale, Pinchot would have gotten a laugh out of the *New York Times's* assertion that he had graduated from archrival Harvard: *New York Times,* October 10, 1946, 27.

48. McGeary, *Gifford Pinchot: Forester-Politician,* 434–35, on the posthumous honors; George B. Sudworth, "A New Species of Juniper for Texas," *Forestry and Irrigation,* May 1905, 206; George B. Sudworth, "Check List of the Forest Trees of the United States: Their Names and Ranges," Miscellaneous Circular 92 (Washington, D.C.: U.S. Department of Agriculture, 1927), 42; Cyrus Longworth Lundell, *Flora of Texas,* vol. 1 (Renner, Tex.: Texas Research Foundation, 1966), 342–46; Barton H. Warnock, *Wildflowers of the Big Bend Country Texas* (Alpine, Tex.: Sul Ross State University Press, 1970), xii–xiii, 15; "Pinchot Juniper," *Texas Highways,* January 1990, 48–49.

Acknowledgments

This book owes its completion, at least in part, to a garden. During the spring of 1997, to celebrate our daughter Rebecca's bat mitzvah and, yes, to quickly beautify the rather neglected eastern side of our home before family came to town, I put pitchfork to ground. Following the landscape designs that a friend had drawn up, I dug the beds, planted an array of drought-resistant shrubs and flowers indigenous to south-central Texas, and hauled in wheelbarrows full of compost and mulch. The labor was fun, all the more so because it often occurred during thunderstorms that marked an end to a devastating two-year dry spell.

The rains are now gone, but the surviving plants have continued to grow—it has been astonishing to watch the coral honeysuckle wind its way up the lattice and the pavona, Blackfoot daisy, and wine cup leaf out and flower. Just as amazing is that this Xeriscape has subsequently attracted bees, tiger swallowtails, and ruby-throated hummingbirds that zip, flutter, and flit through a maze of color. Their daily search for pollen and food, framed by the windows of our bedroom, has given me good reason to sit before this keyboard; their beguiling and animated lives have nourished my writing in ways I could never have imagined when I first started turning over the hard soil.

There are many human beings I need to thank, too, without whom this project would not have gotten off the ground. The oldest of my debts is to the participants in a graduate seminar at The Johns Hopkins University led by Kenneth S. Lynn in the spring of 1976; the critical insights and encouragement of Linda Long Ramsey, Carolyn Ditte Wagner, Nicole White, and especially Dan Wilson, all of whom carefully read my seminar paper on Gifford Pinchot, helped to inspire my return to the project more than a decade later.

Since then, I've piled up a staggering list of people and institutions to whom I owe considerable thanks. I have been blessed with an amazing set of colleagues and staff in the history department at Trinity University: Gary Kates read and commented on multiple versions of the evolving manuscript, while John Martin, John McCusker, Alida Metcalf, and Linda Salvucci have freely given of their time and energy, shared their ideas and laughter, and put up with a lot; so have secretaries Eunice Herrington, Evelyn Luce, and Sherea Norris, whose commitment and friendship have made the department such a fun environment in which to work. The university's generosity has been remarkable, too. Former president Ron Calgaard, former vice president Ed Roy, and former dean William O. Walker, as well as their successors—John Brazil, Michael Fisher, and Gary Kates (again)—have provided, in combination with the Faculty Development Committee, ample funds for travel, research, and reflection.

Librarians everywhere I've worked have helped immeasurably. Craig Likness (now at the University of Miami), Chris Nolan, and Maria McWilliams at Trinity's Elizabeth Huth Coates Library went well out of their way to answer my endless queries. My cousin Nixie Miller at the Duke University Library not only opened her home to me but has been a wonderful guide through her library's important collections. The staff at the Library of Congress, the Bancroft Library at the University of California at Berkeley, the Minnesota Historical Society, North Carolina State University, and the Sterling Memorial Library at Yale University provided remarkable support over the past decade. Of particular aid was the late Joe Miller, librarian at the Yale School of Forestry & Environmental Studies, whose knowledge of the scholarship in forestry and conservation was surpassed only by his willingness to help me understand its significance.

The staff at Grey Towers National Historic Landmark in Milford, Pennsylvania, have been the source of ongoing and considerable help. Former director Ed Vandermillen gave me my first opportunity to speak about Pinchot's life. The current head, the energetic Ed Brannon, has offered me innumerable forums in which to work through my arguments and has critiqued almost every one of them, becoming a wonderful friend in the process. So, too, have his colleagues Gary Hines, Kimo Kimokeo, Rebecca Philpot, and Carol Severance; their knowledge of the Pinchot family's past, and their willingness to share their insights, made this a much richer book.

Giving me the benefit of their knowledge of the politics of American forestry, and of Pinchot's place within that oft-fraught landscape, have been Al Sample, executive director of the Pinchot Institute for Conservation; the institute's senior fellow Jim Giltmier; and Rebecca Staebler, director of publications at the Society of American Foresters. Early conversations with Jean Pablo and Barry Walsh were fruitful, as have been discussions with forester Orville Daniels, John Gable of the Theodore Roosevelt Association, and scholars William Cronon, Sally Fairfax, Stan Goldman, Paul Hirt, James G. Lewis, the late Harold Pinkett, Donald Pisani, John Reiger, Dennis Roth, Hal Rothman, the late Terry West, and Jerry Williams, among many others. At the Forest History Society (FHS), former director Pete Steen graciously drew upon his enormous knowledge of the history of the Forest Service to help place the agency's activities in perspective; its current head, Steven Anderson, has been every bit as supportive. It is impossible to know how to thank FHS librarian Cheryl Oakes, who has given me so much bibliographic aid and advice for so long; she is a gem. In the final stages of research, James G. Lewis, Kevin O'Connor, and Sarah Phelps located and/or shared crucial documents.

Some of this book's arguments originally appeared in different form in a variety of publications, and I am indebted to a host of editors for the chance to work out some of my arguments in their journals, magazines, or anthologies. Thanks, then, to *Arnoldia, Electronic Green Journal, Environmental History, Forest & Conservation History, Forest History Today, In These Times, Journal of American History, Journal of Forestry, Pennsylvania History,* and the *Texas Observer.*

And then there is Jonathan Cobb, executive editor of Shearwater Books. His literary instincts, prodigious knowledge, and deft editing have made the process of writing and rewriting a real joy. Without his patient and gentle nudging, this book would still be in manuscript form, still much less than what I hope it has become. Jonathan is an author's dream.

Great as well are my obligations to my family, extended and nuclear. My mother and my sisters, along with my in-laws and relatives of varying connections, have listened patiently as I regaled them with one last anecdote about Pinchot's life. I am only sorry that this book did not appear while my father and mother-in-law were still alive, though they would have appreciated this promise—with the publication of *Gifford Pinchot,* I swear I'll finally shut up about him.

That's not a vow easily made or fulfilled, and the first to know whether I can stick to it will be my best friend and wife (and wondrous in-house editor), Judi Lipsett. She and our children, Ben and Rebecca, will not miss the piles of books or stacks of papers that have cluttered our home in San Antonio for these many years, and surely will not mind a change in conversation. Maybe we should have thought of digging that garden a long time ago.

Index

Note: In the body of the index, Gifford Pinchot is referred to as "Pinchot." References to illustrations are printed in boldface type.